The Southern Colonial Backcountry

The Southern Colonial Backcountry

INTERDISCIPLINARY PERSPECTIVES ON FRONTIER COMMUNITIES

Edited by
David Colin Crass
Steven D. Smith
Martha A. Zierden
and Richard D. Brooks

THE UNIVERSITY OF TENNESSEE PRESS / KNOXVILLE

Copyright © 1998 by The University of Tennessee Press / Knoxville. All Rights Reserved. Manufactured in the United States of America. First Edition.

Unless otherwise noted, the illustrations were prepared by the authors of the chapters in which they appear.

The paper in this book meets the minimum requirements of the American National Standard for Permanence of Paper for Printed Library Materials.

∞ The binding materials have been chosen for strength and durability.

LIBRARY OF CONGRESS CATALOGING-IN-PUBLICATION DATA

The southern colonial backcountry : interdisciplinary perspectives on frontier communities / edited by David Colin Crass ... [et al.].—1st ed.
   p.   cm.
Includes bibliographical references and index.
ISBN 1-57233-019-8 (cloth: alk. paper)
   1. Southern States—History—Colonial period, ca. 1600–1775. 2. Southern States—History—1775–1865. 3. Southern States—Antiquities. 4. Excavations (Archaeology)—Southern States. 5. Frontier and pioneer life—Southern States. I. Crass, David Colin.
   F212.S68   1998
   975'.02—ddc21   98-8978

This volume is dedicated to the memory of Edward Fry: mentor, teacher, friend.

Contents

ACKNOWLEDGMENTS	XI
INTRODUCTION: SOUTHERN FRONTIER COMMUNITIES VIEWED THROUGH THE ARCHAEOLOGICAL EYE • David Colin Crass, Steven D. Smith, Martha A. Zierden, and Richard D. Brooks	XIII
1. THE SOUTHERN BACKCOUNTRY: A GEOGRAPHICAL HOUSE DIVIDED • Robert D. Mitchell	1
2. MUDDIED WATERS: A DISCUSSION OF CURRENT INTERDISCIPLINARY BACKCOUNTRY STUDIES • Michael J. Puglisi	36
3. SHADOW LAND: PROVISIONAL REAL ESTATE CLAIMS AND ANGLO-AMERICAN SETTLEMENT IN SOUTHWESTERN VIRGINIA • Turk McCleskey	56
4. FROM CREEKS TO CRACKERS • Edward Cashin	69
5. TAVERNS AND COMMUNITIES: THE CASE OF ROWAN COUNTY, NORTH CAROLINA • Daniel B. Thorp	76
6. ECONOMIC DEVELOPMENT IN THE SOUTH CAROLINA BACKCOUNTRY: A VIEW FROM CAMDEN • Kenneth E. Lewis	87
7. "A FER WAYS OFF FROM THE BIG HOUSE": THE CHANGING NATURE OF SLAVERY IN THE SOUTH CAROLINA BACKCOUNTRY • Monica L. Beck	108

8. "Here Are Frame Houses and Brick Chimneys": Knoxville, Tennessee, in the Late Eighteenth Century • Charles H. Faulkner   137

9. "Seeing" Early Appalachian Communities through the Lenses of History, Geography, and Sociology • David C. Hsiung   162

10. Between Two Cultures: Judge John Martin and the Struggle for Cherokee Sovereignty • Elizabeth Arnett Fields   182

11. Folk Art, Architecture, and Artifact: Toward a Material Understanding of the German Culture in the Upper Valley of Virginia • Donald W. Linebaugh   200

Epilogue: Interdisciplinary Dialogues on the Southern Colonial Backcountry, 1893–1998 • Warren R. Hofstra   221

Selected Bibliography   237

Contributors   249

Index   253

Illustrations

Figures

3.1.	Surveys Completed and Acreage Surveyed in James River and Roanoke River Valleys, 1745–55	61
3.2.	Individuals Acquiring Surveys in James River and Roanoke River Valleys, 1745–55	63
7.1.	Painting of Bratton Plantation, 1840s	115
7.2.	Personal and Clothing Artifacts Recovered from the Slave Cabin Site, Historic Brattonsville	122
8.1.	Remains of West Foundation Wall and Southwest Corner of the James White House, Knoxville	147
8.2.	James White House, Knoxville, ca. 1800	148
8.3.	Test Excavation Unit at Blount Mansion, Knoxville, Showing Post-Hole	150
8.4.	Blount Mansion Compound, Knoxville, ca. 1795	152
8.5.	Ceramic Sherds from Knoxville sites	154
11.1.	First-floor Plan, Andrew Keyser House, Virginia, ca. 1765	206
11.2.	Home of the Geiger Family, York County, Pennsylvania, ca. 1810	207
11.3.	First-floor Plan, Lanier House, Dinwiddie County, ca. 1850	208
11.4.	Mrs. Widow Wade House and Mill, Montgomery County, Virginia, ca. 1850	208
11.5.	Residence of John Craig, Hamten Meadow, Montgomery County, Virginia	209
11.6.	"On the Farm of Missters [sic], Emmeline Craig," ca. 1865	210

11.7.	Residence of Mr. Zoll at New River, Montgomery County, Virginia	211
11.8.	Ingles Farm on the Bank of New River, Montgomery County, Virginia	212
11.9.	Residence of Mr. Haymacker, Montgomery County, Virginia, ca. 1856	213
11.10.	Residence of Mr. Lenard, near Christiansburg, Montgomery County, Virginia, ca. 1870	214
11.11.	Residence of Mr. Etzler, near Christiansburg, Montgomery County, Virginia, ca. 1870	215

Maps

1.1.	Probable Extent of Northern Migrants in Colonial South	17
1.2.	Southern Regional Economies	19
3.1.	Prices Charged by Major Land Speculators, Augusta County, Virginia, 1751–54	57
6.1.	Layout of the Interior Townships Established in South Carolina in 1731	93
6.2.	The Road Network of the South Carolina Backcountry and the Locations of Important Settlements in the Late Frontier Period	95
6.3.	European Settlement at Pine Tree Hill before 1760	96
6.4.	Locations of Eighteenth-Century Structures in Camden, as Revealed by Archaeological Investigations	98
6.5.	Survey Plan of Camden as Laid Out in 1771	99
6.6.	Camden as a Fortified Settlement, 1780–81	100
7.1.	Site Location Map, Historic Brattonsville, York County, South Carolina	117
7.2.	Distribution of Ceramics Recovered from Shovel Tests, by Count	120
7.3.	Archaeological Site Map, John S. Bratton Home, ca. 1823	125
8.1.	Knoxville, ca. 1800, Showing Early Street Names and Original Lots Sold by James White	140
9.1.	Washington County, Tennessee, Study Area	167
9.2.	Washington County, Tennessee, Road Networks	170
11.1.	German and English Immigration into the Valley of Virginia, with German settlements, ca. 1714–45	204

Acknowledgments

Special thanks go to the South Carolina Institute of Archaeology and Anthropology, University of South Carolina, which provided time and staff support. Director and State Archaeologist Bruce Rippeteau was particularly helpful. Mark Brooks, Bruce Penner, George Wingard, and Melanie Cabak of the Institute of Archaeology and Anthropology offered support as well as review comments throughout the manuscript revision process.

Albert Tillson served as a commentator at the conference which was the origin of this volume; our debt to him is substantial indeed.

Bradford Rauschenberg, director of research for the Museum of Early Southern Decorative Arts in Winston-Salem, North Carolina, furnished helpful comments on earlier drafts of the essays as well.

Elizabeth Fields's research was funded by a contract with the Mobile District, U.S. Army Corps of Engineers, as part of its Historic Resource Program at Carter's Lake, Georgia.

Introduction

SOUTHERN FRONTIER COMMUNITIES VIEWED THROUGH
THE ARCHAEOLOGICAL EYE

David Colin Crass, Steven D. Smith, Martha A. Zierden,
and Richard D. Brooks

This book examines communities on the southern frontier from the perspectives of history, geography, archaeology, and material culture. Although the editors are all historical archaeologists, we have broad-ranging interests and believe that an interdisciplinary approach is the most rewarding way to portray the diversity and rapid temporal change that characterized the eighteenth- and early nineteenth-century southern backcountry and its people.

This volume's genesis was a series of informal conversations in the early 1990s involving (among others) historians, archaeologists, and geographers. A consensus emerged from these conversations that interaction among scholars working on problems associated with the southern backcountry was on the increase, and that it might be time for a gathering explicitly oriented around the theme of interdisciplinary studies. The result was a conference held in 1993 at the University of South Carolina, entitled "The Southern Colonial Backcountry: Beginning an Interdisciplinary Dialogue." The studies presented in this volume represent an expansion of presentations at that conference and were chosen by the editors from the perspective of historical archaeology. It is a viewpoint similar to what Loren Eiseley referred to as an "archaeological eye."[1] This eye discerns the past through the lens of material culture (defined broadly) and the provenience of that material culture across a site, landscape, and region. While this eye quite clearly has blind spots, it is a vantage point commanding a wide vista, for historical archaeology is the most interdisciplinary of all the disciplines represented in this volume. There is a very solid basis for this assertion, because, of all viewpoints from which to view the past, historical archaeology is the most dependent discipline. It is also the youngest of the disciplines represented in this volume, having appeared only within the last thirty years. Emerging from the graduate schools of anthropology and with theoretical underpinnings borrowed from prehistoric archaeology, it strove fervently to forge an identity.

The heated debates on what historical archaeology should be—history or anthropology—eventually were won by the anthropologists,[2] not necessarily because of the merits of their arguments, but because the students doing historical archaeology were graduating from anthropology graduate programs. But anthropologists had no time for history, and historians had little interest in the material-culture particularism of single-site excavations, almost universal in the early days of the discipline.

While the fact that historians shunned historical archaeology hurt the discipline, it was wounded even more deeply as a result of its attempts to gain attention within its mother discipline, anthropology. Seeking respect, anthropologically trained historical archaeologists proudly proclaimed that only anthropological questions about the past were important to archaeologists.[3] The result was that historical archaeologists became, in essence, prehistorians excavating historic sites, instead of historical archaeologists or, more clearly stated, historian archaeologists.

The result was that our early efforts often drew rather simplistic conclusions. The discipline had a corner on making the obvious explicit in the 1960s and 1970s, and this problem occasionally still appears today. Historical archaeologists were failing to do their homework by reading the literature from other, related disciplines and for that reason were continually, and perhaps properly, ignored. In seeking an identity, historical archaeology had surgically removed the objects of its study (people, sites, and artifacts) from the context in which they had operated. This context was the known history, folklore, geography, and architecture of those people, sites, and artifacts.

Beginning in the late 1970s, more and more scholars in the discipline began to recognize that it was indeed critical to understand the documentary history of a site before excavating. Archaeologists also recognized that it was important in studies of the more recent past to talk to people who may have lived at the site—that is, to conduct oral history along with the excavations.[4] This approach had obvious advantages in seeking behavioral explanations for the archaeological remains. More important, however, it widened the viewpoint of historical archaeologists and made it acceptable to seek data from other disciplines.

Today the argument that a reliance on historical documents makes historical archaeology the handmaiden of history is heard less and less often. History and geography are seen widely as allowing historical archaeologists to move beyond the sherds and nails which often make up the bulk of the assemblage recovered from a site. For instance, historical geography is a component critical in addressing questions concerning settlement and landscape. Of course, historical archaeology still can be the handmaiden of history if that history is not interpreted through the archaeological eye. But the other disciplines, along with anthropology, provide the light waves which allow historical archaeologists to perceive and distinguish the objects and features found on the ground. That is why historians, geographers, and others are so important to archaeologists, and why historical archaeology is a dependent discipline. The other disciplines provide a background or context within which the archaeology of historic America can be understood.

It is our opinion that this dependency has allowed historical archaeology to progress very well in the final years of the millennium. Instead of becoming the handmaiden of history, as many feared, historical archaeology has become an ally of other disciplines which study our past. The essays in this volume are testimony to that fact, and to the advantages that are to be gained from such partnerships.[5] By drawing on concepts and perspectives from history, geography, and archaeology, we hope to promote a synergy that transcends our respective fields of inquiry. We make no claim to comprehensiveness in terms of the perspectives, or topics, represented herein. Rather, our intent is to provide a series of case studies and overviews which we believe are thought-provoking, and which are linked by twin emphases on community and interdisciplinary studies.

COMMUNICATION AMONG HISTORICAL DISCIPLINES

Several impediments exist to the creation of an interdisciplinary synergy. Perhaps the most significant is that disciplinary lines exist for good reasons. For instance, as noted above, historical archaeologists have for the most part been schooled in the broader field of anthropology, which has undergone a rapid transformation in the last thirty years.[6] Anthropological concepts of such basic issues as what constitutes explanation, for instance, are quite different from historical concepts of explanation.[7] David Hackett Fischer's *Albion's Seed* is a good case in point.[8] While this work has prompted its share of heated discussions in the field of history, it has been largely ignored by historical archaeologists.[9] This is ironic, because Fischer, in tracing the transmission of cultures from hearth areas to North America, presents what in effect are a series of archaeological models. For example, Fischer discusses at some length the distribution of wealth in the backcountry.[10] Historical archaeologists have developed several sophisticated techniques which are thought to track wealth and status in archaeological assemblages.[11] For archaeologists, then, *Albion's Seed* represents a potentially rich source of ideas to be tested against material culture data. How well does Fischer's argument support archaeological models of wealth distribution? And, if there are significant disagreements between the two, what are the origins of those?

The significance of Fischer's work, at least for archaeologists, goes beyond its role as a source of questions; therein, at least in part, lies the reason for the dearth of Fischer citations in archaeological studies. Implicit in *Albion's Seed* is the argument that whole complexes of cultural traits are carried and, in effect, transplanted from one place to another. This is an idea of some antiquity in the discipline of archaeology, reaching its apogee of popularity with the so-called "hyperdiffusionists" of the late nineteenth and early twentieth centuries, who argued (among many other things) that dynastic Egyptian culture was responsible for much of European civilization—an argument that was soundly discredited by Franz Boas and many others.[12]

Albion's Seed, then, is, from an archaeologist's perspective, thought-provoking. On one level, it proposes models which have very specific archaeological implications. On another, it proposes an explanatory framework which is, to say the least, controversial among archaeologists. None of this is to say that Fischer's work is not enormously significant, whether one agrees with him or not. It is, however, important to note that *Albion's Seed* can elicit reactions from archaeologists that are quite different from those it evokes from historians, and that these differences have to do at least in part with the intellectual heritage of the two disciplines.

Differences of disciplinary history, terminology, and intellectual thrust operate to make interdisciplinary studies difficult indeed. There are, however, several strategies which can be used effectively to counter some of these difficulties. Clarity in both thinking and writing is critically important in interdisciplinary studies. Likewise, at least a passing knowledge of other disciplines and their intellectual heritage makes it easier to identify and correct instances of terminological confusion. Perhaps most important, however, is the identification of significant research problems. If areas of common interest cannot be discerned, interdisciplinary studies are doomed to failure from the start.

This volume is an attempt to address one of these areas of intersecting interests: community formation and maintenance in the backcountry. We define the term *community* in the broadest sense—that is, as a group of people with a common characteristic or interest living within a larger society. This is a topic broad enough to engage historians, geographers, and archaeologists, but one not so broad that studies carried out under its rubric are rendered trite and meaningless. Further, it is a topical area that can be addressed with a minimal amount of specialized jargon or terms, thus facilitating cross-disciplinary communication.

Structure of the Volume

The authors in this volume begin their explanation by exploring the meanings, both present and historical, of the terms *backcountry* and *frontier*. The terms are not necessarily interchangeable, and their very use invokes criticism. Both derive their meanings through contrast with other terms referring to already settled areas. Beginning with the century-old work of Frederick Jackson Turner, a *frontier* was considered "a migrating region," a stage of initial occupation and settlement by Europeans. In this volume, Robert Mitchell notes that frontiers were transitory; he emphasizes movement and instability, in a gradual and generally westward flow across the continent. *Backcountry* refers to a more specific place, although its precise boundaries remain open to discussion. Mitchell's chapter gives it a "bounded identity."

The southern backcountry extends from portions of Virginia through the Carolinas and Georgia and pockets of Tennessee. Historically, the backcountry was an area of secondary settlement by Europeans, after initial physical and economic conquest of the coastal regions. Backcountry studies focus on the middle of the eighteenth century, from initial settlement as early as the 1720s through the changes brought by the American Revolution. At its western margins in Tennessee, however, the backcountry survived as a culturally distinct region well into the early nineteenth century.

Despite its fluid boundaries and changing levels of economic development, the backcountry retains social and economic distinctions from previously settled regions. The Europeans who settled the backcountry were in many ways different from those who generations earlier had put down roots in the tidewater areas. Scotch-Irish, Scots, Germanic, and nonconformist English groups traveled down the Shenandoah Valley from Pennsylvania or from Atlantic ports. These individuals and groups tended to establish small farms and, later, grain-processing centers, and they had relatively little need for slave labor.

Other characteristics of backcountry society were its multiracial and multiethnic character, and the way relations and identities of its component groups shifted. To tidewater European Americans, Indians were a distant memory. No longer residents of the plantation lowcountry, Native Americans were simply large, distant confederations of sometimes troublesome people, whose traded deerskins supported the coastal economy. In the backcountry, native and newly arrived people often met face to face, and the battle for lands often was a dangerous business. Indians' continued presence created a different political and economic order; until the advent of ethnohistory, Indians were underrepresented in studies of the backcountry.

Backcountry settlers of African descent also are underrepresented in the historical literature and even in current interdisciplinary studies. Arriving and working in a small-farm economy principally as bonded laborers, they were seen as less necessary, and thus were fewer, than in the plantation-based tidewater. From the cattle herders of the early eighteenth century to the cotton-plantation laborers of the early nineteenth century, though, African Americans made up a significant part of backcountry society.

If the definition of *backcountry* implies relatively stable spatial boundaries, then its functional definition changes as the backcountry evolves. As Robert Mitchell notes, the southern backcountry was "an expanding zone of encounters," among both new environments and new peoples. Power relationships, land ownership, a rise in urbanism and capitalism—all these combined in an evolving society that remained socially, politically, and economically a part of coastal and European communities.

The first two chapters of this volume address the development of interdisciplinary studies of the backcountry from the perspectives of history and geography. Robert Mitchell's examination of geography's part in modern backcountry studies identifies several themes which are ripe for interdisciplinary dialogue and collaboration. His review of community formation processes in the Shenandoah Valley makes it clear that it is only by reconstructing the landscape of the mid-eighteenth century that one can begin to understand occupation of the backcountry at what he calls "points of attachment."

Interdisciplinary research on past landscapes focuses on the relationship of people and land. Landscape studies explore how people shaped, and were shaped by, the land they occupied. As defined by John Stillgoe and others,[13] the landscape is not natural but is modified for permanent human occupation in all forms; this modification is by design, and the landscape embodies natural, material, social, and ideological elements. Although these elements may not be shared equitably, J. B. Jackson suggests that the collective, evolving character of the landscape is agreed on by all generations and all points of view. Landscape creation and use, then, fulfills multiple needs simultaneously, from food production to formal design to explicit statements of dominant social position.[14]

It seems likely that new kin relationships, which crosscut ethnic lines, were responsible for many of the later developments in the Shenandoah Valley, as well as on other frontiers. In several of the South Carolina townships, for instance, German speakers after the first generation intermarried into Anglophone families, leading to the rapid disintegration of spatially discrete ethnic communities and the formation of new communities with their own sets of dynamics. Mitchell's essay makes clear that the concept of landscape is one which can be used fruitfully by geographers, historians, and archaeologists alike. Thus it can serve as one unifying concept in an arsenal of interdisciplinary perspectives.

Michael Puglisi's survey of recent backcountry research points out that, in many ways, the initiation of community studies of the backcountry was dependent upon the incorporation of ideas relating to spatial patterning. While the use of space and the landscape that use produces are concepts relatively new to historians, they have yielded promising results. In one sense Puglisi's essay is reassuring: he points out that many of us, to some extent, already incorporate an interdisciplinary perspective in our work. However, he makes clear, citing examples from ongoing studies of Winchester, Virginia, that the potential for such cross-fertilization is only beginning to be realized.

Turk McCleskey's study of real estate claims in southwestern Virginia is the first of a series of case studies. McCleskey's focus on kin networks and their relationship to land holding patterns runs counter to Frederick Jackson Turner's notion that low land prices drove the frontier settlement process. Rather, as McCleskey notes, attempts to maintain kin networks often overrode simple issues of land availability and price. These attempts to maintain kin groups represented a nexus of social, economic, and political objectives. McCleskey's argument has important implications for both geographers and archaeologists. For instance, his identification of spatially discrete kin groups opens the possibility that archaeological surveys could locate these earliest home sites. By linking specific land holdings with particular families, measures of economic and social status could be applied to the artifact assemblages from related families. Similarly, overlaying plats from family groups over soil distribution maps might reveal patterning not only between, but also within, kin cells.

One of the "points of attachment" referred to by Mitchell was Augusta, Georgia. Founded for the explicit purpose of disrupting the Carolina deerskin traders in the Creek Nation, Augusta was a place where both Indians and European American traders and planters felt comfortable. As Edward Cashin points out, Augusta existed as an island of stability in the backcountry until the coming of a new social class, referred to by their social superiors as "Crackers." Crackers were recognized even by the Creeks themselves as a distinctive type, in large part because, unlike traders, who were interested in the exchange of skins for goods, Crackers were interested in one thing and one thing only—Creek land. The newcomers upset the always tenuous balance among competing interests and provided the context for an emerging axis between Savannah-area merchants and backcountry yeomen. This axis would reach fruition in the American Revolution.

The upper classes in new towns like Augusta brought with them the notion of refined, or gentlemanly, behavior which pervaded European society in the eighteenth and early nineteenth centuries, and which ushered in the consumer revolution of this period. Manners, behavior, and material equipage were studied carefully. People were judged by their manners, their possession of certain material items, and the ability to use them properly. In the twentieth century, the example of improper tea usage cited by Cashin seems mildly humorous. However, for the late-eighteenth-century colonists such rituals held great symbolic significance.

Settlement of the backcountry occurred during the height of the consumer revolution of the eighteenth century. As Chesapeake scholar Ann Smart Martin has suggested, "Great prosperity, improvements in manufacturing and distribution, and a new willingness to spend combined to bring a greater quantity, quality, and variety of objects into the lives of American middling ranks," at a time when traditional notions of class were being challenged by new ideas about social mobility. Martin explores the issue of the eighteenth-century consumer revolution in her study of backcountry Virginia merchants. This impressive interdisciplinary study uses documents, probate records, material culture, and archaeological evidence to note that merchants brought to the backcountry all the trappings of tidewater shore life; moreover, Martin portrays the backcountry merchant as a shaper, not a follower, of local taste. Martin successfully measures differences in the purchasing methods and consumer goods used by backcountry folk and sophisticated easterners, noting that members of the elites and those who aspired to that status invested in social knowledge as well as social goods, thus maintaining social distance.[15]

Studies in this volume echo the results of Martin's research. Augusta's settlers in log cabins and Charleston's merchant-planters in brick single houses all used the same porcelain and pearlware teacups, recovered two hundred years later by archaeologists. Recent research at the township of New Windsor in the South Carolina backcountry has amplified our knowledge of the flow of new consumer goods and accompanying ideas to what was a struggling, and ultimately unsuccessful, frontier settlement. Settled in 1737 and intended to include a town and outlying field systems, New Windsor never amounted to more than a scatter of small farms strung along the terraces of the Savannah River. By the 1760s, Augusta had supplanted New Windsor as the center of the Indian trade. Nonetheless, archaeological and historical data clearly indicate that many New Windsor residents were able to buy the same goods as their "betters" in Charleston; what's more, they understood the social significance and proper usage of the items. The evidence emerging from New Windsor and settlements like it signify the global connectedness of backcountry settlements, and the need to explore market systems, transportation networks, the world economy, and the motivations of outsiders.[16]

The delicate balancing act played out in Augusta, Georgia, in the 1760s was emblematic of tensions throughout the backcountry. In a given individual, social class was inextricably bound up with other characteristics, including, of course, ethnicity. Like humans in any other society, backcountry folk operated on a series of cues, visual and otherwise, in their dealings with each other. Occasionally we are lucky enough to glimpse echoes of those cue systems in operation. All communities include gathering places which are scenes of complex social interactions. Daniel Thorp examines one type of community gathering place—taverns—in order to tease apart the intersecting roles of class, ethnicity, and gender. Thorp's study yields results which are both frustrating and enticing from the standpoint of interdisciplinary studies. For instance, it seems clear that gender roles are nearly invisible in the inventories from a tavern in Bethabara, North Carolina. On the other hand, customer lists indicate that ethnicity may have been a less permeable barrier to social interaction than geographer Mitchell's work in the Shenandoah Valley indicates. The material culture implications for such findings are intriguing, if somewhat unclear. Both gender and ethnicity can be enormously problematical to detect archaeologically.[17] This may be at least partially due to the nature of the archaeological record itself, which has been affected by natural processes which lead to deterioration and the complete loss of some data classes. However, Thorp's essay introduces the notion that, at least in the case of backcountry taverns, our inability to trace ethnicity and gender may be due to their lack of correlates in the material record.

The components of that material record—broken sherds of salt-glazed stoneware teacups, remnants of mirror glass, brass buttons and leaded-glass stemware found at archaeological sites—once were central props in the intricate social dances documented by Thorp. Buying and transporting those props to the backcountry were roles which became increasingly important as the century wore on—roles which led to the formation of a small, wealthy class of merchants. Backcountry merchants had regional impact, as Kenneth Lewis points out in his study of Camden, South Carolina, one of a series of small towns, villages, and crossroads communities which dramatically affected the economic, social, and material life of the surrounding countryside.

In his study of Camden, Lewis explores processes of urbanization and landscape development, enunciates a series of characteristics particular to frontier towns, and identifies those activities involved with collection and redistribution of goods and commodities. A major theme of Lewis's study is that backcountry urban centers were deliberately planned, often the product of land speculation and the politics of development. A second theme is the diversity of the colonial urban population. In some cases the various groups found niches, and conflict was slow to develop. At other times the conflict was more overt, as Edward Cashin points out.

Pine Tree Hill, in the South Carolina backcountry, evolved into the thriving center of commerce called Camden in large part because of the efforts of one man, Joseph Kershaw. Kershaw arrived at the Quaker settlement in 1758. The place was ideally located for the Indian trade, and Kershaw acted rapidly to introduce a range of new economic pursuits. These were underwritten by the growing importance of wheat as a backcountry crop. The influx of capital allowed external commerce to rise, which in turn resulted in an accelerated rate of wealth accumulation in the town. Lewis's adoption of a regional approach to settlement pattern analysis allows us to view Camden within a complex web of backcountry economic relationships. His combination of geographical and archaeological data suggests the power of the interdisciplinary approach in explaining frontier town development.

Camden itself testifies to the power of the individual in influencing regional economic and social trends. Individuals are difficult to detect archaeologically; in fact, an axiom of prehistoric archaeology in the 1960s and 1970s was that "there are no individuals in the past." This perspective was the result of several factors. The first of these was the influence of Marxist thought, which in its classical form de-emphasizes the individual. In addition, cultural ecology, which focuses on the interactions of society and ecological systems, gained currency.[18] Finally, of course, and perhaps most important, the nature of much prehistoric archaeological sites is such that the material record of the individual often is lost—or at least is unrecognizable.[19] Historical archaeologists have an advantage in this regard. We often can link specific artifact assemblages and sites with individuals whom we can know, at some level, through various sorts of archival documentation. Lewis's study thus binds together the three disciplines represented in this volume—history, geography, and archaeology—in such a way that we do not lose sight of the individual within his larger regional context.

Although slavery typically was not a critical component of backcountry economies, some landowners invested heavily in bondsmen, and it is safe to say that many more aspired to be slave holders. George Galphin, for instance, was a Carolina deerskin trader who built a fortune on his dealings with the Creeks in the 1750s and 1760s. His real aspiration, however, was to be a planter—an aspiration he eventually fulfilled. When he drafted his will in 1776, he counted among his possessions 114 slaves. While Galphin was an exception in the sense that not many peltry traders made the transition to gentleman planter, he probably was not alone in his desire to create for himself and his family the kind of plantation kingdom typified by Tidewater Virginia's elite.[20]

Monica Beck, an archaeologist, examines another type of transition—from yeoman farmer to gentleman planter—through an examination of the changing spatial relationships between the big house and the slave quarters. This is an area in which archaeology can contribute much, because recreation of yardscapes and the activity areas they enclose is possible through relatively simple field techniques. The difficulty comes in interpreting the changes that take place through time in such a yardscape, and it is here that her study provides unique insight. Beck's examination of the yardscape at Brattonsville is intriguing, not only because she is able to tease apart the changing nature of backcountry slavery in the late eighteenth century, but also because she incorporates into her study primary documents that give a human voice to the byproducts of everyday life that archaeologists typically recover from shovel tests. Her approach holds promise not only for more detailed examinations of slavery in the backcountry, but also for interpretations of power relationships in other settings as well.

The efforts of backcountry traders and farmers to replicate eastern lifeways often resulted in outcomes that were overtly symbolic in nature. Such was the case of Knoxville, Tennessee. The archaeological manifestations of high-status individuals like William Blount, the first governor, are complex. Charles Faulkner demonstrates that, while certain classes of material culture, such as imported ceramics, seem to be sensitive indicators of economic (and perhaps social) status on the frontier, other indicators are much harder to read. Faulkner points out that architecture in the early town reflected vernacular rules, but that within the log and timber homes might be found imported goods like those available in coastal cities. Faulkner's research opens the possibility of examining status within the context of a developing town. The examination of social and economic classes in frontier settings is fraught with difficulties, one of which is the fact that various sources of information often seem to support contradictory inferences. This study illustrates the fact that these indicators reflect the complexities of frontier social structures.

The transportation networks in Tennessee discussed by David Hsiung reflected the attempt by frontier communities to replicate eastern conditions on the frontier at a regional level. Hsiung's chapter reminds us that such nodes of interaction were part of a widespread communications network from the earliest settlement of the frontier. Hsiung uses the concepts of *Gemeinschaft* and *Gesellschaft* (community and society) to examine the communities in Washington County, Tennessee. By mapping the early road network, Hsiung shows that connectedness varies along several different axes. For instance, while an individual might identify himself as part of a regional economy that includes livestock markets in Charleston, South Carolina, local relationships like militia membership were more inward-directed. His use of sociological and geographical concepts reveals the complex nature of social and economic networks among East Tennessee communities. Hsiung's approach has direct implications for the archaeological record. Like McCleskey's kin-based perspective, it lends itself to settlement pattern analysis, in which population distributions are tracked across the natural and cultural landscape through systematic archaeological survey and limited testing. McCleskey's kin-based networks form one aspect of the connectedness spectrum that Hsiung has documented for East Tennessee.

Men like Tennessee's William Blount attempted to direct community formation through a combination of social prestige, political power, and economic development. However, the native cultures of the backcountry also produced such individuals. Caught in a nexus of conflicting loyalties, tribal leaders (many themselves offspring of European American and Native American parents) often attempted to negotiate a path between outright hostility to the newcomers and base subservience. As if this were not difficult enough, territories and states often had agendas different from those of the central government. Particularly during the confederacy and in the early decades of the federal republic, edicts frequently were subverted or simply ignored by local authorities. Indian leaders traveled to Washington to sign treaties and receive gifts and medals from federal authorities, only to find when they returned to their homes that governors and local militia units had no intention of safeguarding their rights under treaty obligations. Cherokee Judge John Martin typifies these conflicts. Born in the closing days of the southeastern frontier, Martin was a key figure in complex maneuverings involving the national capital, the state of Georgia, and various factions of the Cherokee Nation. Elizabeth Fields places Martin in the context of the rapidly changing early-nineteenth-century backcountry, when the national gaze shifted from the Atlantic seaboard to the Old Southwest. Martin (only one-eighth Cherokee) was a successful planter and slave owner who at one point pledged to uphold the U.S. Constitution and later moved to the Cherokee Nation. Giving up a succession of farms, he lived his final days in the new Trans-Mississippi West.

Fields examines the series of political decisions that Martin made through his life as one of a small group of political leaders, most of whom were of mixed ancestry. Their decisions regarding the Cherokee Nation (most of whose citizens were full-blooded) often reflected their pragmatic views of white-Indian relations. Well versed in the political ways of the new national capital, Martin understood the price he would pay for renunciation of the white world. Yet renounce it he did, choosing instead to lead his mother's people. One cannot help feeling that he and William Blount would have had much in common, despite their diametrically opposed cultural and political backgrounds.

The kin cells identified by McCleskey as so important in the settlement of the Shenandoah undoubtedly were, at least in their initial stages, strongly oriented along ethnic lines. German speakers, in particular, acquired a reputation for community insularity. Donald Linebaugh probes German insularity using the nineteenth-century drawings of Lewis Miller, a German folk artist who recorded his views and experiences in the Shenandoah Valley. Using the ethnological concept of controlled acculturation, Linebaugh presents architectural evidence that supports his contention that German ethnic identity continued to exist and evolve into the late nineteenth century. Perhaps as important, he outlines a range of expectations that other disciplines could address in examining the problem of direction, speed, and degree of cultural mixing among the ethnically diverse backcountry population. Linebaugh is not the first archaeologist to use contemporary art in the analysis of historic features.[21] But he is one of first to go beyond examining art merely for the purpose of artifact and feature identification. He seeks answers to questions of acculturation on a regional level. By taking the data from a particular site and comparing it to Miller's art, Linebaugh shows archaeologists a way to escape the confines of single-site excavation.

Although Linebaugh himself does not fall into this trap, his study brings to mind two false assumptions that are all too easy to make. First, acculturation most often is viewed as a struggle between dominant and subordinate cultures, with the dominant culture forcing change and the subordinate one struggling mightily to preserve its identity. Linebaugh's data, however, do not convince us that German speakers were under significant pressure from their neighbors to adapt to Anglophone culture(s). It may be more accurate to view acculturation as a two-way street (so-called "creolization").

The second assumption made by some modern scholars is a product of the chain stores and shopping malls which impart an identical "look" to all American cities and rural landscapes. There is a largely unconscious assumption that early America was characterized by a similar pan-American landscape; any differences were signs of unique ethnic resistance. In fact, this pan-American landscape is a post–World War II development. In this regard, Robert Mitchell's description of backcountry development as "lumpy" makes much more sense than identifying occasional small areas of ethnic resistance.

Robert Mitchell's call for a shared set of research questions requiring interdisciplinary cooperation is an excellent way to promote the synergism that can illuminate the backcountry. In this volume's epilogue, Warren Hofstra provides examples of the broader questions and concerns that can emerge from such synergisms. He concludes that history is written anew by each generation, conditioned to a large degree by the problems facing that generation. At the same time, we all are influenced by our intellectual forebears, even though we may focus on very different topics. As Hofstra points out, Turner himself recognized that only an interdisciplinary approach can give us the real backcountry. If we acknowledge the necessity of integrating history, geography, and archaeology in order to know the past, we beg the question of how much must be known about what has been done in other disciplines before research can progress beyond the simple compilation of data. When does a variety of disciplinary perspectives muddy, rather than clarify, the water? There is no easy answer to this question. While it is true that interdisciplinary research can make the waters murky, it is equally true that the more disciplines and data available, the broader the *potential* horizon of our knowledge. Still, it is easy to sympathize with the captain of a ship who had all the latest electronic and satellite navigational devices on board but eventually turned them all off, except one. That way he always knew where he was. Unlike our mythical captain, the authors of this volume hope to encourage others studying the backcountry to look outside their own disciplines for inspiration and insight. The degree to which we use perspectives and techniques adopted from other historical disciplines will vary with the questions asked and the data available. This volume is offered in the belief that interdisciplinary perspectives can help us understand the early American past in ways which we are only beginning to explore. But explore them we must. For, as Warren Hofstra notes, only by knowing the past can we fully understand the issues facing our society today.

NOTES

1. Loren Eiseley, *The Night Country* (New York: Charles Scribner's and Sons, 1971).
2. For a sample of the various positions in this debate, see Robert L. Schuyler, ed., *Historical Archaeology: A Guide to Substantive and Theoretical Contributions* (Farmingdale, N.Y.: Baywood Publishing Co., 1978); and Stanley South, ed., *Pioneers in Historical Archaeology: Breaking New Ground* (New York: Plenum Press, 1994).
3. Stanley South, *Method and Theory in Historical Archaeology* (New York: Academic Press, 1977). This book was the most influential treatise for the anthropological movement in historical archaeology at that time.
4. For an example of the integration of archaeology, history, and oral history, see William H. Adams, *Silcott, Washington: Ethnoarchaeology of a Rural American Community*, Reports of Investigations 54 (Pullman: Washington State Univ., Laboratory of Anthropology, 1977); and William H. Adams, ed., *Waverly Plantation: Ethnoarchaeology of a Tenant Farming Community* (Washington, D. C.: National Technical Information Service, 1980).
5. The moderators of the conference included Steven D. Smith, Univ. of South Carolina; Albert Tillson, Jr., Univ. of Tampa; Martha Zierden, Charleston Museum; and Warren Hofstra, Shenandoah Univ., Winchester, Va.
6. See, e.g., D. L. Meltzer, D. D. Fowler, and J. A. Sabloff, eds., *American Archaeology, Past and Future: A Celebration of the Society for American Archaeology, 1935–1985* (Washington, D.C.: Smithsonian Institution Press, 1986).
7. James Deetz, "American Historical Archaeology: Methods and Results," *Science* 239 (1988): 362–67.
8. David Hackett Fischer, *Albion's Seed: Four British Folkways in America* (New York: Oxford Univ. Press, 1989).
9. But see N. C. Landsman, "*Albion's Seed: Four British Folkways in America*—A Symposium," *William and Mary Quarterly* 3d ser. 48, no. 2 (1991): 253–60.

10. Fischer, *Albion's Seed*, 747-53.
11. See, e.g., George Miller, "A Revised Set of CC Index Values for Classification and Economic Scaling of English Ceramics from 1787 to 1880," *Historical Archaeology* 25, no. 1 (1991): 1-26; Suzanne Spencer-Wood, *Consumer Choice in Historical Archaeology* (New York: Plenum Press, 1987); Amy Friedlander, "House and Barn: The Wealth of Farmers," *Historical Archaeology* 25, no. 1 (1991): 3-15; David Crass and D. Wallsmith, "Where's the Beef? Diet at an Antebellum Frontier Post," *Historical Archaeology* 26, no. 2 (1992): 3-23; M. C. Beaudry, ed., *Documentary Archaeology in the New World* (Cambridge, England: Cambridge Univ. Press, 1988); John Solomon Otto, *Cannon's Point Plantation: Living Conditions and Status Patterns in the Old South* (Orlando, Fla.: Academic Press, 1984); R. S. Dickens, ed., *Archaeology of Urban America: The Search for Pattern and Process* (Orlando, Fla.: Academic Press, 1982).
12. E. Hatch, *Theories of Man and Culture* (New York: Columbia Univ. Press, 1973). The coming of the "new" archaeology of the 1960s resulted in the near-complete renunciation of diffusion as an mechanism for explaining culture change. One of the most influential figures in archaeological theory during this time was Lewis Binford, who argued against a normative view of culture and for one which was multivariate and, at its most basic level, materialist. Fischer's claims notwithstanding, materialist explanations of historical phenomena were proposed long before the 1980s; see K. Marx and F. Engels, "The German Ideology," in *Collected Works of Marx and Engels*, 5:19-92 (New York: International Publishers, 1976). See also Lewis Binford, "Archaeological Systematics and the Study of Culture Process," *American Antiquity* 29 (1965): 203-10; and Lewis Binford, *In Pursuit of the Past: Decoding the Archaeological Record* (London: Thames and Hudson, 1983). This is not to say that, at some level, archaeologists *must* view culture as normative.
13. Martha Zierden and Linda F. Stine, "Historical Landscapes through the Prism of Archaeology," in *Carolina's Historical Landscapes*, ed. Linda F. Stine, Martha Zierden, Lesley Drucker, and Chris Judge (Knoxville: Univ. of Tennessee Press, 1997), xi-xvi; John R. Stilgoe, *Common Landscapes of America, 1580-1845* (New Haven, Conn.: Yale Univ. Press, 1982); James Brinckerhoff Jackson, *Discovering the Vernacular Landscape* (New Haven: Yale Univ. Press, 1984).
14. James Deetz, "Prologue: Landscapes as Cultural Statements," in *Earth Patterns*, ed. William Kelso and Rachel Most, 1-4 (Charlottesville: Univ. of Virginia Press, 1990); Stine et al., *Carolina's Historical Landscapes*.
15. Richard Bushman, *Refinement in America: Persons, Houses, Cities* (New York: Alfred A Knopf, 1992); Ann Smart Martin, "Frontier Boys and Country Cousins: The Context for Choice in Eighteenth-Century Consumerism," in *Historical Archaeology and the Study of American Culture*, ed. Lu Ann De Cunzo and Bernard L. Herman (Winterthur, Del.: Winterthur Museum, 1996), 71-102.
16. David Colin Crass, Bruce R. Penner, Tammy R. Forehand, John Huffman, Lois J. Potter, and Larry Potter, *Excavations at New Windsor Township, South Carolina*, Savannah River Archaeological Research Heritage Series 3 (Columbia: South Carolina Institute of Archaeology and Anthropology, Univ. of South Carolina, 1997). See also

John C. Huffman, "Preliminary Investigation of New Windsor Township from the Perspective of the Insular-Cosmopolitan Paradigm" (Master's thesis, Univ. of Idaho, 1997); Bruce Penner, "Old World Traditions, New Word Landscapes: Ethnicity and Archaeology of Swiss Appenzellers in the Colonial South Carolina Backcountry," *International Journal of Historical Archaeology*, in press; David Colin Crass, Bruce R. Penner, and Tammy R. Forehand, "Gentility and Material Culture on the Carolina Frontier," *Historical Archaeology*, in press. See also Martha Zierden, "The Urban Landscape," in Stine et al., *Carolina's Historical Landscapes*, 161–74; Kenneth E. Lewis, *Camden: A Frontier Town in Eighteenth-Century South Carolina*, Anthropological Studies 2 (Columbia: South Carolina Institute of Archaeology and Anthropology, Univ. of South Carolina, 1976).

17. See Leland Ferguson, *Uncommon Ground: Archaeology and Early African America, 1650–1800* (Washington, D.C.: Smithsonian Institution Press, 1992); Donna Siefert, ed., Gender in Historical Archaeology, *Historical Archaeology* 25, no. 4 (1991). For an early effort to probe ethnicity at a historic site, see J. O. Brew, "St. Francis at Awatovi," in *Pioneers in Historical Archaeology: Breaking New Ground*, ed. Stanley South, 27–47 (New York: Plenum Press, 1994). One of the best recent statements on ethnicity in archaeology is Dell Upton, "Ethnicity, Authenticity, and Invented Traditions," *Historical Archaeology* 30, no. 2 (1996): 1–7.

18. For the initial iteration of cultural ecology, see J. Steward, "Basin-Plateau Aboriginal Socio-Political Groups," *Bureau of American Ethnology Bulletin* 120 (1938).

19. The most outstanding example of the removal of individuals from archaeological cultures probably was reached in the 1970s, when "general systems theory" was adopted as an explanatory mechanism by many of the "new" archaeologists. See Kent V. Flannery, "Archaeological Systems Theory and Early Mesoamerica," in *Anthropological Archeology in the Americas*, ed. Betty J. Meggers, 67–87 (Washington, D.C.: Anthropological Society of Washington).

20. David Colin Crass, Bruce Penner, Tammy Forehand, Lois Potter, and Larry Potter, "A Man of Great Liberality: Recent Research at George Galphin's Silver Bluff," *South Carolina Antiquities* 27, nos. 1 and 2 (1995): 26–41.

21. One of the best examples still is Ivor Noël Hume, *A Guide to Artifacts of Colonial America* (New York: Alfred A. Knopf, 1970), but also see Stanley South, *Spanish Artifacts from Santa Elena*, Anthropological Studies 7 (Columbia: South Carolina Institute of Archaeology and Anthropology, Univ. of South Carolina, 1988). Colonial Williamsburg Foundation has been at the forefront of using contemporaneous art to interpret artifacts and past landscapes in its various museums.

The Southern Backcountry:
A Geographical House Divided

Robert D. Mitchell

The ritual of fin de siècle rumination has begun in earnest for the late twentieth century. During the 1980s we witnessed a remarkable flurry of new works proclaiming a grand, revised synthesis of the achievements of early European Americans. Three of these works—Bernard Bailyn's The Peopling of British North America (1986), Jack Greene's Pursuits of Happiness (1989), and David Hackett Fischer's Albion's Seed (1989)—were products of historians. Two studies, Donald Meinig's Atlantic America, 1492–1800 (1986), and The American Backwoods Frontier (1989) by Terry Jordan and Matti Kaups,[1] were creations of geographers. That these reevaluations of early America have tended to cloud rather than clarify our understanding of American society should not surprise us in this age of postmodernist criticism. It is likely, however, that the disagreements that have ensued have more to do with perspective than with philosophy. Historians and geographers, like historical archaeologists, retain the viewpoints of their training and so take diverse disciplinary approaches to common problems and issues.

This condition has existed since the formation of academic disciplines during the last third of the nineteenth century, but the intellectual climate of that era differed markedly from ours today. Frederick Jackson Turner's presentation to the annual meeting of the American Historical Association in 1893, entitled "The Significance of the Frontier in American History," makes this abundantly clear, for it ushered in an age of frontier research that absorbed the energies of America's social historians for the next three generations.[2] American geographers, emerging from their own intellectual heritage of the late nineteenth century, were attracted to this frontier thesis because for them it concerned critical issues in the encounters between environments and societies. Thus began the first cautious communications between historians and geographers over the configuration of land and life during America's initial interior expansion. Despite some vigorous oral and written exchanges between 1904 and 1914, historians and geographers operated from very different philosophical and methodological premises, and the interdisciplinary results were both disappointing and divisive.[3]

It is the cautious premise of this paper that the circumstances facing us a century later, within more intellectually turbulent yet more receptive times, will result in a more constructive outcome. The caution expressed is the result of considering three paradoxes of interdisciplinary research which have emerged since the 1960s. Historical geographers and historians of early America have continued a dialogue that, while occasionally tentative and uneven, has expanded as geographers began to produce their own substantive literature on the American past. This has created the first paradox: as geographers have become more prolific, intradisciplinary contrasts in training and outlook have become more evident and controversy more frequent. The second paradox has to do with the communication between historical geographers and historical archaeologists in the United States, which remains largely undeveloped.[4] Despite an obvious point of attachment in their shared interest in form-process relationships, and particularly in inferring process from form, geographers and archaeologists generally have followed divergent paths. The third paradox derives from the previous two. Although geographers and historians have conversed more frequently, historians have incorporated few geographical concepts or methods in their work, while archaeologists have been industrious borrowers of geographical ideas.[5]

This paper is concerned principally with examining how geographers have determined what and where the southern colonial backcountry is said to be. The general indifference of colonial historians to morphological matters—that is, to human distributions and locations, to environmental relations, to settlement landscapes, and to regional boundaries—suggests that place and form are less important than process and function. Geographers, on the other hand, have expended considerable energy in arguing that place matters and that social processes cannot be understood fully without appropriate attention to their spatial organization. Frederick Jackson Turner understood this argument. Although his ideas about early American development now are largely discarded by historians and strongly criticized by geographers, they continue to provide a convenient base line from which to measure the impact of geographical ideas on our cumulative understanding of the complexities of the southern colonial backcountry.

TURNER'S BACKCOUNTRY: OLD WEST AND NEW SOUTH

The two most significant ideas that Turner introduced into the academic lexicon were those of "frontier" and "section." Use of the term "back country" was contemporaneous with these concepts. Turner rightly has been criticized for his loose and ambiguous use of the term "frontier," but he viewed it most consistently as "a migrating region, a stage of society rather than a place."[6] A frontier, therefore, was an initial but temporary stage of settlement that "passed through" an area, to be replaced by a second, more stable stage. Frontiers were repetitive stages of occupancy through which all western or interior areas went before they emerged as fully developed places. Turner's use of the terms "section" and "back country," however, was more definitive. In 1904, he remarked on "the South":

> Through a long period of our history the "Solid South" did not exist ... [there were] not only differences between the various states of the Southern Seaboard, but also the more fundamental differences between the upcountry (the Piedmont region) and the Atlantic Plains. The interior of the South needs treatment as a unit ... as yet no one has attacked the problem of the settlement, development, and influence of the Piedmont Plains as a whole. This peninsula ... thrust down through the Great Valley from Pennsylvania between the mountains and the seaboard, the land that received the German, Scotch-Irish, and poorer white English settlers, developed in the second half of the eighteenth century, an independent social, economic, and political character. It was a region of free labor upon small farms. It was devoted to cereals rather than to the great staple crops of the seaboard. In its social structure it was more like Pennsylvania than the Southern commonwealths with which it was politically connected. It struggled for just representation in the legislatures, and for adequate local self-government. The domestic history of the South is for many years the history of a contest between these eastern and western sections.[7]

Turner later tried to define this "piedmont area" more precisely:

> The Piedmont Plateau, or upland area of the South, reaches from the fall line, behind the old tidewater, south westward to the Allegheny Mountains, in a long belt running from Pennsylvania to Georgia ... Historically, it was closely associated with the Great Valley of Pennsylvania and its continuation, the Shenandoah Valley, as well as with the Allegheny Mountains ... Thus it happened that from about 1730 to 1760 a generation of settlers poured along this mountain trough into the southern uplands, or Piedmont, creating a new continuous social and economic area, which cut across the artificial colonial boundary lines, disarranged the regular extension of local government from the coast westward, and built up a new Pennsylvania in contrast with the tidewater South. This New South composed [sic] the southern half of the Old West.[8]

Turner also has been criticized, less deservedly, for his limited attention to *place* in the formation of an American national identity. Indeed, historians and geographers have focused so intently on his frontier pronouncements that they have overlooked the way his idea of *sections* contributed to regional geography. I thus concur with Michael Steiner that we have underestimated the degree to which Turner viewed his sectional construct as a refinement of his frontier hypothesis.[9] Frontiers were transitory and emphasized movement and instability; sections were created out of frontiers and expressed community and stability within an emerging national whole. The following remarkable passage, published in 1925, attests to this:

> The United States has the problem of the clash of economic interests closely associated with regional geography on a huge scale. It was evident at the outset of a study of the frontier movement that the American people were not passing into a monotonously uniform space. Rather, even in the colonial period, they were entering successive different geographic provinces; they were pouring their plastic pioneer life into geographic molds. They would modify these molds, they would have progressive revelations of the capacities of the geographic provinces which they won and settled and developed; but even the task of dealing constructively with the different regions would work its effects upon their traits.
>
> Not a uniform surface, but a kind of checkerboard of differing environments, lay before them in their settlement. There would be the interplay of the migrating stocks and the new geographic provinces. The outcome would be a combination of the two factors, land and people, the creation of differing societies in the different sections.[10]

Although geographers may quibble with Turner's delineation of the southern colonial backcountry and his failure to define its boundaries after "obliterating the state boundaries which conceal its unity,"[11] he had given us, by the end of his career in 1933, a portrait of a region which later historians have struggled to improve.[12] Geographers interested in the colonial past also have sought to convey a more definitive configuration and even map the boundaries of the backcountry with a confidence no historian has been interested enough or brave enough to display.

Where Is the Common Ground?

Geographers demonstrated no specific interest in the colonial backcountry until the 1950s. There were three reasons for this. First, the status of historical studies in geography was problematical. During the 1930s, wavering between being ahistorical and antihistorical, the discipline became more inward-looking and stressed the importance of systematic and regional studies of geographic differentiation in the present.[13] Second, such concern with the past was maintained primarily by cultural geographers influenced by Carl Sauer. Sauer, a major critic of both Turner's frontier thesis and the environmental deterministic trends evident in the discipline before 1925, emphasized the importance of studying the past to understand the evolution of cultural landscapes. One achieved this more by examining culture history and seeking artifactual evidence on the landscape than by probing documentary evidence in archives. The geography of the past, therefore, was a means to an end rather than an end in itself.[14] Third, even as some geographers began to demonstrate a more overt historical interest during the 1940s, their leading practitioner, Ralph Brown, was convinced that the documentary record for the colonial era was inadequate for a competent geographical reconstruction.[15] Despite the pioneer work by Herman Friis in 1940 in reconstructing population patterns before 1790, Brown believed that a thorough geographical study of the American past was possible only after the first federal census and the creation of a national archive.[16]

The first to challenge this formidable set of disciplinary traditions and present a comprehensive account of the geography of the colonial period was Donald Meinig. In 1958, his paper "The American Colonial Era" was delivered before an Australian audience and published in the relatively obscure journal of the Royal Geographical Society of Australasia.[17] Arguing for a study of America's colonial origins, Meinig cited the population diversity of the colonies, their religious complexity, and the varied landscapes of regional settlement. He suggested a division of these landscapes into the familiar triumvirate of New England, Middle, and Southern colonies. His commentary on a colonial backcountry occurred in reference to the South. "The Southern Interior," he wrote, "was throughout a region of cattle and hog-raising with but a minimum of subsistence cropping, although by the time of the Revolution, some considerable advances had been made in Piedmont, [sic] Virginia."[18] In a more extended discussion, he differentiated an Upper South into an isolated Appalachian region of mountaineers and pioneer economies and more prosperous surrounding regions of the Piedmont and Central Kentucky and Tennessee, with their emphases on tobacco, corn, grasses, and livestock. The entire region became: "the border zone, displaying many Southern features in population, settlement, some use of slaves, and some emphasis upon the cash staple, yet it was not part of the Plantation South, and had a considerably more diversified, small-farm agriculture."[19]

Although Meinig tended to emphasize it in his disquisition, this Upper South was not, in his view, the backcountry that would be crucial to the nation's future. That distinction he reserved for a "heterogeneous Middle Atlantic region [that] anticipated the design for the rich agricultural complex which later spread across the Appalachians and broadened out over the Midwest: a high quality, balanced, mixed agriculture of grains, grasses, orchards, and livestock."[20] This was a theme to be taken up shortly by James Lemon in his doctoral study of southeastern Pennsylvania, prepared under the direction of Andrew Clark.[21]

It was Clark who, in 1960, initiated a renewed dialogue between geographers and historians by proposing his theme of "geographical change" for consideration by economic historians.[22] Despite its ambiguity (which Clark over the years failed to dissipate), this concept represented a major shift in the status and orientation of historical studies in geography. In contrast to the "culture history" approach advocated by Sauer, under whom Clark had completed his own doctorate, the doctrine of geographical change built on Ralph Brown's attempt to create an explicit agenda for geographers based upon studying the past for its own sake through careful examination of the documentary record. Clark, then, spoke directly to historians and used their methods. One of his first doctoral students, Roy Merrens, was to extend this dialogue specifically to colonial historians five years later.[23] It was among Clark's students, therefore, that the first attempts at redefining the morphology of a southern regional experience were made, and it was the southern colonial backcountry that became the principal arena for subsequent and competing geographical perspectives on the European American past.

The term "backcountry" was not particularly current among this new generation of historical geographers. Its widespread use today, however, evokes the immediate geographical question, "Back of what?" "Backcountry" is a term both Eurocentric and ethnocentric, since it reflects a view of the American past predicated on pioneer English settlement of the Atlantic coast. It is a more concrete term geographically than "frontier," however, because it suggests an area, or at least a zone, with a reasonably distinct regional expression and set of boundaries (the point holds even if we admit that backcountry tends to expand). The following discussion focuses, first, on how geographers have attempted to define those boundaries and, second, on how these attempts reflect contrasting perspectives on the content and symbolism of the backcountry.

Defining the Backcountry in Space: Bounded Identity

Regionalization of the backcountry has revolved around identifying the area's distinctive characteristics and plotting their distribution. Geographers seeking to draw regional boundaries were, until my own research on the Shenandoah Valley was published during the 1970s, limited to interpreting secondary historical sources and identifying settlement relics in the landscape. Some geographers nonetheless were able to define and delineate the boundaries of a distinctive, interior, upland area with no direct access to coastal navigation. They suggested a broad range of criteria that differentiated this interior from a coastal South variously termed "coastal plain," "tidewater," "lowcountry," and "lowland South."

Wilbur Zelinsky, a cultural geographer, most effectively synthesizes such tentative descriptions of the early southern interior. The traits upon which he places most emphasis are settlement patterns, building traditions, and ethnic-folk origins. His map of contemporary culture areas, published in 1973 and unaltered in a revised publication in 1992, contains some interesting conclusions. The early regionalization of the colonial era is evident in the distinction among New England, Midland, and Southern culture areas. The boundary between Midland and Southern regions places most of Maryland and most of the Shenandoah Valley in the Midland region. A curious southward loop into the Shenandoah Valley appears to be based principally on the distribution of relict Pennsylvania forebay barns, a symbolic reminder of Midland influences on the Southern backcountry.[24] The South itself is divided into three subregions based upon historical settlement processes. Inland from a narrow coastal strip, identified as "early British colonial South," is a "Lowland South" that encompasses most of the Virginia piedmont, much of the Carolina lowcountry and piedmont, and most of Georgia. West of this region is an "Upland South," bounded approximately by the Blue Ridge in Virginia, the western Carolinas, northern Georgia and Alabama, and the Ohio Valley, with an outlier in the Ozarks.

Geographers concerned with unraveling this kind of regional structure have suggested an explanatory framework predicated upon ideas of culture areas and the diffusion of culture traits. The principal questions, as expressed by Meinig, have been: (1) Why do major cultural patterns and movements begin where they do (the problem of the "culture hearth")? and (2) How do they spread to other peoples and areas (a problem of "spatial diffusion")?[25]

Most cultural geographers have imagined the early southern interior as a variation on their picture of an Upland South, a term familiar to historical archaeologists but one rarely used by historians. Three comprehensive statements have emerged from this research. Fred Kniffen and Henry Glassie presented the thesis during the mid-1960s that folk traditions of house and barn construction (particularly in wood with half-dovetailing and saddle notching) and the distribution of the "I" house (one room deep, two stories high, and long-side entrance) best defined an Upland South. Kniffen's premise in particular was that form expressed function and defined process. "The great contributions of the Middle Atlantic source area," he wrote, "were the English 'I' house and German log construction and basic barn types."[26] These structures diffused from southeastern Pennsylvania across Pennsylvania to the Ohio Valley, through western Virginia to Kentucky, and southward in the Valley of Virginia to northeastern Tennessee and the piedmont areas of the colonial South. The geographical result, Kniffen believed, was an Upland South whose northern and western boundaries remained unclear but whose eastern boundary bordered the Virginia Blue Ridge and extended across the piedmont to leave only a narrow coastal band of "Tidewater South." Glassie believed, however, that to posit such a boundary was to underestimate tidewater influences on the backcountry.[27]

Milton Newton, in the mid-1970s, extended this line of research on material culture traits by defining a more comprehensive set of Upland South characteristics. Newton saw backcountry settlers as forming a society dominated by evangelical Protestantism and antifederalism and based on commercial farming and pastoralism, strong kinship traditions, an "open" class system, dispersed settlements of log and modular pen construction, and a county system of local government with courthouse towns.[28] The geographical expression of this regional culture was an expansive Upland South whose eastern boundary was even more extensive than Kniffen's, extending from Lancaster, Pennsylvania, southward across the Southern Piedmont to Central Florida. Equally significant, however, is Newton's conviction that this culture area of more than one million square miles represented "the preemption of a vast domain by one preadapted, syncretic American culture."[29] Internal regional variation was insignificant.

A more recent set of suggestions has come from Terry Jordan and Matti Kaups.

Their definition of an "American Backwoods Frontier" contains a primary domain the boundaries of which generally follow those of Zelinsky. They see the influences of this region, however, as extending in some fashion throughout most of the eastern United States, with a core in southeastern Pennsylvania and an eastern boundary encompassing a stretch of territory from western Maryland to northern Georgia. The use of the term *backwoods* illustrates Jordan's conviction that what defined a southern interior was settler adaptation to "an external or insular frontier, distant from and noncontiguous with the motherland." Lying "in mesothermal woodlands," this was "not merely a spatially and temporally impermanent fringe area in which an expanding society adapted to a forested environment and to weakened ties to the European homeland; it was also a zone of contact with alien cultures and ethnic mixing."[30]

Backcountry settlers, in Jordan and Kaups' depiction, appeared distinctly more "Turnerian" than those described by Newton. They were classless, individualistic, antagonistic to authority, strongly bound by ties of kinship, locationally unstable, and distributed widely throughout the woods. In these woods, practicing subsistent, shifting agriculture and open-range livestock herding in dispersed settlements composed of log house and barn forms, they survived on a diet based on meat, corn, vegetables, nuts and berries, and distilled liquor.[31] While Newton's conclusions were based on a range of secondary studies, Jordan and Kaups also relied on impressionistic descriptions from contemporary travel accounts.

Only Meinig, of the culturally oriented geographers who explored the colonial backcountry, did not conceptualize it in terms of an Upland South. By the late 1980s, he had come to depict the interior as a derivative territory, its characteristics defined by the competing western extensions of "Greater Pennsylvania," which dominated western Maryland and the Valley of Virginia; "Greater Virginia," which spread on to the Virginia piedmont and into all of settled North Carolina; and "Greater South Carolina" which controlled the settlement of South Carolina and Georgia.[32]

Insofar as cultural geographers had reached a consensus about the spatial configuration of a southern colonial backcountry, they seemed most in agreement about a perhaps fluid northern boundary as a major transition zone, were in reasonable agreement about an eastern boundary extending up to or beyond the fall line, and remained collectively indifferent to a western boundary still in the process of delineation. No cultural geographer would regard the Mason–Dixon Line as defining a northern boundary, because of the penetration of Pennsylvanian or Midland characteristics into the southern interior. The northern boundary has been portrayed either as a line that extends from northern Delaware and Maryland across to the northern margins of the upper Ohio Valley, or as a zone of transition between Midland and upper Southern culture areas. The eastern boundary has been extended as far as the inner coastal plain of the Atlantic Seaboard between the northern Chesapeake and northern Florida. There has been disagreement, however, based on settlement and artifactual evidence, as to what extent the backcountry (or Upland South) includes the piedmont and upcountry areas of the colonial South. The "core" of the colonial backcountry, in any event, seems to be the forested ridges and valleys, along with the most eastern plateaus, of the southern Appalachians.

Defining the Backcountry in Time: Process and Reconfiguration

In addition to the quest for regional boundaries, a number of other problems remain unsolved by cultural approaches to the backcountry. Geographers of historical persuasion remain uneasy, that is, with a research agenda predicated upon concepts of culture areas and cultural diffusion, with a general belief in an undifferentiated forested "wilderness" as the colonial setting, and with a heavy reliance on artifactual evidence and inferential reasoning. They also question the approach of cultural geographers as to process and timing in the formation of the southern colonial backcountry.

Temporal questions, in fact, are crucial to the matter of defining a western boundary for the region. It has been accepted since Turner's time that the southern colonial interior west of the fall zone was settled effectively by European colonists between the 1720s and the 1770s. But what is the significance of the ending of the colonial era for a definition of the backcountry? While the Revolutionary War period caused considerable disruption in local and regional life and slowed down migration to the interior, did it effect an important geographical break in American development? Cultural geographers seldom have considered the impact of political independence on the continuous evolution of America's cultural landscapes and regions. The drawing of a western boundary for the end of the colonial era, however, has been of much less concern than defining and describing an Upland South cultural region and its interior expansion during the early nineteenth century.

For geographers of more historiographical persuasion, independence signaled not only the end of colonialism and imperialism but also the imposition of a republican institutional framework, founded upon liberalism and rationalism, that had no small effect on the disposition of land. The creation of a national land policy and the formulation of the American Rectangular Land Survey System, for example, had a dramatic, homogenizing influence on nineteenth-century settlement landscapes.[33]

The point of departure for this form of inquiry has been the pioneering work of Herman Friis in reconstructing European American population distribution between 1625 and 1790.[34] On a series of maps, Friis used a dot method of symbolization, each dot representing approximately two hundred rural inhabitants. His map for 1740 shows a relatively continuous zone of settlement on the eastern Virginia piedmont and a second band of settlement stretching from southeastern Pennsylvania through the Cumberland Valley to the southern Shenandoah and upper James River valleys. These two distributions are separated by the Blue Ridge, the easternmost mountain zone of the Appalachians. The maps for 1760 and 1770 are spatial elaborations of this pattern, with notable extensions into western Pennsylvania and northeastern Tennessee. If we accept his 1780 map as delimiting the effective settlement of colonial America, the western boundaries would include a relatively continuous zone from western Pennsylvania through western Virginia to northeastern Tennessee, with two isolated outliers in the Kentucky Bluegrass region and the Nashville Basin. The entire sequence of maps makes clear the significance of the southern colonial backcountry: it was the most dynamic area of interior settlement penetration in early America.

Turner, who did not have such detailed maps available to him, relied upon the Census Bureau's 1890 standard—a population density of two persons per square mile—to locate or define the edge of frontier settlement. One geographer, John Fraser Hart, has suggested that such a low figure "meant only half a family, or less, per square mile; the average county would hardly have had enough heads of households for a good, dishonest election."[35] A more realistic measure for an agricultural frontier, in his opinion, would be six to eighteen persons, or up to four families, per square mile. Historian Warren Hofstra and I have found evidence that pioneer households in Frederick County, Virginia, during the 1730s were located one-half to three-quarters of a mile from each other. This created a density in clustered neighborhoods of five to six families per square mile, with two to four-mile stretches between neighborhoods where there was no permanent settlement.[36] If this was a typical pattern for backcountry distributions, it suggests an overall density of three to four families, or about twelve to twenty persons, per square mile. This standard for population density at the frontier would not place the edges of settlement as far west as they are in Turner's Census Bureau model, but it represents an improvement in precision over Friis's maps, which featured excessively conservative estimates of the interior extent of the southern colonial backcountry. Indeed, the work of historical archaeologist Kenneth Lewis, who has used artifactual evidence to reconstruct settlement expansion in South Carolina between 1771 and 1780, indicates several occupied sites in the northwest farther inland than any line generalized from Friis's cartography.[37]

Friis nonetheless has remained useful. Geographer Carville Earle recently has used Friis to measure rates of settlement expansion during the eighteenth century.[38] Earle's argument, based on a generalized map of Meinig's colonial regions, is that about forty-nine thousand square miles of backcountry territory west of the Blue Ridge were settled between 1720 and 1780. The greatest expansion in area occurred between 1760 and 1780, when thirty-two thousand square miles were occupied; but the most rapid expansion occurred between 1720 and 1740, with an annual territorial increase of almost 20 percent. Earle explains these variable rates as influenced primarily by long-run trends in the Atlantic economy. Rates of immigration and expansion were high during periods of prosperity, producing dynamic and regionally divergent frontiers, and lower during depressions which created slower, more convergent frontiers."The frontier," therefore, was not linear, zonal, and uniform but rather cyclical and pluralistic, a rhythmically evolving "mosaic ... of historically specific landscapes."[39]

This was a conclusion that I had come to during the late 1970s, using more regionally specific evidence. As a result of my work on the Shenandoah Valley, I had begun to question the premises upon which other geographers had approached the backcountry. Certain cultural constructs were not supported by available documentary evidence. Donald Meinig, for example, had proposed a geographical model for the evolution of culture areas, based on his description of the Mormon cultural region in nineteenth-century Utah.[40] Meinig suggested that, under ideal conditions of relative geographical isolation and unimpeded expansion, a culture area would develop in three contiguous zones, which he called core, domain, and sphere. He described the *core* as the initial zone of settlement where cultural distinctiveness is most pronounced; the *domain* he identified as the adjacent zone of more selectively diffused traits; and the *sphere* he saw as the outer margins of the culture's influence, where it has to compete with alternative cultural traditions. Zelinsky, however, taking this hypothesis, concluded that, because conditions in the early settled eastern United States were much more complex, this model "can be made to work only with much stretching and bending in the New England, Midland, or French Canadian cases, and it is almost useless in describing or explaining other North American culture areas."[41]

This conclusion did not deter Terry Jordan from employing the model in his analysis of the Upland South. Milton Newton, on the other hand, embraced a modified version of the Meinig paradigm. He located the core (or hearth) region of the Upland South not in the time and place of original migration (southeastern Pennsylvania), but in the broad swath formed between 1725 and 1775 in the interior territory adjacent to the Philadelphia Wagon Road from Lancaster, Pennsylvania, to Augusta, Georgia. The formation of the Upland South, then, was exactly contemporaneous with the emergence of the southern colonial backcountry.

Despite their differences, Newton and Jordan sought an explanation for cultural distinctiveness in the thesis of cultural preadaptation. Settlers from Europe were predisposed to create a unique backcountry region because the collection of traits which they brought with them enabled them readily to adapt to the forested environments of the southern backcountry.[42] Jordan argued that "some European regional cultures were better preadapted for colonization in particular overseas environments than others." Thus the Finns in the Delaware Valley could mix their traditions with those of local Indians and produce "the prototype backwoods pioneer culture" which was carried through the southern backcountry by the Scotch-Irish during the eighteenth century.[43]

An alternative thesis, simplification in new environments, was proposed by Cole Harris, a geographer of more historiographical persuasion who had done comparative work in French Canada and South Africa. Harris, with Leonard Guelke, argued that the search for colonial origins should begin in the adaptive strategies demonstrated by seventeenth-century colonists under universal conditions of family settlement, easy access to land, and limited access to markets. In the North American interior of the next century, these leveling, egalitarian conditions were altered only when access to land became more difficult and when long-distance trade opened up markets for backcountry commodities.[44]

My own response to these arguments was to employ the culture-area concept to extend my interpretation of conditions in the early Shenandoah Valley to the entire eighteenth-century backcountry.[45] The strategy was to trace the migration patterns of pioneer settlers into the interior and try to identify the kind of "syncretic integration" which Newton argued for in the formation of an Upland South. My evidence, however, consisted of data on economic developments and their social consequences, as well as information on ethnic groups and material culture.

My conclusions were at odds with most existing interpretations. I suggested that the southern colonial backcountry, far from being the unified, homogeneous Upland South posited by other investigators, was actually quite "lumpy" and regionally diverse. This pattern resulted from three processes. First, where relatively faithful duplication of colonial hearth traits occurred, as in the relationship between southeastern Pennsylvania and western Maryland, the interior area was appropriated by the hearth. Second, where some deviation from these traits occurred because of local settlement circumstances, as in the South Carolina upcountry, where the rice cultivation of the lowcountry hearth was not viable, cultural variations would become evident but not sufficiently strong to create an entirely new regional experience. Third, novelty was the result of a fusion process in which areas were occupied by settlers from two different hearths, as in the Shenandoah Valley and the northwestern Carolina piedmont. The selective integration of introduced traits created, between 1740 and 1775, distinct interior regions which were to influence regional patterns in the postcolonial era. Thus, for example, the characteristic features of early midwestern agriculture could not be explained by a simple diffusion process from the southeastern Pennsylvanian or Midland hearth, because the corn–livestock fattening components of Ohio Valley farming were more characteristic of western Virginia than of Pennsylvania. More recent research provides some support for this contention.[46]

My general position struck a chord with a few geographers and historians, although little effort has been made to test the conclusions in other backcountry areas.[47] In a later paper, I expressed skepticism about the utility of the hearth concept in understanding the geography of colonial America.[48] A critical institutional analysis of the seventeenth-century Chesapeake tidewater region led me to believe that the culture-area concept was too crude a device to define the complexity and variability of conditions within the early tidewater. It was clear that the evolution of a tobacco-plantation–slave economy and society by 1700 could not be explained by either a cultural-preadaptation or a simplification thesis. Nor was there a clear process of hearth integration, since the characteristic traits of tidewater life took almost a century to evolve. It also was apparent, finally, that regional variations, particularly between the plantation worlds of Virginia and Maryland, had a significant influence on the differential diffusion of tidewater traits into the southern colonial backcountry. In contrasting features of plantation and nonplantation ways of life, I was reduced to modifying—with some slight advance in sophistication—the regional framework of Turner's time.

A New Regional Alternative

My own tentative conclusions really had combined two long-standing modes of geographical inquiry—comparative analyses of frontiers and regional economies—that owed little to, and indeed contrasted with, conventional cultural approaches to the southern backcountry. As early as 1960, Marvin Mikesell had proposed that American frontier experiences could usefully be compared with those of Canada, Australia, and South Africa.[49] Examination of environments shared by more than one country (mid-latitude grasslands, for example) could prove especially valuable, in his view. So, too, could comparisons of cultural encounters between colonizing and aboriginal populations.

Mikesell suggested that cultural frontiers were of two principal types. There were frontiers of inclusion or assimilation, as occurred in regions colonized by Spain; and frontiers of exclusion, as occurred in North America, Australia, and South Africa. He also argued that the relative dynamism or fluidity of frontiers depended on the degree to which settlement expansion was prevented or inhibited by environmental, technological, or human factors. He noted that "historians have not dealt adequately with such topics as settlement morphology, crop ecology, and resource management," and he expressed the hope that these omissions would "stimulate geographers to make further contributions to the frontier theme."[50]

Response to the implicit call for interdisciplinary scholarship was slow in coming. Not until the mid-1970s did American scholars interested in frontier research create a forum for interdisciplinary communication. The departments of history, geography, and anthropology at the University of Oklahoma initiated such a forum in 1975 with an annual symposium and the publication of a newsletter. Two volumes of published papers resulted from these exchanges.[51] Interestingly, the lead paper in the first volume, published in 1977, was a theoretical approach to frontier studies proposed by John Hudson, a geographer. Hudson argued that comparative research had to progress beyond studies "testing" Turner's frontier thesis. "It would be pleasing," he wrote, "to report that, seventy-five years after [Turner] . . . thinking has been substantially advanced and that these early attempts have been improved with our increased knowledge of urbanization, migration, and group behavior. Such is not the case. There is a new vocabulary, containing such terms as network, hierarchy, competition, and adaptation, but this has been superimposed on the same old ideas about behavior in space."[52] Hudson suggested that we build a new research model based on duration of residence (persistence and turnover);

migration field (area from which migrants are drawn); and other aspects of time, location, and population. This framework would encourage scholars to focus more on issues of migration rates, land-use competition, and innovation diffusion. Only during the last few years have some of these suggestions borne fruit.[53]

The most fruitful avenue of inquiry has been research on the origins, characteristics, and spread of regional economic systems. This was one of the principal strategies suggested by Andrew Clark in his plea to economic historians in 1960. It is also the only theme so far that has encouraged active collaboration between geographers and historians. James Lemon's study of southeastern Pennsylvania, published in 1972, with its presentation of the thesis of liberal individualism to explain the entrepreneurial behavior of early Pennsylvanians, initiated a prolonged debate with colonial historians, particularly James Henretta, that focused attention on social change and regional economic development.[54] Lemon's research was also important to geographers because his conclusions provided additional evidence for strong Pennsylvanian influences on the social and economic geography of the southern backcountry.

Even earlier, in 1964, another Clark student, Roy Merrens, had published a pioneering geographical study of colonial North Carolina.[55] Merrens made two especially valuable contributions. First, he introduced a methodology into geographical studies of the colonial South which demonstrated what could be achieved by careful and imaginative use of documentary sources, thus refuting Ralph Brown's pessimistic assumptions about the usefulness of colonial records. Second, he highlighted settlement dispersal and decentralized trade as distinctive and related characteristics of southern colonial life. In contrast to those in Pennsylvania, North Carolina's settlement landscapes were dominated by dispersed plantations and farms, with towns virtually absent. In contrast to Virginia, with which it shared an early dependence on tobacco production, North Carolina saw no large-scale movement of planters on into the piedmont. Thus arose the regional contrast between an ethnically mixed, yeoman farming interior and a more homogenous plantation world along the coastal plain. This regional distinction was highlighted by the emergence of commercial wheat production on the eastern piedmont of North Carolina by the early 1760s.[56]

Subsequent collaboration between Merrens and historian Joseph Ernst focused on the relationship between dispersal and decentralization. Together they produced pioneering work on southern urbanization. Critical of the neglect of towns in southern historiography and doubtful, too, of such traditional measures of urbanization as population size and settlement morphology, they proposed a reevaluation of urban processes, using Camden, South Carolina, as a case study.[57] Because previous scholars had neglected urban functions, they argued, they had underestimated the importance of small towns in the settlement fabric of the southern colonies. Their analysis of Camden, founded in 1751, emphasized the regional importance of its site, as reflected in its early public and commercial buildings. The town became a provisioning center during the Cherokee War in 1760; developed county-seat, tobacco-inspection, and flour-milling functions; and emerged as a travel stop on the main backcountry wagon route between Charleston and Philadelphia. Merrens and Ernst concluded that "'urban'... is a traditional category that only confuses the real issues, which are the structure and operation of the regional economies of the period."[58]

Camden, in fact, has become a symbol of missed interdisciplinary opportunities. While Merrens and Ernst were exploring the town's functional growth, archaeologist Kenneth Lewis was relating the town's morphology to cultural processes in the southern backcountry. He concluded that "Camden shared significant functional similarities with frontier centers in general. In contrast to urban centers in contemporary Britain, Camden exhibited a markedly more dispersed settlement pattern, as well as a smaller population, larger land use units, an apparently greater proportion of activities of a nondomestic (e.g., commercial, industrial) as opposed to a domestic (i.e., residential) nature, and a relatively large proportion of high status residents."[59] These conclusions could have been written just as easily by a geographer. Indeed, Lewis's broader interest in the relationship between cultural and settlement processes in the South Carolina backcountry could have been rich fodder for the geographer and historian.[60] Yet his work is rarely cited in their literatures.

Recognition by Merrens and Ernst of the significance of regional economies, on the other hand, was followed up by another collaboration, between geographer Carville Earle and historian Ronald Hoffman. Their examination of the urban South, I believe, provided a major breakthrough in defining the relationship between settlement landscapes and regional economies, by focusing on how activities associated with agricultural staples defined regional settlement systems in the early South.[61] Commodity trade, they argued, structured relations between rural producers and urban providers. Economies based on tobacco or rice production created little need for town-based systems, because the products, relatively low in bulk, required little local processing or storage and were consigned directly overseas. Economies concentrating on grain exports, particularly wheat and corn, involved the movement of much bulkier commodities which required considerable processing, storage, artisanal, mercantile, and transportation services. These services were concentrated in the numerous small market towns or central places distributed throughout commercial grain-producing areas in the backcountry.[62]

Wheat specialization emerged throughout the backcountry from the Maryland piedmont during the 1750s to the South Carolina piedmont a decade or so later. Since towns were being founded at approximately the same time, grain production and central-place systems became distinct expressions of the southern colonial backcountry. The more localized research that Warren Hofstra and I have been conducting in the Shenandoah Valley generally confirms this thesis, although it does not explain the origins of individual towns.[63] This line of inquiry, therefore, suggests a powerful strategy which supersedes Turnerian thinking about colonial frontiers and promises more fruitful results than the culture-area perspective is ever likely to approach.

The first step in the strategy is to map the areas occupied by migrants moving into the backcountry from the north between the 1720s and 1775 and to compare that distribution with the distribution of principal agricultural specializations and of slaves. The second step is to analyze the pattern of town founding in the South up to the Revolutionary era and to create maps of the backcountry population according to national origins. The extent of geographical overlap between migration areas and grain-based farming systems should provide a measure of the relative strength of plantation and nonplantation agricultural and labor systems. The presence or absence of a network of towns should reinforce the degree of coincidence between the other two patterns. And the distribution of ethnic groups should provide some measure of nonconformity in the backcountry.

The probable extent of northern migration into the southern backcountry is portrayed in map 1.1.[64] Pioneer farmers had begun to move out of southeastern Pennsylvania into the Chesapeake backcountry in search of agricultural land during the late 1720s. Few seem to have lingered in western Maryland because of confusion over land titles and the indeterminacy of the Pennsylvania–Maryland boundary. As a result, the settlement of Frederick County, Maryland, was delayed until the early 1740s—more than a decade after pioneer settlement in Frederick County, Virginia, in the northern Shenandoah Valley.[65] Settlers proceeded to occupy the southern part of the valley during the late 1730s and throughout the 1740s. Other pioneers moved through the valley during the late 1740s but veered eastward through gaps in the Blue Ridge in the vicinity of Roanoke to avoid conflicts with the Cherokees farther to the south. Northern migrants had begun to occupy land south of the Roanoke, or Staunton, River in Old Lunenburg County in the southwestern Virginia piedmont by the late 1740s.[66] Some of these migrants already had moved farther south into Rowan County on the adjacent piedmont of North Carolina by 1747 and were reinforced by Moravian migrants from Pennsylvania beginning in 1753.[67] The first backcountry settlers on the piedmont of South Carolina appeared during the early 1750s, while pioneer yeoman farmers began occupying land on the northern Georgia piedmont by 1755.[68] The arrangement of northern migrants on the southern piedmont, then, would define a potential eastern boundary for the colonial backcountry. This region would include virtually all of the Maryland piedmont but only the southwestern section of the Virginia piedmont. It would also include the central and western sections of the piedmont of North and South Carolina and the upper Savannah River Valley in northeastern Georgia.

Thus, society and economy in the Shenandoah Valley had forty-five years to develop before the outbreak of the Revolution; in the northwest Carolina piedmont, this period was reduced to thirty years; and on the South Carolina and Georgia frontiers colonial settlement was barely twenty years in duration. The

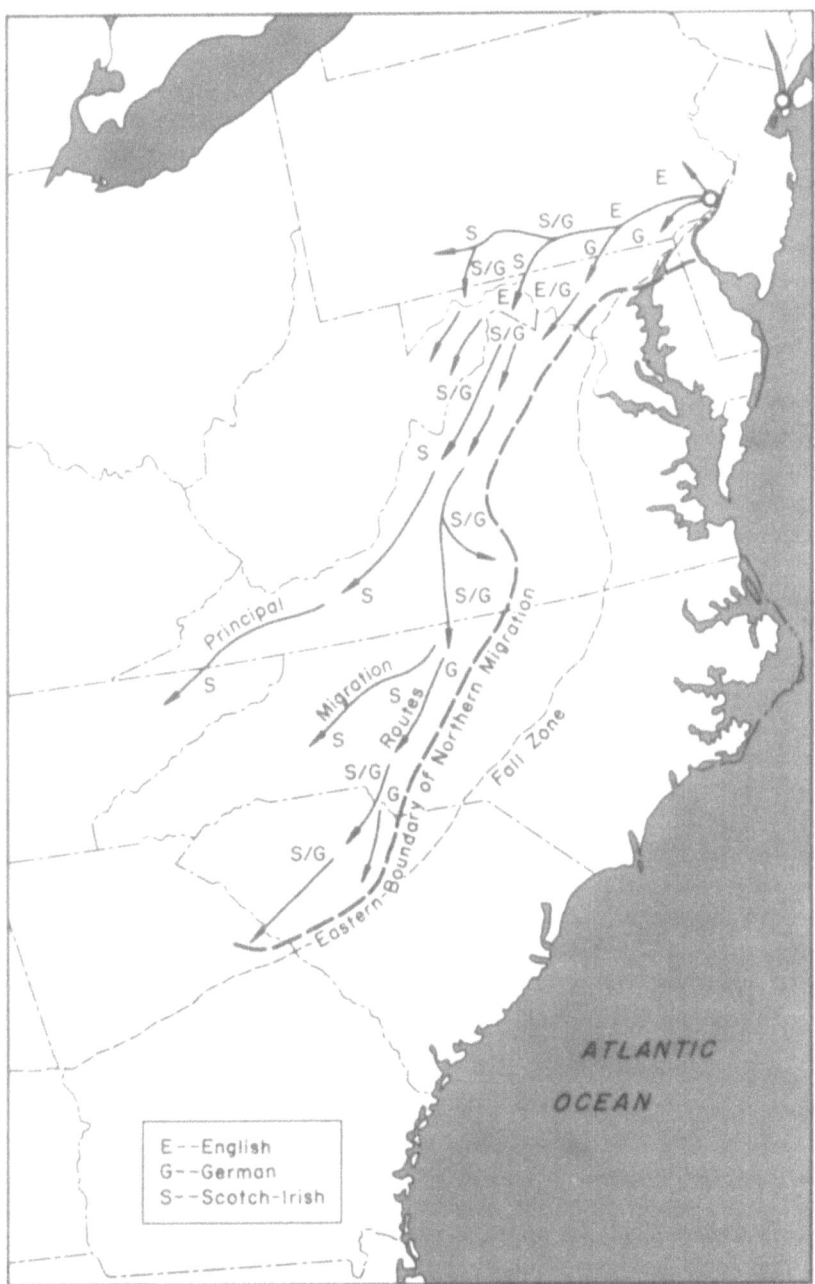

Map 1.1. Probable Extent of Northern Migrants in Colonial South. Cappon, ed., *Atlas of Early American History: The Revolutionary Era, 1760–1790* (Princeton, N.J.: Princeton University Press, 1976).

Shenandoah Valley, therefore, becomes the measure by which to calibrate substantial frontier change in the backcountry.

The distribution of backcountry settlers by national origin further confirms the complex configuration of the backcountry. The pattern of Scottish, Scotch-Irish, German-speaking, and nonconformist English (especially Quaker) immigration, however, must be analyzed with caution. Not all of these groups moved into the southern backcountry from or through Pennsylvania. This was particularly true of Scottish Highlanders on the eastern piedmont of North Carolina, Scotch-Irish who disembarked at Charleston and settled along the coastal plain, and Salzburgers and other German speakers who moved up the Savannah River. Within the backcountry itself, the relative strength of immigrant groups and the degree to which settlements were occupied as mixed ethnic areas created a varied pattern of encounters. Although most areas appear from the beginning to have had ethnically mixed populations, some areas had high concentrations of one national group. Both the Shenandoah Valley and the southwestern Carolina piedmont, for example, were predominantly Scotch-Irish. Yet, because much of the backcountry was settled for such a short time, ethnic identities remained intact until pressures for national conformity and the evangelical movements of the early 1790s began to erode ethnic boundaries. Even before 1775, however, the Baptist church had made considerable inroads into backcountry communities, particularly in southwestern Virginia, North Carolina, and Georgia. Indeed, the dominant denominations along the western boundaries of the colonial backcountry invariably were associated with the Baptists or the Presbyterians.

These observations take on added significance when we examine the distribution of agricultural staples and agricultural regions in the southern colonies by 1775 (map 1.2).[69] The most critical transition zone is the one between the interior penetration of planters and tobacco specialization and the emergence of grain-livestock regions in the backcountry. In Maryland, tobacco production took place along the Potomac Valley but otherwise stopped at the fall line. In the Virginia piedmont, by contrast, tobacco planters dominated commercial agriculture everywhere except in Loudoun County (wedged between the Potomac River and the Blue Ridge) and in Southside south of the Roanoke River. In the broad coastal plain of North Carolina, settlement was sparser and tobacco planters less dominant. Nowhere did the planter world extend on to the piedmont, where range cattle and wheat had become profitable commodities before the Revolution.

The dynamics of staple production in the lowcountry of South Carolina and Georgia were quite different, because rice and indigo were cultivated under more restrictive ecological conditions. Rice, in particular, with its considerable water demands and need for level land, was confined to a narrow strip of coastal plain. Although indigo had a much more extensive distribution, especially along interfluvial areas, it remained a lowcountry staple and was absent from the piedmont. Cattle and wheat in the northern piedmont of South Carolina provided some farmers with marketable commodities by 1775. Within the contested southern piedmont,

Map 1.2. Southern regional economies. Adapted from "Tidewater" map, Map 17, "The Making of America" series, June 1988, National Geographic Society, Washington, D.C.

therefore, only in Virginia were northern migrants overwhelmed by a plantation economy. Loudoun County avoided this assimilation because of its connections with adjacent Frederick County in the "wheat belt" of western Maryland.[70]

These agricultural patterns were closely reflected in the geographical distribution of slaves west of the fall zone. Loudoun County, for example, shared with the counties of the Maryland piedmont and the southwestern Virginia Southside the distinction of being the only counties east of the Blue Ridge with less than 30 percent of their populations as slaves.[71] Another reason the Blue Ridge cannot serve as the major divide between more and less slave-oriented regions is that the slave density of the two northern counties in the Shenandoah Valley, Berkeley and Frederick (with more than 3,500 slaves by the year 1780, or about 16 percent of their populations), resembles that of adjacent piedmont counties.[72] Commercial tobacco had been cultivated along the lower Shenandoah River since the early 1750s and became an important staple in this region during the last thirty years of the century. The pattern of slave distribution is less definitive in the North Carolina piedmont. Granville County's slave proportion of more than 30 percent is an anomaly within a region where most counties had less than 20 percent of their populations as slaves. Because the institution of slavery was so ingrained in the political cultures as well as the plantation economies of all the southern colonies, ownership of slaves was by no means confined to areas dominated by plantation staples. About 25 percent of the inventories recorded in the mixed-farming region of the southern Shenandoah Valley between 1770 and 1780, for example, contained slaves, although usually only one or two per inventory.[73]

In general, therefore, the distribution of agricultural and labor systems in the southern colonies reconfirms the belief that, with the exception of Virginia, the piedmont regions between Maryland and Georgia were dominated by colonists who had little or no experience with plantation agriculture and so had limited use for slaves. The eastern boundary of their world ran along the fall zone in Maryland, along the Blue Ridge in Virginia, and extended across most of the piedmont of the Carolinas into northern Georgia.

The distribution of town foundings in the South after 1730 tends to reinforce the pattern of agricultural regions. There is a distinct difference in the significance of the fall zone, however, between the Chesapeake colonies and the Carolinas.[74] In the Chesapeake, towns on or near the fall zone dominated the urban pattern. Baltimore was the key port in the northern Chesapeake; but, except for Norfolk, all the key centers in eastern Virginia, from Alexandria to Petersburg, were associated with the fall zone. As a result, urbanization was preempted on the Virginia piedmont through a combination of port towns and the tobacco plantation economy. In the Carolinas, however, there was little urban development along the coastal plain or the fall zone, except for Charleston, New Bern, and Fayetteville, and little on the piedmont to compare with the Chesapeake backcountry. The pattern of grain- and livestock-based economies can be followed most clearly from Frederick, Maryland, the largest town in the southern backcountry, through the Great Valley settlements from Elizabethtown (Hagerstown) southward to Lexington, Virginia.

Setting an Interdisciplinary Agenda

The emergence of the southern backcountry is one of the most significant geographical developments of the late colonial era. Between the 1720s and 1780, some 380,000 settlers occupied the piedmont and valley regions of Maryland (62,000), the valley region of Virginia (140,500), and the piedmont regions of the Carolinas (110,500 in North Carolina, 55,000 in South Carolina) and Georgia (12,000).[75] These settlers in total represented approximately 30 percent of the South's population by 1780 and occupied almost 50 percent of the southern region in Revolutionary America.

It would seem obvious from what has been discussed up to this point that we need to examine this varied and dynamic region first on its own terms, rather than viewing it as a geographical extension of earlier coastal and tidewater communities. Only then can we begin to appreciate its wide and often subtle internal variations. Yet such an examination requires a more extensive and comparative data base than currently supports our regional generalizations. To improve our knowledge and comprehension of the overall area, we need more empirical case studies at neighborhood, county, and subregional levels. A comparative framework requires not only examination of particular places or processes but also a shared set of research questions—and this requires interdisciplinary cooperation.

Second, we need to appreciate the backcountry's relations with other regions. The backcountry did not develop in isolation, but rather it acquired settlers from various sources and integrated them into new communities. These communities, in turn, were linked to larger regions, including a forecountry of older settled areas from which were derived many consumer goods and to which were sent surplus agricultural and hunting commodities. At the same time, as settlers colonized Appalachian areas farther west, the late colonial backcountry found itself becoming an interior forecountry serving newer frontiers. We should be able to determine from this framework the singularities that were peculiar to backcountry communities, the regional patterns that were outcomes of these singularities, and the degree of convergence with longer-settled eastern communities. Much of what I propose, therefore, derives from ongoing research work which I have been conducting with colleagues in the northern Shenandoah Valley.

In its broadest sense, the southern colonial backcountry was an expanding zone of encounters. In addition to new physical environments, colonists moving into the interior frequently encountered indigenous populations. Yet much of the southern backcountry, including the Shenandoah Valley during the 1730s, had no resident native occupants at the time of European contact. This absence undoubtedly speeded up pioneer settlement and influenced the direction of migration.[76] The most significant encounters occurred with the Cherokees in the southern Appalachians. To some degree, their strategic importance in the South was analogous to that of the Iroquois in the North. For commercial and diplomatic reasons, interaction with the Cherokees affected the backcountries of all the southern colonies except Maryland.

Such relations are obvious targets for interdisciplinary study. Geographers, unfortunately, have devoted little attention to them. The most prominent study, by Gary Goodwin, is overly descriptive and contributes relatively little to the geography of native-European encounters.[77] Geographers' interest in boundary issues, on the other hand, has been more fruitful. Indeed, the definitive study here is Louis De Vorsey's tracing of the Indian-colonial boundary in the southern colonies after 1763.[78] Late-Woodland archaeologists and ethnohistorians, who have investigated the contact period, also have produced valuable work. Recent studies by Thomas Hatley of the ecological consequences of European–Cherokee encounters, in terms of native borrowings of European agricultural traits and practices, are models of the kind of insightful work that remains to be done on the transformation of the backcountry.[79] Similarly, James Merrell has reminded us of how important trade relations were in maintaining cross-cultural contacts during the late eighteenth century.[80]

Meanwhile, we need to know more about the landscapes encountered by colonial pioneers and how they adapted to them. A team of researchers, including myself, a forester-surveyor, an ecologist, a historical archaeologist, and a social historian, has begun to reconstruct the vegetation cover of the northern Shenandoah Valley between 1730 and 1775. We are attempting to define a base level from which to calibrate environmental changes that affected the settlement decisions made by colonial residents.[81] The Shenandoah Valley has had the reputation of being the most altered section of the Appalachians, as a result of extensive Indian burnings. Much of the valley was presumed to be covered with fire-induced grasslands at contact time. Our research, using the witness-tree designations made by surveyors at each survey point on tract boundaries, as well as land-cover information derived from both the tracts and surveyors' notes, suggests a more complex pattern. The valley floor appears to have been covered with a complex forest-grassland mosaic. Areas of open or lightly wooded grassland were caused primarily by natural processes along river and stream flood plains, not by frequent Indian burning. Indeed, there is little direct evidence of land disturbed by native-induced burning or crop clearances. At the same time, our findings have unearthed a number of opportunities for interdisciplinary research on typical settlement sites above flood plains and with easy access to woodland.[82]

Colonists occupied the backcountry at what might be termed "points of attachment." They sought out suitable settlement sites, claimed these sites through patented or purchased lands, had their properties surveyed, constructed houses and farmsteads, and cleared paths which often became roads linking farms, mills, and churches into loosely organized, open-country neighborhoods. There are two research strategies we need to pursue at this point. First, we have underestimated the importance of frontier land policies within the southern colonies in terms of their impact on migration rates, levels of land speculation, and rates of taking up and developing land tracts. In most colonies, the desire of authorities to settle strategic areas in the backcountry as "buffers" against French and native encroachments led to generous land policies which were designed to induce settlement by groups with little affiliation to tidewater planters. In Lord Fairfax's Northern Neck Proprietary, however, the proprietor's land agents often granted large acreages of the backcountry to absentee planters who showed little interest in active development of these lands until after the Revolution. Thus the impact of plantation life in Frederick County in Virginia's backcountry was delayed.[83]

A second strategy is to examine the formation of backcountry neighborhoods and relate them to the evolution of settlement systems and the development of regional economies. We have identified at least two such neighborhoods in Frederick County, each comprising twenty to thirty farmsteads ranging from one hundred to four hundred acres in size, and focused on a Quaker meeting house and a Presbyterian church respectively.[84] One neighborhood was occupied by a number of British Quaker families, while the other was a more mixed settlement of Scotch-Irish and German-speaking families. Recent work combining land surveys and field reconnaissance has revealed a number of sites suitable for archaeological or architectural investigation.[85] Another outcome of this collaborative research is the production of a cadastral (land survey) map of all the original properties in colonial Frederick County. Though a painstaking and time-consuming task, creating this map was the necessary first step towards being able, beyond vague locational references, to place settlers precisely on the ground.

We are just beginning to understand how pioneer rural neighborhoods functioned in general frontier isolation. We know, for example, that in early Frederick County (founded officially in 1738 but not autonomous until 1743) such dispersed neighborhoods were kin-oriented, economically subsistent, loosely governed, and dependent upon itinerant peddlers and preachers for contact with the outside world. Settlers operated for fifteen years before the siting of a county seat induced the first movement towards village and eventually town life. In contrast to eastern plantation areas, where many county seats supported no more than a courthouse, jail, and lawyers' offices, in the backcountry the entrepreneurial possibilities of combining governmental and market functions at the same sites created an entirely different environment for town founding in advance of the formation of more specialized regional economies.[86]

The creation of town plats with surveyed lots that acquired structures on them provides another opportunity for innovative, interdisciplinary research. We are in the process, for example, of trying to reconstruct the structural and functional characteristics of downtown Winchester in the late eighteenth century as a three-dimensional computer model using surviving property insurance policies and Geographic Information Systems (GIS) techniques.[87] The resulting map will provide further research opportunities for geographers, historians, and historical archaeologists. If, as seems likely, land records and insurance data are available in other colonies and states for the eighteenth century, more such maps could be produced to form an extensive, comparative data base.

If the concept of a settlement system is useful to understanding settlement and spatial organization in the backcountry, its utility rests upon the conviction that what is most important is the reciprocity between town and countryside—not whether people lived in rural or urban settlements. Each component depended upon the other, particularly in the formation of regional economies. Two of our most interesting discoveries about settlement and the economy in the northern Shenandoah Valley concern the impact of the Seven Years' War ("French and Indian" War) and the role of the import trade in creating settlement hierarchies in the backcountry.

This war proved to be a critical threshold in the emergence of the Virginia backcountry, because it stimulated the region's fledgling towns by adding garrison and provisioning functions to governmental and trade functions. Such activities attracted the attention of Philadelphia merchant firms and brought the Maryland and Virginia backcountries into that city's trade hinterland, despite the interest and proximity of Baltimore and the Virginia fall-zone towns.[88] Was this situation unique to the Chesapeake region, or did Charleston perform a similar role in the Carolina and Georgia piedmont?

As the longest occupied backcountry region, the Shenandoah Valley had developed a distinct—and internally varied—regional economy by 1775. Cattle droving to Philadelphia was established as early as the late 1740s and provided commercial opportunities for farmers throughout the region. Wheat, as well as corn, was ubiquitous as a pioneer subsistence crop, although it was not until the early 1760s that a sustained commercial production was available for export, particularly to Alexandria.[89] Custom flour mills began to appear in Frederick County by 1770, with a commensurate increase in the demand for sacks, barrels, and wagons or hauling services. Tobacco, a more limited specialization, was restricted to eastern Frederick County, and its direct consignment to Alexandria or Fredericksburg had little direct impact on the region's settlement or economy. Hemp, as a heavily subsidized crop, emerged during the mid-1760s and reached its greatest importance during the Revolutionary War. Its production, though widespread, was more concentrated in the southern valley (Augusta County) than in the northern valley (Frederick County). Yet its cultivation, like that of tobacco, was a major reason for the early appearance of slavery in the backcountry.[90]

The processing and transport of these staples, however, appears to have had little direct influence on urbanization. Winchester, the largest town in the Virginia backcountry, was a conduit for the cattle trade rather than a cattle market, and its merchants did not handle commodities like wheat or flour, which were sent to Alexandria directly from mills and farms. What sustained Winchester's position as the primary market center for western Virginia was the ability of its merchants to control the import trade in dry goods and to maintain credit worthiness with wholesale merchants in Philadelphia, Alexandria, and Baltimore.[91] By the outbreak of the Revolution, the town had become the backcountry Virginia entrepôt and was poised to become dominant within an integrated central-place system of settlements.

To recapitulate the development of the northern Shenandoah Valley: the first fifteen years saw the establishment of a dispersed, decentralized, open-country neighborhood system; cattle droving began twelve to fifteen years after initial settlement; towns began to be founded twelve to fifteen years after the initiation of droving; crop specialization set in after twenty-five to thirty years; and a central-place settlement system was in place by 1775, or forty-five years after the first farms were established.

This sequential development raises two comparative issues. First, to what extent should we be able to predict the sequence of activities in later-settled backcountry areas from the pattern exhibited in Frederick County? And, second, to what extent can the factors that produced Winchester's founding and growth be extrapolated to other backcountry towns? It seems likely, for example, that Winchester's experiences will shed new light on events in the already well-studied town of Camden, South Carolina.

All these findings suggest new approaches to defining patterns of social organization and social change in the backcountry. Demographically, the newer the frontier area, the younger its population; and, even if the predominant mode of migration was in family units, male-female ratios were on the order of 2:1. Lack of data has prevented us from being more definitive about population profiles in the backcountry, but an effort to produce more case studies would provide more comparable demographic information. Since everywhere in the southern backcountry we are dealing with agricultural frontiers, there is a common economic foundation from which to construct pictures of demographic change. One of the more critical variables appears to be the social cohesiveness of migrant groups. Quakers and sectarian German groups, such as the Moravians, present profiles of older, more gender-balanced populations more rapidly than among other groups, for example.[92]

Measuring population-land ratios has been an important device in deciphering social change in the backcountry. It is clear from available scholarship that even if (as Jordan and others have claimed) many communities began as simplified, egalitarian, almost classless societies, such structures did not endure. Power relationships always were an important dimension of evolving communities. In newly settled areas, the initial source of that power invariably was access to land. We are beginning to discover that, in more isolated valleys and coves in the Appalachians, seemingly unstratified communities still had a power base controlled by early pioneer families who had acquired much of the most productive land, had persisted in place, and had filled most of the local administrative and political posts.[93] In some areas, including the southern Shenandoah Valley, there is also an indication that early landowners and surveyors appropriated many of the best lands and attempted to restrict access to ungranted lands by later migrants. We have underestimated the power of county surveyors, clerks, and other office holders over the appropriation processes in backcountry communities.[94]

Over time, as population increased and good agricultural lands became less available in the most rapidly settled areas, increasing social stratification set in, as distinctions between landowners and renters became more pronounced. By 1775, for example, at least one third of the taxable population of the southern half of the Shenandoah Valley and two-fifths in the northern half owned no land.[95] How does this compare, for example, with conditions in the Carolina piedmont? Should we expect high concentrations of land ownership in more recently settled areas? We know also that, in the neighborhoods we have studied in the northern Shenandoah Valley, land commonly was passed on through family and kinship associations during the first two generations. By the outbreak of the Revolution, however, such associations were less binding: the third generation tended to sell land to unrelated neighbors or strangers as a means of financing emigration to newly developing frontiers in central Kentucky and northeastern Tennessee.[96] Thus the social composition of many pioneer neighborhoods by the 1780s was very different from what it had been in the 1740s and 1750s.

Other factors also were at work in ushering in social change. We are just beginning to understand the impact of the "consumer revolution" on late colonial populations. This would seem to be one of the most fruitful arenas for interdisciplinary research. Our analysis of Frederick County wills and inventories reveals the beginnings of a shift to a more affluent material culture, as indicated by an increase, on the eve of the Revolution, in the consumption of sugar and tea and in the use of pewter, china, and cabinetware. Such consumption patterns present historians and historical archaeologists with rich research opportunities. Geographers and architectural historians also can contribute to our understanding of material culture's evolution by analyzing changing patterns and styles of housing (in particular the increasing appearance of the "I" house during the late colonial era). There is interesting evidence to suggest that some settlers were willing to express their increasing affluence in major changes in house construction and external ornamentation, while retaining a strong domestic conservatism in the arrangement and furnishing of the interior of their homes.[97]

The roles and status of women in backcountry communities remain fertile fields, especially for social historians. It seems likely that women had a considerable degree of autonomy and independence in early backcountry communities, including ownership and inheritance of land in both town and country. Can we determine how extensive this status was in the southern backcountry, and to what degree it was modified as communities became more socially stable and economically developed?[98]

Perhaps the most difficult research to pursue on an interdisciplinary basis in backcountry studies is that of political development. Geographers have contributed little to this issue, other than a few comments on the territorial dimensions of backcountry life, while the absence of material forms as the outcome of political processes seems to have prevented much contribution from archaeologists.[99] We need, nonetheless, to reevaluate interpretations of the colonial backcountry that emphasize only the "marginality" or "buffer zone" characteristics of frontier communities. If we are to interpret such communities on their own terms, it seems imperative to appreciate the range of responses to changing locational circumstances and to perceptions of political representation. By the same token, we need to reexamine the Turnerian issues of backcountry underrepresentation and backcountry-tidewater tensions. Historians have demonstrated clearly the varied responses of individual colonies to changing core-periphery relationships. Why, for example, was there, in the Shenandoah Valley in the late colonial period, little political unrest to compare with the Regulator movement in North Carolina? And why was there such a strong federalist sentiment throughout the Shenandoah Valley after the Revolution, when most backcountry areas demonstrated clear antifederalist sentiments?

In the Shenandoah Valley there is some evidence at the county level, too, of what has been termed "local political culture."[100] The seeming absence of deference to authority and status displayed in both political and military institutions, such as voting patterns and militia discipline, suggests that a different political climate prevailed in the backcountry than in the more disciplined and stratified tidewater. We need more case studies to determine the degrees of political behavior displayed in the backcountry counties and parishes and how they varied between and within individual colonies.

The ultimate issue in backcountry studies is to define the changing relationships between the interior and the larger settled East. This is an issue, however, that transcends the colonial era. How long did the major differences between backcountry and forecountry endure? Turner's frontier methodology did not entertain this question because it always focused on the creation of new frontiers. But attention to a specifically southern colonial backcountry provides a gauge by which to probe larger questions. If this backcountry, as defined by 1775, remains the focus of our inquiry, we can trace its geographical expansion within the early Republic and appreciate its changing spatial relationships to a set of nationally moving frontiers during the nineteenth century.[101] We need to examine whether the colonial backcountry reduced its differences with the East and converged into a new regional framework—or whether the differences remained significant enough for backcountry areas to retain strong regional identities well into the nineteenth century. Framing our questions in terms of a reasonably identifiable and bounded backcountry area in 1775 allows historical geographers to continue to play a crucial part in investigating changing environments and societies through time.

Notes

1. Bernard Bailyn, *The Peopling of British North America: An Introduction* (New York: Alfred A. Knopf, 1986); Jack P. Greene, *Pursuits of Happiness: The Social Development of Early Modern British Colonies and the Formation of American Culture* (Chapel Hill: Univ. of North Carolina Press, 1988); David Hackett Fischer, *Albion's Seed: Four British Folkways in America* (New York: Oxford Univ. Press, 1989); Donald W. Meinig, *The Shaping of America: A Geographical Perspective on Five Hundred Years of History*, vol. 1: *Atlantic America, 1492–1800* (New Haven, Conn.: Yale Univ. Press, 1986); and Terry G. Jordan and Matti Kaups, *The American Backwoods Frontier: An Ethnic and Ecological Interpretation* (Baltimore, Md.: Johns Hopkins Univ. Press, 1989).
2. Presentation as reprinted in Frederick Jackson Turner, *The Frontier in American History* (New York: Holt, Rinehart, and Winston, 1920), 1–38.
3. See, e.g., Frederick Jackson Turner, "Geographical Interpretations of American History," *Journal of Geography* 4 (1905): 34–37; correspondence between Turner and Ellen C. Semple, 1907, in Frederick Jackson Turner Papers, Box 9-A, Huntington Library, San Marino, Calif.; Frederick Jackson Turner, "Report on the Conference on the Relation of Geography and History," *American Historical Association Annual Report, 1907* (Washington, D.C.: AHA, 1908), 1: 45–48; and W. M. Davis to I. Bowman, Jan. 4, 1912 [1914], and D. Johnson to I. Bowman, Apr. 9, 1914, both in Association of American Geographers Archives, National Archives, Washington, D.C.
4. A major exception has been the influence of Karl Butzer, via such publications as *Environment and Archaeology: An Introduction to Pleistocene Geography* (London: Methuen, 1965) and *Archaeology and Human Ecology: Method and Theory for a Contextual Approach* (Cambridge, England: Cambridge Univ. Press, 1982). One of the few examples of direct collaboration is Daniel Elliott and Roy Doyon, *Archaeology and Historical Geography of the Savannah River Floodplain Near Augusta, Georgia*, Report No. 22 (Athens: Laboratory of Archaeology, Univ. of Georgia, 1981), although Doyon, the geographer, really provided geographical background for an archaeological reconnaissance project. Communication has been more fruitful in Britain, as demonstrated in J. M. Wagstaff, ed., *Landscape and Culture: Geographical and Archaeological Perspectives* (Oxford, England: Basil Blackwell, 1987).
5. See, e.g., D. L. Clarke, ed., *Models in Archaeology* (London: Methuen, 1972); L. R. Binford, *For Theory Building in Archaeology* (New York: Academic Press, 1977); and D. L. Clarke, *Spatial Archaeology* (London: Academic Press, 1977). For the views of early American historians, see the praiseworthy comments (which were rarely followed up) in Allan Kulikoff, "Historical Geographers and Social History: A Review Essay," *Historical Methods* [Newsletter] 6 (1973): 122–28; Edward M. Cook, Jr., "Geography and History: Spatial Approaches to Early American History," *Historical Methods* 13 (1980): 19–28; and Bailyn, *Peopling of British North America*, 7–8.
6. Frederick Jackson Turner, *The Significance of Sections in American History* (New York: Henry Holt and Co., 1932), 23.

7. Ibid., 12.
8. Ibid., 292, and F. J. Turner, *Frontier in American History*, 99–100.
9. Michael C. Steiner, "The Significance of Turner's Sectional Thesis," *Western Historical Quarterly* 10 (1979): 437–66. Although geographers have argued that regions and sections are not interchangeable and that the former is the more flexible concept, we continue to emphasize frontier at the expense of section. See Donald W. Meinig, *The Shaping of America: A Geographical Perspective on Five Hundred Years of History*, vol. 2: *Continental America, 1800–1867* (New Haven, Conn.: Yale Univ. Press, 1993), 260–61.
10. F. J. Turner, *Significance of Sections*, 36 and 38–39.
11. F. J. Turner, *Frontier in American History*, 68.
12. Compare the efforts of Carl Bridenbaugh, *Myths and Realities: Societies of the Colonial South* (Baton Rouge: Louisiana State Univ. Press, 1952), 119–96; Jack P. Greene, "Independence, Improvement, and Authority: Toward a Framework for Understanding the Histories of the Southern Backcountry during the Era of the American Revolution," in *An Uncivil War: The Southern Backcountry during the American Revolution*, ed. Ronald Hoffman, Thad W. Tate, and Peter J. Albert, 3–36 (Charlottesville: Univ. Press of Virginia, for the U.S. Capitol Historical Society, 1985); and Fischer, *Albion's Seed*, 605–782.
13. For a brief review of American historical geography, see Robert D. Mitchell, "The North American Past: Retrospect and Prospect," in *North America: The Historical Geography of a Changing Continent*, ed. Robert D. Mitchell and Paul A. Groves, 3–21 (Lanham, Md.: Rowman and Littlefield, 1987). For a more extensive interpretation, see Michael P. Conzen, "The Historical Impulse in Geographical Writing about the United States, 1850–1990," in *A Scholar's Guide to Geographical Writing on the American and Canadian Past*, Research Paper No. 235, ed. Michael P. Conzen, Thomas A. Rumney, and Graeme Wynn, 3–90 (Chicago: Dept. of Geography, Univ. of Chicago, 1993).
14. Carl O. Sauer, *Land and Life: A Selection from the Writings of Carl Ortwin Sauer*, ed. John Leighly (Berkeley: Univ. of California Press, 1963), 315–79.
15. Ralph Hall Brown, "Materials Bearing upon the Geography of the Atlantic Seaboard, 1790 to 1810," *Annals of the Association of American Geographers* 28 (1938): 201–31. See the critique of Brown's position in Harry Roy Merrens, "Source Materials for the Geography of Colonial America," *Professional Geographer* 15 (1963): 8–11.
16. Herman R. Friis, "A Series of Population Maps of the Colonies and the United States, 1625–1790," *Geographical Review* 30 (1940): 463–70; and Herman R. Friis, "A Series of Population Maps," a revised, mimeographed version printed and distributed by American Geographical Society, 1968.
17. Donald W. Meinig, "The American Colonial Era: A Geographical Commentary," *Proceedings of the Royal Geographical Society of Australasia, South Australian Branch* 59 (1957–58): 1–22.
18. Ibid., 15.
19. Ibid., 21.
20. Ibid., 21.

21. James T. Lemon, *The Best Poor Man's Country: A Geographical Study of Early Southeastern Pennsylvania* (Baltimore, Md.: Johns Hopkins Univ. Press, 1972).
22. Andrew H. Clark, "Geographical Change—A Theme for Economic History," *Journal of Economic History* 20 (1960): 607–16.
23. Harry Roy Merrens, "Historical Geography and Early American History," *William and Mary Quarterly* 3d ser. 22 (1965): 529–48.
24. Wilbur Zelinsky, *The Cultural Geography of the United States* (Englewood Cliffs, N.J.: Prentice-Hall, 1973, rev. ed. 1992), 117–28. Richard Pillsbury, in his discussion of the cultural landscape in *Encyclopedia of Southern Cultures*, ed. Charles R. Wilson and William Ferris, 533–44 (Baton Rouge: Louisiana State Univ. Press, 1989), follows Zelinsky's boundaries fairly closely, identifying vernacular house form, religion, individualistic attitudes, diet, and music as distinctive southern traits.
25. Donald W. Meinig, "The Continuous Shaping of America: A Prospectus for Geographers and Historians," *American Historical Review* 83 (1978): 1189.
26. Fred Kniffen, "Folk Housing: Key to Diffusion," *Annals of the Association of American Geographers* 55 (1965): 561.
27. Henry Glassie, *Pattern in the Material Folk Culture of the Eastern United States* (Philadelphia: Univ. of Pennsylvania Press, 1968), 34n. See also Fred Kniffen and Henry Glassie, "Building in Wood in the Eastern United States: A Time-Place Perspective," *Geographical Review* 56 (1966): 40–66.
28. Milton Newton, "Cultural Preadaptation and the Upland South," *Geoscience and Man* 5 (1974): 152.
29. Ibid., 143.
30. Jordan and Kaups, *American Backwoods Frontier*, 19–20.
31. Ibid., 3–4.
32. Meinig, *Shaping of America*, 1:244–54. Bridenbaugh, *Myths and Realities*, 127, suggested the idea of a "Greater Pennsylvania."
33. William D. Pattison, *Beginnings of the American Rectangular Land Survey System*, Research Paper No. 50 (Chicago: Department of Geography, Univ. of Chicago, 1957); and Sam B. Hilliard, "A Robust New Nation, 1783–1820," in Mitchell and Groves, *North America*, 149–71.
34. Friis, "A Series of Population Maps."
35. John Fraser Hart, "The Spread of the Frontier and the Growth of Population," *Geoscience and Man* 5 (1974): 73.
36. Warren R. Hofstra and Robert D. Mitchell, "Town and Country in Backcountry Virginia: Winchester and Frederick County, 1730–1800," *Journal of Southern History* 59 (1993): 619–46.
37. Kenneth E. Lewis, *The American Frontier: An Archaeological Study of Settlement Pattern and Process* (Orlando, Fla.: Academic Press, 1984), 170.
38. Carville Earle, "The Rate of Frontier Expansion in American History, 1650–1890," in *Lois Green Carr: The Chesapeake and Beyond—A Celebration*, ed. L. Simmler, 183–204 (Crownsville.: Maryland Historical and Cultural Publications, 1992).
39. Ibid., 195.

40. Donald W. Meinig, "The Mormon Culture Region: Strategies and Patterns in the Geography of the American West, 1847–1964," *Annals of the Association of American Geographers* 55 (1965): 191–220.
41. Zelinsky, *Cultural Geography of the United States*, 116.
42. Newton, "Cultural Preadaptation," 146–50; and Terry G. Jordan, "Preadaptation and European Colonization in Rural North America," *Annals of the Association of American Geographers* 79 (1989): 489–500.
43. Jordan and Kaups, *American Backwoods Frontier*, 35–36.
44. R. Cole Harris, "The Simplification of Europe Overseas," *Annals of the Association of American Geographers* 67 (1977): 469–83; and R. C. Harris and L. Guelke, "Land and Society in Early Canada and South Africa," *Journal of Historical Geography* 3 (1977): 135–53.
45. Robert D. Mitchell, *Commercialism and Frontier: Perspectives on the Early Shenandoah Valley* (Charlottesville: Univ. Press of Virginia, 1977); Robert D. Mitchell, "The Formation of American Cultural Regions: An Interpretation," in *European Settlement and Development in North America: Essays on Geographical Change in Honour and Memory of Andrew Hill Clark*, ed. James R. Gibson, 66–90 (Toronto, Canada: Univ. of Toronto Press, 1978).
46. Richard K. MacMaster, "The Cattle Trade in Western Virginia, 1760–1830," in *Appalachian Frontiers: Settlement, Society, and Development in the Preindustrial Era*, ed. Robert D. Mitchell, 127–49 (Lexington: Univ. Press of Kentucky, 1990).
47. See, e.g., Jack P. Greene and J. R. Pole, "Reconstructing British-American Colonial History: An Introduction," in *British Colonial America: Essays in the New History of the Early Modern Era*, ed. Jack P. Greene and J. R. Pole, 1–17 (Baltimore, Md.: Johns Hopkins Univ. Press, 1984); Richard Pillsbury, "The Pennsylvania Culture Area: A Reappraisal," *North American Culture* 3 (1987): 37–54; Jordan and Kaups, *American Backwoods Frontier*, 9–10, 27–28; and Robert D. Mitchell and Milton B. Newton, *The Appalachian Frontier: Views from the East and the Southwest*, Historical Geography Research Series No. 21 (London: Institute of British Geographers, 1988), 1–64.
48. Robert D. Mitchell, "American Origins and Regional Institutions: The Seventeenth-Century Chesapeake," *Annals of the Association of American Geographers* 73 (1983): 404–20.
49. Marvin W. Mikesell, "Comparative Studies in Frontier History," *Annals of the Association of American Geographers* 50 (1960): 62–74.
50. Ibid., 74. That such comparative thought remains intellectually important among geographers is evident in Mark Bassin, "Turner, Solov'ev, and the 'Frontier Hypothesis': The Nationalist Significance of Open Spaces," *Journal of Modern History* 65 (1993): 473–511.
51. David Harry Miller and Jerome O. Steffen, eds., *The Frontier: Comparative Studies*, vol. 1 (Norman: Univ. of Oklahoma Press, 1977), and William W. Savage, Jr., and Stephen I. Thompson, eds., *The Frontier: Comparative Studies*, vol. 2 (Norman, Okla.: Univ. of Oklahoma Press, 1979).

52. John C. Hudson, "Theory and Methodology in Comparative Frontier Studies," in David Harry Miller and Steffen, *The Frontier*, 1:11–32.
53. See John Hudson's own research, discussed in "Migration to an American Frontier," *Annals of the Association of American Geographers* 66 (1976): 242–65, and "North American Origins of Middlewestern Frontier Populations," *Annals of the Association of American Geographers* 78 (1988): 395–413.
54. See James A. Henretta, "Families and Farms: *Mentalité* in Pre-Industrial America," *William and Mary Quarterly* 3d ser. 35 (1978): 3–32; James T. Lemon, "Comment on James A. Henretta's 'Families and Farms: Mentalité in Pre-Industrial America,'" with a reply by Henretta, *William and Mary Quarterly* 3d ser. 37 (1980): 688–700; and James T. Lemon, "Early Americans and Their Social Environment," *Journal of Historical Geography* 6 (1980): 115–31.
55. Harry Roy Merrens, *Colonial North Carolina in the Eighteenth Century: A Study in Historical Geography* (Chapel Hill: Univ. of North Carolina Press, 1964).
56. Ibid., 111–19.
57. Joseph A. Ernst and Harry Roy Merrens, "'Camden's Turrets Pierce the Skies!': The Urban Process in the Southern Colonies during the Eighteenth Century," *William and Mary Quarterly* 3d ser. 30 (1973): 549–74.
58. Ibid., 555.
59. Kenneth E. Lewis, *Camden: A Frontier Town in Eighteenth-Century South Carolina*, Anthropological Studies No. 2 (Columbia: South Carolina Institute of Archaeology and Anthropology, Univ. of South Carolina, 1976): abstract.
60. It is interesting to note the broad range of geographical works cited in Kenneth E. Lewis, *American Frontier*.
61. Carville Earle and Ronald Hoffman, "Staple Crops and Urban Development in the Eighteenth-Century South," *Perspectives in American History* 10 (1976): 7–78.
62. Ibid., 51–62.
63. Hofstra and Mitchell, "Town and Country in Backcountry Virginia"; Robert D. Mitchell, "Metropolitan Chesapeake: Reflections on Town Formation in Colonial Virginia and Maryland," in Simmler, *Lois Green Carr*, 105–25.
64. This map is derived from a variety of sources, including Friis, "A Series of Population Maps"; Kniffen and Glassie, "Building in Wood"; and Mitchell, *Commercialism and Frontier*.
65. Frank W. Porter, "From Backcountry to County: the Delayed Settlement of Western Maryland," *Maryland Historical Magazine* 70 (1975): 329–49; and Frank W. Porter, "The Maryland Frontier, 1722–1732: Prelude to Settlement in Western Maryland," in *Geographical Perspectives on Maryland's Past*, Occasional Papers in Geography No. 4, ed. Robert D. Mitchell and Edward K. Muller, 90–107 (College Park: Univ. of Maryland, 1979).
66. Richard R. Beeman, *The Evolution of the Southern Backcountry: A Case Study of Lunenburg County, Virginia, 1746–1832* (Philadelphia: Univ. of Pennsylvania Press, 1984), 14–41.
67. Robert W. Ramsey, *Carolina Cradle: Settlement of the Northwest Carolina Frontier, 1747–1762* (Chapel Hill: Univ. of North Carolina Press, 1964), 23–50.

68. Robert L. Meriwether, *The Expansion of South Carolina, 1729–1765* (Kingsport, Tenn.: Southern Publishers, 1940); Louis De Vorsey, Jr., "The Colonial Georgia Backcountry," in *Colonial Augusta: "Key to the Indian Country,"* ed. Edward J. Cashin, 3–26 (Macon, Ga.: Mercer Univ. Press, 1986).
69. Derived principally from the map "Tidewater," Map 17 in the series entitled *The Making of America* (Washington, D.C.: National Geographic Society, 1988).
70. James B. Gouger, "The Northern Neck of Virginia: A Tidewater Grain-Farming Region in the Antebellum South," *West Georgia College Studies in Social Science* 16 (1977): 73–90, and Elizabeth A. Kessel, "Germans on the Maryland Frontier: A Social History of Frederick County, Maryland, 1730–1800" (Ph.D. diss., Rice Univ., 1981).
71. These remarks are based on the maps in Lester J. Cappon, ed., *Atlas of Early American History: The Revolutionary Era, 1760–1790* (Princeton, N.J.: Princeton Univ. Press, 1976), 25.
72. Mitchell, *Commercialism and Frontier*, 98–100.
73. Ibid., 114–16.
74. Earle and Hoffman, "Staple Crops and Urban Development," esp. fig. 2.
75. Figures compiled from U.S. Bureau of the Census, *Historical Statistics of the United States: Colonial Times to 1970* (Washington, D.C.: U.S. Government Printing Office, 1975), pt. 2, ser. Z1–19. Bridenbaugh, *Myths and Realities*, 121n, suggests a backcountry population by 1776 of about 250,000, or 30% of the South's population.
76. Mitchell, *Commercialism and Frontier*, 19–25.
77. Gary C. Goodwin, *Cherokees in Transition: A Study of Changing Culture and Environment Prior to 1775*, Research Paper No. 181 (Chicago: Department of Geography, Univ. of Chicago, 1977).
78. Louis De Vorsey, Jr., *The Indian Boundary in the Southern Colonies, 1763–1775* (Chapel Hill: Univ. of North Carolina Press, 1966), and Louis De Vorsey, Jr., "Indian Boundaries in Colonial Georgia," *Georgia Historical Quarterly* 54 (1970): 63–78.
79. See esp. Tom Hatley, *The Dividing Paths: Cherokees and South Carolinians Through the Era of the American Revolution* (New York: Oxford Univ. Press, 1993); and Tom Hatley, "Cherokee Women Farmers Hold Their Ground," in Mitchell, *Appalachian Frontiers*, 37–51.
80. James H. Merrell, *The Indian's New World: Catawbas and Their Neighbors, from European Contact through the Era of Removal* (Chapel Hill: Univ. of North Carolina Press, 1989).
81. Robert D. Mitchell, Edward F. Connor, and Warren R. Hofstra, "European Settlement and Land-Cover Change: The Shenandoah Valley of Virginia during the Eighteenth Century," final report, Grant #4381-90, National Geographic Society, 1993.
82. Ibid., 86–92, and Robert D. Mitchell, "From the Ground Up: Place, and Diversity in Frontier Studies," in *Diversity and Accommodation: Essays on the Cultural Composition of the Virginia Frontier*, ed. Michael J. Puglisi, 23–52 (Knoxville: Univ. of Tennessee Press, 1997).
83. Warren R. Hofstra, "Land Policy and Settlement in the Northern Shenandoah Valley," in Mitchell, *Appalachian Frontiers*, 105–26; and Mitchell, *Commercialism and Frontier*, 28–31.

84. Robert D. Mitchell and Warren R. Hofstra, "How Do Settlement Systems Originate? The Virginia Backcountry during the Eighteenth Century," *Journal of Historical Geography* 21 (1995): 123–47; and Warren R. Hofstra, "Land, Ethnicity, and Community at the Opequon Settlement, Virginia, 1730–1800," *Virginia Magazine of History and Biography* 98 (1990): 423–48.
85. Clarence R. Geier and Warren R. Hofstra, "An Archaeological Survey of and Management Plan for Cultural Resources in the Vicinity of the Upper Opequon Creek," report to Frederick County Board of Supervisors, Winchester, Va., 1991; and Clarence R. Geier and Warren R. Hofstra, "The Abrams Creek–Redbud Run Project: A Cultural Resource Inventory Study of Archaeological Sites in the Shale Area East of Winchester, Virginia," report to Frederick County Board of Supervisors and Virginia Department of Historic Resources, Winchester, Va., 1992.
86. Hofstra and Mitchell, "Town and Country in Backcountry Virginia"; and James O'Mara, *An Historical Geography of Urban System Development: Tidewater Virginia in the Eighteenth Century*, Geographical Monographs No. 13 (Downsview, Ont., Canada: Atkinson College, York Univ., 1983).
87. Robert D. Mitchell and Warren R. Hofstra, "Townscape of Winchester, Virginia: The Morphology of a Market Town in the Eighteenth-Century Backcountry" (grant proposal, Columbia: Savannah River Archaeological Research Program, Univ. of South Carolina, 1993–94).
88. Hofstra and Mitchell, "Town and Country in Backcountry Virginia."
89. Ibid.; Mitchell, *Commercialism and Frontier*, 172–78.
90. Mitchell, *Commercialism and Frontier*, 162–72.
91. Hofstra and Mitchell, "Town and Country in Backcountry Virginia"; Thomas M. Doerflinger, *A Vigorous Spirit of Enterprise: Merchants and Economic Development in Revolutionary Philadelphia* (Chapel Hill: Univ. of North Carolina Press, 1986), 82–122.
92. See the suggestive comments in Allan Kulikoff, "Migration and Cultural Diffusion in Early America, 1600–1860: A Review Essay," *Historical Methods* 19 (1986): 153–69, and L. D. Gragg, *Migration in Early America: The Virginia Quaker Experience* (Ann Arbor, Mich.: UMI Research Press, 1980).
93. Mary Beth Pudup, "The Boundaries of Social Class in Preindustrial America," *Journal of Historical Geography* 15 (1989): 139–62; Barbara Rasmussen, *Absentee Landowning and Exploitation in West Virginia, 1760–1920* (Lexington: Univ. Press of Kentucky, 1994); and Paul Salstrom, *Appalachia's Path to Dependency: Rethinking a Region's Economic History, 1730–1940* (Lexington: Univ. Press of Kentucky, 1994).
94. Turk McCleskey, "Rich Land, Poor Prospects: Real Estate and the Formation of a Social Elite in Augusta County, Virginia, 1738–1770," *Virginia Magazine of History and Biography* 98 (1990): 449–96.
95. Mitchell, *Commercialism and Frontier*, 65–72.
96. Hofstra, "Land, Ethnicity, and Community at the Opequon Settlement."
97. Edward A. Chappell, "Acculturation in the Shenandoah Valley: Rhenish Houses of the Massanutten Settlement," *Proceedings of the American Philosophical Society* 124 (1980):

55–89; Warren R. Hofstra, "Adaptation or Survival? Folk Housing at Opequon Settlement, Virginia, 1730–1800," *Ulster Folklife* 37 (1991): 36–61.

98. See the suggestive comments in Lois Green Carr and Lorena S. Walsh, "The Planter's Wife: The Experience of White Women in Seventeenth-Century Maryland," *William and Mary Quarterly* 3d ser. 34 (1977): 542–71; and Frederika J. Teute, "Land, Liberty and Labor in the Post-Revolutionary Era: Kentucky as the Promised Land" (Ph.D. diss., Johns Hopkins Univ., 1988). That gender issues have been given little attention in the backcountry literature is evident in the reviews by Gregory H. Nobles, "Breaking into the Backcountry: New Approaches to the Early American Frontier," *William and Mary Quarterly* 3d ser. 46 (1989): 641–70; Albert H. Tillson, Jr., "The Southern Backcountry: A Survey of Current Research," *Virginia Magazine of History and Biography* 38 (1990): 387–422; and Warren R. Hofstra, "The Virginia Backcountry in the Eighteenth Century: Origins and Outcomes," *Virginia Magazine of History and Biography* 101 (1993): 485–508.

99. Opportunities for geographers and archaeologists to contribute to the political dimensions of backcountry life are discussed in Nobles, "Breaking into the Backcountry," and Hofstra, "Virginia Backcountry in the Eighteenth Century." See also the suggestive comments in J. F. Cherry, "Power in Space: Archaeological and Geographical Studies of the State," in Wagstaff, *Landscape and Culture*, 146–72.

100. Albert H. Tillson, Jr., *Gentry and Common Folk: Political Culture on a Virginia Frontier, 1740–1789* (Lexington: Univ. Press of Kentucky, 1991).

101. See Hofstra and Mitchell, "Town and Country in Backcountry Virginia," and the fascinating sweep of thought in Jack P. Greene, "Mastery and the Definition of Cultural Space in Early America: A Perspective," in Jack P. Greene, *Imperatives, Behaviors, and Identities: Essays in Early American Cultural History* (Charlottesville: Univ. Press of Virginia, 1992), 1–12.

Muddied Waters: A Discussion of Current Interdisciplinary Backcountry Studies

Michael J. Puglisi

Since the appearance, over one hundred years ago, of Frederick Jackson Turner's "The Significance of the Frontier in American History," historians have debated the merits of the so-called "frontier thesis," defending it, refining it, criticizing it, and attacking it outright. More recently, however, students of other disciplines have joined the fray, both complicating and enriching the search for the meaning of the frontier. Archaeologists and geographers, specialists in material culture and folkways, cultural anthropologists and ethnohistorians—all have contributed their particular perspectives to a new and expanding conception of the frontier. Perhaps nowhere is this interdisciplinary collaboration more apparent than in recent studies of the colonial backcountry.

This question of interdisciplinary approaches to the backcountry exists within a larger context. All history, to some degree, ought to be interdisciplinary. What else can it be, in its fullest sense? History is the story of the evolution of human society. To restrict the study of that formidable story to any one methodological approach—or, to phrase it another way, to deny the contributions that other methodological approaches can make in helping to complete the picture—seems incredibly narrow. Within the discipline, we use terms like social history, women's history, and ethnohistory. In an ideal world, however, we would not have to do so; all history would include elements such as social development, gender, and culture, because they all contribute to the whole.

Even the term history is somewhat problematical in the context of this essay; not only professional historians or those trained primarily in the traditional methodology of that discipline are interested in the development of the early American frontier. As is noted above, recent and current scholarship on the topic includes a variety of approaches and methodologies, and scholars need to appreciate all of them for their contributions. The series of conferences devoted to backcountry topics in recent years[1] offers a representative taste of this disciplinary diversity. The conference that initiated this collection included eight presenters trained primarily in history, eight in archaeology, three in geography, and one in architectural history, and they came from colleges and universities, data consulting firms, museums, and public research agencies. Similar disciplinary combinations have appeared in various meetings spread over the preceding several years. Significantly, none of these gatherings of scholars has been confined to historians—or to any other discipline, for that matter. A colleague once suggested that the disciplinary labels someday could be discarded altogether. The intent is positive, but that notion is more idealistic than it is practical or even desirable, because there is value in a multidisciplinary, as well as in an interdisciplinary, approach. Not all scholars have to practice hybrid methodologies, but they do need to be open to the specific skills and perspectives that other disciplines have to offer.

In recent years, the approaches to reconstructing and analyzing the development of the backcountry have been almost as diverse as the experiences they have attempted to study. This essay surveys and discusses some of the best examples of recently produced interdisciplinary work from the fields of history, geography, ethnography, and archaeology. Such diversity makes categorization difficult, but addressing the question from a topical perspective reveals elements of the larger synthesis of interdisciplinary and multidisciplinary scholarship. The focus of this analysis points to *why* these approaches have proven successful and continue to be valuable. Individual recently published works, as well as studies currently in progress, help to illustrate the interdisciplinary methodologies and the topics they approach.

While 1893 is a key date in the historiography of frontier studies, 1989 seems to be an important date in recent interdisciplinary backcountry studies. In that year, three significant works appeared. Two of them have been controversial; all three have influenced interdisciplinary perspectives on the frontier. *The American Backwoods Frontier*, by Terry Jordan and Matti Kaups; and *Albion's Seed*, by David Hackett Fischer, both address the transfer of cultural traditions to the American backcountry; like Turner's original analysis of frontier development, they have elicited strong and sometimes heated debate.[2] Both have been valuable in the evolution of interdisciplinary interpretations, however, and their strengths will be addressed below.

The third work, "Breaking into the Backcountry: New Approaches to the Early American Frontier, 1750–1800," an essay by Gregory Nobles, appeared in the *William and Mary Quarterly*. In this work, Nobles outlines recent themes and new directions in backcountry studies, citing two themes apparent in contemporary scholarship. First, recognition of "significant similarities" in the "social, economic and political development" of different frontier regions allows for more comparative studies of the backcountry.[3] This implies a call for detailed case studies of individual frontier areas, employing the interdisciplinary methodologies that allow scholars delving into the intricacies of local dynamics to lay the foundations for a larger interpretive scheme. The second theme revolves around recognizing the "important lines of social, economic and political connection between the backcountry" and cultural centers back east, as well as in Europe. The ultimate challenge, according to Nobles, "is to explore the relationship between the established culture and the emerging frontier subculture."[4] Again, he implicitly calls for interdisciplinary investigation. Nobles's essay provided, at the time of its publication, important guidance and perspective—if not an explicit agenda—for backcountry studies in the 1990s and beyond, and much of the subsequent scholarship produced in the decade pursued the themes he outlined.

Many topics in backcountry studies have been influenced and enhanced by the trend toward interdisciplinary analysis; one topic has been revolutionized. The rise of the field of ethnohistory has shed light on the importance of cultural contacts in a way that would have been totally foreign to Frederick Jackson Turner, for whom Indians existed on the frontier only to be defeated, transformed, or eliminated as civilization marched inexorably westward. Ethnohistorians, in contrast, emphasize the complexity of frontiers, which they more accurately characterize as cultural contact zones. In fact, this interdisciplinary approach helped to redefine the very understanding of the term frontier. The traditional Turnerian view of frontier was a line of settlement moving across the map, separating chaos and disorder on the far side from order and civility behind. Ethnohistory, with its emphasis on the integrity of all cultures, posits the frontier as a cultural mixing zone, an area of mutual exchange which could take a variety of forms, and in which all groups involved are affected, wittingly or unwittingly.[5]

In applying this perspective specifically to the frontiers of the early British Empire, Bernard Bailyn and Philip Morgan produced the edited volume *Strangers Within the Realm* (1991), a "pioneering" work arguing for a "multicultural, pluralistic approach" to historical scholarship on colonial frontiers and taking into account such factors as ethnography, demography, and material culture. These editors present a picture of "shifting frontiers," with "no firmly set boundaries," in which relationships between groups "were in constant motion." Margin areas, like the southern backcountry, "acquired distinctive and permanent characteristics, and they eventually formed core worlds of their own, that, in many cases, generated margins even more complex than they themselves had been."[6]

Maldwyn A. Jones, in an essay in the above volume, refers to the Scotch-Irish in the backcountry as experiencing a "cultural synthesis" caused by the "various borrowings, adaptations, and compromises" forced by their "interaction with their environments and with other groups."[7] Viewed from this perspective, frontier or backcountry studies must take a cultural approach. The actors of history recognized that cultural diversity existed; although they may not always have appreciated the value of that diversity, they had to accommodate it in their actions. Therefore, it is essential that modern scholars of frontier areas recognize the cultural influences that contributed to the course of events in the past; and any study based on culture, whether European relations with Indians or the transfer of European traditions to America, must employ interdisciplinary methodologies to gain a full picture.[8]

The most notable book published in recent years on the dynamics of cultural contact between natives and Europeans in the southern backcountry is James Merrell's *The Indians' New World: Catawbas and Their Neighbors from European Contact Through the Era of Removal* (1989). Merrell employs archaeological and anthropological sources, in addition to the well-known historical accounts, in convincingly presenting his interpretation that the traditional view of Indians on the frontier has been far too simplistic and one-sided. In this work, he points out that the natives also felt the newness of the encounter and that their perspectives on the changes taking place around them were not wholly unlike those of the Europeans from whose viewpoint historians traditionally have employed the term New World. "Like their new neighbors," Merrell suggests, "Indians had to blend old and new in ways that would permit them to survive in the present and prepare for the future without utterly forsaking their past.... [creating] new societies, each similar to, yet very different from, its parent culture."[9] Merrell finds that trade was the link that tied the cultures together in a two-way mutual exchange system which was "surprisingly fluid and cooperative." Nobles calls this fine work a challenge to "other historians to explore the complex cultural interactions that took place [even] after the initial period of contact."[10]

Tom Hatley has met that challenge. Presenting "a story of intersections," his book, *The Dividing Paths: Cherokees and South Carolinians through the Era of Revolution* (1993), recounts the geopolitical contest between the powerful natives and the expansive colonists, with particular reference to the influence of cultural backgrounds and priorities, world views, and changing social dynamics. What has all too often been lost in traditional accounts of the past, Hatley reminds us, "is the most perishable part of history," in this case "the momentous transactions between two very different peoples, living as neighbors." Chronicles of treaties and battles cannot adequately tell this story, which formed and evolved "as two societies regarded each other across the Piedmont and foothills of South Carolina for a century."[11] Rather, a full understanding of the driving forces behind the conflict—and behind the peaceful interactions and accommodations that existed as well—can be gained only through an interdisciplinary, ethnohistorical approach. Hatley himself epitomizes this approach: with a Ph.D. degree in colonial history and a master of forest science degree, he works as an environmental manager and consultant. It is this type of multidisciplinary perspective, within either an individual or a team, that has invigorated frontier studies.

And the effort continues. Among other scholars who have accepted the challenge, putting interdisciplinary skills to work to gain a better understanding of the cultural dynamics of particular backcountry areas, Michael Barber and Eugene Barfield, forest archaeologists for the Jefferson National Forest, head a team involved in the ongoing investigation, in the upper Roanoke Valley of Virginia, of sites which indicate early trade relations in the region. The early ethnographic record in the backcountry generally tends to be sparse, making archaeological field work and interpretations all the more important. Barber and Barfield's study is based on the recognition that the natives possessed an established, viable cultural system into which European trade intruded. But the combination of archaeological and ethnohistorical evidence confirms that this initial intrusion of trade goods came primarily through Indian "middlemen" east of the mountains.[12] In addition to illuminating the material relations between the cultures, these findings also reveal that Europeans often gained their initial ideas of the backcountry second-hand, by indirect contact, well in advance of actual settlement. Such preconceptions played an important role in guiding the European settlers' approach to the backcountry.

Also in Virginia, archaeologist Jeffrey Hantman is blending archaeological data with the scanty ethnographic record to reconstruct the history and culture of the Monacan tribe, a people who survived in situ physically and biologically, but whose cultural identity was lost at some point in the colonial era.[13] Without collaboration of disciplines, the Monacan story would remain a mystery. These two studies are not unique; they are representative of similar projects taking place in various locations, as scholars in the primary disciplines of history, anthropology, and archaeology develop closer working relationships, filling gaps and supplementing the data they generate individually.

The single topic which has attracted the most attention in frontier studies, from Turner's day to the present, is the development of society as newly settled areas evolved into stabilized neighborhoods. Hence, the search for community has become an integral component of recent backcountry studies—influenced, of course, by the so-called "new social history" and the example of the New England town study genre. Numerous writers have pointed out the inherent difficulties in attempting to impose the town-study model on the backcountry, where geographical, ethnic, demographic, and economic conditions differed vastly from conditions in the colonial Northeast, but the goal of "exploring the network of interactions among inhabitants as a means of identifying the bounds of community" persists.[14] In his 1989 essay, Nobles states that "historians have only begun to explore the process of community building on the frontier," where "communal relations were the most important source of both collective identity and cultural conflict," reflecting the ethnic diversity and the transient nature of the backcountry population.[15] Indeed, historian Warren Hofstra and geographer Robert Mitchell, an interdisciplinary collaborative team that has contributed significantly to the scholarship of the early Virginia frontier, describe the southern backcountry as the birthplace of "hybrid settlement and social systems that influenced the formation of frontier communities west of the Appalachians in subsequent periods."[16] They call for community case studies as the only means of tracing such indicators of development as the transition to urbanization and capitalism in the frontier region.

Daniel Thorp's approach to the Moravian community of Wachovia, North

Carolina, is heavily influenced by the work of Norwegian anthropologist Fredrik Barth, who posits that groups in a heterogeneous society, such as that of the southern backcountry, do not maintain their identity through isolation, but rather "by maintaining peaceful, regulated contact across clearly defined cultural boundaries." This model clearly fits the world of the Wachovia Moravians, who, according to Thorp, protected "many elements of their community from outside influences" while at the same time integrating themselves into the legal, political and particularly the economic systems of the region through "closely supervised links between themselves and other citizens of North Carolina." Thorp calls for scholars to formulate "a fuller picture than we [currently] have of social developments on the eighteenth-century frontier," a picture that can be achieved only through receptivity to models and methodologies of interdisciplinary scholarship which give form to the figures of the past.[17]

Investigation of the regional economy invariably has accompanied the search for society in frontier areas. Recent interdisciplinary studies have allowed scholars finally to refute one of Turner's flawed assumptions, that access to free land on the frontier had a leveling effect, creating an almost classless society. Turk McCleskey's essay, "Rich Land, Poor Prospects" (1990), details a backcountry land system controlled by elites who limited access to land for newcomers and thereby regulated political and economic affairs in the area. A large majority of new arrivals could not become landowners and, without freehold status, could not enjoy the open opportunity traditionally associated with frontier regions.[18] Nobles makes the point that, even in addressing economic matters in the backcountry, scholars must remember that "economic conditions cannot be considered apart from social relations," because "patterns of cultural assumptions and economic expectations" can be just as influential as material conditions.[19]

In a more recent essay included in this volume, McCleskey elaborates on his study of land holding, focusing on purchasers on the fringes of frontier land in the upper Shenandoah Valley. This "shadow land"—imperfect land surveys recorded between 1745 and 1755—reveals surprising relationships between speculator control of land, the price of land, and settlement patterns in extreme frontier areas. Contrary to expected characteristics of inexpensive land and individualistic settlers, McCleskey discovered higher prices in the more remote sections of Augusta County and a pattern of family relations among neighboring farmsteads.[20] Apparently purchasers were willing to pay more to locate in areas where their relations could also find unoccupied land. Speculators capitalized on this desire for the proximity of family. McCleskey's discovery adds a new dimension to considerations regarding settlement patterns, frontier economies, kinship networks, and community formation in the backcountry.

The community study to which Hofstra and Mitchell have devoted their attention involves the dispersed rural communities and the hierarchy of towns, "from rural hamlets to major commercial centers," in that part of the northern Shenandoah Valley centered on the "evolving urban neighborhood" of Winchester. They have analyzed what they call a "town-country settlement system" which is "more complex than central-place theory would suggest" because trade took place not only in towns, but in the countryside as well. Charles Farmer poses a similar theoretical model in his analysis of Southside Virginia, finding the classical central-place model too restrictive in explaining backcountry settlement and economic development in the absence of hierarchical place orientation. Rather, he suggests that country stores, in essence, played the role of towns in the export staple economy of the region. To accomplish an analysis of backcountry communities and their economic systems, according to Hofstra and Mitchell, requires a "holistic approach that appreciates the full reciprocity of town and country."[21]

Hofstra and Mitchell term their methodology a "comparative, interdisciplinary strategy" for community case studies. In their National Endowment for the Humanities grant proposal, "Settlement and Society in the Southern Backcountry: The Northern Shenandoah Valley of Virginia, 1730-1800," they outline a research strategy that consists, first, of a land file of all property holders and transactions, plotted on cadastral maps reflecting patterns of wealth and social status; and, second, a biographical data file to help trace the political economy of the evolving backcountry community. They see this as a research model applicable to subsequent settlement systems in the nineteenth century. In their own words, analysis of the transition to capitalism and urbanism in westward expansion "requires careful tracing and mapping of the career biographies, kinship networks, religious associations, and economic activities" of the residents revealed in the two basic files. "Only a framework that integrates the perspectives of history and geography," they add, can provide answers to these questions of development in the backcountry.[22]

One of the most valuable components of this study, particularly for historians being exposed to the wonders that other disciplines have to offer, is the concept of spatial as well as temporal patterns. Space is a concept relatively new to historians because it is not part of the traditional documentary past, but an understanding of space is essential in deciphering the hidden clues to the story of social development in the backcountry. Space—more accurately, the use of space—reflects how people viewed their landscape (physical, social, economic, and material) and their place in it.[23] Hofstra and Mitchell cite a "new set of perspectives" in the current backcountry research agenda "that can be articulated only by combining history and geography." The spatial dimension revolves around the "integrative functioning of the sites and forms of human activity, the routes that connected them, and the local territorial boundaries within which the activities took place through time."[24] To reconstruct the cultural space of the northern Shenandoah Valley, the research team sponsors field work to verify settlement sites and to assist in the plotting of churches, mills, and taverns, not to mention the roads that connected them.[25]

David Hsiung's study of Upper East Tennessee also focuses on the territorial boundaries of cultural space. Blending historical research, geographical perspective, and sociological theory, Hsiung examines the development of the regional road network, economic connections, and finally the appearance of railroads to analyze various dimensions of social, political, and economic activity. Rather than drawing strictly dichotomous conclusions based on the stereotypical image of Appalachian isolation, he evaluates the dimensions as reflections of "different degrees of connectedness."[26] Contrary to the popular belief that the southern mountaineer was cut off from the outside world, Hsiung suggests that efforts at road building and railroad construction indicate a desire for integration by some residents of the region and that the results, by the early nineteenth century, "connected the residents both internally and externally," placing them not on the side of isolation, but somewhere in the middle of the scale of connectedness. Not all Upper East Tennesseans, however, shared in the desire or the benefits of connectness, preferring instead a more local orientation.[27] In short, the mountaineers valued both Gemeinschaft and Gesellschaft.

"The cultural landscape," according to Hofstra, "represents the outcome of [the] improving process," as human beings modify the terrain around them to reflect their own perspectives, aspirations, and material means. In this sense, landscape represents a "physical artifact," both of individual actions and collective cultural expressions, and the study of space intersects with the study of material culture. As an "artifact of human activity," Hofstra and Mitchell point out, "its provenance must be accounted for in terms of cultural context and the social, economic, and political forces shaping it."[28] One component of this study includes a collaborative effort between public and private agencies—James Madison University, Shenandoah University, the Frederick County (Virginia) Board of Supervisors, and the Virginia Department of Historic Resources—to sponsor a survey of historic and prehistoric sites. In an area of 4,900 acres, the survey identified 127 prehistoric sites, 165 historic sites, and 41 architectural sites.[29]

Connected to this interdisciplinary interest in the landscape is the creation of cadastral maps, reflecting the changes in space over time, and representing what Mitchell calls history "from the ground up."[30] While cartography can be considered a hard, tangible science, for purposes of historical analysis it requires interpretive skills similar to those necessary in dealing with any piece of evidence from the past, whether a written document or an archaeological artifact. All require the interpreter to look below the surface, beyond the outward appearances, to question the meaning and significance behind the data. A comprehensive study based on historical cartography produces an accurate reconstruction of landscape for analysis purposes, and it helps to illustrate contemporary perspectives on that landscape. Innovations in computerized mapping allow scholars to interpret contemporary perspectives on the landscape by reconstructing the inhabitants' usage of the terrain; thereby, studies which employ historical cartography as a resource can provide enhanced analysis of such dynamics as settlement patterns, social interaction, economic activity, and community formation and development.[31]

In a paper he presented at a 1991 conference devoted to "Re-examining America's Frontier Heritage," Gregory Nobles pointed out another aspect of the importance of cartographic studies. Contemporary maps of the frontier were intended not only to depict the geography of the land, but also "to claim and control it, to impose a human, and most important, political order over it." Cartographers incorporated into their creations "preconceived notions of spatial, economic and social organizations" reflecting their own "assumptions about order." In short, the maps represent, to a certain degree, depictions of what authorities wanted to see on the frontier, particularly with reference to "spatial order, social authority, and individual industry."[32] On another level, the manner in which Indian groups were depicted on early maps, in terms of the placement and relative sizes of tribal names with reference to colonial designations, indicates perhaps wishful thinking, in some cases, but also a reflection of beliefs about the proper order of things. Even in the fringes, on frontier land at the time unexplored and uninhabited by Europeans, map makers depicted animals, natural resources, or natives, in "seemingly innocent decorative touches" which in reality were "important part[s] of the message the map conveyed."[33] Maps are material representations of cultural values and prescriptions for social order. Consciously or unconsciously, their makers create a culturally one-sided image of the frontier, one more source for the Eurocentric misconstruction of frontier reality that Michael Barber and Eugene Barfield, as we have seen, address in their research on early intercultural trade networks.

To get off of the parchment and back onto the ground, geographer Mitchell, historian Hofstra, and Environmental Studies scholar Edward Connor produced a report to the National Geographic Society which describes their attempt to reconstruct the natural land cover of the northern Shenandoah Valley in the eighteenth century and to explain the changes that occurred as a result of human activity. The study had to consider natural processes, native practices, and the impact of colonial settlement patterns. The sources of information on land cover include historical literature, such as travel accounts, and land survey records, which often contain references to vegetation.[34]

Despite the location of the Shenandoah Valley in a region of oak, chestnut, hickory, and other hardwoods, early historians generally refer to the valley's open grassland or its prairie-like appearance as the reason why settlers were attracted to the area in the colonial period. But these conditions were the result of two centuries of land clearing and farming; and in fact early travel accounts, which are rich in descriptions of land cover, make no mention of open prairie. Surveyors' records also support the picture of the valley as a wooded mosaic.[35] This example lends additional support to the value of interdisciplinary methodologies in interpreting the backcountry. Like the eighteenth-century colonists, many early historians of the region based their perceptions on superficial or inaccurate information. In contrast, the Mitchell, Connor, and Hofstra study illustrates the corrective and comparative value of new, in-depth, local case studies.

The emphasis on landscape and land cover also suggests the value of ecological history for backcountry studies. Scholars must look at the total exchange of contact on the frontier, including the diffusion of plants and animals; and historians must be open to new sources and new methodologies for interpreting them, so as to erase myths and create a more realistic analysis of the process of frontier development. Doing so successfully requires not only a sensitivity to human perceptions, or misperceptions, of the environment, but also a firm interdisciplinary understanding of the natural processes of particular ecosystems.

In *A New Face on the Countryside* (1990), Timothy Silver achieves that synthesis. He describes environmental changes in the South Atlantic forests from European contact to the nineteenth century, challenging the "simplistic notion of an unspoiled American wilderness ravaged by Europeans." Instead, he "argues that synergism among Indians, Africans, and Europeans altered the vegetation and wildlife" of the region.[36] Silver is convinced that "human history is inevitably intertwined with the history of plants, animals, and micro-organisms." Yet he cites problems in ecological history similar to those encountered in backcountry community studies, noting that "environmental change is frequently a local phenomenon; its scope and scale vary with topography, climate and settlement patterns." Therefore, environmental studies must focus on well-defined areas, to allow for "significant detail and [to] avoid generalizing about environmental change."[37] Inasmuch as ecosystems change on their own, there is also the necessity of distinguishing changes that would have occurred naturally from those actually caused by human activity, and this requires interdisciplinary knowledge.

Silver's study contains information which would be familiar to such diverse professionals as ethnohistorians, plant ecologists, historical geographers, historical demographers, and medical geographers.[38] At its best, then, ecological history clearly illustrates the value of interdisciplinary endeavors. Indeed, we are finding that interpretations of historical materials depend more and more on the specialized information or insights provided by other fields of study. Therefore, works such as Silver's represent one added avenue leading to a more complete picture of the dynamics which influenced backcountry development.

Moving from forests to clearings, architectural history also contributes in significant ways to an understanding of backcountry influences and dynamics. Given the diverse ethnic character of the eighteenth-century backcountry, contemporary vernacular architecture studies, following the example set by Henry Glassie and his students beginning in the 1960s, focus on identifying ethnic influences apparent in houses and related buildings, and assessing how these characteristics reflect the processes of frontier development.[39] Of primary interest to the field of vernacular architecture, of course, are the buildings generally overlooked by early historians of the backcountry, who tended to rely on the outstanding, as opposed to the commonplace, and thereby often misrepresented architectural and social actuality. Again, only individual case research allows a collective image that is reliable.[40]

It goes without saying that a limited supply of buildings, particularly of the vernacular type, survive from the early periods for study purposes, so architectural research must be collaborative. Historical sources provide documentation and descriptions, for both extant and extinct structures; archaeology can indicate location, dimensions, construction techniques, floor plans, and activity patterns. Researchers even tap into more scientific fields for information. Dendrochronology, for instance, allows accurate dating of log structures by matching known tree ring patterns in particular vicinities.[41] The foundation for vernacular studies is survey efforts which provide data bases for analysis, and these surveys must be ongoing, as existing structures succumb to age and neglect.

Recent studies have tied the collection of architectural raw data into the larger context of interdisciplinary backcountry studies by addressing such analytical questions as land use, settlement patterns, and patterns of cultural persistence and change. Ann McCleary, for example, has looked into dwelling plan types in both the Valley of Virginia and in places of origin for German immigrants. She has found great variety in German plans, casting doubt on the assumption that a generic or uniquely characteristic plan type can be used as a fingerprint conclusively to indicate German influence.[42]

Geographer John Morgan also relies on intensive survey field work as a basis for interpretations of cultural processes reflected in architectural practices. Morgan's initial work, *The Log House in East Tennessee* (1990), examines the diffusion of log house construction in the backcountry and its subsequent evolution after the frontier period. He also has surveyed log barn construction in southwestern Virginia and northeastern Tennessee. Morgan's interpretation of survey data points to the counties of southwestern Virginia as a transitional area between the Pennsylvania bank barn common in northern portions of the backcountry and the cantilever barn construction which dominates the region that begins in eastern Tennessee. His twofold goal is to come to a conclusion regarding architectural styles as reflections of cultural dispersion in the region and to continue his analysis of material culture traditions and economic variations in influencing architectural patterns.[43]

For Hofstra, the survival of exact building styles or techniques is not as important as "a way of thinking about housing—a mental attitude toward the arrangement of internal space and the relation of plan to structure and external appearance."[44] Rather than tracing cultural borrowings and exchanges over a geographical path of migration, his survey of early structures built by Ulster settlers of the northern Shenandoah Valley examines adaptations over time in one location. Employing folklore, material culture studies, and vernacular architecture, the survey adds another dimension to the interpretation of the persistence of other cultural traits, such as settlement patterns, kinship networks, and marriage practices, as revealed in the written record. Ultimately, Scotch-Irish residents of the Virginia backcountry adapted their housing styles to reflect the common Georgian "I" house style, itself a symbol of an identifiable regional culture.[45]

One point worth noting is McCleary's statement that newly available interdisciplinary research on vernacular architecture—and this is true of interdisciplinary studies in general—actually "muddies the waters," making definitive conclusions all the more difficult to achieve.[46] Not that this is bad. Placid waters need to be muddied sometimes; a smooth surface can indicate a lack of activity below. Interdisciplinary approaches muddy the waters by making researchers look at new sources and new interpretive methodologies, thereby challenging old assumptions and general principles with intensive individual studies.

Compiling works from a number of the disciplinary perspectives discussed in this paper, the collection of essays, *Appalachian Frontiers* (1991), edited by Robert Mitchell, has been called "the first interdisciplinary attempt to evaluate the settlement and developmental experiences of the Appalachian region prior to the onset of" industrialization.[47] Through the various topics addressed and the multiple disciplines and subfields represented, the unifying theme of the book, which aspires to "sensitivity to place and time," is the vision of "process," of Appalachian areas "becoming" and experiencing phases "of differential change." This process which transformed "place" on the backcountry was "directly related to the unfolding of the social, economic and political interactions . . . [as] the inhabitants of that place interact[ed]."[48]

From Alan Briceland's essay on the Batts and Fallam explorations to Paul Salstrom's chapter on the agricultural economy of the mid-nineteenth century, *Appalachian Frontiers* represents an invaluable contribution to the literature on the backcountry, as well as an important example of the importance of collaborative methodologies and interpretations. The book emphasizes place, process, and the changing, evolving relationships among peoples, cultures, and their economic networks and institutions and ecosystems. In doing so, it identifies the value of, and sets an agenda for, interdisciplinary backcountry studies.

As Mitchell and others maintain, this perspective "cannot be achieved by using traditional historical procedures." His term, "history 'from the ground up,'" a derivative of the social-history phrase "from the bottom up," suggests that place matters because the attributes of places, measured in numerous variables, mattered to the people of the past, the people we study.[49] In this context, it is essential, at least in the short run, that interdisciplinary researchers focus their energies on the kind of well-defined case study referred to many times in this paper. In doing so, they will lay the groundwork for the elevation of particular studies to the comparative level. It is not a simple process and is likely to cause debate, disagreement, and discussion as the individual pieces are brought together in an effort to formulate coherent syntheses. But the results, in the long run, are worth the effort, for, as Mitchell points out:

> If history "from the ground up" is to mean anything, it means multiple histories that may not "fit" very well into a precast mold. It means not only local and regional history but histories of the interaction of communities, ethnicities, and social groups. . . . It means recognizing differences and distinctions, but also seeking similarities and linkages where they can be demonstrated to exist. Perhaps what we are striving for are "place histories," not just "histories of places," locales as transformed by human actions, in all their complexities, known and inferred, and as yet unimagined.[50]

This, in a sense, brings us full circle to the two important and controversial works cited earlier in this essay. Both attempt to base overall explanations of backcountry development on studies focused on interdisciplinary analysis of minute detail, studies that perhaps do not fit very well into any precast mold.

One major section of David Hackett Fischer's *Albion's Seed: Four British Folkways in America* is devoted to the transfer of cultural traditions and practices from the northern British borderlands region to the American backcountry. Fischer's work is cultural history: he employs the "concept of culture as a coherent and comprehensive whole" in analyzing the past.[51] The book is built upon the thesis that "the legacy of [certain] British folkways in early America remains the most powerful determinant of a voluntary society in the United States today." The folkways which were transported by British settlers from northern Ireland, the lowlands of Scotland, and northern England to the colonial backcountry were the major determinants of social development in that region.[52] Defining folkways as the "normative structure of values, customs, and meanings that exist in any culture," Fischer examines and interprets reflections of these social patterns empirically, as they appear in qualitative and quantitative characteristic indicators, such as speech ways, building ways, religious ways, childrearing ways, and food ways. Actually, he cites over twenty such indicators to suggest regional British and American cultural foundations.[53]

Fischer discusses his methodology by comparing "the old and the new history." Clearly interdisciplinary in his perspective, with his emphasis on material data and other folkways, he maintains that there really is no dichotomy separating old and new approaches to studying the past. In fact, Fischer argues, "the progress of historical knowledge is best served by their creative integration."[54] The term "creative integration" characterizes exactly what interdisciplinary studies are all about; the need to fill every gap in drawing the most complete picture possible of social development in the backcountry requires researchers to be creative, integrating useful information from any sources or fields of study which may appear applicable.

Reactions to *Albion's Seed* have varied, but all have been passionate. While one reviewer praised Fischer's "eclecticism" and his reliance on "all forms of legitimate investigation," including "cultural and economic anthropology," another writer decried "an almost total lack of awareness of the relevant work by geographers and anthropologists."[55] Most of the substantive criticisms revolve around Fischer's handling and interpretation of his evidence. Reviewers generally agree that he often stretches his conclusions to illustrate connections between identifiable British folkways and American regional characteristics. But even the book's critics generally credit Fischer with expanding the scope of historical investigation by his ambitious effort.[56] Jack P. Greene applauds Fischer for employing a "theory of the formation of cultures in new immigrant societies" which may be useful in drawing "some general coherence" out of the studies about "discrete areas and populations [which are] being produced in such abundance by social and cultural historians,"[57] including those working on the colonial backcountry.

Like Fischer, Terry Jordan and Matti Kaups have had their critics. *The American Backwoods Frontier* is based upon a diagnostic analysis of essential characteristics, in what the authors call "a cultural ecological methodology." The key questions revolve around the degree to which European traditions were transplanted to the colonies, and to what extent they were influenced by Indians and Africans, the physical environment, and the shaping force of the collective frontier experience. This "cultural ecological methodology" blends the primary fields of geography and anthropology, but avoids the environmental determinist views of historians like Turner and Walter Prescott Webb. In Jordan and Kaups' interpretation, the "cultural preadaptation" of the European immigrants was equal in importance to the other shaping factors awaiting them on the frontier.[58]

These authors cite D. W. Meinig, who states that one goal of cultural geography is to gain "a better grasp of general processes so as to understand an immensely complicated history" by finding "a causal mechanism that is applicable to a specific case."[59] For Jordan and Kaups, that causal mechanism was the immigration of Finnish settlers through the middle colonies during the mid-seventeenth century. From its base in the lower Delaware Valley, what became the midland pioneer culture diffused through a primary domain of intense impact, a secondary domain of less intense impact, and a peripheral zone of penetration, in which it had the least degree of influence. The authors' explanation of why the midland culture went on to dominate the interior is simple; neither the New England culture nor the tidewater southern culture penetrated the backcountry to the extent that the immigrant culture of the middle region did during the colonial period.[60]

While some critics dismiss Jordan and Kaups' conclusions as groundless and their data as thin, other reviewers hail their "solid historiographical research and abundant evidence of material culture," their "painstaking fieldwork ... and archival evidence."[61] Some reviewers even compare the impact of this book to the work of Frederick Jackson Turner in shaping the debate and determining the direction of frontier studies.[62] By all accounts, *The American Backwoods Frontier* is innovatively drawn; William Wyckoff credits the authors with "an independent spirit, a healthy lack of appreciation for traditional authority, and keen, flexible minds." He calls their work "a bold, important, and controversial book," one "sure to stir discussion and dispute."[63] Therein lies the value of this book, as well as Fischer's work. Scholars need not agree fully with their conclusions for these authors to have made a significant contribution to backcountry scholarship.

Both have elicited debate about their conclusions and their methodologies; to refer back to Ann McCleary's insightful statement, both have, in a beneficial way, muddied the waters. Even if neither comes close to pinpointing the one causal mechanism which guided the development of society in the backcountry, their lasting significance is in the novel perspective they have inspired, even in the arguments of their critics. This is exactly what interdisciplinary studies do: by introducing new perspectives and methodologies, they demand response, examination, and further investigation. The outlook for current backcountry research is encouraging, judging by the innovative studies recently produced and currently in progress, the proliferation and ongoing interest in regional conferences devoted to the topic, and particularly the vibrant dialogue between and among the disciplines represented in this volume.

NOTES

1. "The Southern Colonial Backcountry: Beginning an Inter-disciplinary Dialogue," Oct. 15–16, 1993, sponsored by the South Carolina Institute of Archaeology and Anthropology, Univ. of South Carolina. A similar conference devoted to interpreting the backcountry, entitled "Cultural Diversity on the Virginia Frontier," was held at Emory and Henry College in Virginia on Oct. 9–10, 1992. It was sponsored by Emory and Henry College, the Virginia Foundation for the Humanities and Public Policy, and the Institute for Early American History and Culture. There the program participants included twelve who were primarily historians, three geographers, two archaeologists, an ethnohistorian, an architectural historian, a linguist, and a museum curator. Step back further to the conference on "Re-examining America's Frontier Heritage," held Oct. 10–13, 1991, at Shenandoah Univ. Again, the conference featured a healthy mixture of historians, geographers, material culturalists, and professionals from other related fields. Sponsors were Shenandoah Univ., the Univ. of Maryland, the Virginia Historical Society, and the Virginia Foundation for the Humanities and Public Policy.

    Another meeting, called "Upland Archaeology in the East," takes place in Virginia on a biannual basis. Cosponsored by James Madison Univ., the Jefferson National Forest, and the George Washington National Forest, it generally includes sessions ranging from precontact topics to the nineteenth century, and while it attracts mainly archaeologists, invariably there is a representation of ethnohistorians, historians, cultural anthropologists, and geographers who are interested in interpreting the archaeological findings.
2. Terry G. Jordan and Matti Kaups, *The American Backwoods Frontier: An Ethnic and Ecological Interpretation* (Baltimore, Md.: Johns Hopkins Univ. Press, 1989); David Hackett Fischer, *Albion's Seed: Four British Folkways in America* (New York: Oxford Univ. Press, 1989).
3. Gregory H. Nobles, "Breaking into the Backcountry: New Approaches to the Early American Frontier, 1750–1800," *William and Mary Quarterly* 3d ser. 46 (1989): 643.
4. Ibid., 643–44.
5. See Jack D. Forbes, "Frontiers in American History and the Role of the Frontier Historian," *Ethnohistory* 15 (1968): 203–35; J. Frederick Fausz, "By Their Grave Goods and Trash Pits We Shall Know Them" (Paper presented at conference on "Cultural Diversity on the Virginia Frontier," Emory, Va., Oct. 9–10, 1992), 10.
6. Bernard Bailyn and Philip D. Morgan, eds., *Strangers Within the Realm: Cultural Margins of the First British Empire* (Chapel Hill: Univ. of North Carolina Press, 1991), 1, 10, 19.

7. Maldwyn A. Jones, "The Scotch-Irish in British America," in Bailyn and Morgan, *Strangers Within the Realm*, 313.
8. See Fausz, "By Their Grave Goods," 3–5.
9. James Merrell, *The Indians' New World: Catawbas and Their Neighbors, from European Contact Through the Era of Removal* (Chapel Hill: Univ. of North Carolina Press, 1989), viii–ix.
10. Nobles, "Breaking into the Backcountry," 645–47.
11. Tom Hatley, *The Dividing Paths: Cherokees and South Carolinians through the Era of Revolution* (New York: Oxford Univ. Press, 1993), xii, 167. While not focusing exclusively on the southern backcountry, Colin Calloway also presents an ethnohistorical perspective on the "cacophony of languages, peoples, and cultures" that made up the frontiers of American history. He points out that the "boundaries that divided Indians and Europeans in early America were porous; the frontier operated as a sponge as often as a palisade, soaking up rather than separating people and influences." In the end, he suggests, "conquest changed conquered people and conquerors alike." Colin G. Calloway, *New Worlds for All: Indians, Europeans and the Remaking of Early America* (Baltimore, Md.: Johns Hopkins Univ. Press, 1997), xiii, 6, 152.
12. Michael B. Barber and Eugene B. Barfield, "Native Americans on the Virginia Frontier in the Seventeenth Century: Archaeological Investigations along the Interior Roanoke River Drainage," in *Diversity and Accommodation: Essays on the Cultural Composition of the Virginia Frontier*, ed. Michael J. Puglisi, 134–58 (Knoxville: Univ. of Tennessee Press, 1997).
13. See Jeffrey L. Hantman, "Powhatan's Relations with the Piedmont Monacans," in *Powhatan Foreign Relations, 1500–1722*, ed. Helen C. Rountree, 94–111 (Charlottesville: Univ. Press of Virginia, 1993); Jeffrey L. Hantman, "Changing Relations of Power in Virginia: Perspectives on Monacan History" (Paper presented at conference on "Inter-tribal Relations in Aboriginal Virginia," Emory, Va., Mar. 30–31, 1990). In Jan. 1990, the Virginia Foundation for the Humanities and Public Policy, as part of a grant designed to reinvigorate knowledge of the Monacan cultural heritage, sponsored a workshop session between tribal members and a multidisciplinary consultative committee which included three anthropologists, one historian, and a folklife scholar.
14. John McCusker and Russell Menard, *The Economy of British America, 1607–1789* (Chapel Hill: Univ. of North Carolina Press, 1985), 200–202, cited in Robert D. Mitchell and Warren R. Hofstra, "Settlement and Society in the Southern Backcountry: The Northern Shenandoah Valley of Virginia, 1730–1800," grant proposal submitted to National Endowment for the Humanities, Oct. 1989, 4–5; Nobles, "Breaking into the Backcountry," 648–50. Hofstra and Mitchell find that, given the historiographical search for community in New England and the Chesapeake, it is "ironic that the quintessentially American landscape of rural farms and small towns appeared first in" the backcountry. Warren R. Hofstra and Robert D. Mitchell, "Town and Country in Backcountry Virginia: Winchester and the Shenandoah Valley, 1730–1800," *Journal of Southern History* 59 (1993): 622. In fact, early backcountry studies from the middle colonies pointed out that the New England town model was not the only

viable community model which existed in the American past. See James T. Lemon, *The Best Poor Man's Country: A Geographical Study of Early Southeastern Pennsylvania* (Baltimore, Md.: Johns Hopkins Univ. Press, 1972); Stephanie Grauman Wolf, *Urban Village: Population, Community, and Family Structure in Germantown, Pennsylvania, 1683–1800* (Princeton, N.J.: Princeton Univ. Press, 1976).

15. Nobles, "Breaking into the Backcountry," 650.
16. Mitchell and Hofstra, "Settlement and Society in the Backcountry," ii. See also Robert D. Mitchell and Warren R. Hofstra, "How Do Settlement Systems Evolve? The Virginia Backcountry during the Eighteenth Century," *Journal of Historical Geography* 21 (1995): 123–47.
17. Daniel B. Thorp, *The Moravian Community in Colonial North Carolina: Pluralism on the Southern Frontier* (Knoxville: Univ. of Tennessee Press, 1989), 2–5. Thorp cites Fredrik Barth, *Ethnic Groups and Boundaries* (Boston: Little, Brown, 1969) as a major influence in his approach. Barth's influence is also apparent in Michael Zuckerman, ed., *Friends and Neighbors: Group Life in America's First Plural Society* (Philadelphia: Temple Univ. Press, 1982). A. G. Roeber also points to the important work of ethnographers and anthropologists, in his case, "to shed light on how early modern rural and village people reacted to the rise of a political state and became politically conscious." He applies the perspectives of this type of research in his own work on Germans in the colonies. A. G. Roeber, *Palatines, Liberty and Property: German Lutherans in Colonial British America* (Baltimore, Md.: Johns Hopkins Univ. Press, 1993).
18. Turk McCleskey, "Rich Land, Poor Prospects: Real Estate and the Formation of a Social Elite in Augusta County, Virginia, 1738–1770," *Virginia Magazine of History and Biography* 98 (1990): 449–86.
19. Nobles, "Breaking into the Backcountry," 654.
20. See the following chapter in this volume by Turk McCleskey, "Shadow Land: Provisional Real Estate Claims and Anglo-American Settlement in Southwestern Virginia."
21. Hofstra and Mitchell, "Town and Country," 620; Warren R. Hofstra, "Ethnicity and Community Formation on the Shenandoah Valley Frontier, 1730–1800," in Puglisi, *Diversity and Accommodation*, 60; Mitchell and Hofstra, "Settlement and Society in the Backcountry," 19; Charles J. Farmer, *In the Absence of Towns: Settlement and Country Trade in Southside Virginia, 1730–1800* (Lanham, Md.: Rowman and Littlefield, 1993). In fact, Mitchell and Hofstra argue that none of the accepted models—central place theory, long-distance trade theory, or staple theory—alone adequately encompasses the evolution of the backcountry town structures, because each focuses on the towns themselves rather than on the integrated systems within which they developed. Mitchell and Hofstra, "How Do Settlement Systems Evolve?" 124–44.
22. Mitchell and Hofstra, "Settlement and Society in the Backcountry," ii, 11–12, 29, 47. Mitchell, a geographer, is most concerned with patterns of economic development and social change in the valley and in the larger Chesapeake context. Hofstra, a historian, focuses on local political community formation and social history. Their common interest is the "relationship between the material conditions of life and the fabric of social, economic and political relations that define communities." Ibid., 37.

23. See Robert Blair St. George, "'Set Thine House in Order': The Domestication of the Yeomanry in Seventeenth-Century New England," in *Common Places: Readings in American Vernacular Architecture*, ed. Dell Upton and John Vlach, 336–37 (Athens: Univ. of Georgia Press, 1986).
24. Mitchell and Hofstra, "Settlement and Society in the Backcountry," 5–6.
25. Ibid., 10.
26. David C. Hsiung, *Two Worlds in the Tennessee Mountains: Exploring the Origins of Appalachian Stereotypes* (Lexington: Univ. Press of Kentucky, 1997), 5.
27. Ibid., 186–88. Hsiung presents these two outlooks as the cause of the "sense of difference" which "crystallized" into both internal and external perceptions of Appalachian backwardness. Ibid., 188.
28. Hofstra and Mitchell, "Town and Country," 619; Hofstra, "Ethnicity and Community Formation," 60; see St. George, "Set Thine House in Order," 360.
29. Warren R. Hofstra and Clarence Geier, "Prehistoric and Historic Settlement in the Shenandoah Valley: The Opequon Archaeological Survey," abstract presented at Shenandoah Valley Regional Studies Seminar, Staunton, Va., Sept. 1991.
30. Robert D. Mitchell, "'From the Ground Up': Space, Place, and Diversity in Frontier Studies," in Puglisi, *Diversity and Accommodation*, 25.
31. Ibid., 29–30; Robert D. Mitchell, "Introduction: Revisionism and Regionalism," in *Appalachian Frontiers: Settlement, Society and Development in the Preindustrial Era*, ed. Robert D. Mitchell (Lexington: Univ. Press of Kentucky, 1991), 8. For methodology, see Mitchell and Hofstra, "Settlement and Society in the Backcountry," 41.
32. Gregory H. Nobles, "Straight Lines and Stability: The Imposition of Order on the Anglo-American Frontier" (Paper presented at conference on "Re-examining America's Frontier Heritage," Winchester, Va., Oct. 11–12, 1991), 1–2, 12.
33. Ibid., 3, 6. See also Mitchell, "From the Ground Up," 24–25.
34. Robert D. Mitchell, Edward F. Connor, and Warren R. Hofstra, "European Settlement and Land-Cover Change: The Shenandoah Valley of Virginia during the Eighteenth Century," final report, Grant #4381-90, National Geographic Society, June 1993, pp. 1–3.
35. Ibid., 3, 9–11, 49–50.
36. Timothy H. Silver, *A New Face on the Countryside: Indians, Colonists and Slaves in the South Atlantic Forests, 1500–1800* (New York: Cambridge Univ. Press, 1990); Michael E. Lewis, rev. of Silver, *Geographical Review* 81 (1991): 239–41.
37. Silver, *New Face on the Countryside*, ix–x.
38. See Michael E. Lewis, rev. of Silver, *Geographical Review*, 240.
39. Ann E. McCleary, "Ethnic Influences on the Vernacular Architecture in the Shenandoah Valley," in Puglisi, *Diversity and Accommodation*, 255–58; Mitchell, "Revisionism and Regionalism," 17.
40. McCleary, "Ethnic Influences on Vernacular Architecture," 253.
41. Ibid., 257n. 15, 265.
42. Ibid., 259–62.
43. John Morgan, *The Log House in East Tennessee* (Knoxville: Univ. of Tennessee Press,

1990); John Morgan, "The Cantilever Barn in Southwest Virginia," in Puglisi, *Diversity and Accommodation*, 275–94.
44. Warren R. Hofstra, "Adaptation or Survival?: Folk Housing at Opequon Settlement," *Ulster Folklife* 37 (1991): 57.
45. Ibid., 56–57. For a similar conclusion in regard to German settlers of the region, see McCleary, "Ethnic Influences on Vernacular Architecture," 268–70.
46. McCleary, "Ethnic Influences on Vernacular Architecture," 264.
47. Mitchell, "Revisionism and Regionalism," 1.
48. Ibid., 2–5.
49. Mitchell, "From the Ground Up," 25.
50. Ibid., 42.
51. Fischer, *Albion's Seed*, x.
52. Ibid., 7. Similarly, Grady McWhiney argues that settlers from the "Celtic fringe" dominated the southern backcountry, and that Celtic culture and folkways constituted the foundation for southern culture in general. Grady McWhiney, *Cracker Culture: Celtic Ways in the Old South* (Tuscaloosa: Univ. of Alabama Press, 1988).
53. Fischer, *Albion's Seed*, 7–11.
54. Ibid., xi.
55. Bertram Wyatt-Brown, rev. of Fischer, *Albion's Seed*, in *Wilson Quarterly* 14 (1990): 95; Wilbur Zelinsky, rev. of Fischer, *Albion's Seed*, in *Annals of the Association of American Geographers* 81 (1991): 530.
56. Wilbur Zelinsky, one of the book's sharpest critics, admitted: "Admirable is the manner in which the author has broadened the range of historical discourse beyond the traditional historiographic themes of yore to include nearly all aspects of material and nonmaterial culture." He calls the work "a revelation to all those members of the historical guild who are unacquainted with the efforts of historical geographers over the past forty-odd years to chronicle and map the regional cultures of North America . . . and their Old World origins." Zelinsky, rev. of Fischer, *Albion's Seed*, 527. See also Wyatt-Brown, rev. of Fischer, *Albion's Seed*, 94–96; Jack Sosin, rev. of Fischer, *Albion's Seed*, in *Ethnohistory* 38 (1991): 221–24; Jack P. Greene, rev. of Fischer, *Albion's Seed*, in *Journal of Social History* 24 (1991): 909–11.
57. According to Greene, the theory consists of two parts. First, those settlers who are most "strategically situated" among the early arrivals "exert a defining influence upon new cultures." Second, the "precise nature of that defining influence" is a "function of the cultural baggage these strategic elites bring with them." Greene, rev. of Fischer, *Albion's Seed*, 911.
58. Jordan and Kaups, *American Backwoods Frontier*, xii, 1, 19, 35, 247–48; Gregory Graves, rev. of Jordan and Kaups, *American Backwoods Frontier*, in *Journal of American History* 77 (1990): 644.
59. D. W. Meinig, "Spatial Models of a Sequence of Transatlantic Interaction," in Twenty-third International Geographers Congress: Historical Geography, sect. 9 (Moscow: International Geographical Congress, 1976). Cited in Jordan and Kaups, *American Backwoods Frontier*, 19.

60. Jordan and Kaups, *American Backwoods Frontier*, 7, 10, 14.
61. K. B. Raitz, rev. of Jordan and Kaups, *American Backwoods Frontier*, in *Choice* 27 (1990): 207; Graves, rev. of Jordan and Kaups, *American Backwoods Frontier*, 644–45. Lemon found that "the book is without merit"; James Lemon, rev. of Jordan and Kaups, *American Backwoods Frontier*, in *American Historical Review* 95 (1990): 1617–18. See also Allen G. Noble, rev. of Jordan and Kaups, *American Backwoods Frontier*, in *Geographical Review* 80 (1990): 325–26; William Wyckoff, rev. of Jordan and Kaups, *American Backwoods Frontier*, in *William and Mary Quarterly* 3d ser. 47 (1990): 151–53.
62. Noble, rev. of Jordan and Kaups, *American Backwoods Frontier*, 326; Raitz, rev. of Jordan and Kaups, *American Backwoods Frontier*, 207.
63. Wyckoff, rev. of Jordan and Kaups, *American Backwoods Frontier*, 151–52.

Shadow Land: Provisional Real Estate Claims and Anglo-American Settlement in Southwestern Virginia

Turk McCleskey

Social historians who investigate individual communities on the southern colonial frontier face formidable obstacles to any close acquaintance with common settlers. Correspondence, travel accounts, and diaries are relatively scarce and generally terse, while quantifiable public records, though plentiful, are grouped inconveniently not in neighborhoods but in counties—and from Pennsylvania to Georgia, the evolving borders of frontier counties could encompass thousands of square miles.[1] Early counties often generated such an embarrassment of documentary riches that there is no simple way to isolate information concerning a single frontier settlement—all the families who worshipped at a particular meeting house or all the neighbors who lived and traveled on the same stretch of road. Finally, as in every colonial American court system, frontier county court records favored the interests and voices of the powerful and affluent over those of ordinary inhabitants.

In colonial Augusta County, Virginia, no-one was more powerful than the real estate speculators who both promoted and controlled initial settlement. Throughout the eighteenth century, a social and economic elite carefully managed access to land on the Virginia marches, and they were concerned to replicate essential parts of the social structure which had come to prevail in tidewater Virginia. Acquiring clear title to a piece of frontier Virginia therefore usually required a cooperative, deferential stance, not just the price of a plantation.[2] But land speculators could not function or profit without a stream of colonists and trans-Atlantic immigrants who were determined to take up life and land on the frontier. These clients sometimes wanted more than the opportunity to defer and conform. What motives impelled these ordinary people to take up life on the frontier? What can early land records reveal about the concerns and imperatives of individual settlers,

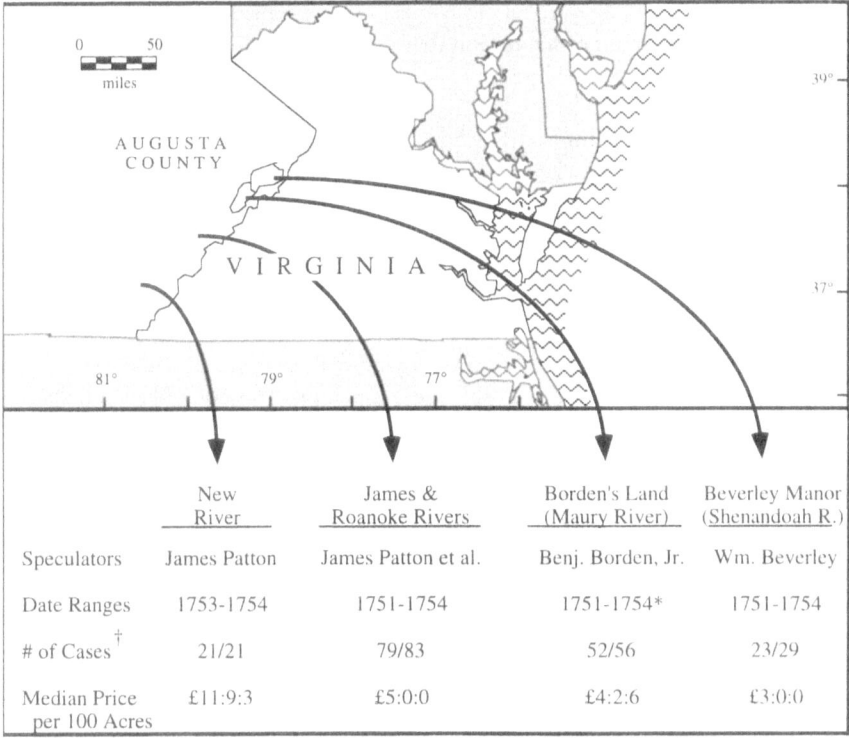

Map 3.1. Prices charged by major land speculators, Augusta County, Virginia, 1751–54. White settlement in Augusta County began in the northeastern section, on the headwaters of the Shenandoah River. Subsequent immigrants moved southwestward through the Maury, James, Roanoke, and New river valleys. Communication with markets in eastern Virginia and Pennsylvania grew increasingly difficult as immigrants moved farther inland, especially in the New River Valley, but prices for southwestern lands nevertheless soared above the norm for more accessible parts of Augusta County. Land price data is drawn from Augusta County Deed Books, vols. 1–7, microfilm, Library of Virginia, Richmond.

† The first number listed in the "# of Cases" row indicates how many deeds included the sale price; the second number indicates the total number of deeds.
* Benjamin Borden, Jr., died in 1753; the sales figures quoted here include transactions by the executors of his estate in 1754.

migrating families, and borderland neighborhoods? As those concerns found expression in hundreds of land transactions, what was their cumulative effect?

Some preliminary answers to these questions reside in the surviving records of territory lying west of the Blue Ridge Mountains in what was once Augusta County, Virginia (map 3.1). White settlers first occupied this region from northeast to southwest, beginning on the headwaters of the Shenandoah River in the late 1730s and moving almost immediately into the upper James River and

Roanoke River valleys. Additional newcomers soon occupied land on the New and Holston rivers in a chain of habitation that by 1755 stretched southwest about as far as the modern Tennessee line.[3]

As newcomers quickly learned, occupying land was not the same as owning it. The process of transforming land into private property—into real estate—began in southwestern Virginia with an authorization to survey. Individuals could obtain such authorizations, known as warrants or entries, directly from the county surveyor if the tract encompassed no more than four hundred acres. Larger tracts required a grant from the Virginia Council, which acted on authority from the Crown. Regardless of the form of authorization—entry or grant—the next step toward ownership was a survey, which produced a literal marking of the tract's borders, as well as a scaled drawing, or plat, depicting the specific parcel of land. Prospective landowners filed the plat with the colonial government and eventually received a freehold patent. Only then were they liable for taxes, known as *quitrents*, on the land. The entire process took anywhere from a couple of years to a generation. Delays sometimes were the result of bureaucratic inefficiency, but settlers not infrequently took their time in securing a patent, the acquisition of which obliged its recipient to begin paying quitrents. In the meantime, the survey represented a significant but still incomplete, or provisional, claim on a specific piece of land. Colonial Virginians might buy and sell grants, entries, and surveys, but such transactions conveyed only a *claim*, not an actual parcel of land. To own land was to own a patented freehold; everything else was only an assertion.[4]

While claims to land based only on surveys were imperfect in a legal sense, colonial Virginians still vested them with considerable economic and political significance. Each survey represented a preliminary step toward the clear or freehold title that secured not only property, but also the rights and responsibilities of citizenship. For Virginians, surveys thus constituted an advance toward two important objectives. Until the patenting process was complete, however, the security of a survey holder's claim depended in large part on the forbearance of elite land speculators. Because this uncertainty sometimes stretched on for years, the tracts depicted in Augusta County's surveys represent a shady realm of ambiguous ownership and competing intentions—and an area ripe for modern investigation of a fundamental aspect of colonial expansion.

The temporal boundaries of this investigation reach from 1745 to 1755, a period beginning with the establishment of an independent Augusta County surveyor's office and covering all but the very earliest white settlements in the upper James River Valley. Official survey records for the first years of white occupation, from about 1739 to 1744, do not survive. From 1745 on, however, surveying records in Augusta County are complete.[5] This study therefore begins after at least sixty-two private individuals and five speculators surveyed land in the James and Roanoke river valleys.[6] The study period closes in flames and flight during the summer of 1755, when Indian raiders overran the New, Roanoke, and James river settlements at the onset of the Seven Years' War.

The temporal scope of this study thus is quite explicit, but the spatial limits are less easily defined. Colonial Virginia's government tolerated such vague descriptions of speculative borderland grants that it is not easy now to locate them. The few exceptions include Beverley Manor and Borden's Land in colonial Augusta County. Both were genuine pieces of property, vast patented holdings that retain aspects of their identity to this day.[7] Nevertheless, most large grants in early Augusta County remained abstractions rather than real estates—gray areas of imperfect claims in which elite speculators enjoyed de facto ownership without the formality of a patent. The masters of this shadow land exercised the rights of ownership, but without actually holding clear title. They traded in surveys, buying and selling provisional claims on land that was not yet liable for quitrents.[8] Colonial Virginia's grants to speculators thus conveyed not ownership, but rather official permission to create a market in individual claims that eventually could transform land into property.

The Virginia Council awarded one such permission in the fall of 1740. It granted to five speculators the land that is the focus of this study: a hundred thousand acres lying "on the River and Branches of Roanoke and the Branches of James River." The Council revised and reissued the award in the spring of 1745, and by early 1748 the original partners were ready to survey this largess.[9] In a move surely calculated to advance their interests, they made a sixth partner of Augusta County's senior magistrate and senior militia officer, Col. James Patton, empowering him "as agent to Survey, Settle and Sell the s[ai]d Land and do all and every other [act] or acts, Thing or Things for the Interest of the Company about the Premises."[10]

Just where were those premises? Unlike Beverley Manor or Borden's Land to the northeast, the James and Roanoke river valleys grant was never surveyed as a single tract, nor was it patented as a single piece of real estate. Instead, under Colonel Patton's supervision, the grant was converted piecemeal into property. Virginia's Gov. Francis Fauquier described the identical process in another of Patton's partnerships a little farther southwest: "Colonel Patton did not immediately make Surveys of the said Lands and mark out his Bounds, but waited till some Persons made choice of particular Spots of rich Land and were willing to purchase of him; then these Spots were surveyed, the Rules of Government comply'd with and patents taken out, to make a Title to the Purchasers."[11] From 1748 through 1754, partnership surveys run in just this fashion dotted the James and Roanoke river valleys. Some surveys adjoined existing patents, while in other places they lay surrounded by vast stretches of unclaimed land.[12] The 1745 James River and Roanoke River valleys grant thus cannot be mapped as one contiguous entity; it is manifest solely as the metes and bounds of individual surveys scattered across an area far more extensive than the authorized hundred thousand acres.

As if definitions of southwestern Virginia land claims were not murky enough, the Augusta County surveyor also began acting on private entries for land along the James and Roanoke rivers, modestly at first—until speculator attention shifted farther southwest—and then much more extensively. By 1755, surveys in the region, based on individual entries, surpassed in both number and acreage the surveys drawn under authority of speculator grants (figs. 3.1a, 3.1b). Taken together, the speculative and private surveys that form the quantitative basis of this study number 465 cases.[13]

These James River and Roanoke River valley surveys appear throughout the first volume of the Augusta County surveyor books. Each record of a survey includes a plat of the tract, its acreage, the name of the individual or partners receiving the survey, the grant under whose authority the survey was made, and—usually—the major river drainage in which the land is located. Sometimes the plat identifies neighbors, and sometimes accompanying notes mention a transfer of the survey to some other claimant. This is rich material, but it can also mislead. The documents provide only a snapshot of an often complex series of transactions. Unlike the conveyance of real estate, the transfer of surveys from one person to the next generated no systematic records. A tract appears once on the day of its survey and once again on the day of its patent; between those dates, the tract could change hands repeatedly and anonymously. Historians can glimpse such conveyances only when the name of the patentee does not match that of the survey recipient, and, even then, any intermediate transactions remain obscure.

Despite these limitations, a quantitative analysis of the James River and Roanoke River surveys between 1745 to 1755 can yield fresh and useful information, especially when shadowy surveys are compared with the records of freehold real estate—patents, deeds, and wills. Three key trends—speculator dominance, familial connections, and rising prices—emerge from this juxtaposition of survey and freehold accounts.

The first trend, speculator dominance, is no surprise. Once the James and Roanoke river valleys partnership rolled into action in 1748, its members received almost every survey in the two valleys for four consecutive years. More precisely, between 1748 and 1751, speculators obtained well over nine out of every ten surveys in the James and Roanoke river valleys (fig. 3.1a).[14] This monopoly on the preliminary step of land acquisition gave James Patton and his partners nearly total control over the creation of real estate in southwestern Virginia.[15] Like other artifacts, the James and Roanoke river valley settlements therefore must signal something about the intentions of their speculative creators.

What kind of buyers looked especially attractive to speculators? A second statistical trend concerning the market for land suggests a useful answer. A total of 192 individuals obtained one or more surveys in the James and Roanoke river valleys between 1745 and 1755. Of these, one-fifth can be documented as related to at least one other resident landowner somewhere in Augusta County. These verifiable connections surely represent only a fraction of kinship on the borderland. Another 121 James and Roanoke river valley survey recipients (63.0 percent) shared a surname—and probably kinship—with established Augusta County freeholders. For example, on November 13, 1754, George Rowland and Thomas Rowland both obtained surveys for James River land.[16] Neither ever had received

Fig. 3.1. Land speculators monopolized the surveying process during Augusta County's first decade as an independent polity. In the James River and Roanoke River valleys, no surveys were conducted during 1746 and 1747, but in 1748 the speculators opened a major sales campaign. Until the speculative boom swept past, the county surveyor and his deputies laid off few tracts for private citizens.

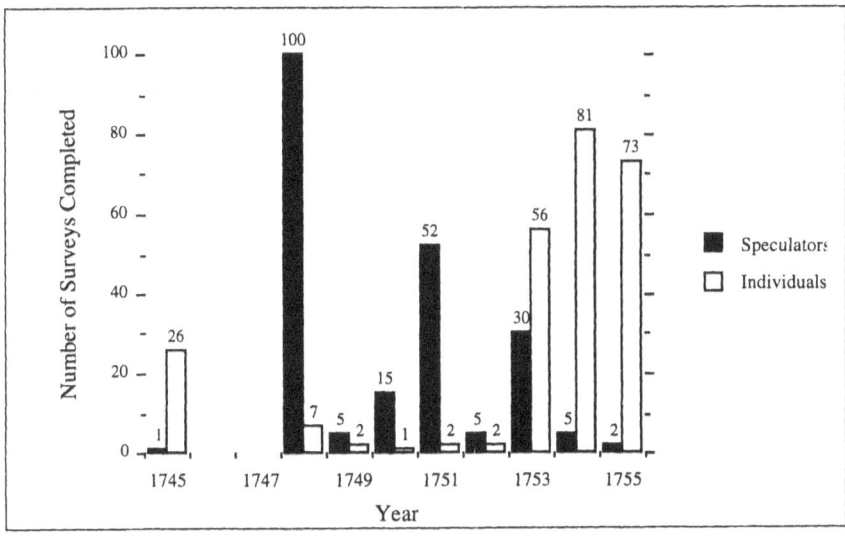

Fig. 3.1a. Surveys completed in James River and Roanoke River valleys, 1745–55. Data from Augusta County Surveyor Book 1, microfilm, Library of Virginia, Richmond.

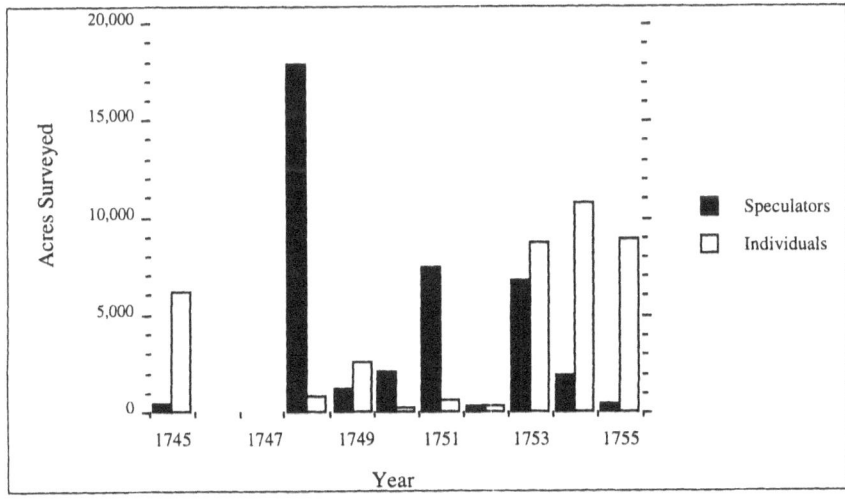

Fig. 3.1b. Acreage surveyed in James River and Roanoke River valleys, 1745–55. Data from Augusta County Surveyor Book 1, microfilm, Library of Virginia, Richmond.

a survey, and neither were freeholders, although neighbor Robert Rowland had owned land in the vicinity since 1746. Robert Rowland also sold land to both George and Thomas Rowland several years later.[17] No documented relationship now can be unearthed among them, but clearly George, Thomas, and Robert Rowland shared a close connection. Of course, not all instances of identical surnames indicate family ties, but cautiously permitting surnames to represent kinship compensates for the undocumented existence of bonds of blood or marriage between settlers with different last names. For a sample of this size, surnames thus provide a rough but serviceable way to estimate the presence or absence of family ties. Altogether, some four-fifths of individual survey recipients probably were related to an established Augusta County freeholder.[18] Speculators surely favored clients with roots in the county, because families reinforced the financial capacity of beginners to purchase land. Established residents also understood and had a stake in maintaining the hierarchical social order which speculators demanded, and they could instruct recently arrived or newly autonomous kinsmen in the prevailing local customs.

Even so, speculator preferences alone cannot account for every trend in the settlement of the James and Roanoke river valleys. The high proportion of relatives among initial recipients of surveys suggests that familial relationships and objectives also shaped the market in provisional land claims. A little additional counting and sorting further illuminates familial objectives for surveying land—or buying existing surveys—in the James River and Roanoke river valleys between 1745 and 1755. A majority of the survey market consisted of beginners. One hundred of the 192 individuals (52.1 percent) who received surveys in this period and place were venturing for the first time into Augusta County's land market. Never before had they surveyed land or owned real estate—not just in the James or Roanoke valleys, but anywhere in this vast county. The hundred survey recipients who never previously had owned a survey or a tract of land included seventy-five individuals who shared kinship with an Augusta County freeholder and twenty-five who had no discernible land-owning relatives in the region (fig. 3.2). Of the seventy-five individuals with probable family connections, fifty-nine (78.7 percent) succeeded in acquiring freehold title to Augusta County land—that is, they parlayed their shadow land into real property. By comparison, only eleven of the twenty-five unconnected newcomers (44.0 percent) eventually obtained a freehold. Familial connection with an Augusta County landowner thus almost doubled a beginner's chances of attaining the economic and political independence of a freeholder.

The third important statistical trend among early southwestern land claims has to do with land prices. It is impossible to determine what speculators charged individuals for surveyed tracts, but when speculators patented their own surveys and then sold the resulting real estate for the first time, the prices they charged increased dramatically from northeast to southwest Augusta County.[19] In the 1750s, median prices paid for unimproved freeholds ranged from £3 per hundred acres

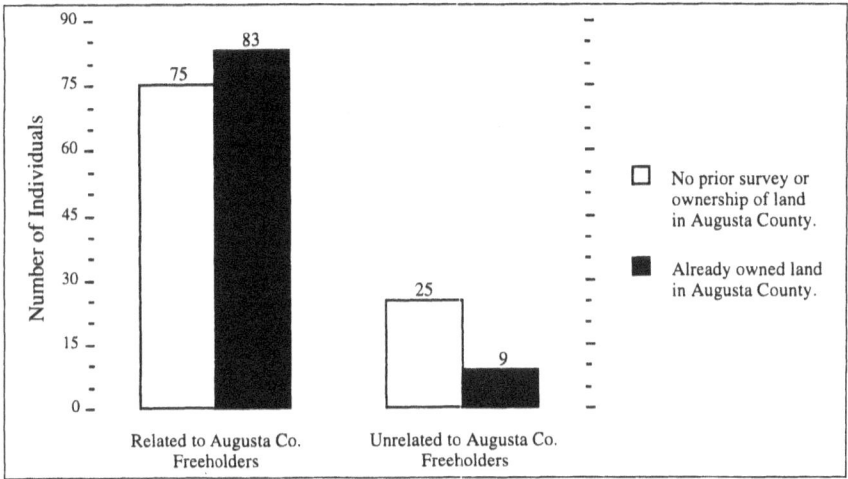

Fig. 3.2. Individuals acquiring surveys in James River and Roanoke River valleys, 1745–55. These figures do not include surveys made for speculators. Relatives of Augusta County landowners dominated land markets in the early James River and Roanoke River valleys. Kinship provided a significant advantage to persons entering the Augusta County real estate market for the first time, and kindred surveyholders were much more likely to convert a claim into a freehold patent. From Augusta County Surveyor Book 1, and Virginia State Land Office County Abstracts, Patents, and Grants; both on microfilm, Library of Virginia, Richmond.

in Beverley Manor to £11:9:3 per hundred acres in the New River Valley (map 3.1). In terms of economic geography, this jump in southwestern land prices appears counterintuitive. The farther new settlers ventured from available markets for their crops and the more flagrantly they encroached on Indian territory, the higher the price they paid for their land.

Two distinct explanations for this trend in land prices are possible. The northeastern part of Augusta County had been open to settlement since the late 1730s, so perhaps by the 1750s immigrants had purchased all of the good, expensive land. A closer look at real estate transactions in this area, however, suggests otherwise. Between 1751 and 1754, William Beverley sold twenty-nine tracts of unimproved real estate on the headwaters of the Shenandoah River in Beverley Manor. His prices varied, but the median was £3 per hundred acres—the exact price paid by five of his purchasers (map 3.1). If these five median-priced tracts are representative, the opportunity to acquire good land still existed in the northeastern part of Augusta County. Four of the five tracts lay within areas characterized by fair to good soil. Only one encompassed soil which was mostly poor in its agricultural potential.[20] If good tracts still could be had for £3 per hundred acres in Beverley Manor, some other factor must explain the willingness of early southwestern settlers to pay such a steep premium for remote, unprotected, and unimproved farmland.

The puzzle's solution begins with the intracolonial context of the frontier land market. Before the Seven Years' War, the owners of Beverley Manor and Borden's Land held their prices below the market value of comparable land in Pennsylvania and elsewhere in Virginia.[21] Their loss-leader pricing stimulated immigration, with the result that sales and settlement boomed during the 1740s and early 1750s. Despite this brisk traffic in unimproved land, good single tracts remained scattered throughout the county among existing freeholds and the provisional claims of earlier surveys.

By the early 1750s, newly arriving or expanding families found it difficult to acquire multiple freeholds—tracts located sufficiently close together to sustain affective bonds and to permit cooperative use of hands and tools. Groups of contiguous or nearby tracts were much easier to acquire in areas just opening to subdivision—and they were more readily developed with the assistance of neighboring kin. A local network of family relations, coupled with the greater availability of additional land, improved the chances that a rising generation of offspring also could successfully establish freeholds in the same rural community.

The argument that rural immigration and labor practices were linked to certain kinds of family interaction is not new, but the juxtaposition of provisional and perfected land claims in the James and Roanoke river valleys does indicate something more: how family ties resonated within a medley of other ambitions seeking frontier fulfillment.[22] The southwestern Virginia borderland thus grew out of the interplay among an intricate bundle of disparate but not mutually exclusive social, economic, and political objectives.

Most important, settlement of the James and Roanoke rivers was a self-amplifying process. In those river basins emerged a powerful confluence of interests, ranging from imperial to personal. Every participant in the colonial conversion of land into property further increased both the tempo and the scope of Anglo-American settlement. Acting in the name of their king, colonial Virginia authorities sought a wider dominion over the North American interior, and so authorized speculative partnerships to claim vast grants of western land.[23] Grant recipients looking for quick profits dodged the expenses of their windfall by trafficking primarily in quitrent-exempt surveys, and returned all the sooner to ask for new grants without paying quitrents on the unmarketable remnants of old ones. Local agents of eastern-dwelling speculators further hastened an already rapid and vast engrossment of frontier land by surveying only prime tracts, so that groups of surveys sprawled over unclaimed areas several times larger than the surveys themselves. The same local agents, concerned with maintaining social stability, sought out not only ideal farmland, but also ideal farmers—purchasers from county families who already knew and presumably accepted the rules of the game. In turn, families continually demanded new, unpartitioned expanses of land, the better to establish settlements of kinsmen with room to grow. Family ambitions on the frontier thus paralleled elite aspirations. This convergence of ambitions produced an explosive momentum for expansion during the Revolutionary era, when the Anglo-American flood into Tennessee and Kentucky demonstrated unmistakably the imperialistic potential of early American family values.

NOTES

1. In colonial Augusta County on the frontier of Virginia, settlers patented over a thousand square miles of land by 1770. All my statistical statements of fact about freehold land ownership in Augusta County are drawn from my quantitative analysis of manuscript records pertaining to land. These include surveys, patents, deeds, mortgages, wills, and intestate administrations. Turk McCleskey, "Rich Land, Poor Prospects: Real Estate and the Formation of a Social Elite in Augusta County, Virginia, 1738–1770," *Virginia Magazine of History and Biography* 98 (July 1990): 449n.
2. Ibid., 449–86.
3. For an overview of early settlement in the Shenandoah Valley, see Robert D. Mitchell, *Commercialism and Frontier: Perspectives on the Early Shenandoah Valley* (Charlottesville: Univ. Press of Virginia, 1977), 8–14. For early settlement in southwest Virginia, see Mary B. Kegley, *Wythe County, Virginia: A Bicentennial History* (Wytheville, Va.: Wythe County Board of Supervisors, 1989), 13–24.
4. For details, see Sarah S. Hughes, *Surveyors and Statesmen: Land Measuring in Colonial Virginia* (Richmond: Virginia Surveyors Foundation, Ltd., and Virginia Association of Surveyors, 1979), esp. ch. 9, "Fieldwork and Officework on the Frontier."
5. The territory that became Augusta County was defined in 1738 and was granted independence from Orange County in late October 1745. For details, see "An Act, for erecting two new Counties, and parishes; and granting certain encouragements to the inhabitants thereof," in William W. Hening, comp., *The Statutes at Large: Being a Collection of All the Laws of Virginia* . . . (1819–23, reprinted Charlottesville: Univ. Press of Virginia, for the Jamestown Foundation of the Commonwealth of Virginia, 1969), 5:78–80; and Wilmer L. Hall, ed., *Executive Journals of the Council of Colonial Virginia*, 2d ed. (1945, reprinted Richmond: Virginia State Library, 1967), 5:191. Augusta County Surveyor Book 1, microfilm (Richmond: Library of Virginia).
6. In 1748, the Virginia colonial government first issued patents for James River and Roanoke River surveys which had been recorded in Augusta County, but by then a number of other patents already had been issued in those valleys. Presumably, each of the pre-1748 patents represents a pre-1745 survey by an Orange County official, but the Orange County Surveyor Book for this period has not survived. Between 1740 and 1750, 54 of the patents issued to individuals for James River land definitely or probably were based on Orange County surveys. Another 30 patents on the Roanoke River, the earliest of which was issued in 1745, fall in the same category. Virginia State Land Office County Abstracts, Patents, and Grants, Library of Virginia, Richmond. In all, 62 individuals received these 84 patents based on Orange County surveys. If each of the 84 total patents represents a single Orange County survey, then, for the period 1740–55, Augusta County surveys of James River and Roanoke River tracts outnumber Orange County surveys by 465 to 84, or over five

to one. For an annual accounting of the Augusta County surveys during this period, see fig. 3.1a.

7. William Beverley patented the 118,941 acres of Beverley Manor in 1736; Benjamin Borden, Sr., patented 92,100 acres adjoining the southwest side of Beverley Manor in 1739. Mitchell, *Commercialism and Frontier*, 31–33. Beverley Manor lies entirely within the bounds of Augusta County; the modern Beverley Manor Fire District surrounds the county seat of Staunton."General Highway Map: Augusta County" (Richmond: Virginia Department of Transportation, 1987). Borden Grant Trail, or Rockbridge County Road 706, roughly traces the southeastern edge of Borden's Land, most of which lies in modern Rockbridge County. Winifred Hadsel, *Roads of Rockbridge County* (Lexington, Va.: News-Gazette, for the Rockbridge Historical Society, 1993), 11.

8. Hughes, *Surveyors and Statesmen*, 127. For an explicit complaint by speculator Benjamin Borden, Jr., about annual quitrent liabilities of two shillings sixpence per hundred acres on unsold portions of Borden's Land, see Samuel McDowell deposition, n.d., Draper Mss. 4ZZ4, State Historical Society of Wisconsin, Madison (microfilm ed., 1980).

9. The original five partners included John Smith, Zachariah Lewis, William Waller, Benjamin Waller, and Robert Green; of these, only Smith was an Augusta County resident. For quoted phrase and original grant, see Hall, *Executive Journals*, 5:38, entry dated Nov. 3, 1740. For subsequent renewal and modification, see ibid., 173, dated Apr. 26, 1745, and ibid., 174–75, dated May 4, 1745. The partnership surveyed its first tract, 220 acres along Poage's Draft adjacent to Borden's Land, on Jan. 10, 1747/8. For Smith's subordinate role in surveying the land, see *John Smith v. Patton's Executors*, May 1767, in Lyman Chalkley, *Chronicles of the Scotch-Irish Settlement in Virginia* (Baltimore, Md.: 1912; reprint, Genealogical Publishing Co., 1980), 1:361.

10. James Patton Joint Land Venture, Apr. 26, 1749, William Preston Papers, item #50, Virginia Historical Society, Richmond.

11. George Reese, ed., *The Official Papers of Francis Fauquier, Lieutenant Governor of Virginia, 1758–1768* (Charlottesville: Univ. Press of Virginia, for the Virginia Historical Society, 1980–83), 3:1076–77.

12. The James River and Roanoke River valleys partnership surveyed a total of 34,925 acres in 201 tracts between 1748 and 1754; the partnership made no surveys in 1755. In addition to these 201 tracts surveyed for the partnership, individual speculators also received surveys for 12 additional tracts in the region between 1748 and 1755. Augusta County Surveyor Book 1, *passim*.

13. Ibid. The river basins in which these surveys were drawn are clearly identified in most cases, but I also included ambiguous surveys for which locations are positively identified in subsequent transactions recorded in the Augusta County Deed Books, vols. 1–17."Positive identification" requires that the courses given in the survey match the courses listed in a later mortgage or deed of sale for which a definitive location is possible. McCleskey,"Rich Land, Poor Prospects," 449n.

14. From 1748 through 1751, speculators received 172 out of a total of 184 surveys in the James River and Roanoke River valleys, or 93.4% of the total.

15. For an analysis of this screening by frontier elites, see McCleskey, "Rich Land, Poor Prospects," 462–65, 478–85.
16. Augusta County Surveyor Book, 1:76.
17. Robert Rowland's 1746 patent and Thomas Rowland's 1754 survey both were located on Looneys Mill Creek, in modern Botetourt County. Augusta County Deed Book, 11:274, dated Jun. 21, 1763, and 15:266, dated Jan. 25, 1769; the latter source gives Robert Rowland's patent date as Jul. 25, 1746, indicating that this tract was an Orange County survey.
18. Thirty-seven out of 192 individuals (19.3%) receiving surveys in the James River and Roanoke River valleys from 1745 through 1755 can be positively identified as related to Augusta County freeholders. In all, 82.3% of individual survey recipients (158 out of 192) either can be positively identified as related to Augusta County landowners or shared the same surname. Relationships are based on explicit statements of kinship in Augusta County Will Books, vols. 1–5, and Augusta County Deed Books 1–19. For the land records identifying Augusta County freeholders, see McCleskey, "Rich Land, Poor Prospects," 449n.
19. As early as the initial surveying of the New River Valley in 1746, James Patton's price exceeded that of clear titles in Beverley Manor; in a proclamation dated Oct. 10, 1746, he and two partners offered their portions of the New River grant for £4:10:0 per hundred acres. Proclamation by James Patton, John Buchanan, and George Robinson, Oct. 10, 1746, item #9846 in Papers of the Breckinridge Family of Grove Hill, Botetourt County, Virginia (microfilm, Alderman Library, Univ. of Virginia, Charlottesville). Between 1745 and 1755, the Augusta County surveyor and his deputies recorded a total of 465 surveys in the James River and Roanoke River valleys. Col. James Patton, acting on behalf of himself as well as his partners, patented 94 of the 465 surveys tracts, of which he sold 83, or 17.8% of the 465-tract total. These sales are the only available systematic source for prices of unimproved land in the James River and Roanoke River valleys.
20. The grantees who paid £3 per hundred acres for Beverley Manor land purchased between 1751 and 1754 include: William Ledgerwood, Jr., 300 acres; Archibald Stuart, 500 acres; John Trimble, 200 acres; John McNutt, 200 acres; and James Hamilton, 200 acres. Augusta County Deed Book, 3:514–518, 4:53–56, 4:300–303, 6:293–295, 6:324–327. I located these five tracts on J. R. Hildebrand's map, "The Beverley Patent," then appraised their agricultural potential with a modern Augusta County soil map. Howard M. Wilson, *The Tinkling Spring, Headwater of Freedom: A Study of the Church and Her People, 1732–1952* (Fisherville, Va.: Tinkling Spring and Hermitage Presbyterian Churches, 1954), endpapers; U.S. Department of Agriculture Soil Conservation Service, in cooperation with Virginia Polytechnic Institute and State Univ., *Soil Survey of Augusta County, Virginia* (Washington, D.C.: U.S. Government Printing Office, 1979).
21. Beverley's median price of £3 per hundred acres almost certainly represents a deliberate effort to undercut competitors. In a letter dated Apr. 30, 1732, Beverley noted that "the northern men are fond of buying land there [northeast of what would be-

come Beverley Manor, in the vicinity of Massanutten Mountain], because they can buy it, for six or seven pounds per hundred acres, cheaper than they can take up land in pensilvania." W. P. Palmer, ed., *Calendar of Virginia State Papers and Other Manuscripts Preserved in the Capitol at Richmond* (1875, reprinted New York: Kraus Reprint Corp., 1968), 1:218. Robert D. Mitchell's modern study confirms Beverley's estimate of land prices just northeast of Beverley Manor. In the first six years of sales, Beverley charged an average price of £2:18:4, or between half and one-third of the price obtained by competitors Jost Hite and Jacob Stover. See Mitchell, *Commercialism and Frontier*, 76. According to James T. Lemon, land in Lancaster County, Pennsylvania, sold for a minimum of £5 per hundred acres in the 1730s, with most prices ranging between £30 and £75 per hundred. Lemon, *The Best Poor Man's Country: A Geographical Study of Early Southeastern Pennsylvania* (New York: Norton, 1972), 69. Lemon's typical prices doubtless reflect improvements to Pennsylvania real estate; the price of £5 per hundred probably was charged for unimproved land like that offered by William Beverley.

22. James A. Henretta set the terms of modern debate over the role of families in rural settlement. See Henretta, "Families and Farms: *Mentalité* in Pre-industrial America," *William and Mary Quarterly* 3d ser. 35 (Jan. 1978): 3–32. For recent summations of historical evidence and thinking on the subject, see Gregory H. Nobles, "Breaking into the Backcountry: New Approaches to the Early American Frontier," *William and Mary Quarterly* 3d ser. 46 (Oct. 1989): 648–50; and David Hackett Fischer, *Albion's Seed: Four British Folkways in America* (New York: Oxford Univ. Press, 1989), 610–12, 759–63.

23. For a recent interpretation of imperial ambitions and Virginia's settlement frontiers, see Warren R. Hofstra, "The Extension of His Majesties Dominions: The Virginia Backcountry and the Reconfiguration of Imperial Frontiers," *Journal of American History* 84 (March 1998): 1281–1312.

From Creeks to Crackers

Edward Cashin

"The present intruders I am informed are persons who have no settled habitation and live by hunting and plundering the industrious settlers," Acting Gov. James Habersham of Georgia wrote to Gov. James Wright, who was in England in 1772. "You will easily distinguish," he continued, that the "people I refer to are really what you and I understand by Crackers."[1] Honest James Habersham was not being supercilious, he was stating a fact. Georgia's backcountry was in the throes of a social revolution. The Creek Indians were even more disturbed than Habersham by what was going on. They called the newcomers "Virginians." "English men and Scotch men I have long been acquainted with," said one chief, "but these Virginians are very bad people; they pay no regard to your laws."[2]

Until the year 1763, Augusta was an Indian town. It was not so much that Indians lived there, but rather that the town was situated in Indian country and was established for the better regulation of the Indian trade. After the Yamasee War of 1715, the Creek headman whom the English called "Emperor" Brims concluded a treaty with the governor of South Carolina which recognized the Savannah River as a boundary between the British and the Creek Nation. During the two decades which followed the Yamasee War, Carolina traders were careful to cultivate the good will of the Creeks. The traders, aware of the competition of the Louisiana French, lived among the Creeks, fathered children of mixed blood, and established bonds of friendship and kinship as well as those of trade. One astonished visitor to the Creek country in 1736 commented that there were more than four hundred racially mixed children in the Creek villages.[3] European wares and European blood changed the social and economic lives of the Creek Indians, tying them more closely to their lifeline, the great trading road which led through Augusta to Charlestown.

Augusta had been established by James Oglethorpe in 1736, in response to Indian complaints that the Carolinians were beginning again to cheat the Indians as they had before the Yamasee uprising. Oglethorpe persuaded Parliament to give him control of the Indian trade by requiring Georgia licenses for anyone doing business west of the Savannah River. Before leaving England to return to Georgia in 1736, he secured another law forbidding the use of rum. In June of that year, he authorized the building of the fort and town of Augusta.

The Creek Indians regarded Oglethorpe as their great good friend for his efforts to regulate the trade and entertained him lavishly when he paid a complimentary visit to Coweta town in 1739. Oglethorpe was equally delighted with his efforts on behalf of the Indians, especially because not much else was working out the way he planned. He ascribed the friendly relationship with the Indians to the establishment of Augusta. "The settlement of Augusta is of great service," he informed his fellow Trustees, "it being 300 miles from the sea and the Key of all the Indian Countrey."[4]

A band of Chickasaw Indians abandoned the land given them on the Carolina side of the Savannah River because they preferred to frequent Augusta and disliked swimming across the river to get there. They set up camp in the area known as New Savannah, around the bend of the river below Augusta. Like the Creeks and the Cherokees from the upper reaches of the Savannah River, the Chickasaws regarded Augusta as their town. The actual trading of goods was supposed to take place out in the Indian villages, where deerskins were exchanged for goods, but the Indians liked to visit Augusta and shop around. They were intimidated by Charlestown but felt comfortable in Augusta.

Augusta gradually assumed the requisites of a proper British town. It acquired a church, a school, and a jail, as well as a twice-repaired fort. However, as the population grew, the attitude of the people remained one of cooperation with the Indian clients and customers. The tradition of friendship paid rich dividends during the Cherokee War of 1759–60. The Cherokees, driven to desperation by encroachments on their lands, took to the warpath. Terrified refugees from the Long Canes district of South Carolina flocked to Augusta and to Fort Moore, across the Savannah River from Augusta. When one Augusta magistrate proposed declaring the town a neutral zone, he reflected a prevailing opinion that Augusta was unwilling to take sides against Indians. However, the Cherokees refused to regard Augusta as neutral. Their war parties attacked people within a few miles of the town. The Creek Indians saved Augusta. This was their land, after all, and they defended it against the invading Cherokees. A few brave locals, Lachlan McGillivray among them, joined the Indians in opposing the hostile warriors.[5]

The British officer sent to take command of Fort Augusta was unaccustomed to the easy familiarity of the Creeks. "Their manner is they come to the fort gate, unsaddle their horses, demand victuals for themselves and their horses, which if not given they are highly affronted," he wrote.[6] Even as the lieutenant penned his dispatch, three of the headmen were seated comfortably at the same table, smoking companionably. They seemed to say that Augusta was their town.

The year 1763 was the crucial year, the year when the great change began. The long war with the French in Louisiana and the Spanish in Florida was over. The British now possessed Florida and all the vast interior as far as the Mississippi and Canada as well. The Indians were called in to Augusta to meet with the governors of Virginia, North Carolina, South Carolina, and Georgia and to be told that the war was over and that the French were gone. Except for Georgia's Governor Wright, the governors grumbled about having to go to a frontier town like Augusta. They preferred Charlestown. The Indians sent the message that they would meet in Augusta or not at all, so the governors had no choice but to go there.

Before the dignitaries reached Augusta, the Creek chiefs worked out an agreement with Lachlan McGillivray and George Galphin. As a gesture of friendship, the new boundary would be the Ogeechee River, some forty-five miles west of Augusta. The surprised dignitaries accepted the cession, presents were distributed, and everyone went home in good humor.[7]

In the same year, the royal proclamation of October 7, 1763, assigned new boundaries to Georgia's southern frontier. The Saint Marys River, rather than the Altamaha River, divided Georgia from the new British province of East Florida. The proclamation forbade settlement across the Appalachian Mountains, reserving the interior for the Indians' hunting grounds.

The effect of the proclamation, together with the Creeks' cession of 1763, was that the pioneer settlers were directed down the mountain valleys and into the Georgia backcountry. The newcomers differed from the older residents of Augusta in their attitude toward Indians. They did not know, or want to know, Indians. Their overriding motivation was to possess the land. The new Georgians, alike in their opposition to Indians, differed among themselves in most other respects. There was a community of Quakers on the Little River who called their town Wrightsborough and were models of good behavior.[8] The town of Queensborough was established on the Ogeechee River for a colony of Irish Protestants who soon scattered in search of better land.[9] Some immigrants were what Governor Wright would call "the middling sort"—not quite the better sort but not the worst, either. Many of them were from Virginia and brought books, good manners, and some slaves with them in the hope of establishing Virginia-style plantations in Georgia's backcountry. Such folks could afford only a log cabin at first, but they planned to erect another cabin when they could and to connect the two with a common roof and porch. Then they would close the breezeway between the two cabins with a front and back door. Still later they would cover the logs with clapboards, so that their houses would resemble those in Virginia. One of these aspiring Virginia gentlemen wrote:

> New Georgia is a pleasant place.
> If we could but enjoy it
> Indians and Rogues they are so great.
> They almost have destroyed it.[10]

Other newcomers brought with them the evangelical religions of the Great Awakening. In 1722, the famous Baptist preacher, Daniel Marshal, with his brother-in-law Shuball Stearns and their families, established Kiokee Church, the first Baptist Church in Georgia.[11] Soon after, evangelists were preaching the exciting gospel throughout the countryside. Their message was simple: If you feel saved, you are saved, and your life will be changed forever. You will be blessed in this life and in the next. You will be selected out from all those who are not saved and are therefore on their way to hell. As one of the favored, God has given you dominion over the land, therefore the land belongs to the Christians and not the heathen Indian. These two influences—that of the Virginia plantation and that of the evangelism of the Great Awakening—flowed together into the Georgia backcountry and were formative in shaping its future social mores.

Some of the newcomers were untouched by the civilizing effects of the Virginia and evangelical attitudes. They were the lower sort, described by Governor Wright as "a set of almost lawless white people who are a sort of borderers and often as bad if not worse than the Indians."[12] Travelers were appalled and fascinated by the behavior of these people. According to one, the men let their fingernails grow and hardened the nails with tallow, the better to scoop out the eyes of an opponent.[13] A French visitor to the Georgia backcountry told of how the woman of the house wanted to impress him with her social amenities. She sent her husband to buy tea. Then she put the tea in a kettle and a large ham in with it. When the ham was cooked, she dumped out the tea and served the leaves on a platter along with the ham. The woman took the first bite of the leaves, spat them out and threw the platter of tea leaves at her husband, accusing him of buying inferior tea and saving the money for whiskey.[14]

The incendiary factor in the backcountry social mix was the fact that the Indians continued to come and go along the old trading road. Inevitably, there was friction. Frontierspeople made no secret of their dislike of the Indian visitors and of the Augusta merchants who sold firearms to the Indians. One Creek chief reminded Governor Wright of the British promise that the trading path "should always be free for their friends the Indians to pass and repass upon."[15]

Soon the Indians had another complaint. The settlers were crossing over the Ogeechee boundary into Indian country. In a futile effort to placate the Indians, Governor Wright had a team of surveyors mark the boundary and invited the chiefs to Augusta in 1768 to celebrate the occasion. The ceremony of marking the trees failed to deter the restless borderers, who regarded laws as rules made for other people. Encroachments over the line grew in number.

In December 1770, the Cherokee Indians informed the Augusta traders that they were willing to cede land on the upper Savannah River in exchange for the cancellation of their debts to the traders. The traders informed Governor Wright, who quickly embraced the plan. The royal government would accept the land, sell it to the better sort of settlers, and with the proceeds pay off the claims of the traders. The Augusta merchants were enthusiastic, their London suppliers added their endorsement, and Governor Wright presented the case in person to the British ministry. Approval was conditional upon agreement by the Creeks, who also claimed the land in question.[16]

The Indians were invited to meet with the governor and Indian superintendent in Augusta in November 1773. The Cherokees came readily, the Creeks reluctantly. Governor Wright hoped to obtain a cession west of the Ogeechee to the Oconee, but the Creeks refused to consider that idea. Only after much talk and many presents did the Creek chiefs agree to the Cherokee cession along the upper Savannah River.[17] Governor Wright had the "ceded lands" surveyed, and he advertised in Great Britain for buyers. Meanwhile, he attempted to clear the region of those people he and James Habersham called "Crackers." The region indeed was cleared, but not by the governor.

Young Creek warriors, angry at their chiefs for yielding their land in the Augusta treaty, attacked the squatters as well as the peaceful Quakers of Wrightsborough. The Augusta militia marched out to do battle, but when its members saw painted, war-whooping Indians, they fled in panic.[18] Governor Wright had only one weapon in his arsenal—he put a stop to the Indian trade. For the moment, he was a hero in the backcountry. When Savannah merchants protested the British Coercive Acts in 1774, the people of the backcountry signed petitions pledging loyalty to the king and governor.[19]

The trade embargo worked. The Creek chiefs came into Augusta to ask for peace. A treaty conference was arranged for Savannah in October 1774. The backcountry was elated; this was an opportunity to acquire the Oconee cession from the chastened Creeks.

The Augusta traders, on the other hand, argued that if the Indian boundary were moved that far away, the Creeks would look to Mobile and Pensacola for their trade goods. Augusta would lose its position as the premier center of Indian commerce.[20]

The governor had a difficult choice. Should he appease the land-hungry settlers, or should he maintain the Indian trade? He decided in favor of the trade and refrained from demanding an additional cession. The decision was fateful. It marked the point when the backcountry leaders joined with the radicals of the lowcountry in the movement which climaxed in the American Revolution.[21]

The Revolution in Georgia can be seen as war against British-allied Indians and against those who did business with Indians. The Revolution was a turning away from the sea lanes which led to Europe and a turning toward the frontier with its promise of new land. The Creeks were displaced by the Crackers, and the Crackers aspired to become planters.

The character of Augusta changed dramatically. Although commerce remained its essential economic enterprise, the town served the convenience of backcountry farmers, not Indians. Augusta lost the deerskin trade, but it gained the tobacco and cotton trades.

Notes

1. Habersham to Wright, Aug. 20, 1772, in Georgia Historical Society *Collections*, Savannah, 6:203–7.
2. Quoted in Louis De Vorsey, Jr., *The Indian Boundary in the Southern Colonies, 1763–1775* (Chapel Hill: Univ. of North Carolina Press, 1966), 160–61.
3. The young man was John Tanner, Oglethorpe's agent to the Creeks; see his letter to Mr. Cadownhead, *South Carolina Gazette*, Oct. 16–23, 1736.
4. Oglethorpe to the Trustees, Mar. 8, 1739, Georgia Historical Society *Collections*, Savannah, 3:68.
5. For McGillivray's heroics, see Edward J. Cashin, *Lachlan McGillivray, Indian Trader: The Shaping of the Southern Colonial Frontier* (Athens: Univ. of Georgia Press, 1992), 194–98.
6. Lt. Lachlan Shaw to William Henry Lyttelton, Mar. 6, 1760, in Lyttelton Papers, William L. Clement Library, Ann Arbor, Mich.
7. *Journal of the Congress of the Four Southern Governors and the Superintendent of That District, with the Five Nations of Indians at Augusta, 1763* (Charlestown, 1764); also in British Public Record Office, Colonial Office 5/65, pt. 3.
8. Robert S. Davis, Jr., *Quaker Records in Georgia: Wrightsboro, 1772–1793, Friendsborough, 1776–1777* (Augusta, Ga.: Augusta Genealogical Society, 1986).
9. E. R. R. Green, "Queensborough Township," *William and Mary Quarterly* 3d ser. 17 (1960): 189–96.
10. Edward Butler, diary, in Hargrett Collections, Univ. of Georgia Libraries, Athens.
11. Waldo Harris III, "Daniel Marshall: Lone Georgia Baptist Revolutionary Pastor," *Viewpoints: Georgia Baptist History* 5 (1976): 51–64.
12. Wright to Shelburne, Aug. 15, 1767, in "Colonial Records of Georgia" (manuscript), 37, pt. 1:240–42.
13. Louis LeClerc de Milfort, *Memoirs, or a Quick Glance at My Various Travels and My Sojourn in the Creek Nation* (Savannah, Ga.: Beehive Press, 1959), 87.
14. Ibid., 88–89
15. Philemon Kemp to Gov. of Georgia, June 6, 1771, in K. G. Davies, *Documents of the American Revolution* (Shannon: Irish Univ. Press, 1972–81), 3:118.
16. "List of Papers Relative to My Memorial about Indian Affairs and with Some Notes and Remarks Thereon," in Wright to Hillsborough, received Dec. 12, 1771, in "Colonial Records of Georgia" (manuscript), vol. 28, pt. 2B, pp. 669–73; Dartmouth to Wright, Dec. 12, 1772, in "Colonial Records of Georgia" (manuscript), vol. 38, pt. 1A, pp. 31–35.
17. Francis Harper, ed., *The Travels of William Bartram* (New Haven, Conn.: Yale Univ. Press, 1958), 22.
18. Wright to Dartmouth, Jan. 31, 1774, in "Colonial Records of Georgia" (manuscript), vol. 38, pt. 1A, pp. 163–71.
19. "A Protest of Declaration of Dissent of the Inhabitants of St. Paul's Parish," (Savannah) *Georgia Gazette*, Oct. 12, 1774.

20. "Petition of the Inhabitants of the Parish of St. George and St. Paul, including the ceded lands in the Province of Georgia," July 31, 1776, in *Collections of the New York Historical Society for the Year 1872* (New York, 1873), 181.
21. Extract of a letter from Savannah to a gentleman in Philadelphia, Dec. 9, 1774, in *American Archives*, ed. Peter Force, 6 vols. (Washington, D.C.), 4th series (1837–46), 1:1038–39.

 Taverns and Communities: The Case of Rowan County, North Carolina

Daniel B. Thorp

Inns, taverns, ordinaries, dram-shops, groggeries, alehouses—public drinking establishments went by a variety of names in colonial America. But whatever they were called, such establishments appeared early and spread fast in virtually every community established by Europeans or Euro-Americans during the seventeenth and eighteenth centuries, including those of the southern colonial backcountry. From the lower Shenandoah Valley to the Savannah River, taverns were among the earliest and most common economic and social institutions established in the backcountry, which should make them one of the most promising windows onto the culture of the region.

The problem, of course, is that the keepers and patrons of backcountry taverns were no more likely than any other residents of the frontier to record their activities or to preserve their records. Without such records and without the announcements and advertisements found in newspapers—none of which were published in the colonial backcountry—it is difficult to produce the sort of close analysis that Peter Thompson offered of Philadelphia taverns or Peter Clark of English alehouses or Thomas Brennan of public drinking in Paris.[1]

In the case of Rowan County, North Carolina, however, taverns are more accessible to historians than is generally the case on the southern colonial frontier. Public records for the county are as good as those for any other county in the region: deeds, wills, inventories, county court minutes, trial dockets, and civil action papers are all quite complete. In addition, two county publicans left private papers—letters or account books—that offer insight into taverns in the county,[2] and the Moravian settlers of Bethabara—near what is now Winston-Salem—left a variety of documentary and archaeological evidence that is unmatched on the southern frontier.[3] Together, these sources provide an unusually rich portrait of tavern culture in one part of the southern colonial backcountry and reveal quite clearly the divisions that existed in that region's population during the earliest years of its settlement by European colonists.

Rowan County was established in 1753 and initially included the entire northwestern quarter of what is now North Carolina. The new county's settled portion, of course, was much smaller. Most of its four thousand or so residents had arrived from Virginia, Maryland, or Pennsylvania via the Great Wagon Road, which crossed the county from northeast to southwest; or from eastern Carolina and Virginia along the Western Great Road, which entered the county on its eastern border and joined the Wagon Road southwest of the Forks of the Yadkin. As a result, they settled first in the Y-shaped corridor on either side of those roads—part of what Carville Earle and Ron Hoffman called a "linear urban network."[4]

Over the next twenty years, the population quadrupled, grew denser in the central corridor, and spread up the Yadkin and Catawba rivers toward the Appalachian Mountains. It remained, however, largely rural. The only towns to emerge before the Revolution were the county seat, Salisbury, and the congregation town of the Moravians' Wachovia settlement—Bethabara until 1772 and Salem thereafter. It also remained largely agricultural; other than a few hundred people in Salisbury, Bethabara, or Salem, nearly all of the early settlers were small farmers. Many of the latter, however, also were part-time artisans or retailers of some kind; and a number were tavernkeepers.[5]

For the purposes of this paper, a "tavern" is any establishment that regularly offered alcohol, meals, and/or lodging to the public for a fee. Any resident might occasionally provide travelers with dinner and a place to sleep, but my focus here is on those places where members of the public—traveling or resident—knew they could gather regularly. This definition makes irrelevant what was probably an artificial distinction between taverns, ordinaries, and public houses. Between 1753 and 1776, the Rowan county court used all three terms to describe what it was licensing.[6] As far as I can tell, though, it used the three interchangeably. There is no evidence that one word simply replaced another; they were all used throughout the period. Nor, apparently, did usage depend on what the licensee actually did. William Steele, or his widow Elizabeth, received licenses to keep a tavern in 1764 and 1771 and an ordinary in 1769 and 1774, yet nothing in their papers suggests there was any change in the business itself. In the case of Bethabara's Moravian community, the variety of licenses was even greater—nine for an ordinary, three for a tavern, and one for a public house—but all issued for exactly the same business in exactly the same building.

Nor does it seem useful in this paper to distinguish sharply between licensed and unlicensed establishments. Among the latter, there were certainly some that do not meet my definition of a tavern. In 1754, for example, the county court instructed the sheriff to order those selling liquor at the courthouse contrary to the law to remove "their boothes in harbours [sic]."[7] Vendors like these were certainly part of the public proceedings surrounding the court's quarterly sessions, but their booths and arbors did not provide the sort of established, public space that a tavern did. I therefore have chosen to ignore them. Other unlicensed dealers, however, are virtually indistinguishable from their legal counterparts. Alexander and John Lowrance never held a license of any kind, but they sold liquor by the drink, probably in their house, for forty years. Technically, perhaps, the Lowrances ran a grog shop, but for the purposes of this paper it was a tavern.

Unlicensed operators like the Lowrances are one reason it is impossible to say how many taverns there were in colonial Rowan County. There must have been a significant number of illegals, though. Peter Thompson estimates that, in Philadelphia at that time, there was one public house, legal and illegal combined, for every 77 to 130 inhabitants; while Peter Clark calculates that, in the English counties of Kent and Warwickshire, the rates were 1 to 104 and 1 to 109, respectively.[8] On the basis of its licensed taverns alone, Rowan never came close to these ratios. In its best year, 1754, the rate was about one tavern for every 300 people (71 taxables), and it was usually closer to 1 to 1,000. Even taking into account the backcountry's lower population density and less developed economy, I have to believe there may have been as many unlicensed taverns in the county as there were licensed ones.

Unlicensed operators are not the only obstacle to an accurate count of taverns in the county, though. The effort is further complicated by the fact that well over half the individuals who did obtain licenses did so just once, for a single year. These may be people who did run a tavern for just one year. But they may also be people who, for some reason, took out a license one year and operated illegally in others. William Temple Coles certainly falls into this category. He received a tavern license just once, in 1774, yet in 1767 he had sued John Holland for refusing to pay a debt incurred largely for small purchases of rum, toddy, or sling.[9]

Nor is it possible to say with certainty how the taverns of colonial Rowan were distributed, although one seems to be on safer ground here than in trying to count them. One would expect their distribution to reflect that of the county's population: densest in Salisbury, Bethabara, and Salem, where the combination of a concentrated resident community, regular visitors attracted by the towns' many services, and travelers on the Great Wagon Road provided the largest clientele; less dense along the rural portions of the Wagon Road and the Western Road; and steadily thinner with increasing distance from that "linear urban network." And, with one anomaly, this seems to be the pattern found among licensed tavernkeepers in the county. The anomaly was the Moravian settlements at Bethabara and Salem. Between them, these communities probably could have supported several taverns, but the Moravian Church tightly controlled their economies and limited each to a single tavern, in order to avoid competition among church members and to limit contact between outsiders and members of the Moravian community. Otherwise, the predicted pattern seems to hold. Salisbury, with perhaps 5 percent of the county's population,[10] was home to at least a quarter of its tavern licensees. The only other marked concentration of licenses was at the Shallow Ford, where the

Great Wagon Road crossed the Yadkin River. The rest seem to have been scattered throughout the county.

Whatever their precise number and location, though, taverns were clearly the most common public places in the county. Except for magistrate's court, which required only one justice of the peace, and some militia drills, political and governmental offices and functions were confined to Salisbury or the provincial capital. There also was a small number of churches in the county, but outside the Moravian community most residents probably lived closer to several taverns than they did to a church or chapel. This is what makes taverns such a tantalizing source of information about social dynamics in colonial Rowan County. Probably they were the places in which people most often gathered and the most important nodes around which neighborhoods developed. Thus, they should reflect the principal divisions among early residents of this frontier county.

The most visible division was along ethnic lines. Observers of the backcountry since the region was settled have agreed that one of its distinguishing features was the mixed ethnicity of its immigrant population. English, German, and Scots-Irish groups each contributed a significant share of the region's population, together with smaller numbers of French, Welsh, Irish, Scottish, and African American settlers. There has been less agreement, however, on the ways in which these different groups interacted. To Carl Bridenbaugh, the backcountry was a Tower of Babel and "the scene of cultural conflict for many decades." To Robert Mitchell, German settlers may have been somewhat isolated from their neighbors, but, in general, "the creation of a landscape of dispersed rural settlements and individual family farms transcended differences in national origins." Greg Nobles recently concluded that we still do not know how different groups reacted to one another; in Nobles' words, "understanding both the commingling and continuity of those [groups'] traditions remains one of the critical tasks for historians of the early American frontier."[11]

The evidence of Rowan County taverns suggests that Mitchell was right to identify Germans as the most closed group but that he may have understated the extent of the boundary between them and their neighbors. It is notoriously dangerous to base ethnic identification on people's surnames, but nevertheless I have tried to do it with two lists of customers from Rowan County taverns. William Steele drew up a record in 1768 of the amounts due him from approximately 319 patrons of his Salisbury tavern, while Alexander and John Lowrance kept running accounts for 205 individuals who came to their tavern in the county's Irish Settlement, ten miles west of Salisbury, between 1755 and 1776.[12] In both cases, German names are conspicuously absent. Among the Lowrances' customers were 24 ethnically distinctive surnames, one of which was German. In Steele's case, of 35 distinctive surnames, one was German and one was Dutch.[13] In the Lowrances' case, the absence of Germans may simply reflect the ethnic makeup of the tavern's neighborhood; most of its patrons came from a region of the county in which Germans made up less than 5 percent of the population. William Steele's customers, however, were drawn from virtually the entire county, which was 27 percent German in 1759 and 30 percent in 1778.[14]

Ethnic divisions may also be evident in what people drank.[15] Throughout Rowan County, distilled spirits—whiskey, rum, and brandy—were served more often than beer, but the ratio of spirits to beer varied from place to place.[16] The more Scottish a tavern's clientele, the more spirits it served; and the more German or English its patrons, the more beer it served. In the Lowrances' ledger, 71 percent of the ethnically distinctive surnames were Scottish, while English and German names, together, made up just 12.5 percent. The Lowrances never mentioned beer in their twenty years of tavern keeping before 1776; except for a little mead one year, rum and whiskey were all they served. In William Steele's case, where Scottish surnames were 54 percent and English or German 17 percent, servings of spirits still outnumbered those of beer by about three to one. For Bethabara's tavern, unfortunately, no list of customers has survived, but evidence from the Moravian community itself, which was overwhelmingly German, supports the link between ethnicity and drinking. Spirits were served there just slightly more often than beer in 1762–63 and actually were below the level of beer in 1764–65.[17] Some ethnic stereotypes, then, held true. German and English settlers in Rowan County drank tankards of beer, while Scots had a wee dram of whiskey; and historians may be able to use this fact to identify ethnic enclaves within the mixed population of the backcountry.

Ethnicity was not the only factor dividing the populace of the colonial backcountry. There were also economic or class differences. These were first highlighted by students of North Carolina's Regulator Movement, although more recent writers, such as Richard Beeman and Rachel Klein, have discussed their significance in times and places less riven by conflict.[18] All these scholars, however, have focused largely on politics, showing a correlation between wealth and office holding, for example. Evidence from taverns, on the other hand, allows us to gauge the extent to which such differences influenced patterns of social activity and did or did not divide the frontier community in an arena that was closer to the average person on a daily basis.

In the case of Rowan County, there is no evidence that whole taverns catered to a particular class or economic group. Most of the county's 1778 tax list has survived, and approximately a third of the customers named in the Steele and Lowrance account books can be identified on it.[19] In both cases the same pattern is apparent. Few account holders came from the ranks of those with little or no taxable property, but neither Steele nor the Lowrances seem to have drawn their customers disproportionately from the upper segments of the community. Each seems to have served mostly middling taxpayers and a smaller but significant number of wealthy ones. Judging from the credit they extended, neither establishment seems to qualify as a gentlemen's club or a working-class tavern.[20]

Inside a particular tavern, though, class differences were more evident. Only the Moravians left an inventory of their tavern's furnishings,[21] but in their tavern, at least, "gentlemen" and others enjoyed distinctly different experiences, and the differences widened during the 1760s.

When the Bethabara tavern opened, in 1757, it was a simple log structure, 20 feet by 15 feet, with a half-story loft, and both the main floor and the loft were divided into two rooms.[22] When its furnishings were first inventoried, two years later, they were as plain and undifferentiated as the tavern itself. The taproom [my term] contained "a large table," "5 benches, 1 armchair, and a stool"—none of them described as old, new, nice, or worn. All of the plates and bowls were wooden or earthen, all the spoons were tin, and the table was covered with one of three apparently identical tablecloths. At night, guests slept either on a "sleeping bench" or on one of the two-person straw ticks in the loft.[23] Whatever a patron's class or economic standing, all enjoyed the same level of comfort in the tavern's early years.

Such democracy began to fade in the 1760s. Early in the decade, the Moravians enlarged their tavern, adding at least one more room and a "gallery" across the front; and in 1764 they decided to find new quarters for Brother and Sister Shaub, who ran the tavern, so that "the present tavernkeeper's room can be used for gentlemen."[24] These facilities for gentlemen were not only separate from those of other patrons, but also more refined. In the summer of 1766, when a second inventory of the tavern was produced, many of its furnishings existed in both rough and fine versions. There was now a "round walnut table" worth twice as much as two other "large tables." There were "rush-bottomed walnut chairs," "small and inferior" versions of the same, and simple benches on which to sit. Both "flowered tablecloths" and "oznabrug tablecloths" were available, and the tables could be set with glassware and pewter plates or with pottery items too inferior to inventory. At bedtime one could retire to a feather bed, a straw tick, or a wooden bench.[25]

Another aspect of class differentiation that emerges from the record of Rowan County's early taverns is the apparent spread of metropolitan fashion to that remote corner of the Empire. This is most visible, perhaps, in a comparison of the drinks sold at the Lowrances' tavern in the Irish Settlement and those offered by William Steele at his Salisbury establishment.[26] The vast majority of the Lowrances' sales involved unmixed alcoholic beverages. The mainstay of their trade, identified usually as "liquor" in their account book, was a form of whiskey made from corn and rye, although they also sold significant amounts of brandy, apparently peach and perhaps locally made; rum brought from Charles Town; and, for a few months in 1767, a batch of locally produced *mathiglein*—a type of mead. The only other drink they offered was "toddy," rum or whiskey mixed with sugar and hot water.[27] Steele, on the other hand, sold a much greater variety of drinks and fewer local products. From merchants in Charles Town he purchased two kinds of rum, plus Madeira, claret, and another unnamed wine. Some of these types of beverages his patrons drank straight, but most went into toddies, punch, eggnog, juleps, sling, club, and sanger. The last of these, sanger, is particularly interesting. According to the *Oxford English Dictionary*, it was a mixture of red wine and lemon water, and the dictionary's first example of its usage is the statement by *Gentleman's Magazine* in 1736 that the drink had been devised by a punch seller in the Strand. If sanger was new to England in 1736, then its presence in a Salisbury tavern thirty years later seems to represent the spread of genteel culture from center to periphery as described by Richard Bushman. Moreover, Steele did not sell the locally produced beverages, whiskey and brandy, as the Lowrances did, a fact which seems to illustrate Bushman's distinction between high-style and vernacular cultures in colonial America.[28]

The Moravians' tavern inventories, however, show that metropolitan fashion did not always take when transferred to the backcountry. The 1759 inventory includes a coffee pot, a writing table, and pen and ink. These may represent an effort on the Moravians' part to establish in Bethabara's tavern a rudimentary version of the coffee houses or rooms in which London and Philadelphia businessmen met to discuss and conduct their affairs.[29] If so, the effort failed. Customers at the tavern still may have done deals, but by 1766 the only item in the tavern to evoke images of a coffee house was a coffee mill, and it came last on the list of ironwork—after a musket and a manure fork—with no value listed.

Finally, the evidence from Rowan County taverns shows that the community there was sharply divided by gender. Unfortunately, the exact nature of that division remains unclear. On the surface, taverns seem to have been almost exclusively male preserves, but that appearance could be the result of biased sources rather than house-bound women.

Women certainly did not hold tavern licenses in colonial Rowan County; Elizabeth Steele, William Steele's widow, was the only woman in the county to obtain a license before 1776. That may actually mean that Elizabeth Steele was the only female tavernkeeper in colonial Rowan County, but it also may mean that she was the only one not hidden to historians by the *femme couverte* status of married women. Writing about eighteenth-century England, Peter Clark concluded, "Although no more than a small minority of alehouses had female licensees, there can be little question that women were still pivotal figures in the day-to-day running of popular drinking establishments."[30] Was the southern frontier really more scrupulous in the maintenance of gender roles than the metropolis?

Nor did women generally have accounts at Rowan County taverns. Among William Steele's 319 accounts, no more than six, and perhaps only five, belonged to women; and only ten of the Lowrances' 205 account holders were female. Moreover, an unusually high percentage of the women who did have accounts were widows. Of the fifteen or sixteen female account holders, at least half were widows; five were explicitly identified as such, while three others first appeared in the Lowrances' book only after the death of a male account holder with the same surname. With the others, it is impossible to tell their marital status. This phenomenon could indicate a society that tried to keep women out of public places, such as taverns. It could also be, however, the result of businessmen's limiting credit to people they could sue, by recording wives' purchases under their husbands' names.

Nor do women's accounts reflect the sort of drinking behavior suggested by most men's accounts. Fifty-seven percent of the Lowrances' male account holders purchased a toddy or a dram—drinks that were probably consumed in the tavern—

at least once. No woman ever did. They might buy liquor, but they did so in quantities that suggest it was for home consumption. This could indicate that no women were allowed to drink at the Lowrances' establishment, but it could also be the result of a selective ban on social drinking by unaccompanied women, as was found in many English alehouses of the time.[31] If widows and unmarried women could have accounts but could not drink in the tavern, while married women with their husbands could drink in the tavern but could not have accounts, then female social drinking would remain invisible.

I wish I could say that material culture research has solved the dilemma with clear evidence of women's presence or absence in backcountry taverns. Several years ago, Laurel Thatcher Ulrich expressed the hope that "a more realistic appraisal of the relationship between documents and the actual structures of early American life" would lead historians to see that "in the small communities of seventeenth- and eighteenth-century America, women were everywhere."[32] Inventories of the Bethabara tavern, however, are remarkably ungendered. Except for the fact that there were no chamber pots on the 1759 inventory and only one in 1766, nothing about the tavern's material culture seems particularly male. Nor does any item on either inventory seem uniquely female. So for now the mystery remains. Clearly, men and women were not equal in colonial Rowan County or in its taverns, but whether the difference between them was a legal technicality or a more deeply rooted cultural pattern is impossible to say.

Looking inside the taverns of early Rowan County, one can see that residents of the southern backcountry were neither homogeneous nor xenophobic. Ethnicity, class, and gender all divided the backcountry population into overlapping groups, but none of the boundaries between these groups was impermeable. Germans did, evidently, prefer to socialize with other Germans—probably because of the language barrier between themselves and English-speaking Britons. Aspiring gentlemen could distance themselves from their less refined neighbors. And women, if their culture allowed them to operate or frequent taverns, still did so in the face of legal restrictions. But none of these divisions threatened the basic stability of backcountry society.

NOTES

1. Peter J. Thompson, "A Social History of Philadelphia's Taverns, 1683–1800" (Ph.D. diss., Univ. of Pennsylvania, 1989); Peter J. Thompson, "'The Friendly Glass': Drink and Gentility in Colonial Philadelphia," *Pennsylvania Magazine of History and Biography* 113 (1989): 549–73; Peter Clark, *The English Alehouse: A Social History, 1200–1830* (London: Longmans, 1983); Thomas Brennan, *Public Drinking and Popular Culture in Eighteenth-Century Paris* (Princeton, N.J.: Princeton Univ. Press, 1988).
2. William and Elizabeth Steele left a variety of letters and business records from their Salisbury tavern that are now part of the John Steele Papers, Southern Historical Collection, Univ. of North Carolina at Chapel Hill. Alexander and John Lowrance

left a ledger from the tavern they ran in rural Rowan County that is now in the Manuscript Department of Perkins Library, Duke Univ., Durham, N.C.
3. For a discussion of documentary material relating to Bethabara, see Daniel B. Thorp, *The Moravian Community in Colonial North Carolina: Pluralism on the Southern Frontier* (Knoxville: Univ. of Tennessee Press, 1989), 4 and 208n8. Reports of the archaeological excavations at Bethabara are in Stanley South manuscript, "Discovery in Wachovia," P.C. 1585.1, North Carolina State Library, Raleigh.
4. Robert W. Ramsey, *Carolina Cradle: Settlement of the Northwest Carolina Frontier, 1747–1762* (Chapel Hill: Univ. of North Carolina Press, 1964); Carville Earle and Ronald Hoffman, "Staple Crops and Urban Development in the Eighteenth-Century South," *Perspectives in American History* 10 (1976): 7–78, quotation on 56.
5. Harry Roy Merrens, *Colonial North Carolina in the Eighteenth Century: A Study in Historical Geography* (Chapel Hill: Univ. of North Carolina Press, 1964), 162–66.
6. Tavern licenses can be found in the minutes of Rowan County Court of Pleas and Quarter Sessions. The original minute books are in the North Carolina State Library, Raleigh; for published abstracts, see Jo Linn White, *Abstracts of the Minutes of the Court of Pleas and Quarter Sessions, Rowan County, North Carolina, 1753–1762* (Salisbury, N.C.,1977); Jo Linn White, *Abstracts of the Minutes of the Court of Pleas and Quarter Sessions, Rowan County, North Carolina, 1763–1774* (N.p., 1979); and Jo Linn White, *Abstracts of the Minutes of the Court of Pleas and Quarter Sessions, Rowan County, North Carolina, 1775–1789* (Salisbury, N.C., 1982).
7. Rowan Court Minutes, Oct. 9, 1754, in White, *Abstracts of the Minutes, 1753–1762*, 30.
8. Thompson, "Social History of Philadelphia's Taverns," 209; Peter Clark, *English Alehouse*, 58.
9. Rowan Court Minutes, May 3, 1774, in White, *Abstracts of the Minutes, 1763–1774*, 150; [petition of William Temple Coles], Oct. 15, 1767, in 1768 File, Rowan County Civil Action Papers, 1755–1774, C.R. 085.325.1, North Carolina State Library.
10. Robert W. Ramsey, *Carolina Cradle*, 169; "A Table of North Carolina Taxes (1770)," in *Some Eighteenth-Century Tracts Concerning North Carolina*, ed. William K. Boyd, 412–17 (Raleigh, N.C.: State Dept. of Archives and History, 1927; reprint, Spartanburg, S.C.: The Reprint Co., 1973).
11. Carl Bridenbaugh, *Myths and Realities: Societies of the Colonial South* (Baton Rouge: Louisiana State Univ. Press, 1952; New York: Athenaeum, 1963), 134; Robert D. Mitchell, *Commercialism and Frontier: Perspectives on the Early Shenandoah Valley* (Charlottesvile: Univ. Press of Virginia, 1977), 239; Gregory H. Nobles, "Breaking into the Backcountry: New Approaches to the Early American Frontier," *William and Mary Quarterly* 3d ser. 46 (1989): 641–70, quotation on 651–52.
12. "A Memorandum Book for the Year of Our Lord 1768," in folder 153, John Steele Papers, Southern Historical Collection, Univ. of North Carolina, Chapel Hill, includes 221 different surnames; the Lowrance Ledger includes 122 different surnames.
13. Ethnic identity based on: English and Welsh lists in American Council of Learned Societies, "Report of Committee on Linguistic and National Stocks in the Population of the United States," *Annual Report of the American Historical Association for the Year*

1931 (Washington, D.C.: n.p., 1932), 1:177; Scottish and Irish lists in Forrest McDonald and Ellen Shapiro McDonald, "Ethnic Origins of the American People, 1790," *William and Mary Quarterly* 3d ser. 37 (1980): 192–94 and 196–98; and German, Dutch, and French lists in Thomas L. Purvis, "The European Ancestry of the United States Population, 1790," *William and Mary Quarterly* 3d ser. 41 (1984): 89–91n.

14. Mikle Dave Ledgerwood, "Ethnic Groups on the Frontier in Rowan County, North Carolina, 1750–1778" (Master's thesis, Vanderbilt Univ., 1977), 96–97.
15. See David Hackett Fischer, *Albion's Seed: Four British Folkways in America* (New York: Oxford Univ. Press, 1989), 729–30, for another example of this.
16. I base this on servings—a quart of beer or a half-pint of spirits—rather than total volume or monetary value.
17. [Bethabara accounts, June 1, 1762–May 31, 1763, and June 1, 1764–May 31, 1765], Papiere die Wachau betreffend, 1762–1764, Wachovia VI, Archives of the Moravian Church in America–Northern Province, Bethlehem, Pa.
18. A. Roger Ekirch, *"Poor Carolina": Politics and Society in Colonial North Carolina, 1726–1776* (Chapel Hill: Univ. of North Carolina Press, 1981); James P. Whittenburg, "Planters, Merchants, and Lawyers: Social Change and the Origins of the North Carolina Regulation," *William and Mary Quarterly* 3d ser. 34 (1977): 215–38; Richard R. Beeman, *The Evolution of the Southern Backcountry: A Case Study of Lunenburg County, Virginia, 1746–1832* (Philadelphia: Univ. of Pennsylvania Press, 1984); Rachel N. Klein, *Unification of a Slave State: The Rise of the Planter Class in the South Carolina Backcountry, 1760–1808* (Chapel Hill: Univ. of North Carolina Press, 1990).
19. "List of Taxable Property in the County of Rowan North Carolina Anno 1778," typescript in the North Carolina State Library, includes 85 of Steele's 319 legible names and 74 of the Lowrances' 205.
20. Any discussion of the taverns' "patrons" is complicated by the fact that neither the Lowrances nor Steele left a daybook; so there is no record of purchases that were paid in full at the time of the transaction. I suspect that such purchases were rare in colonial Rowan County, but I cannot prove it. For more on this, see Daniel B. Thorp, "Doing Business in the Backcountry: Retail Trade in Colonial Rowan County," *William and Mary Quarterly* 3d ser. 48 (1991): 387–408.
21. They actually left two. One, dated 1759, is in Moravian Church Records, R.14.Ba.Nr.2c, 832–833, Manuscript Division, Library of Congress. The other, from 1766, is in File G 260:1a, 62–65, Archives of the Moravian Church in America–Southern Province, Winston-Salem, N.C.
22. [Inventory of buildings in Bethabara], March 27, [1758], in Moravian Church Records, R.14.Ba.Nr.2c, 222–225, Library of Congress, Washington, D.C.
23. [Bethabara tavern inventory], Oct. 3, 1759, in Moravian Church Records, R.14.Ba.Nr.2c., 832–33, Library of Congress.
24. Protocol der Helfers Conferenz, July 10, 1764, in Archives of the Moravian Church in America—Southern Province.
25. Inventarium das Gasthoff oder Tavern, 1766 der 30 Aug., pp. 62–65 of Mobillien

Inventaria des Diaconats von der Wachau, July–Aug, 1766, in File G 260:1a, Archives of the Moravian Church in America—Southern Province.

26. Alternatively, this phenomenon may have had more to do with a growing difference between urban and rural parts of the county than with economic or class differences.
27. W. J. Rorabaugh, *The Alcoholic Republic: An American Tradition* (Oxford, England: Oxford Univ. Press, 1979), 19.
28. Richard L. Bushman, "American High-Style and Vernacular Cultures," in *Colonial British America: Essays in the New History of the Early Modern Era*, ed. Jack P. Greene and J. R. Pole (Baltimore, Md.: Johns Hopkins Univ. Press, 1984), 345–83.
29. Peter Clark, *English Alehouse*, 13–14, 214; Thompson, "Social History of Philadelphia's Taverns," 285–87; Penelope Batcheler, *Independence National Historical Park, Pennsylvania, Historic Structure Report, Architectural Data Section, City Tavern* (Denver, Colo.: National Park Service, 1973), 21.
30. Peter Clark, *English Alehouse*, 205.
31. Ibid., 131–32, 225, 311.
32. Laurel Thatcher Ulrich, "Of Pens and Needles: Sources in Early American Women's History," *Journal of American History* 77 (1990): 200–207, quotation on 201.

Economic Development in the South Carolina Backcountry: A View from Camden

Kenneth E. Lewis

By the time of the American Revolution, much of the South Carolina interior had been occupied by immigrants of European origin, and the region was well on its way toward becoming an integral part of the expanding European world economy. During the previous half-century, the backcountry had undergone a transition as a result of its colonization and the establishment of commercial export production as a primary adaptive strategy. Such a process occurs among complex societies as they attempt to recreate themselves in the face of the attenuated conditions encountered at the periphery of settlement.

Colonization is strongly influenced by economic variables. The form it takes is influenced heavily by the form of production that the colonists attempt to establish and the manner in which they are able to implement their intentions. The evolution of the South Carolina backcountry was, to a significant degree, a result of economic adaptation to the particular conditions encountered in this region at the time of its settlement.

The study of a region, especially in terms of its material record, is an examination of its settlements as components of a larger landscape. By its very nature, the occupation of a frontier region involves the planned creation of settlements whose purpose it is to consolidate control over an area and its resources. If we assume that settlements collectively represent a functionally interrelated system, then it should be possible to examine structure and change in the region's economy by observing the form and development of individual settlements, particularly those with central roles in the system.

It is the purpose of this paper to explore the development of the backcountry by examining the nature of regional economic change on the frontier through its manifestations in a particular colonial settlement. The changing organization of a frontier economy, such as that in eighteenth-century South Carolina, may be observed in the evolving structure of component settlements playing key economic roles during the period in which colonization took place. Evidence relating to Camden, a central settlement on the South Carolina frontier, will be reviewed to demonstrate the extent to which changes associated with the evolution of the backcountry economy may be observed in the development of a single site.

Frontier Processes, Landscapes, and Settlement Patterns

Frontier colonization is a process integral to explaining the historical development of regions occupied as a consequence of the expansion of Europe after the fifteenth century.[1] Although all colonization involves an expansion of organized settlement, its form varies with its purpose. It is especially important to distinguish between colonization carried out largely for the purpose of extracting resources and that intended to replicate and expand the home civilization. In the former, a focus on the production of specific commercial commodities ties the colony immediately to narrow external markets, limits immigration to those associated directly with production, and discourages reinvestment in the region. These colonies remain foreign enclaves closely linked to the homeland and its economy. As such, they do not evolve except in response to alterations in external demand and technological change.[2] Agricultural frontiers, on the other hand, are established for purposes of resettlement, and their populations migrate largely for the purpose of replicating the parent society abroad. Production here is diverse and not directed solely to external markets. Although such colonies are formed with the idea of extending the capitalist world economy, their initial focus is internal. This is reflected in the development of regional trade and reinvestment and in the formation of complex colonial institutions. Agricultural frontiers are dynamic entities that represent a transitional stage between an initial intrusive presence and a region's incorporation into a larger international economy.[3]

The evolution of agricultural frontiers is a general adaptive response to low population density, inadequate transportation within the area of colonization, and attenuated economic and political interaction. These factors result in the establishment of an entrepôt that serves as the focus of economic and political activity and, by means of a dendritic network of transportation, as the principal link between areas of interior settlement and the outside world. Meanwhile, the expansion and enlargement of the colony precipitates change in older settled areas over time. The area of colonization contains a hierarchy, or "gradient," of settlements, the size and function of which diminish as their access to the entrepôt increases. These settlements do not remain static over time. As regional population density increases and networks of trade and communication become more complex, they may assume new roles as necessitated by the evolving economy.[4]

Agricultural colonization creates a changing cultural landscape characterized by varying distributions of people and activities. Settlement patterning in a frontier landscape involves the distribution of people and activities, as well as the functions of settlements and the interrelationships among them. Such patterning reflects an adaptation to frontier conditions, and a study of its form is crucial to examining the process of frontier change.

Determining the spatial distribution of past settlements is important; similarly, information pertaining to settlement function is necessary when dealing with material evidence and is particularly useful in the case of archaeological data. Because archaeology is site-specific in nature, the acquisition of material evidence becomes difficult unless the past functions of the sites examined can first be determined. Consequently, a knowledge of settlement patterning and its relationship to the processes that produced it is integral to the effective employment of the material record in studies of frontier change.

The Frontier Town and Colonial Settlement

The relatively low population density of agricultural frontier regions dictates their settlement structure. The small number of settlements resulting from the distribution of immigrant settlers over a wide area does not allow formation of the complex hierarchy of community types found in stable, settled areas.[5] On the frontier, the services normally performed by settlements at the lower levels of the hierarchy are shifted upward to those at a higher level and are concentrated in "frontier towns." These settlements serve as centers of trade and communications within the colony; because they possess the most direct connections with the entrepôt, they also provide crucial links to the outside world.[6]

Because of their central positions, frontier towns play a vital role in the colonial economy. They serve as distribution points for imports, jumping-off places for immigrants entering the area of colonization, processing and storage sites for agricultural products from the dispersed farms, and regional markets.[7] Frontier towns are ideally suited to be centers of internal economic activity. Situated at the hub of an interior trade and communications network, they are natural locations for redistributive and other specialized activities. The frontier town is linked closely to the development of the frontier economy and should be a sensitive indicator of its evolution over time.

The Evolution of Frontier Economies

Agricultural frontier development is the curious product of an attempt to extend the capitalist economy of the parent society into a region where the conditions essential to that economy are largely absent. One of the most important of these is the ability to participate in larger world markets. Because of the isolation of frontier farms and the poorly developed state of transportation and processing infrastructure, the volume and extent of trade is limited, and the size and certainty of external markets are likely to be reduced. These conditions would limit not only the amount of profit generated by agricultural activities, but also the reliability of investment in farm production. Until reliable external markets are firmly established, a frontier economy must sustain itself by the large internal market created by continuing immigration.

The limitations of frontier agriculture are temporary, in the sense that continuous population growth and the development of processing and transportation facilities eventually will overcome the isolation of the initial settlement period. In the meantime, however, farmers in the area of colonization, obliged to adapt their production to minimize the risks of operating in a world of limited access and uncertain markets, may follow several concurrent strategies to support frontier households. They may, for example, reduce dependence on outside sources by increasing the amount of subsistence products raised. Although an emphasis on subsistence is necessary to alleviate deficiencies resulting from isolation, it does not preclude exchange in a wider community whose requirements are greater than mere survival. Pioneer households are not isolated and usually, from the beginning, participate in a regional economy.[8] Another strategy involves diversifying production within the region. Because the time and skills necessary to produce a variety of crops and goods lie beyond the capability of most pioneer households, individual specialization appears early, accompanied by regional exchange.[9] Regional diversification has the advantage of increasing production efficiency and applies not only to agriculture but also to the work of craft specialists and others whose work is crucial to sustaining settlement.

The exchange of the diverse products necessary to the success of agricultural colonization anticipates the complex organization typical of settled regions; however, both production and exchange are affected by the initial absence of a capitalist market. Under these circumstances, goods and services are exchanged not as commodities but as material manifestations of labor. The labor involved in production is directly coordinated, in a decentralized way, and exchange is controlled by need rather than price. In such an economy, manufacture and distribution are governed by a product's use value rather than by its exchange value as a commodity.[10]

Well adapted to the conditions of early settlement, the mechanisms of frontier production and exchange help to establish and expand agriculture while creating networks helpful in maintaining the region without reliance on substantial external trade. A frontier region is not a static phenomenon, and changing conditions inevitably affect the pioneer economy. Although growth in population and enlargement of the production base do not by themselves alter the nature of exchange, they do create conditions that invite the intrusion of a larger economy that begins to impose its own market relations on frontier goods and services. This change marks a crucial transition in the development of the frontier economy.

The integration of a frontier region with a larger external economy occurs when the expansion of demand for the region's agricultural commodities results in an extension of trade and communications links between the area of colonization and the older settled area. Increasing external demand for frontier products provides an impetus for capitalist expansion, which is abetted by the opening of adequate transportation routes linking pioneer producers to larger markets. The intrusion of outside markets extends the larger economy into the hinterlands, creating competition for regional products.

As frontier producers become participants in networks leading to external markets, the structure of earlier regional exchange systems is disrupted, obliging their members to seek new sources and recipients for their products. Such people now find their relationships with one another increasingly mediated by markets which establish exchange values for their products. More and more, goods and labor become commodities, the values of which are dictated by market demand, not need.

In response to competition from a wider market, the diversity of frontier agriculture diminishes. Farmers begin to concentrate their attention on the potential cash returns of crops—that is, on exchange rather than use value. Consequently, farm production becomes increasingly specialized throughout the region, as the network of external exchange expands.[11] Thus a shift occurs toward items that can be produced more efficiently or inexpensively.

To integrate the production of crops into the larger economy, however, a processing infrastructure must be established for the collection and preparation of raw commodities in quantities sufficient for export.[12] The key to creating such an infrastructure in an area of colonization is the introduction of investment capital. It is necessary to construct collection, storage, and processing facilities, as well as more efficient transportation links within and out of the region.[13] In general, bulky, perishable crops requiring more elaborate processing demand a higher capital investment to accommodate their more complex marketing arrangements. The creation of such an infrastructure is likely to be reflected in the settlement structure of the frontier.

The evolution of the frontier economy is responsible for changes in the settlement system that supports it. An examination of the latter over time should reveal the impact of the colonization process in a particular region. Because of their central role in the frontier economy, frontier towns experience the most profound alteration as a result of regional economic change. Therefore, functional change observed in such settlements should provide evidence for alterations in the region as a whole. Camden was the principal inland frontier settlement in South Carolina during the eighteenth century, and its development is likely to reveal the economic change occurring in the region as a result of the region's growth as an agricultural frontier. This change and this growth will be thrown into relief by an examination of documentary and material evidence pertaining to this settlement.

Camden and the Economy of the South Carolina Backcountry

The settlement of the interior of British South Carolina occurred well after the coastal region of the province was occupied. In contrast to the lowcountry, which developed as a specialized rice-growing region centered in large-scale plantation production for export markets, the backcountry was settled largely by small farmers who produced a variety of crops for which initially there existed no outside demand. This expansion was promoted by a provincial government anxious to consolidate its position on the southern Atlantic Seaboard and uneasy about the presence of a large slave population in the coastal region. The creation, in 1731, of nine large inland settlement tracts, called townships, was intended to colonize each of the major river drainages in South Carolina.[14]

Fredericksburg Township, on the east side of the Wateree River, lay near the center of the province and was one of the townships farthest from Charleston (see map 6.1). Its placement astride the Catawba Path, linking the entrepôt to the upper Wateree and adjacent river drainages, not only established a strategic political presence in the backcountry, but also encouraged settlement in a location ideally suited to control the region's internal trade.[15]

The survey of the township was completed in early 1734.[16] As in most of the other townships, a nucleated settlement did not develop. Instead, the earliest settlers occupied scattered tracts on or near the river. The first immigrants arrived within two years of the survey, but a large influx of colonists did not take place until the late 1740s. This abrupt increase in settlement included the arrival of a group of Irish Quakers, who settled in the vicinity of Pine Tree Creek. Their presence would have a pivotal role in the area's economic development.[17]

The Quakers chose a site for their meeting house on high ground near the mouth of Pine Tree Creek, situated on the land of Samuel Wyly, who by 1753 also had established an inn near its location. Several years later, he erected saw and grist mills nearby to accommodate the local demand for processing grain and lumber.[18] These services were needed to provision the growing number of agriculturists on the upper Wateree. Immigrants occupying the highlands had begun to produce a variety of crops, including corn, wheat, barley, flax, and garden vegetables.[19] At this time, the economy was largely regional in scope, without either a market for export crops or substantial surplus production.[20] The processing of grain, however, was dependent upon the existence of mills at locations convenient to the inhabitants of the region. Placement of mills around a centrally located site such as Pine Tree Hill would have made it a focal point for backcountry trade and a center for the redistribution of products.

The geographical extent of Pine Tree Hill's early trade is difficult to determine, but it is likely to have included much of the upper Wateree and Pee Dee river drainages, which then were undergoing settlement. Trade even extended as far as the Moravian settlement of Bethabara, in North Carolina, which exchanged its distinctive, locally made ceramics over a wide portion of the backcountry. (Existence of this exchange is confirmed by archaeological specimens of Bethabara ceramics recovered at the site of Pine Tree Hill.)[21] The settlement's role as a regional marketing center was also reflected in its acquisition of facilities for tanning and the manufacture of leather goods.[22]

Pine Tree Hill's location on the Catawba Path also situated it ideally as a collection point for those products that could be exported and as a distribution center for imported manufactured goods. Deerskins obtained from the Catawbas and

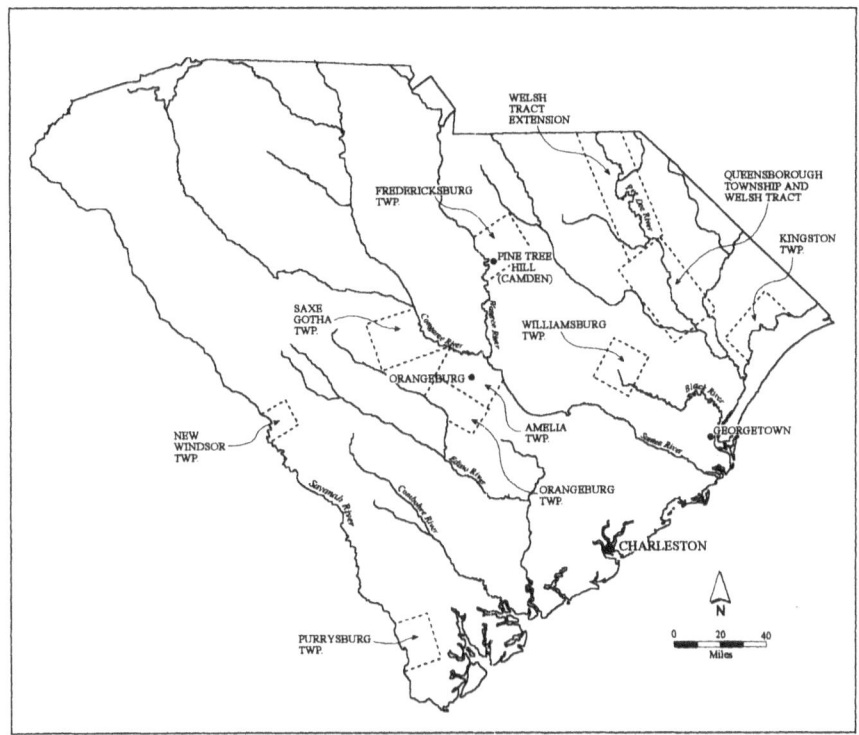

Map 6.1. Layout of the interior townships established in South Carolina in 1731. Adapted from Judith J. Schulz, "The Rise and Decline of Camden as South Carolina's Major Trading Center, 1751–1829: A Historical Geographic Study" (Master's thesis, University of South Carolina, 1972), 14.

other Indian peoples were gathered and shipped from here. It is not surprising that Samuel Wyly, the principal trader, was also the colonial agent to the Catawbas.[23]

The rapid growth of settlement during the 1750s set the stage for an increase in the scale of agricultural production in the South Carolina backcountry. The introduction of wheat as a staple crop offered the opportunity for participation in the larger colonial economy. Wheat had been grown as one of a number of food crops in the backcountry; however, a rise in demand for foodstuffs in the British West Indies and a constant need for imported flour in the coastal region of South Carolina created an extensive outside market for this crop.[24]

In order to take advantage of this situation, two developments had to occur. The first was the *introduction of sufficient capital and organization* to develop backcountry production. The second was the *creation of adequate transportation links* to permit the scale of traffic necessitated by the greater volume of trade. Both these conditions were met by 1760, resulting in the transformation of the frontier settlement of Pine

Tree Hill into a regional export center. Concomitant changes in the settlement's size, form, and composition occurred.

Perhaps the seminal event in the transformation of Pine Tree Hill was the arrival there in 1758 of Joseph Kershaw, initially as an agent for, and partner of, Charleston merchants Ancrum, Lance, and Loocock. This firm maintained ties to influential and wealthy Quaker mercantile families in Philadelphia. Kershaw's appearance coincided with a major mid-century shift in capital to South Carolina, because of the province's increasing importance in international trade.[25] The establishment of an additional store and mills at Pine Tree Hill and their ownership by a Charleston mercantile firm provided not only the resources and facilities for processing quantities of backcountry wheat, but also a direct economic link to entrepôt markets. Flour from this settlement was advertised in Charleston by Ancrum, Lance, and Loocock as early as 1760.[26] Kershaw subsequently formed a new partnership and, as its head, extended his business widely in the backcountry. In addition to his store and mills, at Pine Tree Hill he operated a bakery, a brewery and distillery, and a brickyard. He also owned a tobacco warehouse and an indigo works there, which afforded distributive control of two additional emerging frontier exports. These activities established Pine Tree Hill as a multifunctional center in the backcountry and acted to attract millers and other craft specialists and tradespeople to the settlement.[27] Apparently at Kershaw's instigation, in 1768 the settlement's name was changed to Camden.[28]

Kershaw's success at Camden coincided with the rise of wheat as the staple crop of the backcountry and the focusing of agriculture on the production of export commodities. By the late 1760s, Camden's mills were shipping 2,000 barrels of flour and 1,500 of shipbread to Charleston annually, amounts indicative of a grain-growing hinterland of considerable size.[29] Through a network of stores at Camden, Cheraw on the upper Pee Dee, and Granby at the head of the Congaree, Kershaw's economic influence spread over a wide portion of the South Carolina interior (map 6.2).[30] By the early 1770s, the radius of his intensive business activity extended about sixty miles from Camden, with lesser activity occurring at nearly twice that distance.[31] Largely as a result of the flow of investment capital through Camden and the establishment there of a processing infrastructure, the town dominated the backcountry economy in the period prior to the Revolution.

Camden's success also required a transportation network to link its parts and enable the efficient movement of necessary goods and services. The development of this network occurred rapidly in the pre-Revolutionary period. Camden's situation along a major interior land route permitted shipment of products directly to Charleston. The Catawba Path was improved as far inland as Camden by 1755, and within the next five years the road was extended north to the Waxhaws.[32] By the 1770s, the backcountry road network also provided lateral connections in both directions from Camden, permitting the settlement access to a wide area. Although the Wateree River was navigable to Camden, its outlet on the coast near Georgetown required an uneconomical transfer of cargo to coastal vessels before reaching Charleston. Consequently, the volume of river traffic remained low.[33]

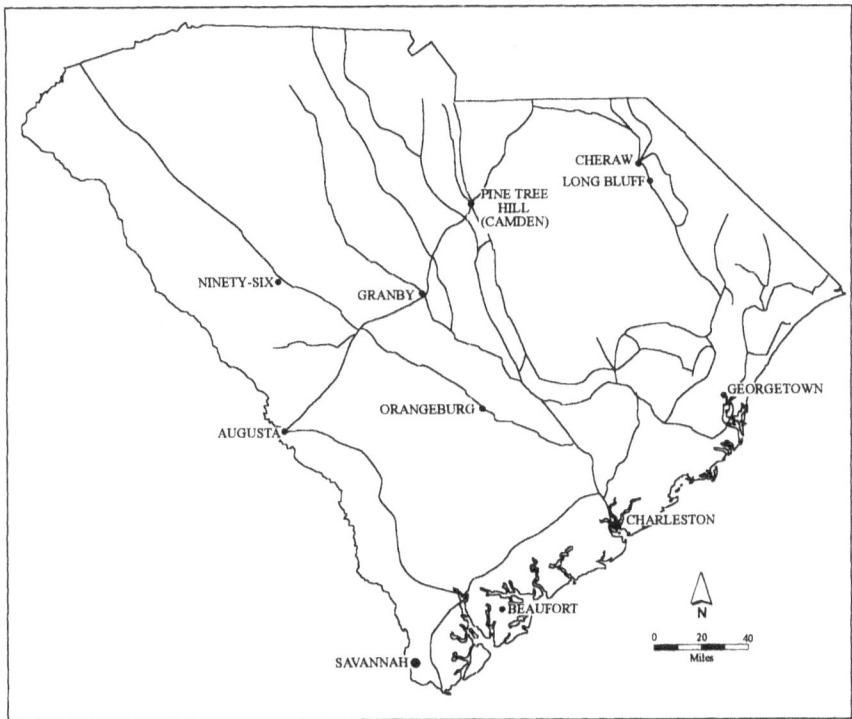

Map 6.2. The road network of the South Carolina backcountry and the locations of important settlements in the late frontier period. Adapted from Julian J. Petty, *The Growth and Distribution of Population in South Carolina* (Columbia: South Carolina State Planning Board, 1943; reprinted, Spartanburg, S.C.: The Reprint Co., 1975), 38. Used by permission.

Neither overland nor water transportation offered the South Carolina backcountry ideal access to entrepôt markets, and transportation improvement would be a dominant concern in the postcolonial economy.³⁴ The value of merchandise carried on the interior roads, however, was adequate to justify the cost of its shipment during the time of Camden's rise. Together with the processing infrastructure, the development of these overland routes supported the economic emergence of the backcountry and the distinctive development of its principal settlement.

Camden's Development in the Pre-Revolutionary Period

In the decade before the Revolution, Camden underwent considerable change as a result of its role as a frontier town in the South Carolina backcountry. The settlement underwent a transition from largely intra-regional redistributive activity to the collection, processing, and storage of staple exports. The 1760s saw the con-

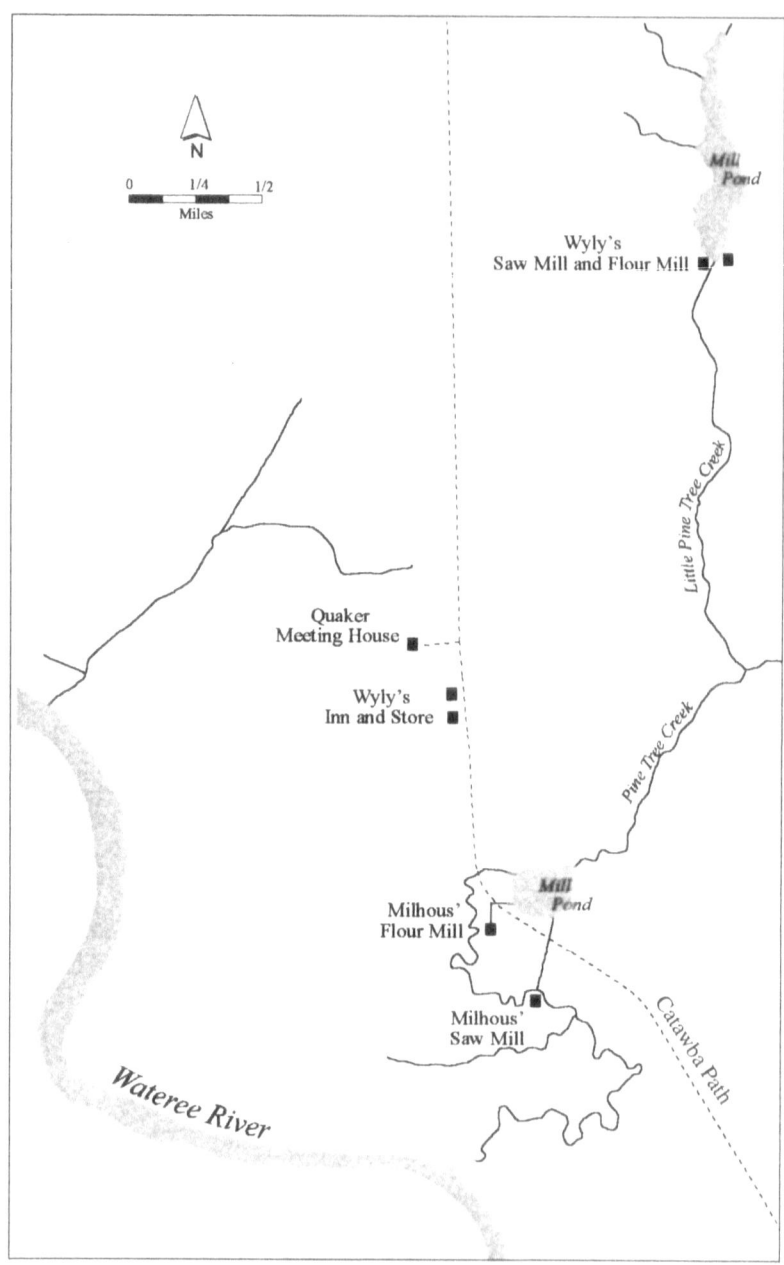

Map 6.3. European settlement at Pine Tree Hill before 1760. Adapted from Judith J. Schulz, "The Rise and Decline of Camden as South Carolina's Major Trading Center, 1751–1829: A Historical Geographic Study" (Master's thesis, University of South Carolina, 1972), 17. Used by permission.

struction of more mills, warehouses, and stores. Because of the wealth these activities engendered, the decade also witnessed an investment in various integrative institutions associated with nucleated settlements. Changes in the size, form, and composition of Pine Tree Hill/Camden during the first three decades of its existence reflected the development of such institutions and are discernible in the material remains, documents, and graphics pertaining to the settlement. Given that little above-ground evidence of early Camden exists, archaeological investigations carried out over portions of the townsite have been useful in providing information regarding its physical aspects.

Although portions of the site of Camden were granted as parts of large parcels in the 1740s and 1750s, the first settlement took place on Samuel Wyly's tract and consisted of his store and inn and the Quaker meeting house and cemetery.[35] These lay on the west side of the Catawba Path and are represented by the present Quaker cemetery and by archaeological remains lying directly to the east of it. The latter contained structural remains and assemblages of artifacts that indicate an occupation of that area prior to 1750 (map 6.3).[36]

Wyly's mills and those of fellow Quaker Robert Milhouse were built on streams removed from this nucleus but in close proximity to it, and they established a pattern of dispersed industrial development that would continue to characterize Camden.[37]

The settlement's rapid growth in the pre-Revolutionary period is revealed by archaeological evidence. Based on the distribution of structural debris and associated occupational refuse obtained in sample excavations of the townsite, a number of areas were defined. An analysis of temporally sensitive artifacts permitted the initial time of occupation of each of the latter to be determined and displayed graphically. The results produced a pattern indicating that a cluster of structures north of the initial settlement appeared in the 1750s, followed by an expansion over much of the intermediate area in the following decade. The occupation of the townsite was completed in the 1770s, at which time Joseph Kershaw's large house immediately east of Camden, a jail structure just north of the settlement, and a magazine on the southeastern edge of the town also had been constructed (map 6.4).[38]

The growth of the settlement and its concentration within a relatively confined area confirm suggestions in documentary sources that Pine Tree Hill expanded around the site of Kershaw's store on the Catawba Path. An examination of deeds revealed that the land the town occupied was in the hands of Joseph Kershaw or his mercantile partners. The archaeological remains of two stores, the locations of which correspond to properties owned by several of these individuals, were identified in the western half of the settlement.[39]

The form of the growing settlement also suggests the orderly growth dictated by a 1771 survey, which laid out the townsite on a grid pattern centered on a square that, in the 1770s, marked its northern extent (map 6.5).[40] Such a design controlled expansion and created a settlement the compactness of which permitted efficient access for economic activities as well as social interaction. The development of the

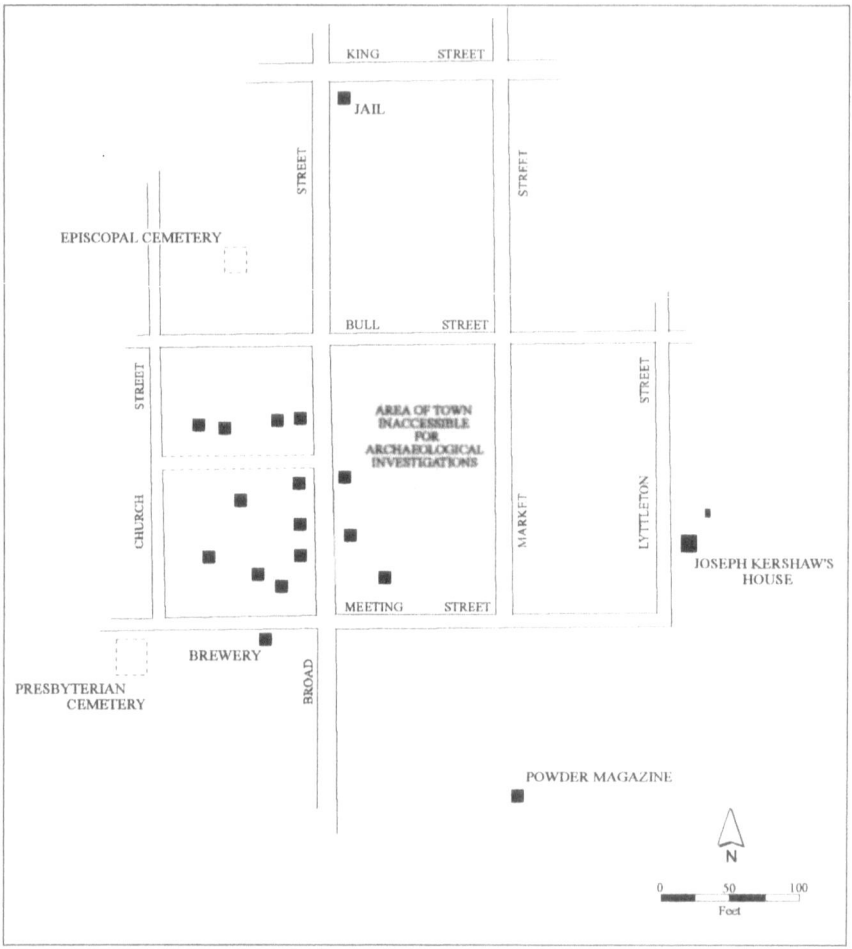

Map 6.4. Locations of eighteenth-century structures in Camden, as revealed by archaeological investigations. Adapted from Lewis, *American Frontier*, 254–55; Lewis, Kershaw House Site, 98; Lewis, Camden Jail and Market Site, 22; Calmes, "Fortifications at Camden," 51–55.

town along a grid pattern is evident not only in the archaeological data but also in a 1781 plan drawn at the time of Camden's occupation during the Revolutionary War (map 6.6).[41] This map clearly reveals a number of structures and outbuildings arranged in parallel with, or at right angles to, the Catawba Path and testifies to the role of planning in the growth of the settlement.

The use of a grid layout also permitted the incorporation of a variety of activities into the pre-Revolutionary community. Tracts allocated for the Anglican Church, a courthouse, a jail, a market, and a fairground reveal the settlement's acquisition of additional centralizing functions. Religious, political, and economic

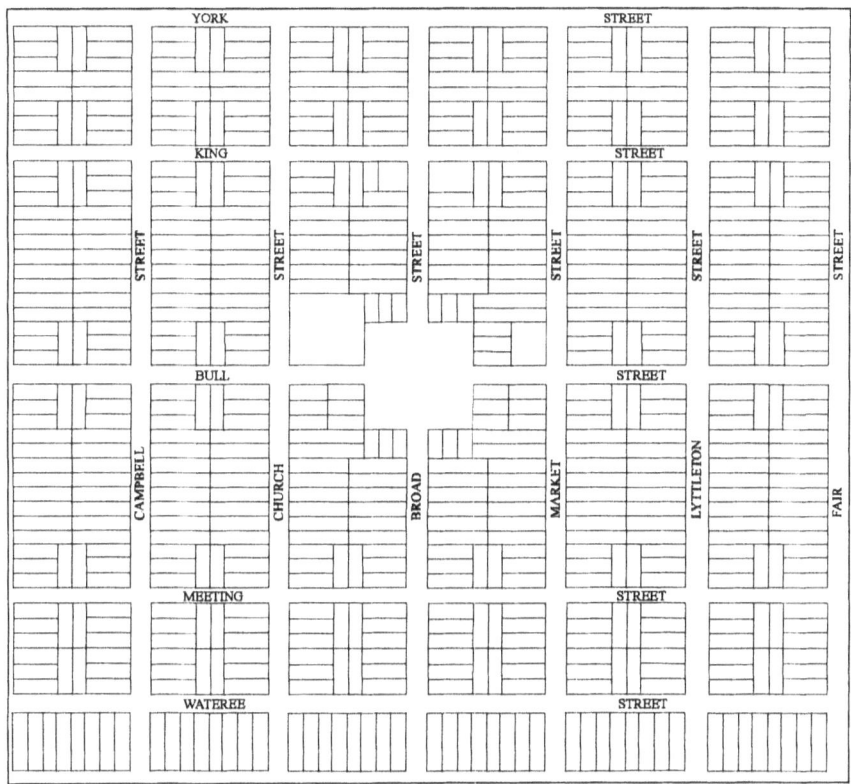

Map 6.5. Survey plan of Camden as laid out in 1771. The town was bisected by the Catawba Path, or Broad Street, which passed through the central square that marked the northern edge of the nucleated settlement. Adapted from Cooper, *Statutes*, 1798, Act 1702.

institutions all appeared in Camden in the early 1770s, reflecting its rapid development as the initial center of urban activities in the South Carolina backcountry.[42]

Camden's preRevolutionary War development was marked by the spread of diverse economic activities that accompanied its rise as an inland agricultural processing center. By the late 1770s, a tailor, a shoemaker, a lawyer, two blacksmiths, and at least three merchants carried on business in a settlement that also contained two taverns, a bakery, an inn, a brickyard, a brewery and distillery, and a pottery factory. The ceramics, manufactured there in quantity by expatriate British master potter John Bartlam, rivaled contemporary imported fine earthenwares and were distributed widely throughout the province.[43]

Camden's expansion and acquisition of ancillary activities are only part of the story of the settlement's growth and increasing importance. The town's prominence is also indicated by the extent to which its inhabitants increasingly invested in the material wealth of the community, a phenomenon expressed in the evolution of

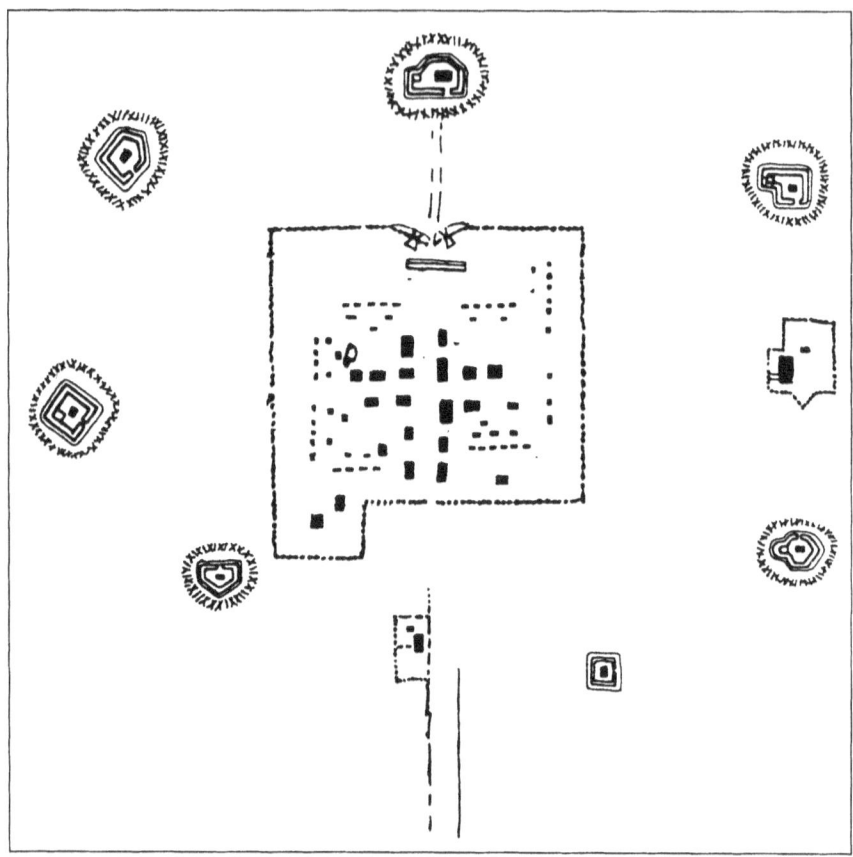

Map 6.6. Camden as a fortified settlement, 1780–81. The area lying within the palisade wall corresponds roughly to that enclosed by Bull, Market, Meeting, and Campbell streets. The brewery was situated in the extension at the southwestern corner of the wall. A number of redoubts surrounded the town. Several of these enclosed existing structures, including the jail to the north, Joseph Kershaw's mansion to the east, and the magazine to the southeast. From Nathaniel Greene Papers, Letters, 1774–89, Papers of the Continental Congress, Roll 175, 2, 161.

its architecture. Early structures at Pine Tree Hill mirrored the newness of settlement in the region and consisted of small log structures. Archaeological investigations in the town suggested that many of its structures were small wooden buildings with insubstantial foundations.[44] Even the 1771 courthouse was of rough-hewn construction.[45] The introduction of brick architecture in the 1770s, notably in large buildings incorporating contemporary high style, indicates an increase in capital investment for both public and private purposes. These buildings, which include Joseph Kershaw's house, the Camden jail, the Kershaw brewery, and the town magazine, were designed not only to carry out the utilitarian functions for which they were built, but also to advertise the social, political, and economic status of their builders and occupants.[46]

In the thirty years before the Revolution, Camden's development exhibited the characteristics of a settlement created by the growth of an export economy centered in the specialized production of grain for an outside market. The early location of mills in the vicinity of Pine Tree Hill to serve the regional backcountry economy provided an impetus for economic growth that led to the site's expansion, its enlargement as a planned settlement, and its acquisition of various urban functions. Camden's emergence as a frontier town in the 1770s marked its movement from the economic isolation of early settlement to a fuller participation in the larger colonial economy.

Conclusions

Camden developed successfully as a central settlement in the evolving frontier economy of South Carolina largely because of its accessibility and the decision by investors to develop its location as a focus of economic activity. *Accessibility* is important because the geographical situation of a frontier town must offer convenient transportation to the entrepôt and to the producers within the region it serves. The degree of accessibility is measured not only in distance, but also in ease of travel. Settlements connected by roads, navigable water, or easily traversed terrain offer greater access than those with intervening physical or social barriers.

Fredericksburg Township was situated along an established network of overland routes that tied it to the entrepôt of Charleston, as well as to a wide area encompassing several major river drainages. This network placed the township in a position central to settlement on the Broad, Saluda, and upper Pee Dee and Wateree rivers; most of this area was devoted to small farms which produced diversified food crops for consumption within the region. The Pine Tree Hill settlement emerged as a focal point for the milling of backcountry grain. In the absence of outside demand, its external commerce was restricted to the reshipment of products obtained in the Indian trade.

Pine Tree Hill's position in the regional economy of the backcountry was insufficient alone to bring about its subsequent development as a central settlement. This change was contingent upon an increasing external demand for wheat, a crop well suited to cultivation in the backcountry. A second condition necessary to exploit this demand was the *introduction of capital* to create an infrastructure capable of collecting, processing, and shipping this staple to the entrepôt. The development of a site as a center for export trade involved more than the reorientation of backcountry production. It introduced a higher level of external commerce that permitted the accelerated accumulation of wealth on the frontier—a process that not only encouraged the development of ancillary economic activities, but also supported the establishment of social and political institutions necessary to accommodate increasing growth and differentiation.

Access and capital investment serve to promote the development of frontier towns that serve as regional centers and as primary links between the area of colonization and the larger external economy. They are not, of course, the only factors that affect the form of colonization. Political, social, ideological, and environmental variables also may influence the patterning of settlement and activities on the frontier. The significance of access and investment, however, lies in the fact that they reflect the economic basis of agricultural colonization. They also demonstrate the importance of considering the *evolutionary* aspect of frontier economies when attempting to explain the form of agricultural colonization in a particular region.

A central point emphasized here is that the investigation of *single settlement components* holds substantial potential for studies of the regional systems of which they are a part. In this examination of a frontier town, it was possible to investigate aspects of the backcountry as a whole because of our knowledge of the role played by that type of settlement in a larger regional context. If one is aware of the structure of a regional system and the function of its parts, it should be possible to focus research on those components that will yield information concerning the question at hand. The obvious advantage, of course, is that a researcher can study large-scale processes without having to exhaust all potential sources and can investigate regional problems even if some information is unavailable or lost. To no one is this more beneficial than the archaeologist.

Settlement-oriented research has important implications for archaeology and other material culture studies. Because of the intensive character of its work, archaeology is by nature a site-specific activity. The expense and time involved in field work make extensive investigations lengthy and regional problems difficult to approach, unless such work can be concentrated where it is likely to yield data relating to something more than the conditions particular to one settlement. If such settlements are seen as components of larger integrated behavioral phenomena, then an assemblage of artifacts from one site may be employed to address a question of regional significance. Thus, the excavation of a Camden mill might reveal data pertaining to the specialization of backcountry production, or the analysis of pottery from that settlement's as-yet-undiscovered kilns might yield information about colonial industry and its competition with that of the homeland. Adopting a regional approach in archaeology requires the analysis and classification of settlements and an understanding of the operation of the systems of which they were a part. The results of such an approach promise to make archaeological findings more relevant to questions of wider historical interest and to enhance the contribution of material culture studies to our knowledge of the past.

Notes

I wish to thank several individuals for their assistance in the preparation of this article. The results of a regionally oriented study are difficult to convey without clear and accurate maps. Computer-generated graphics that appear with this article accomplish both these tasks and are the result of painstaking efforts by Frank Krist. The text has also benefited from the careful review and comments of David Colin Crass, Martha A. Zierden, and Steven D. Smith.

1. For general summaries of the development of the frontier as a concept for the explanation of European expansion and adaptation in the New World, see: William W. Savage, Jr., and Stephen I. Thompson, "The Comparative Study of the Frontier: An Introduction," in *The Frontier, Comparative Studies*, vol. 2, ed. William W. Savage, Jr., and Stephen I. Thompson, 3–24 (Norman: Univ. of Oklahoma Press, 1979); Kenneth E. Lewis, *The American Frontier: An Archaeological Study of Settlement Pattern and Process* (Orlando, Fla.: Academic Press, 1984), 8–27.
2. Jerome O. Steffen, *Comparative Frontiers: A Proposal for Studying the American West* (Norman: Univ. of Oklahoma Press, 1980), xii–xvii, introduced the terms "cosmopolitan" and "insular," respectively, to describe these two broad types of colonization. The distinction is based on the assumption that the nature of the colony is determined by the economic and political links it maintains with its homeland. The closer the ties, the lesser is the degree of insularity and the more responsive the nature of colonization is to external demands. Conversely, the greater the degree of insularity, the higher is the likelihood that the colony will develop economic interests divergent from those of the homeland, together with separate political institutions. Donald L. Hardesty, "The Evolution of the Industrial Frontier," in *The Archaeology of Frontiers and Boundaries*, ed. Stanton W. Green and Stephen M. Perlman, 213–15 (Orlando, Fla.: Academic Press, 1985), explored the concept of the cosmopolitan frontier further, in his examination of the evolution of industrial settlements in the American West. Employing concepts derived from cultural ecology, he emphasized the adaptiveness of cultural standardization and episodic development in regions with a low degree of isolation from outside influences.
3. Steffen, *Comparative Frontiers*, xii–xxiii, xvii–xviii, 23–25, viewed the insular frontier as a response to conditions exclusive to the region under settlement itself, factors that promoted fundamental indigenous change which is expressed in the colony's economic diversity, as well as in the development of distinct social and political institutions. Agricultural frontier change as a process in time and space is discussed by Joseph B. Casagrande, Stephen I. Thompson, and Philip D. Young, "Colonization as a Research Frontier," in *Process and Pattern in Culture: Essays in Honor of Julian H. Steward*, ed. Robert A. Manners, 283–84 (Chicago: Aldine, 1964). In their study of colonization in modern Ecuador, they introduced a model which linked the distribution and function of settlement to the conditions imposed by low population density, limited access, and inadequate infrastructure development in the area of colonization. Observed at any given time, a "colonization gradient" of increasing complexity is visible as one moves from the periphery toward the entrepôt connecting the colony to the homeland. The gradient also may exist over time in a single settlement, as the latter evolves toward greater complexity in response to the region's increasing level of sociocultural integration. Stephen I. Thompson explored pioneer adaptations to agricultural frontiers further in his *Pioneer Colonization: A Cross-Cultural View*, Addison-Wesley Modules in Anthropology 33 (Reading, Mass.: Addison-Wesley, 1973), 7.
4. Kenneth E. Lewis, *American Frontier*, 25–26.
5. Brian J. L. Berry, *Geography of Market Centers and Retail Distribution* (Englewood Cliffs, N.J.: Prentice-Hall, 1967), 33–34.

6. Casagrande, Thompson, and Young, "Colonization as a Research Frontier," 312–13.
7. Kenneth E. Lewis, *American Frontier*, 23.
8. Andrew Hill Clark, "Suggestions for the Geographical Study of Agricultural Change in the United States, 1790–1840," *Agricultural History* 46 (1972): 165, emphasized that the requirements of subsistence in a complex industrial society precluded the existence of self-sufficient colonies in British North America. Intensive regional studies of agricultural colonization, such as Robert D. Mitchell's examination of the Shenandoah Valley of Virginia, have revealed that initial colonization was motivated by the intent to enter commercial production and always was characterized by organized regional exchange. See Robert D. Mitchell, "The Shenandoah Valley Frontier," *Annals of the Association of American Geographers* 62 (1972): 475–76; Robert D. Mitchell, "The Commercial Nature of Frontier Settlement in the Shenandoah Valley of Virginia," *Proceedings of the Association of American Geographers* 1 (1969): 109–13; Robert D. Mitchell, *Commercialism and Frontier: Perspectives on the Early Shenandoah Valley* (Charlottesville: Univ. of Virginia Press, 1977), 4–6.
9. For a discussion of the nature of regional economics in early America, and esp. the role played by market forces, see Carole Shammas, "How Self-Sufficient Was Early America?" *Journal of Interdisciplinary History* 13 (1982): 252–53; James T. Lemon, "Household Consumption in Eighteenth-Century America and Its Relationship to Production and Trade: The Situation among Farmers in Southeastern Pennsylvania," *Agricultural History* 41 (1967): 59–70; Winifred B. Rothenberg, "The Market and Massachusetts Farmers, 1750–1855," *Journal of Economic History* 41 (1981): 283–313.
10. The distinctive nature of exchange in regional economies and its association with modes of production is discussed by Michael Merrill, "Cash Is Good to Eat: Self-Sufficiency and Exchange in the Rural Economy of the United States," *Radical History Review* 3 (1977): 52–54; Michael Merrill, "So What's Wrong with the 'Household Mode of Production'?" *Radical History Review* 22 (1979–80): 141–46. For further discussion of agrarian modes of production and their development in capitalist economies, see Harriet Friedmann, "Household Production and the National Economy: Concepts for the Analysis of Agrarian Reforms," *Journal of Peasant Studies* 7 (1980): 161–64.
11. Hill, "Farm Management," *Michigan History* 22 (1938): 312.
12. See Douglass C. North, *The Economic Growth of the United States, 1790–1860* (New York: Norton, 1966), 154, for a discussion of the role of infrastructure in the development of the American economy.
13. Carville Earle and Ronald Hoffman, "Staple Crops and Urban Development in the Eighteenth Century South," *Perspectives in American History* 10 (1976): 11, 67.
14. Lewis Cecil Gray, *The History of Agriculture in the Southern United States to 1860*, 2 vols. (Washington, D.C.: Carnegie Institute, 1933; reprinted, Gloucester, Mass.: Peter Smith, 1958), 286; Julian J. Petty, *The Growth and Distribution of Population in South Carolina* (Columbia: South Carolina State Planning Board, 1943; reprinted, Spartanburg, S.C.: The Reprint Co., 1975), 35.
15. Robert L. Meriwether, *The Expansion of South Carolina, 1729–1765* (Kingsport, Tenn.: Southern Publishers, 1940), 99.

16. South Carolina, Office of the Surveyor General, Colonial Plats, in Drawer 4, Folder 8, South Carolina Archives, Columbia.
17. Meriwether, *Expansion of South Carolina*, 102–4; Thomas J. Kirkland and Robert M. Kennedy, *Historic Camden*, vol. 1: *Colonial and Revolutionary* (Columbia, S.C.: State Printing Co., 1905), 67–71.
18. Judith J. Schulz, "The Rise and Decline of Camden as South Carolina's Major Trading Center, 1751–1829: A Historical Geographic Study" (Master's thesis, Univ. of South Carolina, 1972), 16–17.
19. Meriwether, *Expansion of South Carolina*, 106, 166–67; Richard J. Hooker, ed., *The Carolina Backcountry on the Eve of the Revolution: The Journal and Other Writings of Charles Woodmason, Anglican Itinerant*, with an introduction by Richard J. Hooker (Chapel Hill: Univ. of North Carolina Press, 1953), 7.
20. Petty, *Growth and Distribution of Population in South Carolina*, 57.
21. These distinctive ceramics appear to have been unique in the South. Representing an Eastern European tradition, these earthenwares were produced for use in the Moravian settlements in North Carolina, as well as for trade. Their manufacture continued through the eighteenth century, at which time they were superseded by the production of ceramics similar to the fine earthenwares made in Britain. For a discussion of the history of Moravian ceramic production, see John F. Bivens, Jr., *The Moravian Potters of North Carolina* (Chapel Hill: Univ. of North Carolina Press, 1972), 257; and Stanley South, "The Ceramic Forms of the Potter Gottfried Aust at Bethabara, North Carolina, 1755–1771," *Conference on Historic Site Archaeology, Papers* 1 (1967): 33–52. The appearance of Moravian ceramics in archaeological deposits at Pine Tree Hill was noted by Kenneth E. Lewis, *Camden: A Frontier Town in Eighteenth-Century South Carolina*, Anthropological Studies No. 2 (Columbia: South Carolina Institute of Archaeology and Anthropology, Univ. of South Carolina, 1976), 171.
22. Kirkland and Kennedy, *Historic Camden*, 1:77.
23. Ibid., 1:51.
24. Leila Sellers, *Charleston Business on the Eve of the American Revolution* (Chapel Hill: Univ. of North Carolina Press, 1934), 31; Joseph A. Ernst and Harry Roy Merrens, "The South Carolina Economy in the Eighteenth Century: A View from Philadelphia," *West Georgia College, Studies in the Social Sciences* 12 (1973): 19.
25. Ernst and Merrens, "South Carolina Economy," 24–25. For a summary of Joseph Kershaw's life and activities in South Carolina, and particularly at Camden, see Kirkland and Kennedy, *Historic Camden*, 1:376–81.
26. Meriwether, *Expansion of South Carolina*, 106; Kirkland and Kennedy, *Historic Camden*, 1:376.
27. Walter B. Edgar and N. Louise Bailey, *Bibliographical Directory of the South Carolina House of Representatives*, vol. 2: *The Commons House of Assembly, 1692–1775* (Columbia: Univ. of South Carolina Press, 1977) 385; Schulz, "Rise and Decline of Camden," 21, 23, 25–26; Judith J. Schulz, "The Hinterland of Revolutionary Camden, South Carolina," *Southeastern Geographer* 16 (1976): 93–94.
28. Hooker, *Carolina Backcountry*, 49.

29. *Boston Chronicle*, Dec. 5, 1768, quoted in "The Backcountry in the 1760s," in *The Colonial South Carolina Scene: Contemporary Views, 1697–1774*, ed. Harry Roy Merrens (Columbia: Univ. of South Carolina Press, 1977), 247; Harvey S. Teal, ed., *Rides about Camden, 1853 and 1873* (Columbia, S.C.: McDonald Letter Shop, 1961), 21.
30. Sellers, *Charleston Business*, 89.
31. Schulz, "Hinterland of Revolutionary Camden," 94–95.
32. Meriwether, *Expansion of South Carolina*, 106–7.
33. Schulz, "Rise and Decline of Camden," 18–20; Thomas J. Kirkland and Robert M. Kennedy, *Historic Camden*, vol. 2: *Nineteenth Century* (Columbia, S.C.: State Printing Co., 1926), 35–36.
34. David Kohn, *Internal Improvements in South Carolina, 1817–1828* (Washington: Published by the author, 1938).
35. Kirkland and Kennedy, *Historic Camden*, 1:78–81.
36. Kenneth E. Lewis, "Report of a Survey at the Southwest Redoubt and the Presbyterian Cemetery, Camden," on file with the Camden Historical Commission, Camden, S.C. (1983); Kenneth E. Lewis, *American Frontier*, 254–55.
37. Schulz, "Rise and Decline of Camden," 17, 26, 30.
38. Kenneth E. Lewis, *A Functional Study of the Kershaw House Site in Camden, South Carolina*, Research Manuscript Series 110 (Columbia: South Carolina Institute of Archaeology and Anthropology, Univ. of South Carolina, 1977), 98; Kenneth E. Lewis, "The Camden Jail and Market Site: A Report on Preliminary Investigations," in *Notebook* 16 (Columbia: South Carolina Institute of Archaeology and Anthropology, Univ. of South Carolina, 1984), 22; Alan Calmes, "The British Revolutionary War Fortifications at Camden, South Carolina," *Conference on Historic Site Archaeology, Papers* 2 (1968): 51–55.
39. The remains of at least two structures were found to be situated on tracts owned by John Adamson, Eli Kershaw, and John Chesnut, all of whom are known to have operated businesses in Camden. For a discussion of land ownership in Pine Tree Hill/Camden during the eighteenth century, see Kenneth E. Lewis, *Camden: A Frontier Town*, 53–61.
40. Thomas Cooper, ed., *Statutes at Large of South Carolina*, vol. 5 (Columbia, S.C.: A. S. Johnson, 1839), 1798, Act no. 1702.
41. Nathaniel Greene Papers, Letters, 1774–1789, Papers of the Continental Congress, Microfilm, Roll No. 175, Vol. 2, Item 161, South Carolina Archives, Columbia.
42. Kirkland and Kennedy, *Historic Camden*, 2:12–13; Joseph A. Ernst and Harry Roy Merrens, "'Camden's Turrets Pierce the Skies,' The Urban Process in the Southern Colonies," *William and Mary Quarterly* 3d ser. 30 (1973): 565.
43. Schulz, "Rise and Decline of Camden," 26, 29. For a discussion of Bartlam's ceramics recovered at Camden, see Kenneth E. Lewis, *Camden: A Frontier Town*, 132. Recent archaeological investigations by Stanley South at the site of Bartlam's earlier pottery factory at Cain Hoy, in Berkeley County, have revealed an extensive collection of his wares, which in turn has provided much information about the nature and extent of his production in South Carolina. An analysis of the Cain Hoy collections and a comparison to those

specimens found in Camden and the sites of other contemporary settlements is reported by Stanley South, *The Search for John Bartlam at Cain Hoy: America's First Creamware Potter*, 2 vols., Research Manuscript Series 219 (Columbia: South Carolina Institute of Archaeology and Anthropology, Univ. of South Carolina, 1993). See also Bradford L. Rauschenberg, "John Bartlam, Who Established 'New Pottworks in South Carolina' and Became the First Successful Creamware Potter in America," *Journal of Early Southern Decorative Arts* 17, no. 2 (1991): 1–66; Bradford L. Rauschenberg, "'A Clay White as Lime … of Which There Is a Design Formed by Some Gentlemen to Make China': The American and English Search for Cherokee Clay in South Carolina, 1745–75," *Journal of Early Southern Decorative Arts* 17, no. 2, (1991): 67–80; Bradford L. Rauschenberg, "Escape from Bartlam: The History of William Ellis of Hanley," *Journal of Early Southern Decorative Arts* 17, no. 2, (1991): 81–102.

44. Hooker, *Carolina Backcountry*, 7, 16; Kenneth E. Lewis, *Camden: A Frontier Town*, 107.
45. Richard Maxwell Brown, *The South Carolina Regulators* (Cambridge, Mass.: Belknap Press of the Harvard Univ. Press, 1963), 111.
46. Kenneth E. Lewis, *Kershaw House Site*, 38–42; Kenneth E. Lewis, "Camden Jail and Market Site," 25–31; Kenneth E. Lewis, *Camden: A Frontier Town*, 98; Calmes, "Fortifications at Camden."

"A Fer Ways Off from the Big House": The Changing Nature of Slavery in the South Carolina Backcountry

Monica L. Beck

The settlement of the South Carolina interior, an area commonly referred to as the backcountry, began after 1730. Pioneers migrated into the frontier via the Great Wagon Road from northern colonies and, within a relatively short period of time, prosperous economic centers were established. By the 1790s, the cultivation of short-staple cotton required a larger workforce than subsistence farming, a need that was satisfied by slave labor. This multiethnic experience, which transformed the South Carolina interior from a frontier economy of fur trading, husbandry, and subsistence farming into an expanding cash-crop economy, left an indelible mark upon the backcountry landscape.

This study explores the transition of a frontier farmstead into a prosperous cash-crop plantation. Archaeological and historical data from this late-eighteenth to early-nineteenth-century backcountry plantation, today known as Historic Brattonsville, are used to examine elements of culture change. Through this examination, I trace the changing relationship between master and slave. This cultural transformation is illustrated in spatial and architectural changes within the original frontier period farmstead, as compared with the later antebellum plantation. Using interpretive theories developed by folklorist Henry Glassie and archaeologists James Deetz and Mark Leone, we can see how architecture and plantation layout express social order and reinforce the institution of slavery.[1]

As Deetz notes, the homeplace "reflect[s] the shared beliefs and behavior of [its] owners and users, . . . [and] embodies the worldview of the society at large."[2] Thus, architecture, use of space, and landscape can be used to investigate and interpret social organization and cultural beliefs. Patterns of segmentation, control over nature, and spatial order that are visible in the archaeological record reflect social relationships and worldview during life. Additionally, the proximity of particular structures, such as slave cabins to the main house, should reflect relationships between landowners and their slaves. Analysis of these house patterns allows us to draw inferences regarding the institution of slavery in the backcountry.

Folk Versus a Georgian Worldview

As units of analysis, households include not only the inhabitants and their behavior, but the structures, use of interior and exterior space, and placement of buildings on the landscape. According to Michael Ann Williams, "The house is 'home,' the center of family life. It is the container of social activity and a cultural symbol ... study of spatial use provides insight into both the social and symbolic nature of the dwelling. Spatial use represents a system of culturally transmitted ideas, including ideas about both the nature of space and the nature of social relationships."[3] These culturally transmitted relationships, or worldview, define what the appropriate hierarchical interactions should be between people within society and their surroundings.

The structuralist approach to archaeology and vernacular architecture, pioneered by Glassie and built upon by Deetz and Leone, was developed to infer a nineteenth-century worldview.[4] Binary choices broadly represent the opposition between culture and nature, since, as Deetz summarizes it, "material culture is the prime mediator between people and the natural world."[5] Components of houses, such as stone or brick fireplaces, naturally weathered siding or white paint, and floor plans, illustrate the mediation of widespread unconscious cultural rules. Glassie argues for a transition from choices favoring nature in the early 1700s, which exemplified the continuation of communal folkways, to opposing choices in the early 1800s, which represented the desire to dominate nature and exemplified a new, controlling, private, individual, and segmented mindset. The transition from folk asymmetric design and cultural view to a formal, controlled, symmetrical design that culminated in a Georgian architectural style and worldview was documented by Glassie.[6] Building on the structuralist interpretations of Glassie, Deetz argues for a set of conditions consisting of symmetry, segmentation, and standardization that constitutes a Georgian worldview.[7] Leone continues to develop this approach by focusing on the extent and reflexive nature of Georgian worldview at a local level.[8]

These models provide a theoretical framework to explore the appearance of a Georgian worldview at the local level of an individual homeplace. As Deetz notes, the acceptance of a Georgian worldview marked a striking change in the relationships "among the individual, his family, his house, and his community."[9] The appearance of Georgian traits is thus interpreted to signal cultural change through the abandonment of folk traditions. This study focuses on the extent of segmentation, asymmetrical versus symmetrical architectural design, spatial patterns of outbuildings, and historical evidence of domestic self-sufficiency versus a more active participation in the market economy, to track this changing worldview.

Previous Backcountry Plantation Research

Although the archaeological study of African American slave material culture is a relatively new pursuit, interest in the large homes of the "Old South" began as early as the 1930s.[10] The emergence of plantation archaeology has paralleled developments in historic archaeology. Initial historic archaeology focused on early European settlements in the New World, such as Williamsburg, Plymouth, Saint Augustine, Brunswick Towne, Charles Towne, and Santa Elena.[11] Similarly, plantation archaeology started with magnificent homes of the wealthy and famous, such as Monticello,[12] Kingsmill,[13] the Hermitage,[14] and Kingsley Plantation.[15]

The archaeological investigation of ethnic groups and non-elites resulted from the turbulent years of political and civil unrest during the 1960s and 1970s. The rising voices of minorities, largely represented by the African American community, forced the recognition that history was not a singular European American experience. Federal laws, such as the National Historic Preservation Act, combined with pressure from African Americans, compelled "bureaucrats and archaeologists alike ... to consider African American archaeological sites as sources of information important to history."[16] This newly created interest in documenting the "history of the inarticulate" initiated the archaeological study of African Americans.[17]

Initial archaeological research in South Carolina focused on the large rice plantations of the coastal lowcountry. These studies contributed to our knowledge of large, cash-crop plantations,[18] as well as African American slave life.[19] However, the majority of South Carolinians lived on small farmsteads and plantations located in the interior of the state. As Joseph observes, "Given the size of the upcountry, these plantations were certainly more numerous than those of the coast, but upcountry cotton plantations have not been archaeologically studied as intently as the coastal rice plantations."[20]

Although backcountry archaeological research is not abundant, excavation has been conducted in various counties of the region. Farmstead and plantation research includes residences ranging in occupation dates from the frontier to postbellum periods. Initial research, primarily conducted in the mid-1970s and early 1980s, investigated the time of occupation and the spatial layout of existing homes and yards, such as the Howser House (ca. 1803) in King's Mountain State Historic Site,[21] Redcliffe Plantation State Historic Site (ca. 1850s) in Aiken County,[22] Rosemont Plantation (ca. 1850s) in Laurens County,[23] the frontier town of Camden,[24] and the Bratton House outbuildings (ca. 1820s) in York County.[25] By the mid-1980s, larger projects included those at Millwood Plantation (ca. 1860s) in Abbeville County,[26] Allen Plantation and Clinkscales Farm (ca. 1890s) in Abbeville County,[27] Finch Farm (ca. 1890s) in Spartanburg County,[28] Lethe Farm (ca. 1770s) in McCormick County,[29] New Windsor Township (ca. 1730s) in Aiken County,[30] and Saxe-Gothe Township (ca. 1730s) in Lexington County.[31] These investigations, as well as master's and doctoral research, focused on the ethnic composition of backcountry residents and the transition of the backcountry from frontier to modern occupation.[32]

Of this research, four projects were successful in uncovering artifacts and features clearly associated with backcountry African Americans.[33] Groover's work uncovered the remains of a 1780s slave kitchen at the Howell Plantation, originally located in the Saxe-Gotha Township.[34] He explored the interaction between Europeans and African American slaves by identifying the creolized practices of African and European folk traditions. Kenion's work focused on one of the antebellum slave dwellings at Historic Brattonsville and contributed to our knowledge of the material culture of African Americans.[35]

Research by Crass et al. at the frontier township of New Windsor also unearthed the remains of an African American dwelling. Post molds, roughly five feet apart, indicate the presence of a structure measuring approximately 14.1 by 9.8 feet in diameter. There was no evidence of a chimney, but inside the cabin were the remains of a small hearth in the earthen floor. Artifacts recovered from an associated refuse pit suggest a forty- to fifty-year occupancy.[36]

At Millwood Plantation, Orser used the spatial location of tenant farm houses to argue for postbellum power relations between landowners and free tenant farmers.[37] Orser explored late antebellum slave dwelling size and artifacts, and investigated the continuity of power relations beyond slavery.[38] One structure, near James E. Calhoun's antebellum home, is considered to be the residence of Caroline Walker "Calhoun," Calhoun's long-time house servant.[39] Despite a promising start, the creolized culture that developed as a result of frontier interaction is still poorly documented.

Historic Context

The South Carolina interior historically has been referred to as the *backcountry*. During the eighteenth century, this term referred to the land west of the nineteen coastal parishes. As settlement grew in the area just above the fall line, the concept of the backcountry changed. By the 1790s, new terms, such as *mid-country* and *upcountry*, were used to distinguish regional differences within the backcountry.[40] Presently, these terms often are used interchangeably. However, I shall use the term *backcountry* to refer to the interior as a whole, while the term *upcountry* will be used to refer to the northwestern portion of the South Carolina backcountry.

Although several ethnic groups settled the backcountry, the majority of pioneers were Scots-Irish entering the South Carolina interior through inland routes from northern colonies. Living as squatters, these pioneers began clearing land to build log cabins and raise subsistence crops. The log cabin has become an icon representing frontier life. A study of American log construction determined that this particular form of architecture originated in northern Europe and appeared in America as early as 1650.[41] This construction type soon was adopted by immigrants passing through northern colonies and was used on the Carolina frontier.

These pioneers migrated from established colonies where labor demands were satisfied through indentured servitude and slavery. In the late 1600s, African slaves lived and worked alongside Native American slaves and European indentured servants. African slaves long had been in contact with Native Americans. Essentially pioneers, African slaves interacted with Native Americans in daily colonial life and in hunting and trading ventures. Peripheral Native American communities were obvious refuges for runaway slaves. As relations between Native Americans and Europeans disintegrated, African American slaves were likely to benefit from Native American contact, due to the low status they both possessed. The absorption of Native American culture and knowledge made African slaves important mediators for European backcountry settlers.[42] As late as the 1720s, Africans and Native Americans continued to share quarters.[43]

By 1730, the slave population of the lowcountry numbered almost twice the population of free European residents.[44] The possibility of slave rebellion, combined with the colony's vulnerability to Indian attacks, created considerable anxiety among Charles Town leaders. In contrast, pioneers in the South Carolina backcountry brought few, if any, slaves with them. Inventories recorded in 1754–74 indicate that the wealthiest of upcountry planters owned, on average, only eight slaves.[45] Yeoman farmers typically were not slave holders, although some did own one slave. By the mid-1760s, African American slaves represented only 8 percent of the backcountry population.

The majority of backcountry settlers established stable farmsteads, occasionally assisted by one or two slaves. Initial survival, including clearing land, building houses, and hunting, necessitated interracial cooperation.[46] Wood refers to the "case of a Huguenot named Elias Horry who ... took up land among other French refugees near the Santee River ... and worked many days with a Negro man at the Whip saw."[47] On farmsteads or small plantations, masters and slaves shared interconnected lives.

The small number of slaves owned by backcountry farmers made impossible isolated, self-contained African American communities like the large African American slave communities on the rice plantations of the lowcountry. Instead, the backcountry slave community was larger, extended far beyond the plantation boundaries, and operated as a "wider, underground spiritual and social community."[48] Intimate relationships among Europeans, Native Americans, and African Americans developed and were to some degree tolerated on the backcountry frontier. Often wives and children from mixed marriages were afforded the lifestyle and status of free whites;[49] in rare instances, these relationships meant freedom, considering that "one-third of all recorded colonial manumissions were mulatto children and three-fourths of all adult manumissions were females."[50]

Gideon Gibson and his descendants in Craven County (present day York County) are an example of a family with a culturally mixed ancestry that passed into free white society. Gibson, a free person of color, was a carpenter from Virginia. After explaining his family's presence in the South Carolina upcountry to the governor in 1731, Gibson's wife and children were classified as "white." With the labor of seven slaves, Gibson established a 1,100-acre plantation and became a prominent leader in the Regulator movement.[51]

Social tolerance in the backcountry became strained with the onset of the profitable cultivation of short-staple cotton in the late 1790s. Racism was the defining element forcing the "Negro" classification on those with any Native American or African heritage. Charles Ball, a slave on a large plantation in the early 1800s, addressed the nature of slave-owner relationships by noting the underlying injustice of bondage: "The slave sees his master residing in a spacious mansion, riding in a fine carriage, and dressed in costly clothes, and attributes the possession of all these enjoyments to his own labor; whilst he who is the cause of so much gratification and pleasure to another, is himself deprived of even the necessary accommodations of human life."[52]

By the 1760s, settlers of the South Carolina backcountry struggled with the process of maturing from a rugged frontier existence to a more organized social community. This region was caught between independent local leaders, who attempted to organize and control settlers, hunters, traders, squatters; and the growing "Gangs of Rogues . . . composed of Runaway negroes, free mulattoes and other mix'd Blood" who inhabited the frontier.[53] Strong yet fiercely independent upcountry leaders worked to extract greater governmental representation, walking the fine line between government intervention and the existing vigilante Regulator system of law and justice.[54] As will be discussed below, it was in this social and political milieu that William Bratton bought land in the South Carolina upcountry.

Archaeological Investigation at Historic Brattonsville

Historic Brattonsville (38YK21), located in York County, South Carolina, provides an excellent setting for investigating cultural continuity and change within three generations of one family. Beginning as a small farmstead in the 1770s, the Bratton estate eventually became an affluent antebellum plantation in the upcountry. The original log house was constructed by Col. William Bratton and his wife Martha between 1774 and 1780. Within eight years after their deaths, William and Martha's youngest son, Dr. John Simpson Bratton, and his wife Harriett began the construction of their own home, located on an elevated knoll across the road. It was during John and Harriett's lifetime that the Bratton homeplace expanded from a subsistence farmstead into an estate that included a thriving short-staple cotton plantation. They also incorporated a medical practice, a female academy, and a mercantile operation. In 1870, after the Civil War, Napoleon Bonaparte Bratton, the youngest child of John and Harriett Bratton, reopened the Brattonsville General Store. Prior to the Civil War, Napoleon and his wife, Minnie Mason, lived in a large frame house built north of his father's house. After choosing to become a merchant rather than a planter, "Bona" and Minnie moved into a brick structure next to the frame store.[55]

The preservation of Historic Brattonsville began in 1974, with the intention of preserving and restoring the six extant structures for the public. These structures include Col. William Bratton's frontier-period log house, the antebellum house, a doctor's office, a brick slave cabin, the general store, and another brick structure used as a store, post office, and dwelling. Three of these structures—the frontier house, the antebellum house, and the doctor's office—are owned by the York County Historic Commission and have been renovated to interpret the Bratton family's upcountry experience during the frontier and antebellum period. Historic Brattonsville is operated as a living history museum, which includes raising sheep and pigs, subsistence gardening, and cotton cultivation. "De Brattons was always sheep raisers," commented Jim Henry, a former slave who had been owned by Colonel Bratton's grandson, Gen. John Bratton of Winnsboro, "and us had woolen blankets and clothes in de winter."[56]

The antebellum spatial and architectural patterns are well preserved at Historic Brattonsville and offer a unique opportunity to study the transition from a subsistence farmstead to a cash-crop plantation. However, as there are no extant structures associated with the frontier-period house, an original landscape painting aided in reconstructing the antebellum landscape (fig. 7.1). The painter, thought to be Martha Bratton, granddaughter of Col. William Bratton, appears to have completed the painting in the early 1840s. Although artists may exercise creative license, the positions of existing structures depicted in the painting suggest that the rendition of the plantation landscape is fairly accurate.

Of particular interest was the depiction of a small log cabin in the far left corner of the painting. This small outbuilding is located next to the Colonel Bratton house, which had been freshly renovated with clapboard siding in the 1840s for use as a girls' school. This painting provides the only known historic reference to any outbuilding associated with this early residence. These ephemeral structures are typically difficult to locate, but the painting indicated an area that could be tested archaeologically. Therefore, to establish the early farmstead spatial pattern, archeological investigation was conducted to locate this outbuilding.

EVIDENCE FOR THE PRESENCE OF A STRUCTURE

Images of upcountry slave dwellings emerge from existing buildings, ex-slave narratives, and archaeological and historical research. Charlie Robinson, an ex-slave from Winnsboro, South Carolina, commented that they "Had good 'nough houses, though they was made of logs,'cup and saddled' at both ends, and covered wid white oak board shingles. Had stick and mud chimneys."[57] The majority of upcountry slave cabins were of log construction with plank wood or dirt floors and had wood shingled roofs. Bill Williams, of Blackstock, South Carolina, stated, "Us lived in rows of log houses, a path 'twixt de two rows. Us lived close to de spring, where us got water and mammy did de white folks washin' every week. We had a good rock chimney to our house, plank floors, movable bedsteads wid good wheat straw ticks, and cotton pillows."[58] Some dwellings had mud and stick chimneys, while other chimneys were constructed from rock or

Fig. 7.1. Painting of the Bratton Plantation, ca. 1840s. Reproduced with the permission of the Historical Center of York County and the York County Historical Commission, York, S.C.

brick. Josephine Stewart, also born on a plantation in Blackstock, South Carolina, explained in her WPA interview, "Us lived in Marse Wade's quarter, to the east of de white folks' house. Dere was a row of log houses, 'bout ten I think. Mammy and me lived in one dat had two rooms. De chimney was made of sticks and mud, but de floor was a good plank floor."[59]

By the mid-1800s, most slave houses were one-room cabins occupied by one family, although multifamily structures still existed. Aleck Woodward, born in Woodward Station, South Carolina, described the house he lived in as a four-room log house occupied by approximately sixteen people. As he explained, "Well, dat's de number piled in dere at night in de beds and on de floors. They was scandlous beds; my God, just think of my grands, old as I is now, tryin to sleep on them hard beds and other folks piled 'scriminately all over de log floors! My Gran'pappy Henry was de carpenter, and old marster tell him 'if you make your beds hard, Henry,' 'member you folks got to sleep on them.'"[60]

Slave dwellings had a minimum of furniture, pieces so mundane that only basic human needs were served. "All us had was a table, benches, and beds," Zack Herndon, an ex-slave born at the Herndon plantation outside Union, South Carolina, summed it up.[61] He explained further, "My paw made benches fer us to set by the fire on [and] we had a large plank table dat paw made. Never had no sech things as dressers in dem days. Never had no mirrors. Went to de spring to see ourselfs on a Sunday morning."[62]

At Historic Brattonsville, existing structures provide evidence that in the mid-1800s slaves working in association with the antebellum house, such as house servants and skilled artisans, lived in one-room brick dwellings with raised plank floors and brick chimneys. Unknown, however, are the location and type of houses occupied by the Brattons' slaves on the small frontier farmstead of the late 1770s. The 1840s painting depicts a small cabin located next to the Colonel Bratton house. This cabin appears to be of log construction, with a brick chimney and a small shed addition (fig. 7.1).

From archaeological fieldwork conducted in 1994, the location and use of the cabin were confirmed in the area denoted in the painting, which is between fifty and seventy feet north of Colonel Bratton's house (map 7.1). Archaeological evidence recovered from test units and block excavation indicates the existence and location of this building. This evidence consists of domestic artifacts, a refuse pit, and architectural artifacts such as nails, flat glass, bricks, and stone piers, combined with features including a brick-salvaging area and the remains of stone piers.

The number and types of nails recovered from excavation provide a picture of the building form and construction. A relatively low frequency of recovered nails and nail fragments, compared to other documented slave cabins, indicates that the cabin was of log construction.[63] The high frequency of siding, sheathing, and flooring nails suggests that siding may have been added to the exterior of the original structure after creation of the 1840s painting, which depicts it as a log structure (fig. 7.1). Moreover, the nail assemblage indicates that the log cabin, situated on stone piers, had a raised, wooden plank floor and a shingle roof. Further supporting the presence of a wood floor is the absence of a substructural, prepared-clay floor, even though, as ex-slave Bill Williams commented, "Other folks' slaves was complainin' 'bout dirt floors in de houses, boards to sleep on, no ticks, and rags for pillows" as late as the mid-1800s.[64]

The 1840s painting does not depict any windows in the north wall of the cabin. A low frequency of excavated flat glass indicates that, if the cabin had windows elsewhere, these did not hold glass panes. However, it is likely that the cabin had no windows at all, especially given the description of Josephine Stewart, born on a plantation in Blackstock, South Carolina, who commented, "Dere was no windows in de house, so it was warm in de winter and blue blazing hot in de summer time."[65]

Fireplaces were the focal point within slave cabins, not only for heat and light, but also for cooking meals. Zack Herndon, from Union, South Carolina, recalled, "Pots biled in de back o' de chimney a hanging from a pot rack over de blazing fire. Had plenty wood fer fire and pine knots fer lights when de fire git low or stop blazing."[66] Commonly, chimneys were constructed of mud and sticks, local rock, and brick. Alexander Robertson, an ex-slave born at the Stewart plantation in Winnsboro, commented, "On dat plantation was many two-room houses, brick chimneys in de middle, for de plantation slaves."[67] The chimney of the cabin depicted in the 1840s painting appears to be a red-clay color with fine lines suggesting layered courses of brick. The concentration of brick fragments recovered from

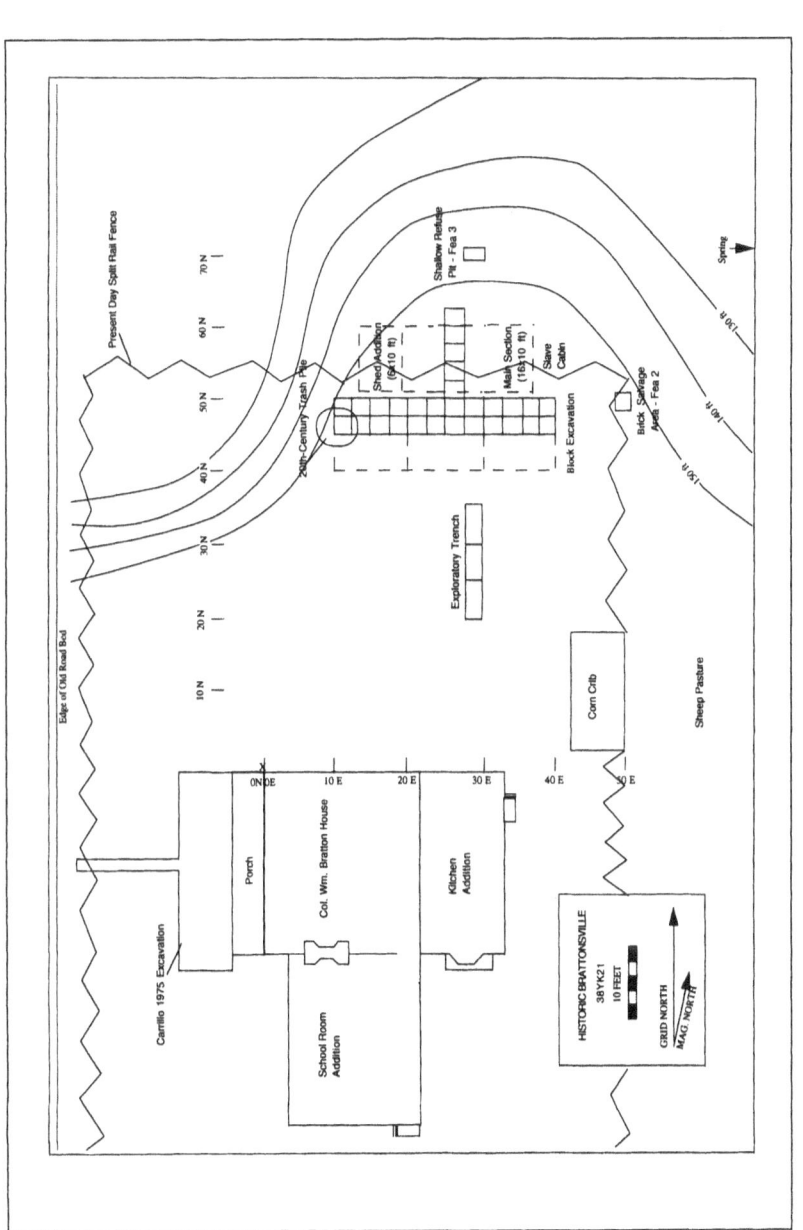

Map 7.1. Site location map, Historic Brattonsville, York County, South Carolina.

the cabin area, combined with a nearby brick-salvaging feature, created when the chimney was torn down, indicates that the cabin had a brick chimney along the east wall, as represented in the 1840s painting (fig. 7.1).

Domestic Artifact Density and Feature Pattern

The archaeological study of plantations, including slave dwellings and activity areas, the overseers' house, and the main house complex, has focused on uncovering material patterns that would differentiate the various residences and outbuildings from each other.[68] Even so, differences in material patterns are not always clear. In particular, Lewis and Haskell state that, "despite cultural differences which should be evident in the archaeological record, the living standards of white overseers were not much above those of their African charges."[69] More commonly, research has demonstrated that material patterns of planters, white or black slave overseers, free blacks or whites, and Native American sites are similar or overlap in particular artifact classes. These distinctions are all the more obscure at small farmsteads characteristic of frontier settlement. However, archaeological research combined with historic documentary sources, interpretive theory, and ethnohistoric accounts has achieved success in locating and investigating slave dwelling sites.

Colono Ware, a low-fired, hand-built earthenware, while manufactured by both Native Americans and African Americans, has been recovered in significant amounts from slave contexts, particularly in South Carolina and Virginia.[70] Ferguson successfully has argued that a portion of these sherds, previously classified as Colono-Indian ware, likely were produced by African American slaves.[71] Considering the existence of an African pottery tradition, hand-built earthenware pottery would have been a familiar and welcome cooking and serving vessel to enslaved Africans.

High frequencies of Colono Ware are recovered primarily from large rice plantations in the South Carolina lowcountry, "where most African Americans lived relatively isolated lives in largely black communities."[72] The low frequencies of Colono Ware recovered from North Carolina and Georgia have been attributed to the predominant presence of self-sufficient farmsteads of the colonial period.[73] Similarly, the colonial South Carolina upcountry was characterized by small self-sufficient farmsteads.

Currently, six upcountry farmsteads and plantations have been archaeologically tested, and their ceramic assemblages have significantly lower frequencies of Colono Ware than the volume recovered at lowcountry sites.[74] By the early 1800s, archaeological evidence indicates a decline in the use and manufacture of plantation-produced Colono Wares, and an increased use of European ceramics.[75]

Crude and poorly made pottery recovered from early South Carolina lowcountry slave sites was easily differentiated from the higher quality pottery made by the Catawba Nation. Catawba pottery is relatively thin-walled and burnished. However, as African American slaves became accustomed to the local clays, the craftsmanship of their pottery improved. Therefore, sherds that are relatively thin and burnished are simply classified as River Burnished, rather than assigning them an ethnic affiliation.[76] The ethnic affiliation of the Colono Ware potter often is difficult to determine; this does not, however, negate the correlation between Colono Ware and African American sites.

Researchers have begun investigating "African" usage of the predominantly European materials found at slave sites.[77] A high frequency of bowl-shaped vessels has been found at African American sites. At Cannon's Point Plantation in the Georgia Sea Islands, Otto noted that 44 percent of tableware recovered from nineteenth-century slave quarters consisted of serving bowls, while Drucker and Anthony also documented that 44 percent of tablewares recovered from the early nineteenth-century Spiers Landing site were bowls.[78]

Ethnoarchaeological research of West African foodways indicates that meals commonly consist of a main starchy food served in large bowls. This main food often is picked up by hand and dipped into small bowls of spicy sauces. Beverages are consumed from small bowls or gourds. Ferguson comments, "In the archaeological record, this West African pattern of foodways would leave many fragments of small bowls as well as sherds of cooking pots."[79]

Artifacts relevant to this study are those indicating that the structure was occupied as a dwelling. Domestic items indicating a household include Foodways artifacts such as ceramics, glassware, ammunition, and faunal remains; clothing and personal items.[80] The distribution of domestic trash recovered from shovel test pits was plotted by frequency and, as expected, a dense concentration is present in the area of the cabin. However, the most interesting aspect of the domestic artifact pattern is a diagonal concentration connecting the back entrance of the Colonel Bratton house, thought to have been the kitchen, to a "doorway" depicted in the 1840s painting of the proposed outbuilding (map 7.2). This "walkway" pattern is interpreted to reflect interaction between the two structures. The distribution of ceramic refuse alone reflects the diagonal pattern, which likely was the result of dishes being carried back and forth between the two structures. Zack Herndon explained that his job "As house-boy dar, I mind de flies from de table and tote dishes to and fro from de kitchen"[81]

A shallow refuse pit was detected only six feet to the north of the cabin remains (map 7.1). Seventy-five percent of the artifacts recovered in this feature were related to foodways, consisting of ceramics, Colono Ware, glassware, glass bottles, and faunal remains. The percentage of bowl-shaped vessels recovered from the shallow refuse pit is 92 percent of identifiable vessels, or eleven out of twelve vessels. The Mean Ceramic Date calculated for the ceramic assemblage is 1796 and the bracketed occupation date range is 1765 to 1820. Pipe fragments and clothing artifacts such as a decorated brass buckle, a bone button, and a faceted glass jewel button also were recovered from this feature (fig. 7.2).

Based on recovered information, the small cabin located next to the Colonel Bratton house most likely was occupied as a slave dwelling and secondary kitchen.

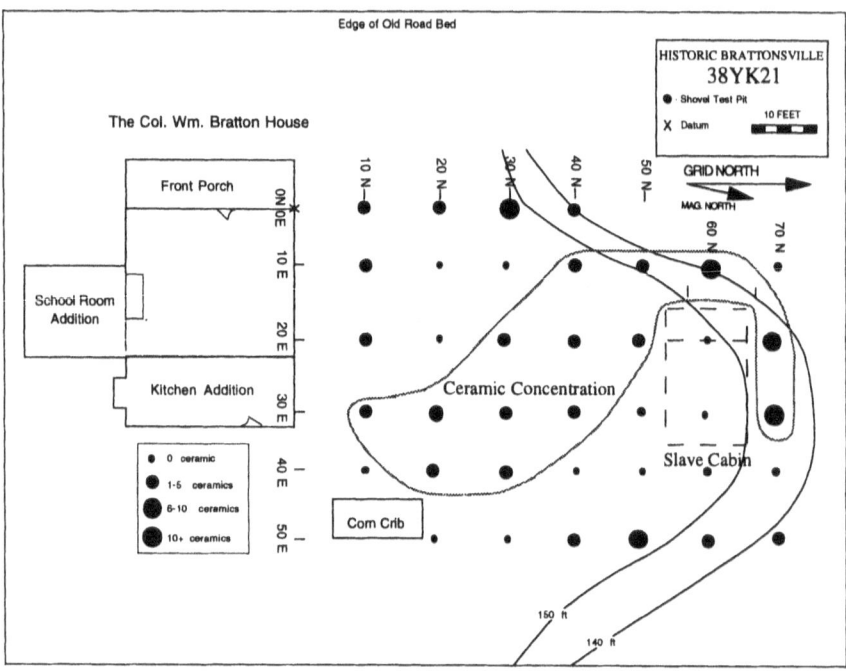

Map 7.2. Distribution of ceramics recovered from shovel tests, by count.

This conclusion is supported by (1) the high proportion of foodways artifacts from the yard midden around the cabin and the refuse pit, (2) the Mean Ceramic Date calculated from the ceramics, (3) the presence of Colono Ware, which was recovered only in this area, (4) a high frequency of bowl-shaped vessels, and (5) the presence of personal artifacts. Establishing the location and function of this early slave cabin (ca. 1790) allowed the investigation of the continuity of folk, vernacular, and spatial traditions at the early Bratton farmstead.

Continuity of Folk Traditions

The Bratton's frontier-period house, initially constructed of log in the mid-1770s, displays material and spatial elements that demonstrate a continuity of folk traditions. Consistent with other Scots-Irish homes, the Bratton house is an example of folk vernacular design. Deetz explains that a vernacular building is one that is constructed without the use of formal or "academic" plans.[82] These structures "are the immediate product of their users and form a sensitive indicator of these persons'... ideas of what is or is not suitable to them."[83]

The original portion of this house was a rectangular, single-pen room with opposing front and back entrances (map 7.1). This layout is similar to that of houses in northern and western Ireland and Scotland. Functionally, this floor plan created ventilation for the chimney and guided the direction of livestock when farmers and their animals lived under the same roof.[84] However, the front door of the Bratton home is not in the center of the façade, but rather is north, or to the left, of center. The position of the chimney also is off-center. Consistent with vernacular construction, house design was based on need or convenience.[85] In this case, the offset chimney and doorway allowed room for a corner stairwell.

A room used as the kitchen was added in the rear, probably before 1780.[86] Other Scots-Irish families used interior kitchens until it became the practice to build safer detached kitchens in the early 1800s.[87] The choice to expand the rear of the house is another example of folk design. Since the Brattons' land extended behind the house, a rear kitchen probably provided direct access to the garden and backyard activities related to meal preparation. While additions on either side of the house would have made the house look bigger, it was most likely easier to add a room underneath the existing roof eaves.

The asymmetrical design of this house is characteristic of vernacular or folk tradition.[88] The single-pen house, or the lack of interior room segmentation, is a significant indicator of an adherence to folk tradition. Interior evidence suggests that the kitchen addition was divided into two rooms at one time. An existing window on the northern side of the addition, not depicted in the painting (fig. 7.1), most likely was added to allow light into one of the newly created rooms. This suggests that the addition was partitioned into two rooms after the painting was completed, reflecting the Georgian worldview of the renovator, John Bratton, Col. William Bratton's youngest son.[89]

The spatial location of the slave cabin also reflects a communal folk lifestyle. Interaction between the two structures, as well as between the two families, was facilitated by the close proximity of the cabin, which was fifty feet from the Bratton's house. This arrangement illustrates the open, or public, concept of communal space. Density patterning of domestic trash also illustrates the interaction that occurred between these two households. A "walkway" pattern of domestic artifacts, particularly ceramics, exists between the two structures and connects the doorway depicted in the 1840s painting of the slave cabin to the kitchen door of the Bratton's house.

At the time of William and Martha Bratton's deaths in 1815 and 1816, respectively, they had eight adult children and owned a thriving farmstead. With the advent of Eli Whitney's cotton gin in the 1790s, short-staple cotton had become the cash crop of the upcountry, and the number of Bratton slaves had increased from twelve in 1790 to twenty-three by 1816.[90]

Interestingly, the disposition of William and Martha's estate illustrates the retention of Scottish inheritance tradition. From the wills of early Scottish colonists, Landsman identified an adapted Scottish inheritance practice. In North America, the equal division of property among male heirs shifted to a pattern in which the

Fig. 7.2. Personal and clothing artifacts recovered from the slave cabin site, historic Brattonsville.

youngest children inherited the largest portion of property. Landsman argues that older sons were assisted in establishing homes of their own during their parents' lives, in order to maintain extended kinship networks.[91] Retention of this folk tradition was expressed in Col. William Bratton's will and, based on the distribution of his wealth described in the probate inventory, his wishes were executed after his death. The probate records indicate the property including slaves that Colonel Bratton bequeathed to his children. The children are listed here by age, from oldest to youngest:

> Elsie Bratton Sadler
>   2 slaves—Peter and Betty
> William Bratton, Executor
>   2 slaves—Col. Bratton's "negroe Boy" Harry
> Jane Bratton Simpson
>   2 slaves—June and Lydia
> Elizabeth Bratton Erwin
>   2 slaves—Butler and Moses
> Nancy Agnes Bratton McCaw
>   2 slaves—Archy and Luce
> Mary Bratton
>   5 slaves—Jack, Winny, Isey, Limus, and Harriott
> $541 in cash
>   200 acres of land
>   Riding chair and harness
>   Bed and bed furniture
>   Household and kitchen furniture
>   1 Horse, saddle and bridle
> John Simpson Bratton
>   4 slaves—Watt, Polly, Jim, and Nelson
>   860 acres of land
>   Mill
>   The entire stock of cattle, sheep, and hogs
>   Wagon and gears
>   Plantation tools
>   Loom and appurtinances
>   Rifle gun, sword, and pistols
>   Cotton machine
>   Smith tools
> Martha Bratton Foster
>   4 slaves—July, Cloe, Kitty, and Pat

The Acceptance of a Georgian Worldview

In 1823, Colonel Bratton's son John and his wife Harriett constructed a Federal-style, double-parlor, central-hall I-house up the road from his father's log house. Georgian traits are visible in the symmetry and segmentation of rooms on either side of the central hall. Windows were symmetrical and evenly spaced on both sides of the centrally positioned front door.

The Georgian architectural style was introduced from England to America in the late 1600s. Georgian homes first became popular in large coastal cities such as Boston, Providence, Charleston, and Savannah by the middle to late 1770s. Deetz argues that the introduction and spread of this style was influenced by the popularity and availability of a large number of architectural style books published from the late seventeenth century onwards.[92] These plan books provided landscape and house floor layouts to local craftsmen. This "academic" form of construction marks a movement away from traditional vernacular design. Elements of the Georgian architectural style were incorporated with traditional vernacular design to form unique regional architectural styles.[93] The Brattons, as well as their neighbors, began incorporating elements of the Georgian architectural style in the upcountry by the early 1800s.[94]

The Brattons' house was completed and occupied in 1826. Within two years, the Brattons added symmetrical wings (map 7.3). Additional segmentation of living space occurred with the construction of a formal brick rear dining room, attached by a breezeway to the central hall. The Georgian house plan created separate rooms for specific activities through segmentation. In contrast to his father's one-room house that was openly accessible, John and Harriett's house contained five segmented rooms accessible from the central hall. The floor plan of John and Harriett's house controlled accessibility from public to private space. The dining-room addition is an example of privileged interior access. Guests were directed through the imposing Greek revival porch, past the segmented private rooms, and, via the central hall, through the house to the private inner sanctum of the dining room.

A substantial number of brick dependencies also were constructed in the main complex. The continued construction of residential upgrades and the careful placement of additional dependencies expressed the Brattons' belief in an "ideal" model of plantation landscape representing an elite social standing. Vlach summarizes the worldview of the planters' controlling plantation design as "highly rational formalism": "The world was, in their view, suitably improved only after it was transformed from its chaotic natural condition into a scene marked by a strict hierarchical order. The planters' landscapes were laid out with straight lines, right-angle corners, and axes of symmetry, their mathematical precision being considered as a proof of individual superiority."[95]

John and Harriett chose to have the brick dependencies symmetrically constructed on each side of the house. Four dependencies visible from the road, each measuring 16 by 22 feet, were larger than the rear structures, which measured 16

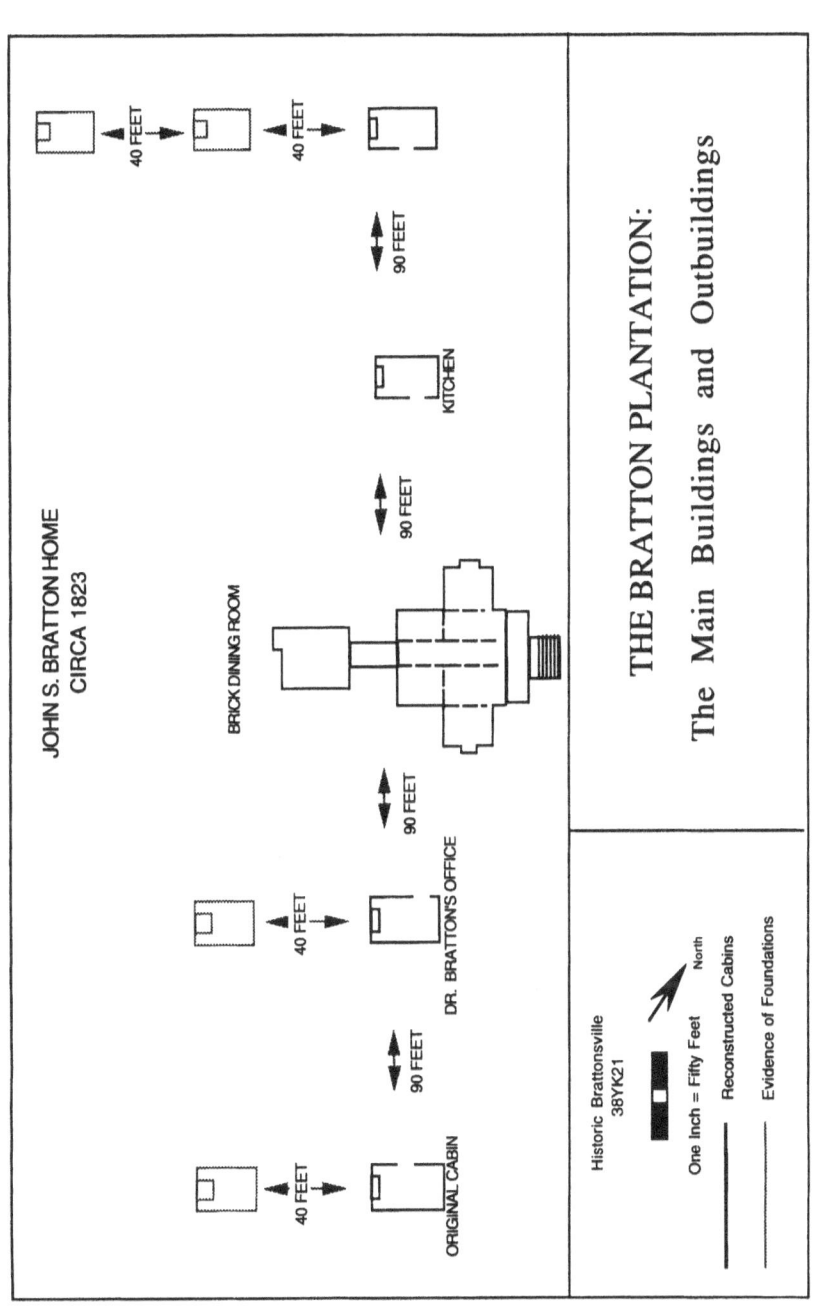

Map 7.3. Archaeological site map of John S. Bratton home, ca. 1823.

by 16 feet. The closest structures, located 90 feet from the main house, were associated directly with the use of the Bratton family. For example, one building was used as the doctor's office, while the other building, located on the other side of the main house, served as a detached kitchen. The outer structures, occupied as slave dwellings, were located at least 180 feet from the main house.

During the antebellum period, the nature of slave housing became an important aspect of "ideal" slave management. The growing abolitionist movement criticized small, dirty, and poorly constructed slave dwellings. Breeden asserts that reform demanded "every justification for slavery [through] duty, humanity, . . . as well as self-interest."[96] Agricultural journals became vehicles for planters to disseminate their views on improvement, including cabin size, wood-plank floors, and ventilation. While accommodating abolitionist criticism, nineteenth-century planters continued to use housing size and location to regiment their slaves and to express control of the plantation landscape.[97] The different sizes of cabins constructed for house servants and skilled slaves indicates that hierarchy existed among house servants and skilled slaves living in the main house complex.

The placement of slave cabins, clustered around the planter's house, enabled visitors to "inventory at a glance a portion of the plantation's labor force."[98] A decision to construct outbuildings and slave cabins out of brick may have been an aesthetic choice; however, a recorded transaction of seven hundred dollars for several loads of brick indicates that brick was a costly option. The brick dependencies provided a striking contrast to the Brattons' white-washed frame house and "served to underscore the Brattons' prestige in the local community . . . at a time when most planters built log [slave] cabins."[99] Further, the permanence and quality of brick cabins, as opposed to impermanent log structures, reinforced the hierarchical status of domestic slaves in relation to field slaves.[100]

The brick dining hall, attached to the Brattons' house by a breezeway, is the most prominent structure in the rear yard. This building was positioned in the center of the yard, establishing a vantage point with a clear view of the domestic slave activity. Moreover, the Brattons and their guests dined above the warming kitchen, being served by slaves laboring below in subterranean space. The symbolism of this arrangement expresses the institutionalization of a rigid social code intended to elevate the position of the master and subordinate that of domestic slaves.[101]

Architectural and spatial elements indicate that the location of slave housing was used to express the Brattons' wealth and social standing. Viewed from the road, the clustering of numerous brick outbuildings around the Brattons' Georgian-style home was impressive, implying the presence of a successful and powerful family in control of its landscape. Hierarchy among slaves was expressed by the location and construction of larger, brick slave cabins close to the Brattons' house. Orienting cabin entrances toward the Brattons' interior yard enabled family members to monitor the movement of slaves in and out of their cabins during the antebellum period, which had not been the case in the earlier frontier-period slave cabin located next to Colonel Bratton's house.

The house servants, including valets, maids, cooks, waiters and servers, children's nurses, drivers, seamstresses, and laundresses, were expected to wait on the Brattons and their children. Although there may have been degrees of household specialization, quite frequently domestic servants performed any tasks that were deemed necessary.[102] John Collins, an ex-slave born in Chester County, explained, "Best I 'member, dere was about twenty men, women, and chillun to work in de field and five house slaves. Dere was no good feelin's 'twixt field hand and house servants. De house servants put on more airs than de white folks. They got better things to eat, too, than de field hands and wore better cleaner clothes."[103] Joyner argues that, despite the advantages of better food and personal items given to house servants by the master's family, their behavior was constrained to reflect their master's wishes, and they were expected to be on constant call.[104]

Reflexive Aspect for African American Slaves

The location of the colonial period slave cabin in relation to the Colonel Bratton house reflects a communal folk lifestyle. Interaction between the two families would have been facilitated by the close proximity (fifty to seventy feet) of the slave cabin to the Brattons' log house. The density patterning of domestic refuse in the open space between the two structures illustrates the interaction between these two households. A "walkway" pattern of domestic artifacts, particularly ceramics, was detected between the two structures and connects the doorway depicted in the 1840s painting of the slave cabin to the rear kitchen door of the Brattons' house.

One reason for the close proximity of the Brattons' house and the slave cabin may have been for safety against the violent conflicts presented by Native American hostility and roving marauders. The gun ports or slit windows on the second story of the Brattons' original log house confirm the perceived presence of danger. However, locating domestic structures close together for safety is another example of communal reliance and folk tradition. The main house was a haven for the Bratton family, including the slaves, who likely were expected to protect Mrs. Bratton and her children when her husband was not home.

A communal environment would have been as familiar to the Brattons as it was to their African American slaves. The structure of power relations would appear to reflect a form of family hierarchy. This structure is not an implication of paternalism, nor does it overlook the harsh reality of enslavement. Rather, the application of a family hierarchy provided a relatively informal structure necessary to achieve the self-sufficiency of a small farmstead. The slaves had their own space separate from the Bratton family, yet their cabin was located close enough to be convenient and functional. The location of the slave cabin expressed the slave family's position in the hierarchy of the farmstead. Although interdependent, the placement of the doorway depicted on the side of the slave cabin farthest from the Brattons' house in the 1840s painting (fig. 7.1) implies a sense of respect between the two families and the lack of need to monitor the slaves' movements. Oral tradition regarding two of the Brattons' slaves is supportive of an intimate relationship between master and slave, suggesting that both parties may have held a mutual sense of ownership of their shared space. Within the small unit comprising the Brattons and one to three house servants, it is likely that their lives were highly interconnected and stifling at times, making it difficult for the slaves to participate in the larger African American culture.

The reflexive empowerment of distanced slave dwellings within the antebellum main complex enabled slaves an amount of control over their own households. From the big house to the boundary edges of the plantation and beyond, slaves created their own landscape.[105] Within this landscape were pathways connecting house slaves to the quarters of field slaves, to secret meeting places, or to other plantations where a spouse and children lived. As Benjamin Russell, an ex-slave from Chester County, explained, news was spread throughout the plantation by house servants. "Many plantations were strict about [news], but the greater the precautions the alerter became the slaves, the wider they opened their ears and the more eager they became for outside information. The source were: Girls that waited on the tables, the ladies' maids and the drivers; they would pick up everything they heard and pass it on to the other slaves."[106]

This network made it possible to arrange clandestine meetings and participate in the growing African American culture within the larger field slave community. As M. E. Abrams, an ex-slave explained, they would secretly meet on Saturday nights "down in de pastur' . . . dat wuz de place whar us colored folk . . . would have our lil' mit o' fun frum de white folks hearin."[107]

African American acceptance of Christianity likely provided more empowerment than spiritual salvation. Supported by the European elite, slaves were encouraged, if not forced, to participate in religious services in order to hear the moral and ordained message of servitude. Many slaves accepted this moral code, however, and, as Norrece Jones, Jr., asserts, this belief system must have provided some sense of satisfaction from "knowing that those who called themselves 'master' were morally inferior and would one day suffer interminably at the hands of Him who accepted nothing less than total morality."[108] Even for nonbelievers, religious affiliation provided advantages, such as passes to attend worship services, enabling slaves the opportunity to meet with friends and family.[109] The displaced location of house-slave dwellings increased accessibility to the outer limits of the landscape, facilitating participation in late-night African American revivals or meetings. Often, attendance at church services was used to explain detected absences, as ex-slave Abrams commented, "Us would tell some lie bout gwine to a church 'siety meetin."[110]

Conclusions

Architectural, historical, and archaeological evidence demonstrates the changing relationship between the Bratton family and their African American slaves between the late eighteenth and the mid-nineteenth centuries. Architectural change reflected the replacement of folk vernacular traditions with the expression of Georgian traits, or the acceptance of a Georgian worldview. Prior to the antebellum period, folk traditions defined the relationship between the Brattons and their house slaves as communal and interdependent, interacting in close proximity to each other.

The profitable production of cotton resulted in an increased number of Bratton slaves, from 23 in 1816 to 112 in 1840.[111] With a cash-crop plantation, a girls' school, and a mercantile operation, the Bratton family abandoned a self-sufficient, subsistence lifestyle and increasingly participated in the market economy. Archaeological and architectural research at the Bratton plantation documents the transition from an incipient to a formal institution of slavery. Rigid roles reflecting this new formality were defined and reinforced by architecture and landscape use. Domestic slave dwellings were located over 180 feet away from the main house, in a position that created an impressive view from the road. The size and location of these cabins suggests that the Brattons established a hierarchy among their domestic slaves.[112] The architecture and landscape of the Brattons' estate demonstrated to their upcountry neighbors their new socioeconomic position and their control over their land, slaves, and property. This Georgian layout gave bondsmen access to *their* own landscape, allowing them to participate in a vibrant African American culture.

NOTES

This research was funded in part by the Archaeological Society of South Carolina, through a Grant-in-Aid award. Additional funding and support, for which I am very grateful, was contributed by Historic Brattonsville and the Savannah River Archaeological Research Program. I would especially like to thank Keith Stephenson for the time and effort he spent editing previous drafts of this paper.

1. James Deetz, "Material Culture and Worldview in Colonial Anglo-America," in *Recovery of Meaning: Historical Archaeology in the Eastern United States*, ed. Mark P. Leone and Parker Potter, Jr., 219–34 (Washington, D.C.: Smithsonian Institute Press, 1988); James Deetz, *In Small Things Forgotten: The Archaeology of Early American Life* (New York: Anchor Press/Doubleday, 1977); Henry Glassie, *Pattern in the Material Folk Culture of the Eastern United States* (Philadelphia: Univ. of Pennsylvania Press, 1968); Henry Glassie, *Folk Housing in Middle Virginia* (Knoxville: Univ. of Tennessee Press, 1975); and Mark P. Leone, "The Georgian Order as the Order of Merchant Capitalism in Annapolis, Maryland," in Leone and Potter, *Recovery of Meaning*, 235–62.
2. James Deetz, "Households: A Structural Key to Archaeological Explanation," *American Behavioral Scientist* 25 (1982): 721.
3. Michael Ann Williams, *Homeplace: The Social Use and Meaning of the Folk Dwelling in Southwestern North Carolina* (Athens: Univ. of Georgia Press, 1991), 141.
4. Deetz, "Material Culture and Worldview," 219–34; Deetz, *In Small Things Forgotten*; Glassie, *Pattern in Material Folk Culture*; Glassie, *Folk Housing in Middle Virginia*; Leone, "Georgian Order as the Order of Merchant Capitalism," 235–62.
5. Deetz, "Material Culture and Worldview," 222.

6. Glassie, *Pattern in Material Folk Culture*; Glassie, *Folk Housing in Middle Virginia*.
7. Deetz, "Material Culture and Worldview," 219–34; Deetz, *In Small Things Forgotten*.
8. Leone, "Georgian Order as the Order of Merchant Capitalism," 235–62.
9. Deetz, *In Small Things Forgotten*, 115.
10. James A. Ford, "An Archaeological Report on the Elizafield Ruins," in *Georgia's Disputed Ruins*, ed. E. Coulter, 191–225 (Chapel Hill: Univ. of North Carolina Press, 1937).
11. Leland Ferguson, *Uncommon Ground: Archaeology and Early African America, 1650–1800* (Washington, D.C.: Smithsonian Institution Press, 1992), 5–6.
12. William M. Kelso and Rachel Most, eds., *Earth Patterns: Essays in Landscape Archaeology* (Charlottesville: Univ. Press of Virginia, 1990); Larry McKee, "Ideals and Realities Behind the Design and Use of Nineteenth-Century Virginia Slave Cabins," in *The Art and Mystery of Historical Archaeology: Essays in Honor of James Deetz*, ed. A. E. Yentsch and M. C. Beaudry, 195–214 (Ann Arbor, Mich.: CRC Press, 1992).
13. William M. Kelso, *Kingsmill Plantations, 1619–1800: Archaeology of Country Life in Colonial Virginia* (New York: Academic Press, 1984).
14. Larry McKee and Brian Thomas, "Twenty Years of Research on the Hermitage Slave Community: A Summary of Archaeological Findings," (Paper presented at the annual meeting of the Society for Historical Archaeology, Cincinnati, Ohio, Jan. 1996); Brian Thomas and Larry McKee, "Twenty Years of Research on the Hermitage Slave Community: Interpreting the Archaeological Findings" (Paper presented at the annual meeting of the Society for Historical Archaeology, Cincinnati, Ohio, Jan. 1996).
15. Charles H. Fairbanks, "The Kingsley Slave Cabins in Duval County, Florida, 1968," in *Conference on Historic Site Archaeology, Papers 7*, ed. Stanley South (Columbia: South Carolina Institute of Archaeology and Anthropology, 1987).
16. Ferguson, *Uncommon Ground*, xxxix.
17. Robert Ascher and Charles Fairbanks, "Excavation of a Slave Cabin: Georgia, USA," *Historical Archaeology* 5 (1971): 10.
18. William B. Lees, *Limerick, Old and in the Way: Archaeological Investigations at Limerick Plantation*, Anthropological Studies No. 5, Occasional Papers of the Institute (Columbia, S.C.: South Carolina Institute of Archaeology and Anthropology, Univ. of South Carolina, 1980); Lynne Lewis, *Drayton Hall: Preliminary Archaeological Investigation at a Lowcountry Plantation* (Charlottesville: Univ. of Virginia, 1978); James L. Michie, *Richmond Hill Plantation, 1810–1868: The Discovery of Antebellum Life on a Waccamaw Rice Plantation* (Columbia, S.C.: The Reprint Co., 1990); James B. Stoltman, *Groton Plantation: An Archaeological Study of a South Carolina Locality*, Monograph of the Peabody Museum No. 1 (Cambridge, Mass.: Peabody Museum of Harvard Univ., 1974); Michael Trinkley, *Archaeological and Historical Examinations of Three Eighteenth- and Nineteenth-Century Rice Plantations on the Waccamaw Neck*, Research Series 31 (Columbia, S.C.: Chicora Foundation, 1993); and Martha A. Zierden, Lesley M. Drucker, and Jeanne Calhoun, *Home Upriver: Life on Daniel's Island, Berkeley County, South Carolina* (Columbia, S.C.: Carolina Archaeological Services, 1986).
19. Natalie P. Adams, "Early African-American Domestic Architecture from Berkeley

County, South Carolina" (Master's thesis, Univ. of South Carolina, 1990); Richard M. Affleck, "Power and Space: Settlement Pattern Change at Middleburg Plantation, Berkeley County, South Carolina" (Master's thesis, Univ. of South Carolina, 1990); David W. Babson, "Plantation Ideology and the Archaeology of Racism: Evidence from the Tanner Road Site (38BK416), Berkeley County, South Carolina," *South Carolina Antiquities* 19 (1987): 35–47; Lesley M. Drucker and Ronald W. Anthony, *The Spiers Landing Site: Archaeological Investigations in Berkeley County, South Carolina* (Columbia, S.C.: Carolina Archaeology Services, 1979); Thomas R. Wheaton, Amy Friedlander, and Patrick H. Garrow, *Yaughan and Curriboo Plantations: Studies in Afro-American Archaeology* (Atlanta, Ga.: Soil Systems, Inc., 1983); and Zierden, Drucker, and Calhoun, *Home Upriver*.

20. J. W. Joseph, "The Early American Period and Nineteenth Century in South Carolina Archaeology," *South Carolina Antiquities* 25 (1993): 70.

21. Richard Carrillo, *The Howser House and the Chronicle Grave and Mass Burial: King's Mountain National Military Park, South Carolina* Research Manuscript Series No. 102 (Columbia: South Carolina Institute of Archaeology and Anthropology, Univ. of South Carolina, 1976).

22. James D. Scurry, *Archaeological Investigations at Redcliffe Plantation, Aiken County, South Carolina*, Research Manuscript Series, Vol. 14, Nos. 3 and 4 (Columbia: South Carolina Institute of Archaeology and Anthropology, Univ. of South Carolina, 1982).

23. Michael Trinkley, ed., *Plantation Life in the Piedmont: A Preliminary Examination of Rosemont Plantation, Laurens County, South Carolina*, Research Series 29 (Columbia, S.C.: Chicora Foundation, 1992).

24. Kenneth E. Lewis, *Camden: A Frontier Town in Eighteenth-Century South Carolina*, Anthropological Studies 2 (Columbia: South Carolina Institute of Archaeology and Anthropology, Univ. of South Carolina, 1976).

25. Rita B. Kenion, "Investigation of a Brick Dependency at Historic Brattonsville District: An Archaeological Study," 1994, manuscript on file, York County Historic Commission, McConnells, S.C.; S. Gayle Russell, Lesley M. Drucker, and Rebecca Fulmer, *Archaeological Testing and Architectural Interpretation of the Homestead House Kitchen, Well and Servants' Dwelling, and the Revolutionary House Spring, Historic Brattonsville, York County, South Carolina* (Columbia, S.C.: Carolina Archaeological Services, 1981); and Joseph C. Wilkins, Howell C. Hunter, Jr., and Richard Carrillo, *Historical, Architectural, and Archaeological Research at Brattonsville (38YK21), York County, South Carolina*, Research Manuscript Series No. 76 (Columbia: South Carolina Institute of Archaeology and Anthropology, Univ. of South Carolina, 1975).

26. Charles E. Orser, Jr., "Toward a Theory of Power and Space," in Leone and Potter, *Recovery of Meaning*, 313–43; Charles E. Orser, Jr., *The Material Basis of the Postbellum Tenant Plantation: Historic Archaeology in the South Carolina Piedmont* (Athens: Univ. of Georgia Press, 1988); Charles E. Orser, Jr.; Annette M. Nekola; and James L. Roark, *Exploring the Rustic Life: Multidisciplinary Research at Millwood Plantation, a Large Piedmont Plantation in Abbeville County, South Carolina, and Elbert County, Georgia*, Russell Papers, Archaeological Services, National Park Service, Atlanta, Ga., 1987.

27. Lesley M. Drucker, Woody C. Meizner, and James B. Legg, *Testing and Data Recovery at Allen Plantation (38AB102) and Thomas B. Clinkscales Farm (38AB221), Richard B. Russell Multiple Resource Area, Abbeville County, South Carolina*, Russell Papers, Archaeological Services, National Park Service, Atlanta, Ga., 1982.
28. J. W. Joseph, Mary Beth Reed, and Charles E. Cantley, *Agrarian Life, Romantic Death: Archaeological and Historical Testing and Data Recovery for the I-85 Northern Alternative, Spartanburg, South Carolina*, Technical Report 39 (Stone Mountain, Ga.: New South Associates, 1991).
29. Carl Steen, Dan Elliott, Rita Folse-Elliott, and Anthony Warren, *Further Excavations at John de la Howe's Lethe Farm* (Columbia, S.C.: Diachronic Research Foundation, 1996).
30. David Colin Crass and Bruce R. Penner, "The Struggle for the South Carolina Frontier: History and Archaeology at New Windsor Township," *South Carolina Antiquities* 24 (1992): 37–56; David Colin Crass, Bruce R. Penner, Tammy R. Forehand, Lois J. Potter, and Larry Potter, "A Man of Great Liberality: Recent Research at George Galphin's Silver Bluff," *South Carolina Antiquities* 27 (1996): 26–41; David Colin Crass, Bruce R. Penner, Tammy R. Forehand, John Huffman, Lois J. Potter, and Larry Potter, *Excavations at New Windsor Township, South Carolina*, Savannah River Archaeological Research Heritage Series 3 (Columbia: South Carolina Institute of Archaeology and Anthropology, Univ. of South Carolina, 1997).
31. Natalie P. Adams and John S. Cable, *Intensive Archaeological Survey of the Otarre Tract, Cayce, S.C.*, Technical Report 99 (Atlanta, Ga.: New South Associates, 1997), 32; Mark D. Groover, *Of Mindset and Material Culture: An Archaeological View of Continuity and Change in the Eighteenth-Century South Carolina Backcountry*, Volumes in Historical Archaeology No. 20, ed. Stanley South (Columbia: South Carolina Institute of Archaeology and Anthropology, Univ. of South Carolina, 1992); Benjamin Resnick, *The Williams Place: A Scotch-Irish Farmstead in the South Carolina Piedmont*, Volumes in Historical Archaeology No. 3, ed. Stanley South (Columbia: South Carolina Institute of Archaeology and Anthropology, Univ. of South Carolina, 1988); Linda F. Stine, "Social Inequality and Turn-of-the-Century Farmsteads: Issues of Class, Status, Ethnicity, and Race," *Historical Archaeology* 24 (1990): 37–49.
33. Crass et al., *Excavations at New Windsor Township*; Groover, *Of Mindset and Material Culture*; Kenion, "Investigation of a Brick Dependency at Historic Brattonsville District"; and Orser, Nekola, and Roark, *Exploring the Rustic Life*.
34. Groover, *Of Mindset and Material Culture*.
35. Kenion, "Investigation of a Brick Dependency at Historic Brattonsville District."
36. Crass et al., *Excavations at New Windsor Township*.
37. Orser, "Toward a Theory of Power and Space," 313–43; Orser, *Material Basis of the Postbellum Tenant Plantation*; Orser, Nekola, and Roark, *Exploring the Rustic Life*.
38. Orser, "Toward a Theory of Power and Space," 313–43; Orser, *Material Basis of the Postbellum Tenant Plantation*.
39. Orser, "Toward a Theory of Power and Space," 313–43; Orser, *Material Basis of the Postbellum Tenant Plantation*.

40. Rachel N. Klein, *Unification of a Slave State: The Rise of the Planter Class in the South Carolina Backcountry, 1760–1808* (Chapel Hill: Univ. of North Carolina Press, 1990), 7.
41. Glassie, *Pattern in Material Folk Culture*; Terry G. Jordan, *American Log Buildings: An Old World Heritage* (Chapel Hill: Univ. of North Carolina Press, 1985); Terry G. Jordan and Matti Kaups, *The American Backwoods Frontier: An Ethnic and Ecological Interpretation* (Baltimore, Md.: John Hopkins Univ. Press, 1989); Fred B. Kniffen and Henry Glassie, "Building in Wood in the Eastern United States: A Time-Place Perspective," *Geographical Review* 56 (1966): 40–66.
42. Peter H. Wood, *Black Majority: Negroes in Colonial South Carolina from 1670 through the Stono Rebellion* (New York: Norton, 1974), 114–17.
43. Ibid., 99; and John Solomon Otto, *The Southern Frontiers, 1607–1860* (New York: Greenwood Press, 1989), 18.
44. Wood, *Black Majority*, 152.
45. Klein, *Unification of a Slave State*, 20.
46. Richard Maxwell Brown, *The South Carolina Regulators* (Cambridge, Mass.: Belknap Press of Harvard Univ. Press, 1963), 31; Drew G. Faust, "Slavery in the American Experience," in *Before Freedom Came: African-American Life in the Antebellum South*, ed. E. D. C. Campbell, Jr., and K. S. Rice (Charlottesville: Univ. Press of Virginia, for Museum of the Confederacy, Richmond, 1991), 4; Robert L. Meriwether, *The Expansion of South Carolina, 1729–1765* (Kingsport, Tenn.: Southern Publishers, 1940),178; Wood, *Black Majority*, 96–97.
47. Wood, *Black Majority*, 97.
48. J. William Harris, *Plain Folk and Gentry in a Slave Society: White Liberty and Black Slavery in Augusta's Hinterlands* (Middletown, Conn.: Wesleyan Univ. Press, 1985), 43.
49. Richard M. Brown, *South Carolina Regulators*, 31; Wood, *Black Majority*, 98.
50. Wood, *Black Majority*, 100.
51. Richard M. Brown, *South Carolina Regulators*, 31, 54–56; Wood, *Black Majority*, 100–101.
52. Norrece T. Jones, Jr., *Born a Child of Freedom, Yet a Slave: Mechanisms of Control and Strategies of Resistance in Antebellum South Carolina* (Hanover, N.H.: Univ. Press of New England, 1990), 197–98.
53. Richard J. Hooker, ed., *The Carolina Backcountry on the Eve of the Revolution: The Journal and Other Writings of Charles Woodmason, Anglican Itinerant* (Chapel Hill: Univ. of North Carolina Press, 1953), 277.
54. Richard M. Brown, *South Carolina Regulators*, 6–12, 29–31, 38–52; Jordan and Kaups, *American Backwoods Frontier*, 68–69; and Klein, *Unification of a Slave State*, 14, 61–64, 82–84.
55. Wade B. Fairey, *Historic Brattonsville: A Wedge of County History* (McConnells, S.C.: York County Historical Commission, 1993).
56. George P. Rawick, ed., *The American Slave: A Composite Autobiography*, vols. 2–3: *South Carolina Narratives, Parts 1–4* (Westport, Conn.: Greenwood Publishing Co., 1972), 2:266.
57. Ibid., 3:35.

58. Ibid., 3:199.
59. Ibid., 3:151.
60. Ibid., 3:253.
61. Ibid., 2:272.
62. Ibid., 2:272.
63. Natalie P. Adams and Cable, *Intensive Archaeological Survey of the Otarre Tract*, 32; Groover, *Of Mindset and Material Culture*.
64. Rawick, *American Slave*, 3:199.
65. Ibid., 3:151.
66. Ibid., 2:271–72.
67. Ibid., 3:32.
68. Frederick W. Lange and Jerome S. Handler, "The Ethnohistorical Approach to Slavery," in *The Archaeology of Slavery and Plantation Life*, ed. Theresa A. Singleton, 15–34 (New York: Academic Press, 1985); Lees, *Limerick, Old and in the Way*; Kenneth E. Lewis and Helen Haskell, *Hampton II: Further Archaeological Investigations at a Santee River Rice Plantation*, Research Manuscript Series No. 161 (Columbia: South Carolina Institute of Archaeology and Anthropology, Univ. of South Carolina, 1980); and John Solomon Otto, *Cannon's Point Plantation, 1794–1860: Conditions and Status Patterns in the Old South* (Orlando, Fla.: Academic Press, 1984).
69. Kenneth E. Lewis and Haskell, *Hampton II: Further Archaeological Investigations*, 2.
70. Drucker and Anthony, *Spiers Landing Site*; Ferguson, *Uncommon Ground*; Lees, *Limerick, Old and in the Way*; Wheaton et al., *Yaughan and Curriboo Plantations*; and Zierden, Drucker, and Calhoun, *Home Upriver*.
71. Leland Ferguson, "Looking for the 'Afro' in Colono-Indian Pottery," in *Archaeological Perspectives on Ethnicity in America*, ed. Robert L. Schuyler, 14–28 (Farmingdale, N.Y.: Baywood Publishing Co., 1980); and Ferguson, *Uncommon Ground*.
72. Ferguson, *Uncommon Ground*, 32.
73. Ronald Anthony, "Colono Ware," in Zierden, Drucker, and Calhoun, *Home Upriver*, 22–50.
74. Monica L. Beck, "Upcountry Pioneers: Archaeological Investigation of a Slave Cabin at the Bratton Farmstead, ca. 1770s," *South Carolina Antiquities* 27 (1995): 1–25; Crass et al., *Excavations at New Windsor Township, South Carolina*; Groover, *Of Mindset and Material Culture*; Kenion, "Investigation of a Brick Dependency at Historic Brattonsville District"; Orser, Nekola, and Roark, *Exploring the Rustic Life*; Steen et al., *Further Excavations at Lethe Farm*; and Trinkley, *Plantation Life in the Piedmont*.
75. William B. Lees and Kathryn Kimery-Lees, "The Function of Colono-Indian Ceramics: Insights from Limerick Plantation, South Carolina," *Historical Archaeology* 13 (1979): 1–13; Theresa A. Singleton, "The Archaeology of the Plantation South: A Review of Approaches and Goals," *Historical Archaeology* 25 (1987): 70–77; Wheaton et al., *Yaughan and Curriboo Plantations*; and Zierden, Drucker, and Calhoun, *Home Upriver*.
76. Ferguson, "Looking for the 'Afro' in Colono-Indian Pottery"; Ferguson, *Uncommon Ground*.

77. Drucker and Anthony, *Spiers Landing Site*; Ferguson, *Uncommon Ground*; Groover, *Of Mindset and Material Culture*; Charles Joyner, *Down by the Riverside: A South Carolina Slave Community* (Urbana: Univ. of Illinois Press, 1984); Lange and Handler, "Ethnohistorical Approach to Slavery"; Otto, *Cannon's Point Plantation*.
78. Drucker and Anthony, *Spiers Landing Site*; and Otto, *Cannon's Point Plantation*.
79. Ferguson, *Uncommon Ground*, 97.
80. Orser, *Material Basis of the Postbellum Tenant Plantation*.
81. Rawick, *American Slave*, 2:274.
82. Deetz, *In Small Things Forgotten*, 93.
83. Ibid.
84. E. Estyn Evans, *Irish Folk Ways* (New York: Routledge, 1957), 44–45; Glassie, *Pattern in Material Folk Culture*, 355; and Ned C. Landsman, *Scotland and Its First American Colony, 1683–1765* (Princeton, N.J.: Princeton Univ. Press, 1985), 18–21.
85. Deetz, *In Small Things Forgotten*, 99.
86. Fairey, *Historic Brattonsville*, 8; Wilkins, Hunter, and Carrillo, *Historical, Architectural, and Archaeological Research at Brattonsville*, 21.
87. Groover, *Of Mindset and Material Culture*; Resnick, *The Williams Place*; Wilkins, Hunter, and Carrillo, *Historical, Architectural, and Archaeological Research at Brattonsville*.
88. James Deetz, *In Small Things Forgotten*; Deetz, "Material Culture and Worldview"; Glassie, *Pattern in Material Folk Culture*; Glassie, *Folk Housing in Middle Virginia*.
89. Fairey, *Historic Brattonsville*, 9; Wilkins, Hunter, and Carrillo, *Historical, Architectural, and Archaeological Research at Brattonsville*, 21–24.
90. Fairey, *Historic Brattonsville*, 18–19, 25.
91. Landsman, *Scotland and Its First American Colony*, 151–58.
92. Deetz, *In Small Things Forgotten*, 112.
93. Ibid.; Glassie, *Folk Housing in Middle Virginia*; John R. Swanson, "Georgian Symmetry in the South Carolina Upcountry: An Architectural Analysis of the Bratton's Homestead Plantation, 1823–1830," 1995, manuscript on file, York County Historical Commission, McConnells, S.C.
94. Swanson, "Georgian Symmetry in the South Carolina Upcountry."
95. John M. Vlach, *Back of the Big House: The Architecture of Plantation Slavery* (Chapel Hill: Univ. of North Carolina Press, 1993), 5.
96. James O. Breeden, *Advice among Masters: The Ideal in Slave Management in the Old South* (Westport, Conn.: Greenwood Press, 1980), 114.
97. Natalie P. Adams, "Early African-American Domestic Architecture from Berkeley County," 70, 89–92; and McKee, "Ideals and Realities Behind the Design and Use of Nineteenth-Century Virginia Slave Cabins," 200–201.
98. Vlach, *Back of the Big House*, 26.
99. Lesley M. Drucker and Ronald W. Anthony, "On the Trail: An Examination of Socioeconomic Status at Late Historic Piedmont Farmsteads," *South Carolina Antiquities* 20 (1986): 15–22; and Russell, Drucker, and Fulmer, *Archaeological Testing and Architectural Interpretation of the Homestead*.
100. Swanson, "Georgian Symmetry in the South Carolina Upcountry," 15–16.

101. Ibid., 13.
102. Joyner, *Down by the Riverside*, 80–85.
103. Rawick, *American Slave*, 2:243.
104. Joyner, *Down by the Riverside*, 80–85.
105. Vlach, *Back of the Big House*, 1, 13.
106. Rawick, *American Slave*, 3:52–53.
107. Ibid., 2:1–3.
108. Norrece T. Jones, *Born a Child of Freedom, Yet a Slave*, 158.
109. Ibid., 140.
110. Rawick, *American Slave*, 2:1–3.
111. Fairey, *Historic Brattonsville*, 25.
112. Ferguson, *Uncommon Ground*; Otto, *Cannon's Point Plantation*; Theresa A. Singleton, "Archaeological Implications for Changing Labor Conditions," in *The Archaeology of Slavery and Plantation Life*, ed. Theresa A. Singleton, 291–308 (New York: Academic Press, 1985).

"Here Are Frame Houses and Brick Chimneys": Knoxville, Tennessee, in the Late Eighteenth Century

Charles H. Faulkner

Urban historians have recently suggested that the "western movement was made possible by urban impulses—by townsmen hoping to convert strategic positions in the continental wilderness into cities, putting down checkerboard streets with hotels and public buildings where Indian trails had run irregularly through the forest."[1] Many towns on the southern frontier, like Knoxville in East Tennessee, started out as forts or stations but soon became speculative enterprises in a vast reservoir of unexploited land. In this high-stakes game, where some towns won and others lost, Knoxville held some high cards. While the Blue Ridge–Smoky Mountains and the Cumberland Mountains were formidable barriers to the east and west, respectively, the Great Valley provided a gateway to the Mid-Atlantic states, and the Tennessee River breached the eastern escarpment of the Cumberlands. The town's trump cards, however, may have been the men of vision and wealth who founded and promoted Knoxville. One was William Blount, who, after being named governor of the Territory South of the River Ohio by President Washington, chose the site of Knoxville as his new capital and named it after Henry Knox, the secretary of war. Blount's political connections, in other words, were impressive, but he was also a land speculator and a shrewd negotiator with the often suspicious and restless Cherokee. Another critical player was James White, a modest yet insightful entrepreneur, who owned all of what is now downtown Knoxville.

Several historians have traced the growth of Knoxville from its beginnings in the Appalachian wilderness to its emergence, late in the nineteenth century, as the "Queen City of the Mountains." Emphasizing its estrangement from kindred Mid-South cities because of its Union sympathies and Republican politics, none of these scholars concentrated on Knoxville's early development and character as a southern frontier town. Such research requires both archival and archaeological data, the latter being crucial because there are so few existing standing buildings and written records that document early Knoxville lifeways. However, archaeological remains have become accessible only since the early 1980s, when urban archaeological projects began in the city.

Since Knoxville is over two hundred years old, historians have divided these two centuries into several "periods" of growth and development, although no-one has ever defined a specific frontier period. In this study, the early settlement or frontier period begins in 1786, when James White built his fort in what is now downtown Knoxville, and it ends in 1815, when Knoxville received her first city charter.[2]

What is the place of Knoxville on the expanding southern frontier and how does it fit the pattern of a frontier town? Numerous studies of the frontier have appeared in the United States since Frederick Jackson Turner's seminal essay in 1893. Many of these studies present models that attempt to explain the dynamics of frontier development. One model relevant to the study of frontier Knoxville is the model of "adapted spread" of Upland South culture.[3] In this model, "preadaptation" to the Southern Appalachian environment occurred in a core area, then the entire complex of Upland South traits spread southward, allowing its carriers quickly to come to terms with the new environment.

Knoxville is within the Upland South culture area, first demarcated by Frederick Jackson Turner.[4] Distinctive cultural characteristics of this area remained vague, however, until Henry Glassie defined what he called the Southern Appalachian culture. He visualized this as a synthesis of Pennsylvania German and Scotch-Irish strains, especially in the construction of houses and outbuildings.[5] A recent study by Jordan and Kaups[6] of log houses in both North America and Europe demonstrates that Fenno-Scandian log buildings served as models for later settlers, who added both German and British architectural features to their log houses. In the adapted-spread model, the rapid diffusion of the Upland South culture is exemplified particularly by log construction; log carpentry skills derived from northern Europe gave the settlers the ability to conquer the semitropical Southern Appalachian forest quickly and efficiently. Additional Upland South culture traits include a reliance on diversified farming, the importance of the cooperative family unit, an oligarchic political system centered on the county court, and a stratified social system with slaves as the lowest class.[7]

The first settler to clear the forest in Knoxville was the redoubtable James White, who in 1786 built a fort above First Creek a short distance above its confluence with the Tennessee River. This fort was described as quadrangular in plan, with an eight-foot-high stockade connecting "strong cabins" at the corners, one of which was the White log house.[8] A successful land speculator, White owned all the high ground between the Tennessee and First and Second creeks. This "beautiful eminence," described in a 1792 promotional article in the *Knoxville Gazette*, was chosen by Governor Blount for the capital of the Territory South of the Ohio River. On October 3, 1791, this eminence was laid out in a grid of streets and sixty-four lots of a half-acre each. This has been accepted by historians as the founding date for the city. The lots were drawn by lottery among subscribers (map 8.1).

By early 1792, several houses and business establishments were under construction. The earliest description of the town was written two years later by Abishai C. Thomas: "Here are frame Houses and Brick Chimneys [and] there is in it ten stores & seven taverns, besides tippling Houses, one Court House [and] no prison which they boast of as not being an article of necessity."[9] One of these houses certainly was the timber frame residence that Governor Blount built on a lot overlooking the river. By 1796, there were forty houses and businesses, the latter including four stores and the *Knoxville Gazette* printing office.[10]

With the exception of the Blount Mansion, most of the town buildings extant in 1796 appear to have been built of logs. A nineteenth-century historian in that year said, "The buildings were, without exception, of logs, not weather boarded."[11] As late as 1802, the town commissioners found it necessary to prohibit the construction of log and clay chimneys.[12] But there is also substantial evidence from eyewitness accounts—and from a few early structures still standing in the twentieth century—that new architectural styles were appearing by 1800. According to the Moravians Abraham Steiner and Fredrick C. De Schweinitz, visiting in 1799:

> Knoxville lies in Knox county, on the north side of the Holston, on several hills, and consists of about 100 houses all built of wood; the newest are, mostly, two-story frame structures. A new two-story building is being put up by Governor Sevier. The Courthouse, a two-story structure of limestone, is not yet completed. The former barracks are not far away on the highest place, are of two stories with wings, and are used for sessions of the Assembly. At the north end, on a high level place, stands a great, not yet completed frame house, first intended to be an academy; now the town school is conducted there.... Stores there are many; near our hotel we counted no less than five, some of which make a good appearance.[13]

In addition to the timber frame buildings which apparently were replacing some log houses by 1800, masonry was also introduced as a building material at this time. The dressed-limestone courthouse already has been mentioned; although this stone was abundant in the region, it was never popular for construction except for foundations and chimneys. Brick often was the building material of choice for later nineteenth-century houses and commercial establishments, but, with the exception of chimneys, it was used infrequently for construction until the second decade of the nineteenth century. It was said that "the pioneers had much amusement in witnessing the efforts to make a house of 'daubs of mud.'"[14] One of the earliest brick houses that is still standing in Knoxville is Gov. John Sevier's house, which was under construction when the Moravian missionaries visited the city in 1799. This two-story, brick I-house of Federal design finally was completed in 1804 by James Park. According to one historian, the Sevier-Park house was the third brick house built in Knoxville, the earliest being the old Webb house on the corner of Central and Cumberland streets.[15]

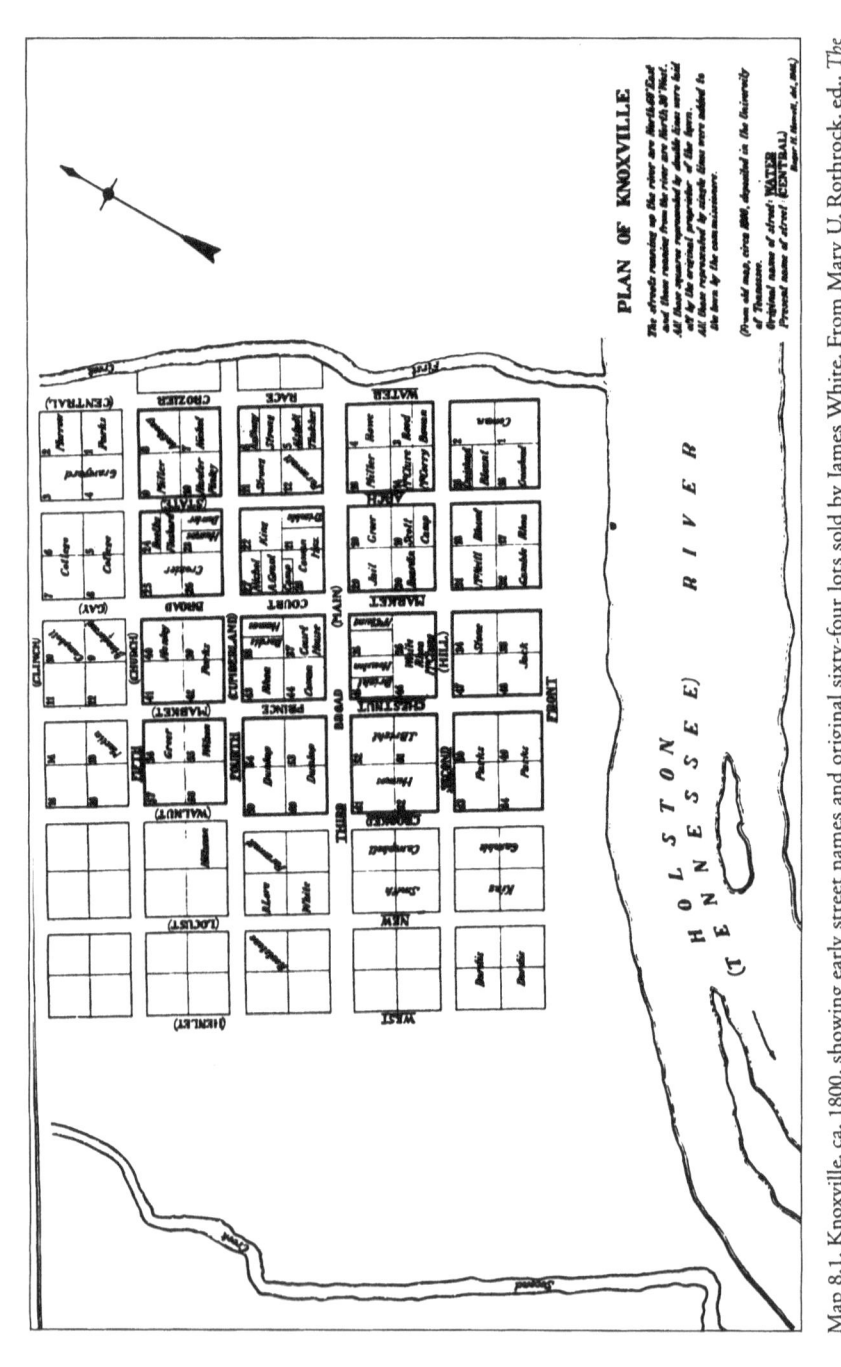

Map 8.1. Knoxville, ca. 1800, showing early street names and original sixty-four lots sold by James White. From Mary U. Rothrock, ed., *The French Broad–Holston Country* (Knoxville, 1946). Courtesy of the East Tennessee Historical Society.

Churches were built very early in what became Knox County: at Lebanon-in-the-Fork (1791), Little Flat Creek (1796), and Ebenezer (1796).[16] But a church building was not erected in Knoxville for several years after its founding. James White set aside two lots, the present site of the First Presbyterian church, for a "meeting house" and cemetery. A Presbyterian congregation was organized as early as 1793, with the Rev. Samuel Carrick conducting services in the court house.[17] However, it did not begin building a church on the White lot until 1812—a brick building not completed until four years later.[18] Despite the absence of a formal church building for several years, however, spiritual life in Knoxville did not seem to have been markedly affected. Methodist Bishop Francis Asbury visited Knoxville in November 1800 and wrote that he "preached in the state-house on Isai. iv, 6, 7. I was very unwell, but was enabled to bear the cross of public speaking; we had about seven hundred people in and about the house."[19]

It has been suggested that the "material concerns of the settler were necessarily so great that there seemed to be little time for cultivating the spiritual life."[20] While there is little doubt that the hardships of frontier life caused a certain amount of moral laxity (Thomas's description of the town suggests that there were more taverns and tippling houses than stores), the fact that seven hundred persons attended Bishop Asbury's sermon attests to a considerable spiritual concern among the townsfolk. Many pioneers seem to have resisted a strong parish organization, preferring a more emotional folk faith.[21] Also they apparently did not believe it necessary to worship in a formally sanctified building.

One of the characteristics of Southern Appalachia is that buildings—from farmstead outbuildings to public edifices—usually served multiple functions.[22] A church in this region often doubled as a meeting hall or a school, or it served more than one denomination.[23] This could be interpreted as another practical adaptation on the southern frontier, where multiple uses of buildings saved labor and raw materials, and the sharing of public space strengthened community bonds.

While Knoxvillians did not seem particularly concerned to have a formal church in their midst as long as they had a public building to worship in, they apparently were eager to build schools. In 1794, the Territorial Legislature granted a charter for the establishment of Blount College (later to become the University of Tennessee), and in the next year a city block (four lots) across the street from the church lot was sold for a nominal fee to the nonsectarian college. A building of some sort was erected on the property a year later.[24] Four years later, Moravian missionaries described the building as a large frame house, not yet completed.[25] In 1810, a school later known as the Knoxville Literary Institution was established and offered classes in Latin, Greek, and the sciences. Hampton Sidney Academy opened in 1817.[26]

Commercial establishments were among the earliest buildings in Knoxville. The earliest mercantile stores were established by Hugh Dunlap, Samuel and Nathaniel Cowan, and John Crozier and James King. Hugh Dunlap occupied one of the government "shanties" which had been erected on the corner of State and Front streets in 1791.[27] On February 11, 1794, the Cowans advertised: "The subscribers have just received a general assortment of goods, suitable to the season, and are in daily expectation of a larger from the Philadelphia market; all of which they will sell at their former seats in Jonesboro and Knoxville, on moderate terms for corn, rye, oats, bees wax, flax, old congress money, and Martin's certificates."[28]

The type of merchandise available to Knoxvillians as early as 1795 is suggested by an advertisement of King and Crozier:

> In addition to their former assortment, have just come to hand, Irish Linens; Saddles and Bridles; Books and Stationary; Steel; Nails; Window Glass; Queen's Ware; Glass Ware; Pipes; Lead; Gun Powder; coffee; chocolate; Bohea, Green, Sequin, and Hyson Teas; Loaf and Brown Sugar; Pepper; All spice; Allum; Brimstone; Copperas, &c.&c. They have also for sale, as usual, Salt and Castings; and shortly expect a further supply of Bar Iron, All of which they will sell on reasonable terms, for Cash, Deer and Bear Skins, Furs, Hemp, Bees' Wax, Keg Butter, Tallow, Country linen, Flax, &c.&c.[29]

Among the earliest commercial establishments in Knoxville were taverns, inns, ordinaries, and tippling houses. The county court minutes contain a number of permits for persons to operate a "public house" in their homes.[30] In 1794, a mere three years after the town was founded, Thomas counted seven taverns, plus tippling houses. Six frontier-period taverns mentioned in Knoxville histories include Chisholm's, Carmichael's, Stone's, McNamee's, Wood's, and Bearden's.[31]

Ramsey[32] calls Chisholm's the pioneer tavern in Knoxville. The first mention of this tavern is found in the September 14, 1793, issue of the *Knoxville Gazette*, where Chisholm requests that people indebted for "Liquors, Eating, Beef, &c" settle their accounts with him. Later he announced, "The subscriber has opened a house of entertainment, at No. 17, State Street—Boarding may be had by the quarter, half year, or year, on the usual terms."[33] No. 17 State Street was the lot immediately behind Blount Mansion. Since Chisholm was the original purchaser of the lot in the lottery, it is possible that he immediately erected a temporary building to ply his trade, then a couple of years later completed a larger structure that also served as an inn.

John Stone purchased the lot on the northwest corner of Cumberland and Gay streets, where he built a tavern described as a large log structure.[34] Some idea of the complex of outbuildings associated with this establishment is described in an 1800 deed as "gardens and stables, yards, backsides, ways, paths, passages, houses [and] outhouses."[35] The Moravians Steiner and De Schweinitz stayed in Stone's Tavern when they visited Knoxville, remarking, "We stopped with a Capt. Stone, a German, who received us in a courteous manner."[36]

Besides providing food and drink to the public, Knoxville's taverns also served as meeting places for legislative bodies before suitable governmental buildings were constructed. Ramsey[37] notes that the Territorial Legislature met in the large room of Anthony Carmichael's Tavern, which was located at the southeastern corner of Cumberland and State streets.

In 1802, the French botanist F. A. Michaux described the state of commercial business in Knoxville:

> Although founded eighteen or twenty years ago, this little town does not yet possess any kind of establishment or manufactory, except two or three tan yards. Trade, notwithstanding, is brisker here than at Nashville. The shops, though very few in number, are in general better stocked. The tradespeople get their provisions by land from Philadelphia, Baltimore, and Richmond in Virginia; and they send in return, by the same way, the produce of the country, which they buy of the cultivators, or take in barter for their goods. Baltimore and Richmond are the towns with which this part of the country does most business.[38]

A characteristic of frontier towns is the early establishment of basic industries to provide the settlers with necessities crucial for their survival: corn meal and wheat flour, iron tools and horseshoes, harness and saddles, firearms, and furniture being among the most obvious. James White owned two early grist mills on First Creek. We know that a mill was already in place as early as 1793, for there is a court entry that "ordered that the upper Mill Dam of James White be broke down [sic], against the first day of July next."[39] An early Knoxville historian stated that, soon after the founding of the town, several blacksmith shops opened. So did a goldsmith and jeweler, the latter advertising that he "made rifle guns in the neatest and most appropriate fashion."[40] In early 1794, merchant Nathaniel Cowan advertised that he "WANTED to purchase, a quantity of BARK, to be delivered on the North East side of the creek, opposite the town spring of Knoxville . . . I am determined to carry on the tanning business in this place, the ensuing fall."[41] In January 1795, David Lard and Stephen Duncan advertised that they had shoe, saddle, and bridle leather for sale at their tan yard on Second Creek,[42] and five months later a saddler's shop was opened in the house of Stephen Duncan.[43] In 1794, Thomas Hope, an architect, house carpenter, and cabinetmaker from Charleston, arrived in Knoxville and in 1796 advertised for an apprentice to learn the joiner's business.[44] Furniture maker Asa Hazen advertised in *Wilson's Knoxville Gazette*: "Having acquired a thorough knowledge of his business in the seaports and most approved shops he assures the public his work will be inferior to none."[45]

Household goods that required a more complex manufacturing process—refined ceramic tableware, for example, or luxury foodstuffs—had to be imported from the coastal cities. Although the closest seaports were Charleston and Savannah, the eastern Appalachian barrier initially forced merchants to depend on the long route down the Great Valley from the Middle Atlantic ports. Evidence that the journey was arduous is found in the statement of merchant Hugh Dunlap, who complained, "I left Philadelphia with my goods in December 1791, and did not reach Knoxville until about the 1st of February, 1792."[46] That these transportation barriers were being overcome, however, is suggested by a promotional piece in the *Knoxville Gazette* three years later:

> We have the pleasure to inform the public that the waggon road from this place to Nashville is so far completed, as that a waggon with a ton weight has actually passed it; and that the commissioners have entered into a contract for its thorough completion in the month of October, in whose hands ample funds are provided for that purpose....
>
> We have also the pleasure to inform our readers, that two waggons arrived here two days past from South Carolina, having passed through the mountains by way of the warm springs of French Broad; so that a waggon road is now open from Georgia, South Carolina, North Carolina, and the other Atlantic states by way of this place to Nashville, the capitol of the rich Cumberland country.[47]

What kind of commodities were being traded to the eastern cities and coastal ports from the frontier Knoxville area? Michaux observed that: "They send flour, cotton and lime to New Orleans by the river Tennessee; but this way is not so much frequented by the trade, the navigation of this river being very much encumbered in two different places by shallows interspersed with rocks."[48]

Early editions of the *Knoxville Gazette* provide a list of produce taken in by merchants and exchanged for luxury goods and some staples sold in their shops: corn, rye, oats, flax, butter, pork, hog's lard in white walnut kegs, tallow, furs, new feathers, seven hundred linen, and horses.[49]

What was the ethnic origin of these people who built homes and opened businesses in early Knoxville, and how might this ethnicity have affected community patterns and material culture? Henry Glassie has pointed out the fallacy of the "pure Anglo-Saxon blood" in Southern Appalachian culture.[50] However, an examination of the surnames of the fifty-one persons who acquired the sixty-four lots in the 1791 lottery suggests that all but one—Thomas Amis, who was of French descent—appear to be English, Scottish, or Scots-Irish. The same Anglo-American heritage is evident in the 1806 Knoxville tax list: the fifty-three legible surnames suggest that only three persons did not have an ancestry in the British Isles. Unfortunately, we know much less about the ancestry of the propertyless European American craftspersons and laborers who also contributed considerably to the development of the town in the frontier period.

We know even less about the African Americans, the other disenfranchised group that constituted a significant proportion of the early population and probably provided most of the back-breaking labor in the town. An 1801 census for Knoxville lists 146 slaves, out of a total population of 381 persons—38 percent of the population. This census lists no free persons of color in town.[51] In 1806, 26 of the 52 property owners had an average of 3 slaves apiece, but some persons owned many more.[52] Governor Blount owned 27 slaves when he died in 1800.[53]

It can be assumed from their numbers that much of the town construction and maintenance was done by African Americans. However, except for an occasional Christian name in a runaway advertisement or estate inventory, persons of color are virtually invisible in the frontier period of Knoxville.

How do the social and community patterns of early Knoxville compare to those of other towns on the southern frontier? The most comprehensively studied towns on this frontier are on the South Carolina Piedmont. Basically, the form and structure of the Piedmont settlement emerged in the movement of an agricultural system inland from coastal ports through a dendritic overland transportation network.[54] Descriptions of early Knoxville reveal a close similarity to the South Carolina frontier patterns.[55] The forty houses and businesses described in 1796 are within the range of South Carolina inland settlements—between twenty-eight and fifty structures. The gridiron plan of streets in both areas provided easy access for the maximum number of people. Specialized, nondomestic activity areas were an integral part of the earliest settlement. Finally, both areas had markedly stratified populations, ranging from persons like Governor Blount to the large number of slaves who often constituted the majority of the work force.

What was the mechanism at work that made frontier towns so similar? Similarities between Knoxville and the South Carolina frontier towns can be attributed in part to their unique positions in regional and national agricultural and transportation systems. The similarities among these communities seem to owe something, too, to their origins as speculative enterprises. To assure the growth of frontier towns, promoters had to offer incentives to settlers and have the capital for investment. The power of these land speculators harks back to the colonial period, as described by McCleskey in this volume. On the late-eighteenth-century southern frontier, capital was land and commodities. Both Governor Blount, who chose Knoxville for his capital, and James White, who laid it out, were land speculators; some historians have even argued that White was an agent of the governor.[56] Such intrigues aside, Blount, White, and the merchants who were attracted to the young town saw Knoxville as a strategic base for regional development. They promoted it as a "civilized" place like the secure towns they had left behind east of the mountains. It was necessary to establish order and security quickly and to provide a dependable supply of goods. This was made possible by wealth and by an authoritarian control of town development.

The idealized view of the frontier is of egalitarian pioneers carving out their niches in the wilderness, but in reality their destinies often were controlled by an oligarchic ruling class of white males in the nascent towns. Before the Civil War, Knoxville's ruling class was almost exclusively Anglo-American in ethnic origin and was composed largely of merchants, professional men, and large real-estate holders who were descendants of the town's original settlers. Women also were discriminated against. They could not vote; and, while single women possessed the property rights accorded to men, married women had no rights under the laws of coverture. The town's elite presided over local affairs virtually unchallenged, and it was not until 1839 that the mayor became an elected official.[57] Such undemocratic, authoritarian control was found in other southern frontier towns as well.

This control of town development resulted in an interesting mix of values and patterns. For example, the attempt to recreate the coastal urban centers in the frontier environment produced planned streets and town squares lined with log houses in which people ate their meals on imported Chinese porcelain. The street grid and establishment of courthouses and other public buildings symbolized order and security, as well as the town's central position in the frontier economy. Log houses often continued to be the homes of choice, even for the ruling elite. Nevertheless, while adhering to a vernacular preadaptive code of house building, members of the elite were assured a constant supply of the latest and often the most expensive consumer goods to advertise their high status. This availability of expensive consumer goods also has been documented on the eighteenth-century Kentucky frontier, where such objects allowed settlers to recreate the pleasant, secure lives they had left behind, imbuing them with optimism concerning the future.[58]

Archaeology of Frontier Knoxville

What does the archaeology of early Knoxville tell us about its architecture, social status, foodways, and other material culture? Due to the destructive impact of urbanization on archaeological remains in the central city, very little evidence of early Knoxville lifeways before 1815 has been recovered. Only two late-eighteenth-century sites, the James White Second house site and Blount Mansion, have been excavated extensively. Both were homes of the ruling elite, although work at the Blount site from 1992 through 1996 concentrated on what were believed to be slave quarters. Unfortunately, analysis of the thousands of artifacts from this structure has not been completed. The James White house possibly was built as early as 1786 and was occupied by the White family until James's death in 1821.[59] Blount Mansion was the home of Gov. William Blount from 1792, when the house was built, until his death in 1800.[60]

An early-nineteenth-century domestic midden was excavated on the Jourolman site in 1990.[61] This trash dump was located at the rear of a large two-story timber frame house adjacent to Blount Mansion, a structure probably built by one John McNeil, who purchased the property in 1793 and sold it in 1821. The mean ceramic date for the ceramics excavated in the midden is 1812. The house, later owned by the Jourolman family, was razed between 1871 and 1884.

We know very little about John McNeil. He served in the Revolutionary War in a Virginia company and is listed on the 1806 tax list for Knoxville. According to this list, McNeil owned six slaves and 1,327 acres in the county—a large tract of land. He was not living in Knoxville when he died in 1833.[62] Because his home was an impressive structure near Governor Blount's, it is likely that McNeil was either a merchant or a professional.

Only one additional archaeological feature dating from the twenty-nine years

Fig. 8.1. Remains of west foundation wall and southwest corner of the James White house, Knoxville. From Charles H. Faulkner. *An Archaeological and Historical Study of the James White Second Home Site*, Department of Anthropology Report of Investigations No. 28 (Knoxville: Department of Anthropology, University of Tennessee, 1984).

of Knoxville's frontier period has been excavated professionally. During the construction of the River View Towers in 1983, a privy pit was exposed containing a large sample of ceramics with a mean ceramic date of 1802.[63] This privy was on the rear line of Lot 20, owned in 1800 by one Joseph Greer. One of the earliest purchasers of a lot in Knoxville, Greer was appointed justice of the peace for Knox County by Governor Blount in 1793[64] and was one of five town commissioners appointed by the governor in 1794.[65] He appears on the 1806 Knoxville tax list, which shows that he owned 410 acres in the county, four city lots, and nine slaves. Joseph Greer obviously was a member of the town elite.

Both the James White house and Blount Mansion were modest dwellings, certainly not overt expressions of these families' elite status. The former house, moved

Fig. 8.2. James White house, Knoxville, ca. 1800. From Charles H. Faulkner, *An Archaeological and Historical Study of the James White Second Home Site*, Department of Anthropology Report of Investigations No. 28 (Knoxville: Department of Anthropology, University of Tennessee, 1984).

in 1854, was described as a two-pen log saddlebag house with front piazza, or porch.[66] While only the west end of the White house site was excavated, the architectural remains and spatial distribution of artifacts conform to the historic description of this house. The remnants of limestone footers indicate that the house was eighteen feet wide (fig. 8.1). The absence of a fireplace base at the west gable end suggests a central fireplace in the structure. Small limestone fragments scattered along the wall line could be chinking for interstices in the log walls, and a concentration of flat glass indicates a window in the west gable end. A heavy deposit of domestic debris at the southwestern corner of the house probably accumulated under a porch and also suggests an off-center doorway in a double-pen house[67] (fig. 8.2).

Blount Mansion, while constructed with the more intricate timber framing, also was a simple building of Anglo-American design. An architectural and archaeological study of the house, carried out in 1992 and 1993, revealed that the original home of the governor was a two-room, story-and-a-half, hall-and-parlor structure. The second story of the central block and the wings were shown to be nineteenth-century additions to the original eighteenth-century building.[68] Archaeological excavations within the quadrangle of outbuildings, dug from 1992 through 1996, reveal that one of the structures, a probable slave domicile, was moved after 1800 to become the west wing of the mansion.[69]

Restored outbuildings and recent archaeological testing in the rear yard of Blount Mansion reveal that timber-frame and weatherboarded buildings were arranged in a quadrangular pattern behind the house, with the governor's office and slave quarters anchoring the southeast and southwest corners, respectively (fig. 8.3). A large cistern provided a self-contained source of drinking water, filled by a conduit from the detached kitchen.[70] Given the number and arrangement of its outbuildings, the Blount Mansion lot (like the Stone tavern lot, with its similar diversity) seems typical of what recently has been defined as "the urban farmstead."[71] These farmsteads allowed for food production and storage, the stabling of animals, a source of drinking water, and waste disposal areas, until such necessary functions could be supplied by urban public and private services. These services were not available to Knoxvillians until well after the end of the pioneer period.[72]

While both houses and outbuildings were built in simple vernacular form, some of the latest construction materials were used in them. At the James White house were found a large number of window-glass sherds dating to the eighteenth century. Hand-headed cut nails recovered indicate that these early machine-produced fasteners were available in Knoxville at an early date.[73] Window glass was used extensively in Blount Mansion, too. In January 1792, Governor Blount wrote that he expected a box of window glass to be sent to Knoxville from Richmond.[74] Eighteenth-century window glass was ubiquitous around the mansion, even in the slave quarters.[75]

One of the most important discoveries of the four field seasons at Blount Mansion was the presence of large postholes at two corners of the slave quarters and

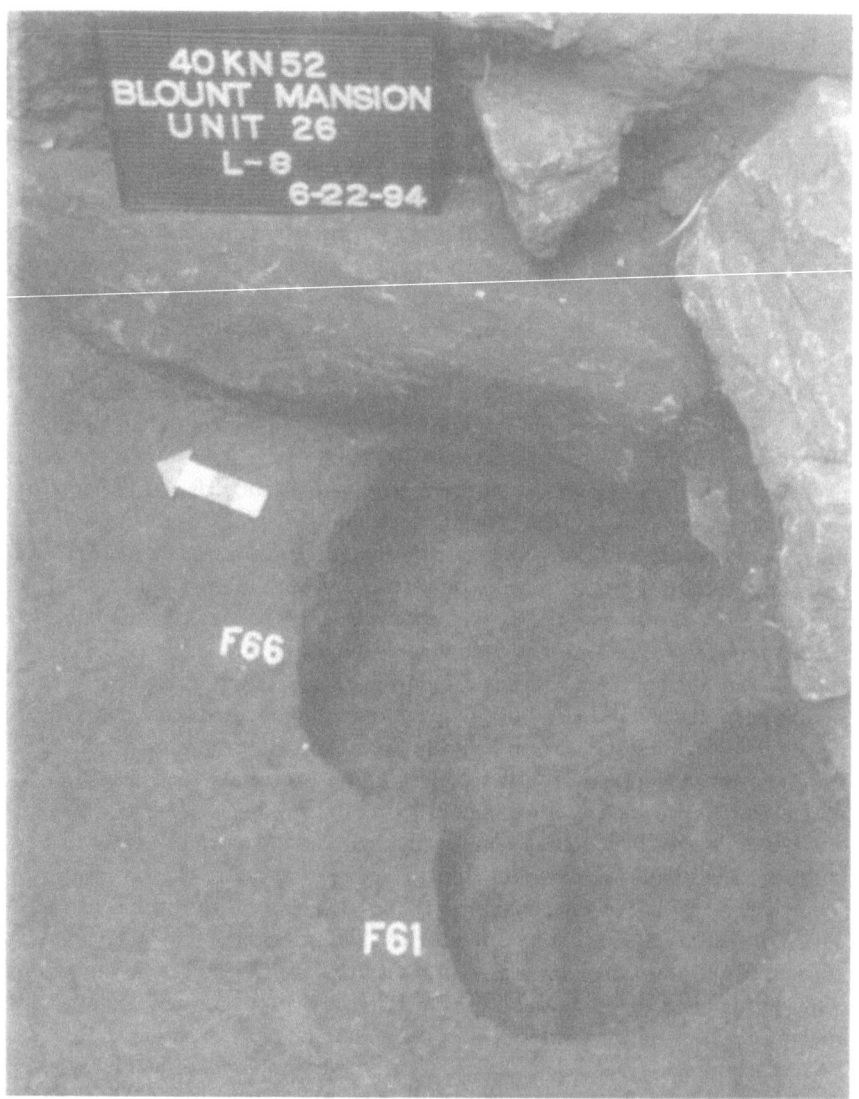

Fig. 8.3. Test excavation unit at Blount Mansion, Knoxville, showing posthole from defensive fence in northeast corner of office.

one corner of the office. These are believed to be part of a substantial defensive fence or palisade around the compound. Like the James White fort, the defensive enclosure had outbuildings integrated into the corners. The post at the northwest corner of the quarters was well chinked with limestone rock; the posthole was over one foot in diameter. The posthole at the southeast corner of the building also was over one foot in diameter, and the bottom of the deeply set post could not be reached, due to its location so close to the unit corner. The large posthole at the northeastern corner of the office was truncated by later excavation, but the base of this feature, which contained late-eighteenth-century artifacts, was about one foot in diameter (fig. 8.4).

Such a defensive enclosure may have been nothing more than a symbol that reaffirmed elite control of property, but its massive scale suggests a felt need to keep intruders out. That is, the townspeople of Knoxville may not have had complete confidence in the garrison of United States troops that arrived in February 1793, although the *Knoxville Gazette* reported on March 9, 1793, "On Tuesday, the 27th ult. arrived here, after a long and tedious march from Salisbury in North Carolina, a company of federal troops commanded by M. Rickard. The order and discipline displayed by this company, affords a new proof of the military abilities of this war-worn veteran, as well as his attention to duty."[76] On September 25 of the same year, over a thousand hostile Creek and Cherokee warriors gathered near the edge of town but decided against an attack. It was said later that they erroneously believed their position had been discovered, but perhaps they also were daunted by proliferating fortifications.[77]

While the archaeological record supports historical evidence that Knoxville's early architecture, even among the elite, was an efficient vernacular adaptation to the frontier environment, the archaeological remains of domestic artifacts reveal that the town leaders enjoyed a cosmopolitan way of life. Analysis of the numerous ceramic sherds found on the four sites demonstrates that the latest wares manufactured in England appeared in Knoxville almost as early as they did in the coastal cities.[78] High status was expressed in the use and display of expensive ceramics, and ceramics were used in the same social ceremonies here as in the metropolitan areas of the cultured East.

At the earliest levels of the James White site, researchers found that the most commonly recovered refined earthenware—45 percent of the sherds—was pearlware.[79] In two test excavations at Blount Mansion, pearlware constituted 31 percent and 36 percent of the ceramics in the deepest strata of the site.[80] Since pearlware was reaching North America by 1790 at the latest,[81] this means that women in Knoxville were serving tea in this new ware almost at the same time it appeared in the coastal cities. That the tea ceremony was commonplace is indicated by the fact that almost 50 percent of the decorated pearlware sherds at the James White house are from tea sets.[82] Twenty-seven percent of the identifiable vessel forms in an early stratum at Blount Mansion are tea bowls and saucers.[83] Only about 7 percent of the sherds from the Jourolman site are from tea sets, but this percentage is from a very small collection of twenty-nine sherds.[84] Unfortunately, vessel form was not recorded from the 1802 privy.[85]

Not only were the latest ceramic styles readily available to frontier Knoxvillians, but more expensive wares were acquired as well. Although Chinese porcelain is said to have become more common and of lower quality by the end of the eighteenth century,[86] recent comparisons of ceramic assemblages on early sites in

Fig. 8.4. Blount Mansion compound, ca. 1795. Drawn by Teresa J. Faulkner.

Tennessee identify porcelain as a high-status indicator.[87] At the James White and Blount Mansion sites, sherds of Chinese export porcelain dinner service constitute about 5 percent of the ceramics in the early levels (fig. 8.5).[88] The ceramic assemblage from the privy on Lot 20 contained about 19 percent Chinese porcelain.[89] While we cannot unequivocally identify this feature with Joseph Greer, the high percentage of Chinese porcelain in it suggests that it belonged to a high-status household. No porcelain was recovered at the Jourolman site; but, again, the small sample may be responsible.[90] Further research on Knoxville domestic sites undoubtedly will reveal other status indicators. The proliferation of tea wares suggests one way frontier women could express their independence from the dominance of males in frontier society.

Virtually no historic information exists about daily diet in frontier Knoxville. From only one archaeological site, the James White house, have the faunal and floral remains been completely analyzed; and at this site it is difficult to separate late-eighteenth-century remains from those dating to the later nineteenth century. Only a preliminary analysis of faunal and floral materials has been made on the other sites. Nevertheless, some general conclusions about early Knoxville foodways can be drawn from these limited data. These conclusions are based upon subjective observations of animal bones, especially as they reveal which species were butchered most frequently.

A large number of fragmentary long bones of large mammals are found (probably pigs and cattle), with virtually no evidence of their having been sawed into specific cuts of meat.[91] While the possibility exists that post-depositional forces (trampling, freezing, etc.) fragmented these bones, the presence of bones in the same condition at the rural late-eighteenth-century Gibbs site near Knoxville has been interpreted as the deliberate crushing of these elements to obtain marrow.[92] This intensive extraction activity and a prevalence of chopping in the butchering process suggest what Deetz[93] has identified as a medieval butchering pattern, which largely had disappeared in New England by the late eighteenth century.

Skeletal elements that occurred consistently on all the Knoxville domestic sites were pig teeth and other cranial parts. This is good evidence that these animals were butchered on these sites, an activity typical on an urban farmstead where animals were penned up and slaughtered, and where their meat was preserved in a smokehouse.

One can also conclude that the earliest settlers, at least the wealthy, had both the quantity and variety of domestic stock needed to meet their daily dietary requirements without having to rely on hunting. Wild animal species were only minimally present at the James White site and thus far have not been identified at the other sites. The identifiable faunal remains are dominated by pig and cow, with chicken a distant third in frequency.[94] Other identified species include sheep at the James White site and goat and mallard duck in the Lot 20 privy.[95]

Another conclusion, though tentative, is that pork was more common in the diet than beef. This, of course, has been a standard interpretation of the southern diet,[96]

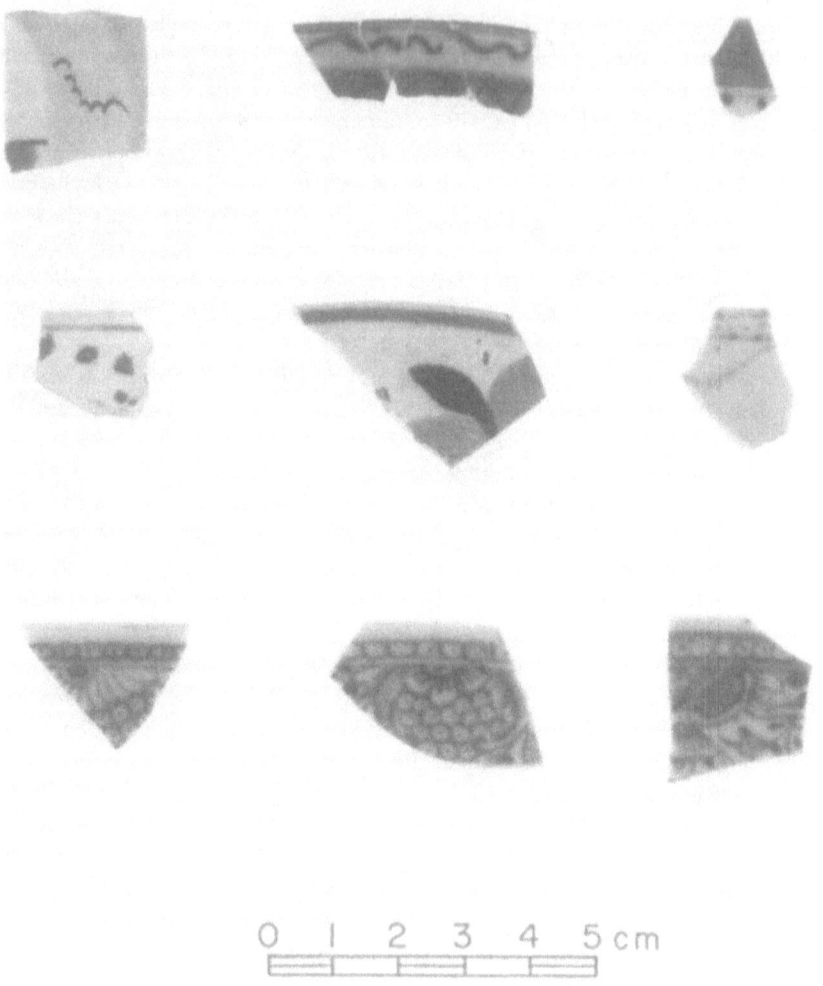

Fig. 8.5. Ceramic sherds from Knoxville sites. Top row, cups from the James White house site, left to right: underglaze polychrome pearlware, underglaze blue handpainted, underglaze blue Chinese porcelain. Middle row, saucers from Blount Mansion, left to right: overglaze enameled creamware, underglaze polychrome pearlware, overglaze enameled Chinese porcelain. Bottom row: underglaze blue Chinese porcelain plates from Blount Mansion.

but it is also relevant to preadaptation on the Southern Appalachian frontier. Pigs are extremely self-sufficient, free-ranging animals that were ideally suited to the forested uplands of the Southern Appalachians. In addition, pork can be preserved much more easily than beef and in more palatable forms. The diversified farming of the Upland South culture did, however, provide for the raising of cattle, and fresh beef was available to Knoxvillians who could afford it. In the June 5, 1794, issue of the *Knoxville Ga-*

zette, John Chisholm advertised: "The subscriber gives notice to the inhabitants of Knoxville and its vicinity, that he intends to open a beef market on the first of June next, where they may be supplied with beef every third day of the season. The cash must be paid on delivery of the beef."

Conclusions

The archival data on frontier Knoxville, and the limited archaeological excavations carried out on sites of this period, suggest that the layout, or town plan, of the early village was strongly influenced by the Southern Appalachian cultural tradition and by the economic power of the male Anglo-American town leaders. This rectilinear design reinforced social order and assured economic prosperity in the frontier towns. Similar patterns can be seen in town plans and public architecture in other areas of the southern frontier.

That these frontier community patterns sometimes may have been more symbolic than substantive is indicated by their unkempt occurrence in Knoxville. While streets were laid out in a grid pattern when the town was founded, they were not surfaced at that time, nor was their location clearly established. It was not until 1826 that the first systematic effort was made to improve them.[97] Although bids for the construction of a masonry courthouse were sought as early as 1793, this important building still was not completed six years later. J. G. M. Ramsey reports that the courthouse where the Territorial Assembly met was a small one-story building with floor space about thirty by twenty-four feet, and that this body sometimes held its sessions in the barrack or blockhouse.[98] Thomas Humes reported, "The Court-house . . . became highly obnoxious by its dilapidation to the citizens, but more particularly to the lawyers. One of the latter, a frolicsome Irishman, determined to remove the universal pest by fire . . . And so, on a quiet winter night, when a deep snow was upon the earth it was burned down, to the great satisfaction of the town."[99]

While town planning and public buildings were used by the town's founders to symbolize stability and thereby to stimulate economic prosperity, their log and timber-frame houses did not symbolize power and wealth. Whether this was due to a powerful influence of the Southern Appalachian architectural tradition, a greater difficulty in obtaining masonry construction materials and specialized labor to work them, or simply the need to erect solid houses quickly and efficiently, their homes often continued to be built in the vernacular style. Wealth and social status seem to have been expressed more easily by the luxury goods present in significant quantities on domestic sites. These artifacts provide considerable data for the study of social and economic relationships in these towns. While men controlled the estate, frontier women apparently were in charge of hearth and home, to judge by the elegant ceramics that graced their tables. While women take a back seat to men in early historical accounts, their importance in frontier social interaction is marked in the archaeological remains of the times.

Frontier towns appear to have softened the cutting harshness of the eastern woodlands wilderness, where many so-called "backwoodsmen" have been characterized as uncouth, antigovernment, irreligious, and anti-intellectual.[100] In towns such as Knoxville, and even in rural areas like the Kentucky frontier, the documented availability of luxury goods and services, and perhaps more importantly the social ceremonies those goods represent, indicate that many pioneers followed and adopted the latest eighteenth-century fashions. In addition, schools were established, and there was bustling governmental and religious activity. Perhaps a tea set does not a cultured person make, but there is little doubt that most of these early settlers, in town and on farm alike, yearned for security, salvation, and the amenities of life that eighteenth-century progress could bring, at the same time that they were seeking independence and personal freedom in the wilderness. Frontier towns, as "backwoods" as the rural people they served, provided both survival necessities and luxury creature comforts. Ironically, though, in the process, the early settlers became dependent on the very power structures and centralized authority which many were trying to escape.

While wealth, power, and politics played important roles in the early development of Knoxville, the sweat and blood of the usually faceless persons who built, maintained, and defended the town were just as significant in the development of this future city. Unfortunately, America's infatuation with the wealthy and powerful is a major reason we know more about persons who ate their meals from Chinese porcelain than about those who served them. The houses of the elite, such as Blount Mansion, have become veritable shrines, preserved and restored by historical associations for a devoted public. In undertaking such preservation, these groups also preserved surrounding yards and outbuildings, where archaeological evidence of daily lifeways was protected in an oasis surrounded by modern urban development. Because these are the only frontier sites accessible in downtown Knoxville, it is not surprising that archaeological research has focused on them.

Unfortunately, most of the Euro-American working class and the African American slaves remain nameless. Few of them left written records, since most were illiterate; the recorders of early events neglected to describe what they undoubtedly felt were the mundane, workaday lives of these people. In the absence of their own written history, the lifeways of the laboring class can be studied most effectively through archaeology. However, none of their small, undistinguished houses are preserved, and their home sites are buried under two hundred years of fill in the heart of downtown Knoxville. It is imperative that future archaeological research in Knoxville not be locked into opportunistic projects like Blount Mansion, but be directed toward answering questions about the Euro-American working class and African American slaves. The current research on the slave quarters at Blount Mansion is a step in this direction. Relevant questions include: What other culture traditions besides the Upland South are in evidence? And how did these thus far "invisible" people adapt to the frontier environment and elite power structure? Considering the nature of the urban archaeological record, answering these questions will be a difficult but not impossible task. Half the battle is realizing where biases exist in the historical and archaeological records, and what we need to do to compensate for them.

NOTES

1. Charles N. Glaab and A. Theodore Brown, *A History of Urban America* (New York: Macmillan, 1967), 28.
2. Aelred J. Gray and Susan F. Adams, "Government," in *Heart of the Valley: A History of Knoxville, Tennessee*, ed. Lucille Deaderick (Knoxville: East Tennessee Historical Society, 1976), 75.
3. Milton B. Newton, "Cultural Preadaptation and the Upland South," *Geoscience and Man* 5 (1974): 143–54.
4. Frederick Jackson Turner, *The Frontier in American History* (New York: Holt, Rinehart, and Winston, 1920), 164.
5. Henry Glassie, *Pattern in the Material Folk Culture of the Eastern United States* (Philadelphia: Univ. of Pennsylvania Press, 1968), 78–79.
6. Terry G. Jordan and Matti Kaups, *The American Backwoods Frontier: An Ethnic and Ecological Frontier* (Baltimore, Md.: Johns Hopkins Univ. Press, 1989).
7. Roger D. Mason, *Euro-American Pioneer Settlement Systems in the Central Salt River Valley of Northeast Missouri*, Publications in Archaeology No. 2 (Columbia: Dept. of Anthropology, Univ. of Missouri, 1984), 91.
8. J. G. M. Ramsey, *The Annals of Tennessee* (Knoxville: East Tennessee Historical Society, 1967), 374.
9. Alice B. Keith, ed., *The John Gray Blount Papers*, vol. 2: *1790–1795* (Raleigh: North Carolina State Dept. of Archives and History, 1959), 447–48.
10. Thomas W. Humes, "An Address Delivered before the Citizens of Knoxville, on the 10th Day of February, 1842, the Semi-Centennial Anniversary of the Settlement of the Town" (Knoxville, 1842), 21. Univ. of Tennessee Special Collections.
11. Ibid.
12. Gray and Susan F. Adams, "Government," 72.
13. Samuel Cole Williams, ed., *Early Travels in the Tennessee Country, 1540–1800* (Johnson City, Tenn.: Watauga Press, 1928), 454–55.
14. William Rule, *Standard History of Knoxville, Tennessee* (Chicago: Lewis Publishing Co., 1900), 92.
15. Ibid.
16. Mary U. Rothrock, ed., *The French Broad–Holston Country* (Knoxville: East Tennessee Historical Society, 1946), 279.
17. Ibid., 281.
18. Rule, *Standard History of Knoxville*, 424–25.
19. Samuel C. Williams, *Early Travels in the Tennessee Country*, 312.

20. Clifton H. Olmstead, *History of Religion in the United States* (Englewood Cliffs, N.J.: Prentice-Hall, 1960), 221.
21. Jordan and Kaups, *American Backwoods Frontier*, 74.
22. Randall W. Moir, "Farmstead Proxemics and Intrasite Patterning," in *Historic Buildings, Material Culture, and the People of the Prairie Margin*, Richland Creek Technical Series, vol. 5, Archaeology Research Program, ed. David H. Jurney and Randall W. Moir, 229–37 (Dallas, Tex.: Institute for the Study of Earth and Man, Southern Methodist Univ., 1984).
23. Michael A. Williams, *Homeplace: The Social Use and Meaning of the Folk Dwelling in Southwestern North Carolina* (Athens: Univ. of Georgia Press, 1991), 131.
24. William J. MacArthur, Jr., "Knoxville's History: An Interpretation," in Deaderick, *Heart of the Valley*, 10–11.
25. Samuel C. Williams, *Early Travels in the Tennessee Country*, 454–55.
26. Rothrock, *French Broad–Holston Country*, 255.
27. Rule, *Standard History of Knoxville*, 56.
28. *Knoxville Gazette*, Feb. 11, 1794.
29. *Knoxville Gazette*, May 22, 1795.
30. Rothrock, *French Broad–Holston Country*, 59.
31. Amy L. Young, *The Knoxville Archaeological Mapping Project: Final Report* (Knoxville: Dept. of Anthropology, Univ. of Tennessee, 1993), 19.
32. J. G. M. Ramsey, *Annals of Tennessee*, 560.
33. *Knoxville Gazette*, Feb. 13, 1794.
34. Jeffrey L. Holland and Phillip Thomason, *Final Preliminary Phase I Archaeological and Architectural Resources Investigations of the Gay Street Site of the Proposed United States Courthouse in Knoxville, Knox County, Tennessee* (Atlanta, Ga.: Garrow & Associates, 1992), 14.
35. Knox County Deed Book, F1, 2:161.
36. Samuel C. Williams, *Early Travels in the Tennessee Country*, 454.
37. J. G. M. Ramsey, *Annals of Tennessee*, 630.
38. Ruben G. Thwaites, ed., *Travels West of the Alleghenies* (Cleveland, Ohio, 1904), 266.
39. Knox County Court, Minute Book No. 21, 1793.
40. Rule, *Standard History of Knoxville*, 194.
41. *Knoxville Gazette*, Mar. 27, 1794.
42. Ibid., Jan. 23, 1795.
43. Ibid., June 5, 1795.
44. Susan Tate, "Thomas Hope of Tennessee, ca. 1757–1820, House Carpenter and Joiner" (Master's thesis, Univ. of Tennessee, Knoxville, 1972).
45. *Wilson's Knoxville Gazette*, May 11, 1808.
46. Rule, *Standard History of Knoxville*, 57.
47. *Knoxville Gazette*, July 31, 1795.
48. Thwaites, *Travels West of the Alleghenies*, 266.
49. *Knoxville Gazette*, Feb. 13 and 27, 1794.
50. Glassie, *Pattern in Material Folk Culture*, 79.
51. "Letter of Robert Hays to President of the U.S. on the Population of Knoxville and East Tennessee, 1801." East Tennessee Historical Society's *Publications*, no. 26 (1954).

52. Knoxville, Tenn., Tax List for 1806.
53. Lisa Oakley, *Interpretive Supplement: The African-American Experience at Blount Mansion, Summer 1990* (Knoxville: Blount Mansion Association, 1990).
54. Kenneth L. Lewis, *The American Frontier: An Archaeological Study of Settlement Pattern and Process* (Orlando, Fla.: Academic Press, 1984).
55. Ibid., 181–200.
56. MacArthur, "Knoxville's History: An Interpretation," 70.
57. Michael J. McDonald and William B. Wheeler, *Knoxville, Tennessee: Continuity and Change in an Appalachian City* (Knoxville: Univ. of Tennessee Press, 1983).
58. Elizabeth A. Perkins, "The Consumer Frontier: Household Consumption in Early Kentucky," *Journal of American History* 78, no. 2 (1991): 509–10.
59. Charles H. Faulkner, "James White's Second Home: A Historical Site in Knoxville," East Tennessee Historical Society's *Publications*, nos. 56 and 57 (1986).
60. Stanley J. Folmsbee and Susan H. Dillon, "The Blount Mansion: Tennessee's Territorial Capitol," *Tennessee Historical Quarterly* 22 (1963): 103–22; Kent Whitworth, "Blount Mansion: Parking Lot or Landmark?" *Journal of East Tennessee History* 62 (1991): 80–92.
61. Amy L. Young and Charles H. Faulkner, *Phase II Archaeological Excavations at the Blount Mansion Visitor's Center, the Jourolman Site* (Knoxville: Dept. of Anthropology, Univ. of Tennessee, 1991).
62. Ibid., 2.
63. Linda F. Carnes, *Archaeological and Historical Investigations of the River View Towers Site (Formerly the C&C Plaza Site), Knoxville, Tennessee* (Knoxville: Dept. of Anthropology, Univ. of Tennessee, 1983), 48–52.
64. Territory of the United States, South of the River Ohio, 1790–1796, *The Blount Journal, 1790–1796* (Nashville: Tennessee Historical Commission, 1955), 71.
65. Rule, *Standard History of Knoxville*, 50.
66. Nancy Scott, *A Memoir of Hugh Lawson White* (Nashville, 1856).
67. Charles H. Faulkner, *An Archaeological and Historical Study of the James White Second Home Site*, Department of Anthropology Report of Investigations No. 28 (Knoxville: Dept. of Anthropology, Univ. of Tennessee, 1984); Faulkner, "James White's Second Home: A Historical Site in Knoxville."
68. Michael Emrich and George T. Fore, *Historic Structure Report, Blount Mansion, Tennessee* (Nashville: Office of Michael Emrich, 1992).
69. Charles H. Faulkner, "Archaeology at Blount Mansion: Architectural Metamorphosis of a Frontier Landmark" (Paper presented at the 11th Symposium on Ohio Valley Urban and Historic Archaeology, Giant City State Park, Ill., Mar. 13, 1993).
70. Charles H. Faulkner and Deborah German, *Archaeological Excavation of the Blount Mansion Cistern Conduit* (Knoxville: Dept. of Anthropology, Univ. of Tennessee, 1990).
71. Leslie C. Stewart-Abernathy, "Urban Farmsteads: Household Responsibilities in the City," *Historical Archaeology* 20 (1986): 5–15.
72. Charles H. Faulkner, "The Urban Farmstead in Knoxville, Tennessee: Pattern and Process in a Mid-South City," *Ohio Valley Historical Archaeology* 7–8 (1993): 17–23.

73. Faulkner, *Archaeological and Historical Study of the James White Second Home Site*, 116–24.
74. Philip M. Hamer, ed., "Letters of Governor William Blount," East Tennessee Historical Society's *Publications*, nos. 3–4 (1931–32): 126.
75. Faulkner, "Archaeology at Blount Mansion: Architectural Metamorphosis."
76. *Knoxville Gazette*, Mar. 9, 1793.
77. Ibid., Oct. 12, 1793.
78. Charles H. Faulkner, "An Archaeological Study of Fences at the Gibbs House," Tennessee Anthropological Association Miscellaneous Paper No. 16, in *Proceedings of the Tenth Symposium on Ohio Valley Urban and Historic Archaeology* (Knoxville: Tennessee Anthropological Association, 1992), 32.
79. Faulkner, *Archaeological and Historical Study of the James White Second Home Site*, 60–68.
80. Charles H. Faulkner, *A Final Report on Archaeological Testing in the Garden of Blount Mansion, Knoxville, Tennessee* (Knoxville: Dept. of Anthropology, Univ. of Tennessee, 1985), table 1; Mary Foster, "Analysis of Ceramics and Glass from Unit 5, Blount Mansion, 1992 Field Season," 1992, research paper on file, Historical Archaeology Laboratory, Department of Anthropology, Univ. of Tennessee, Knoxville, p. 235.
81. Ivor Noël-Hume, "Creamware to Pearlware: A Williamsburg Perspective," in *Ceramics in America*, Winterthur Conference Report, 1972, ed. Ian M. G. Quimby (Charlottesville: Univ. Press of Virginia, 1973), 235.
82. Faulkner, *Archaeological and Historical Study of the James White Second Home Site*, 65–68.
83. Foster, "Analysis of Ceramics and Glass from Unit 5," table 6.
84. Young and Faulkner, *Phase II Archaeological Excavations at Blount Mansion*, table 12.
85. Carnes, *Archaeological and Historical Investigations of the River View Towers Site*, table 4.
86. Ivor Noël-Hume, *A Guide to Artifacts of Colonial America* (New York: Alfred A. Knopf, 1969), 261.
87. Samuel D. Smith, *Historical Background and Archaeological Testing of the Davy Crockett Birthplace State Historic Area, Greene County, Tennessee*, Division of Archaeology Research Series No. 6, Tennessee Department of Conservation (Nashville: Tennessee Division of Archaeology, 1980), table 1A; Faulkner, *Archaeological and Historical Study of the James White Second Home Site*, table 6.
88. Faulkner, *Archaeological and Historical Study of the James White Second Home Site*, table 7; Foster, "An Analysis of Ceramics and Glass from Unit 5," table 4.
89. Carnes, *Archaeological and Historical Investigations of the River View Towers Site*, table 4.
90. Young and Faulkner, *Phase II Archaeological Excavations at the Blount Mansion*, table 12.
91. Ibid.; Faulkner, *Archaeological and Historical Study of the James White Second Home Site*, 102–14.
92. Charles H. Faulkner, *Archaeological Testing at the Nicholas Gibbs House: Season I* (Knoxville: Dept. of Anthropology, Univ. of Tennessee, 1988), 23–24.
93. James Deetz, *In Small Things Forgotten: The Archaeology of Early American Life* (New York: Anchor Press/Doubleday, 1977).
94. Faulkner, *Archaeological and Historical Study of the James White Second Home Site* 102–14; Faulkner, *Final Report on Archaeological Testing in the Garden of Blount Mansion*, 13.

95. Carnes, *Archaeological and Historical Investigations of the River View Towers Site*, 50.
96. Lewis Cecil Gray, *The History of Agriculture in the Southern United States to 1860*, 2 vols. (Washington, D.C.: Carnegie Institute, 1933; reprinted, Gloucester, Mass.: Peter Smith, 1958).
98. J. G. M. Ramsey, *Annals of Tennessee*, 630.
99. Rothrock, *French Broad–Holston Country*, 52.
100. Jordan and Kaups, *American Backwoods Frontier*.

 "Seeing" Early Appalachian Communities through the Lenses of History, Geography, and Sociology

David C. Hsiung

The name "Appalachia" evokes a host of popular images and stereotypes: feuds, individualism, moonshine, subsistence farming, quilting bees, illiteracy, and dueling banjos, to name just a few. Both complimentary and derogatory images generally arise from two important concepts, "isolation" and "community." John Fox, Jr., one of America's most popular novelists at the turn of the twentieth century, wrote, "In the march of civilization westward, the Southern mountaineer has been left in an isolation almost beyond belief. He was shut off by mountains that have blocked and still block the commerce of a century, and there for a century he has stayed." As for the mountaineer's social world, Fox wrote that "his interest centered in himself, his family, his distant neighbor, his grist mill, his country store, his county town."[1] Ever since Will Wallace Harney in 1873 identified Appalachia as "A Strange Land and Peculiar People," Americans in large part have attributed local characteristics to tightly knit communities well removed from the mainstream of American society.[2]

To understand Appalachia and its accompanying stereotypes, one must look critically at the notions of isolation and community. How are such terms defined? What physical and social forces unite or fragment a community? In what ways can a region be "isolated" from surrounding areas? To answer the questions and examine the origins of the images, one must go back before the twentieth and nineteenth centuries to the beginnings of permanent white settlement. After all, isolation can make the recent mountaineer "the pioneer of the Revolution, the living ancestor of the Modern West," only if such isolation took hold from first settlement.[3]

This essay focuses on Washington County, in upper East Tennessee, the northeastern tip of the state, from 1780 to 1800. This rural area formed an important part of the southern backcountry soon after permanent settlers arrived in the late

1760s. Using a framework for analyzing isolation (and its corollary, integration) in conjunction with different theories of community, this chapter will look at an early Appalachian region through the complementary lenses of history, geography, and sociology, to help see the southern backcountry in new ways and in a new interdisciplinary light.

Interdisciplinary Frameworks and Theories

A theoretical framework for measuring a region's internal and external "connectedness" with the larger society can help one evaluate the degree to which a community is "isolated" or "integrated." Social psychologists would call this framework a "multidimensional construct," one composed of several distinct "dimensions" and "measures." More simply, "connectedness" contains a variety of parts, each in turn consisting of smaller pieces. One must consider each dimension in relation to, rather than separate from, the other dimensions. Otherwise, blanket statements proclaiming a region "isolated" or "integrated" miss the different ways in which a region can be isolated in one respect but not in others. By paying close attention to how a region exhibits a range of characteristics, one can arrive at a more holistic, synthetic, and realistic understanding of a region.

The framework separates connectedness into several component parts. Each of these "dimensions" must be placed on the isolation-integration continuum before drawing any conclusions about the region as a whole. For example, upper East Tennessee may be broken down into its political, social, economic, geographical, and perceptual elements. The region may be more isolated in one dimension (such as political structure) and more integrated in others (such as economy and transportation). Therefore, the region can be both isolated and integrated during the same time period. Only after one examines all of these dimensions can upper East Tennessee be assigned a spot on the continuum of connectedness. Several cautions must be noted, however. The framework may convey the sense that the dimensions are distinct from and unrelated to one another, but such a separation did not exist in upper East Tennessee (or anywhere else); each dimension shares important characteristics with every other dimension. Furthermore, variations may exist *within* the region. Towns located along the railroad, for example, might be more integrated in certain respects than those tucked within the folds of mountain ridges and valleys. The sum of these geographical variations shapes our larger understanding of upper East Tennessee.

A similar process of evaluation takes place at a more detailed level, for each dimension must be examined through several "measures." These different forms of evidence must be weighed before judging the degree of connectedness for a given dimension. For example, upper East Tennessee's economy may be more isolated regarding subsistence agriculture, but more integrated with respect to iron manufacture and livestock trade. One might then conclude that the region's economy should be placed more toward the side of integration than of isolation on the continuum of connectedness. Many of these measures, too, address more than one dimension. As this essay will show, the early road network is influenced by geographical conditions, provides a context for the development of a community, and shapes the perceptions of those living within the region.

This framework, therefore, provides a complex way to study a theoretical notion like connectedness. "Isolation," often regarded in monolithic terms, can be broken down into its interrelated parts and analyzed more clearly and critically. To refer to the metaphor used in this essay's title, this framework serves as a camera lens through which one can take a wide-angle shot of the forest as well as zoom in on the trees. But as experienced photographers know, different lenses help clarify certain subjects while obscuring others. The polarizing filter removes the sun's disconcerting glare, but it also darkens the sky to an artificial shade of blue. The lens of "community theory"—ground and polished over the decades by historians, anthropologists, and sociologists—helps us understand society in the southern backcountry, but it too carries a coating of assumptions that distorts our view of the past.

When George A. Hillery, Jr., surveyed the social science literature in 1955, he found *ninety-four* definitions for "community." While the majority of these definitions agreed on certain elements, they shared only one obvious and simplistic concept—that "all of the definitions deal with people."[4] Many current definitions of *community* are based on identifying social structures and activities in a particular locale. For example, Gideon Sjoberg calls a community "a collectivity of actors sharing in a limited territorial area as the base for carrying out the greatest share of their daily activities."[5] Although specific physical location unquestionably plays an important role, some argue that it need not be a prerequisite for community. As Thomas Bender makes clear, "the concept means more than a place or local activity. There is an expectation of a special quality of human relationship in a community, and it is this experiential dimension that is crucial to its definition." Community, therefore, "is best defined as a network of social relations marked by mutuality and emotional bonds" that "may or may not be coterminous with a specific, contiguous territory."[6] A community of *interests* may exist, as, for example, among researchers of the early southern backcountry. Gunnar Almgren argues in a recent survey of the topic of community that "the dominant discriminating element and point of debate among definitions remain the role of territorial arrangements."[7] Although this essay pays close attention to geographical details, it takes a flexible approach towards analyzing community in terms of location. Networks of social relations are not limited to a single town, cove, valley, or mountain top, but instead overlap these different areas and change form under different circumstances.

In addition to freeing the concept of community from this geographical anchor, one must also liberate it from its romanticized theoretical tradition. Scholars often have seen societies as evolving from a "rural" or "traditional" stage to an "urban" or "modern" one.[8] Such views are rooted in Ferdinand Tonnies's early analysis, *Gemeinschaft und Gesellschaft* (1887), translated as *Community and Society*. At one end, community is bound together by close personal ties where "[a]ll intimate, private, and exclusive living together . . . is understood as life in Gemeinschaft (community)." At the other extreme, "Gesellschaft (society) is public life—it is the world itself." An atomized society of unconnected individuals characterizes Gesellschaft, the "mere co-existence of people independent of each other."[9] The point can be illustrated by comparing the colonial New England town with modern Manhattan. Similarly, the familiar world of the mountain hollow can be contrasted with the disconcertingly alien character of emigrant destinations such as Detroit. In each case, one associates a positive value with the Gemeinschaft image of society. Almgren notes that sociologists have had difficulty with the concept of community for several reasons, "not the least of which has been nostalgic attachment to the idealized notion that the existence of community is embodied in the village or small town where human associations are characterized as *Gemeinschaft*—that is, associations that are intimate, familiar, sympathetic, mutually interdependent, and reflective of a shared social consciousness."[10]

This biased analysis of community also has seeped into the field of rural sociology, where two divergent perspectives compete for interpretive dominance. The first, emerging out of the Country Life movement at the beginning of this century, sees rural societies and communities as backward and seeks to improve them. This view encouraged movements designed to modernize and transform rural society through Cooperative Extension Services, agricultural colleges, and sociological research. The second perspective, conversely, sees rural society as superior to urban society, and therefore its existence must be protected and preserved against the forces of industrial capitalism. Both outlooks have driven research on rural areas, especially rural communities.[11] Students of Appalachian communities in the southern backcountry must be aware of these coatings on the sociological lens before they can see with any degree of historical precision how such communities have changed.

Tonnies's ideas, and the use to which historians subsequently put them, have come under sharp attack. Historians disagree as to the particular period during which the shift from Gemeinschaft to Gesellschaft took place in America. In his perceptive survey of this issue, Thomas Bender examines the works of Bernard Bailyn and Darrett Rutman (who locate the change sometime during the seventeenth century), Gordon Wood and Richard Bushman (who find it in the eighteenth century), and Stephan Thernstrom and Robert Wiebe (who place the change during the early and late nineteenth century, respectively).[12] How can the crucial shift in American society occur at different points in time, let alone different centuries? Further complicating the picture, more recent studies stress the continuation, not the destruction, of earlier social relationships. For the colonial period alone, studies of Massachusetts (Concord, Gloucester, and Marblehead) and Maryland (Saint Mary's County) argue for the persistence of communal relations that resemble Tonnies's Gemeinschaft.[13]

Other critics take issue with the utility of the concepts of Gemeinschaft and Gesellschaft. Christopher Lasch, for example, invites readers to "consider some of the many contrasting typologies that Tonnies piled on the basic contrast between community and 'society' or contractual 'association.'" After listing half a dozen of these abstract and ambiguous "contrasting dichotomies" (to use Tonnies's words), Lasch emphasizes "their uselessness either as instruments of sociological analysis or as categories of moral judgment."[14]

Thomas Bender, also a target of Lasch's criticism, nonetheless clears a path through this conceptual jungle. Instead of conceiving Gemeinschaft and Gesellschaft as mutually exclusive conditions, he reminds us that Tonnies "described these two patterns of social relations that coexisted in everyone's social experience. *Gemeinschaft* and *Gesellschaft* were not places; they were forms of human interaction."[15] Tonnies wrote that a society's "whole development tends toward an approach to Gesellschaft in which ... the force of Gemeinschaft persists, although with diminishing strength, even in the period of Gesellschaft, and remains the reality of social life."[16] An entire society need not shift from "traditional" and "rural" to "modern" and "urban"; instead, certain portions of that society may exhibit more of one interaction than the other. Similarly, every segment of society (which may be based in different geographically settings) contains a particular mixture of Gemeinschaft and Gesellschaft at any given time. Even at the individual level, certain persons may view their relationships with society from both perspectives. This insight allows us to use a basic element of Tonnies's ideas without getting mired in shifting definitions of vague terms.

The framework for connectedness and the theories of community can be brought together in upper East Tennessee by analyzing the road network that developed from 1780 to 1800. Examining the geographical dimension of transportation and communications reveals the physical nature of isolation and integration. At the same time, the roads describe the shifting territorial boundaries of the community, where the network of social relations fostered by the roads fit imperfectly with the political and physical units of town, county, and valley. The road system reveals that both Gemeinschaft and Gesellschaft operated during the late eighteenth century, forcing us to rethink not only notions of "isolation" and "community" but also the image and development of Appalachian communities more generally.

Mapping the Early Road Network

The road system in upper East Tennessee helped shape the character and boundaries of the region. A network had developed by the turn of the nineteenth century that connected the residents both internally and externally. Settlements on different creeks and rivers were tied to each other by many small roads, while larger routes linked upper East Tennessee with different states. These roads, however, served some areas better than others, and certain portions of the region remained fairly inaccessible. Furthermore, overland travel during this period, no matter how well constructed the road, involved considerable effort and expense. A broad analysis

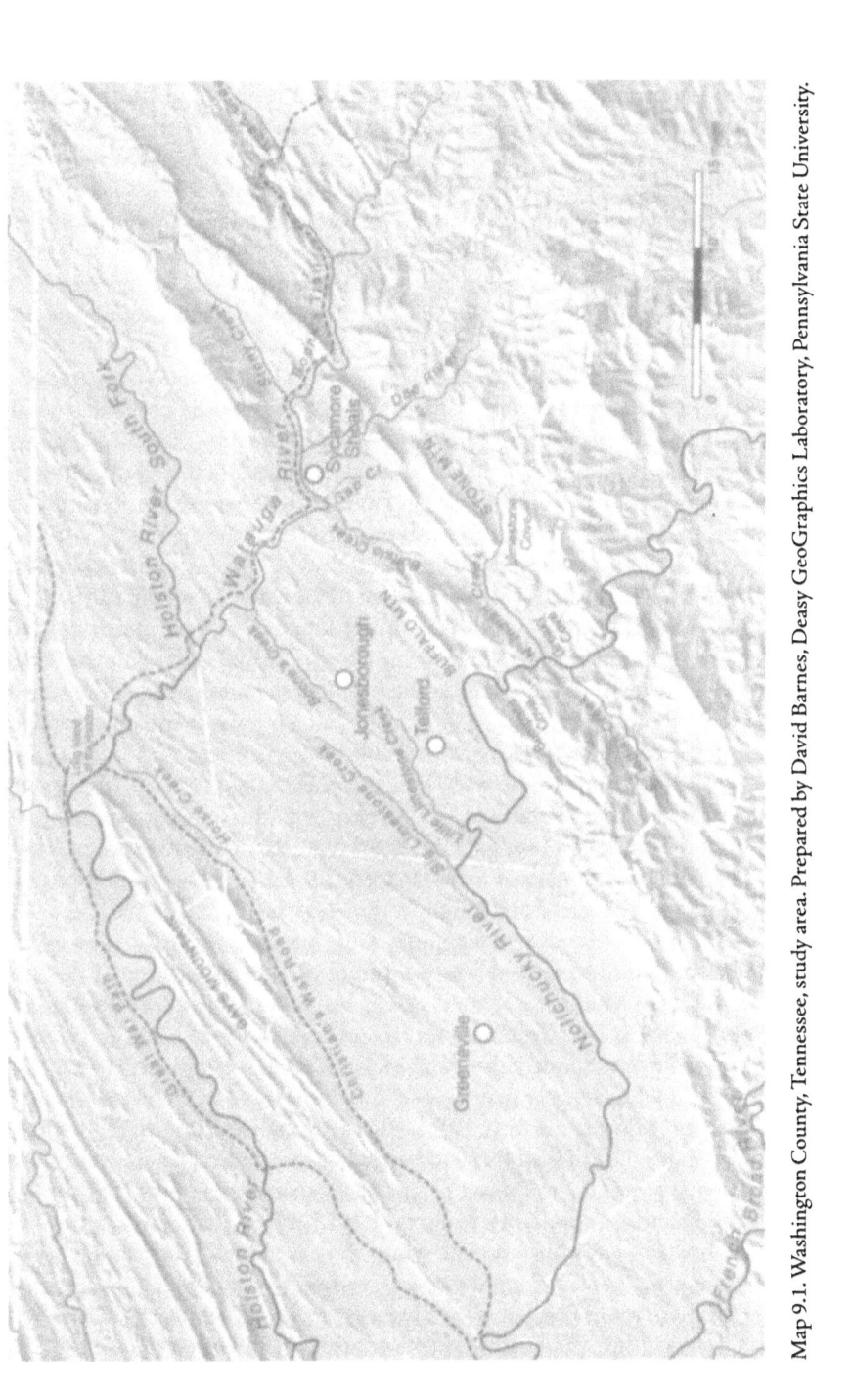

Map 9.1. Washington County, Tennessee, study area. Prepared by David Barnes, Deasy GeoGraphics Laboratory, Pennsylvania State University.

of transportation—not only where and when roads were built, but also the difficulty people had traveling on those roads—reveals the degree to which the residents in upper East Tennessee were isolated geographically from, or integrated with, others. The network also describes the arena within which the social and psychological ties of community most likely would be formed. The various steps settlers took to link themselves with neighbors both near and far demonstrate that, by 1800, they were "connected" geographically and emotionally, albeit tenuously in places, to points scattered across the map. These ties argue against any early historical basis for modern depictions of Appalachian residents as a people isolated from first settlement.[17]

Colonists moved into Washington County from regions both to the north and to the east. The majority of the first settlers followed the Shenandoah Valley south from Virginia. Jacob Brown arrived from western Virginia in 1771 and arranged a long-term lease from the Indians for large tracts of land in the river valleys. By trading and sub-letting portions of this land to those who settled after him, Brown acquired the financial resources to buy this property when the opportunity arose.[18] John Sevier, who eventually settled near Jacob Brown, also migrated south from Virginia. After visiting the region in 1771 or 1772 with the intent to trade, he settled first in Sullivan County and then in Washington.[19] David Deaderick, like the others, came to upper East Tennessee as a trader. Before the end of the Revolutionary War, he established a mercantile business in Jonesborough, the seat of Washington County. Born in 1754 in Winchester, Virginia, at the northern end of the Shenandoah Valley, Deaderick probably took the Great Wagon Road and followed the valley south to the wide Holston River valley of East Tennessee.[20] This ancient trade route, established by Cherokee and other Indians, passes within twenty-five miles of Jonesborough. Christian's War Road, however, loops south of Bay Mountain and comes ten miles closer to the town.[21] The connections between upper East Tennessee and Virginia, therefore, were well established in the late colonial period and provided a popular route for emigrants from the north.

Settlers also arrived by moving westward from North Carolina across the crest of the Appalachian Mountains. Daniel Boone blazed a trail in 1769, entering the eastern tip of what is now Tennessee via Roan Creek and following the Watauga River westward to the south fork of the Holston River.[22] Early settlers like Andrew Greer and Julius Dugger may have followed this route to the Watauga River, where they settled during the early 1770s. Charles Robertson, dissatisfied with the poor soil in central North Carolina and harried by the political persecution of the British colonial government, moved nearby at about the same time.[23] Fewer settlers came over the mountains from North Carolina than came along the Shenandoah Valley, but transmontane routes were established early in the period of permanent settlement. In its physical connections to outside regions, then, upper East Tennessee was crossed from northeast to southwest by the Great War Path and from southeast to northwest by Boone's Trail and other routes.

Internal road connections enabled residents not only to reach these routes, but also to link themselves with one another. This network fell under the control of the Washington County Court of Pleas and Quarter Sessions, which in 1778 served about 2,500 residents (the number grew to 5,862 in 1791 and to 11,192 by 1800) within an area of approximately 1,150 square miles.[24] A typical resident such as David Deaderick, from his residence in Jonesborough, would have had ample opportunity to see the court at work, ordering residents to survey, clear, and oversee 161 different roads from 1778 to 1800. A detailed examination of when these roads were cleared, where they went, and how they were administered makes it possible to map the region's growing physical connections.

Deaderick undoubtedly knew where these roads went, but the modern historian must wrestle with several methodological problems that complicate the process of pinpointing the exact location of each. Consider a typical entry in the court's minute book: "Ord that Adam Willson, Robert Willson, James Stinson, Jos Gest, & James Rodgers be appointed to make and Lay out a road the most convenient & best way from the Court House of Washington down to Benja Gest Esqrs & Make return to our next Court." One endpoint can be easily located (Jonesborough, the county courthouse), but the other is far more difficult to place accurately. Although Benjamin Gest could not be located using primary and secondary sources, he could be placed by knowing that surveyors and workers on roads usually lived near the proposed road and by using primary and secondary sources to locate Adam Wilson and James Stinson in the Telford region, six miles southwest of Jonesborough on Little Limestone Creek.[25] While the road cannot be placed exactly, one can be fairly confident of its general location.

Several problems arise from locating people and roads according to such methods. The primary documents, including other road requests and the occasional tax list which mentions property location, are seldom specific enough to allow exact placement. The secondary materials cite few of their sources, contradict each other at times, and give vague descriptions.[26] Maps can be used when physical landmarks such as Greasy Cove and Rock Creek are given as end points, but the names of such places may have changed over time or been given to multiple locations.[27] Despite such complications, these roads can be mapped with some accuracy. Whenever possible, an individual was located using two independent sources. By using internal evidence from the road requests to supplement the sources mentioned above, one may follow a typical resident like David Deaderick on the routes he might have taken during the first two decades of settlement.

The Washington County road system may be described best by spatially organizing the myriad routes around the two population centers, Jonesborough and Sycamore Shoals, and the most important physical landmarks surrounding them. In the mountains south of Jonesborough lay the Nolichucky River, which begins at the juncture of North and South Indian Creeks in Greasy Cove and flows westward into Greene County. Big and Little Limestone creeks, with tributaries spreading throughout western Washington County, also flow into the Nolichucky. The South Fork of the Holston River and the Watauga River form a diagonal

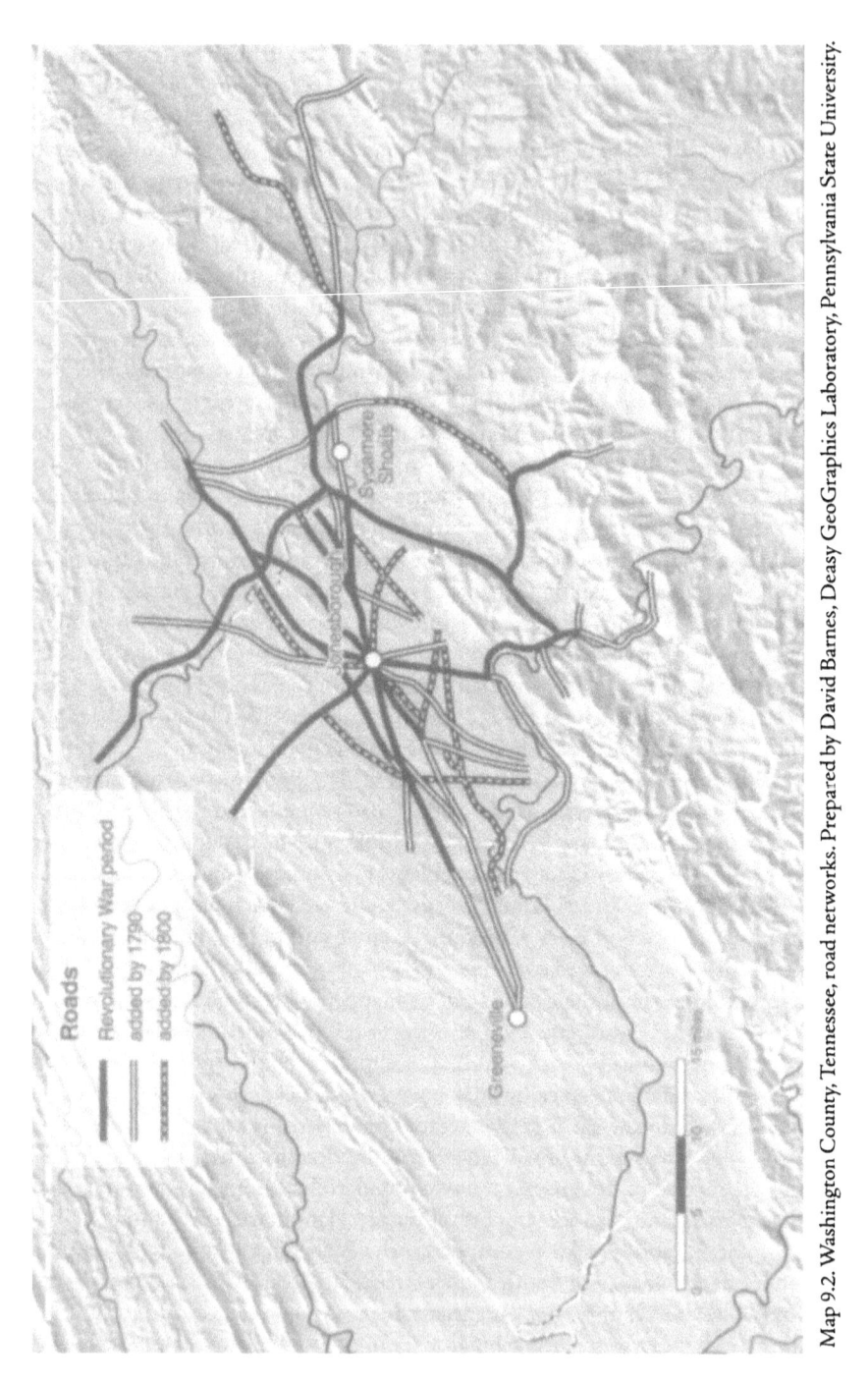

Map 9.2. Washington County, Tennessee, road networks. Prepared by David Barnes, Deasy GeoGraphics Laboratory, Pennsylvania State University.

boundary northeast of Jonesborough which is perforated by several fords. From Sycamore Shoals on the Watauga, settlements and mills on the Doe River to the southeast, the Watauga River and Roan Creek to the east, and Stony Creek to the northeast all served as important focal points for the early road system.

During the Revolutionary War, David Deaderick could travel from his home in Jonesborough to many of these surrounding areas. He could venture north into Sullivan County, south to Greasy Cove, and west to Big Limestone Creek and Greene County. Many roads linked up with the Great War Path, the region's major trade route. In fact, residents from all over Washington County, not just Jonesborough merchants like Deaderick, could reach the Great War Path and thereby connect with regions to the west and in Virginia. Merchants also were attracted by customers living towards the east. Roads connected Jonesborough to Sycamore Shoals, and then further into the steep mountain valleys along the Doe River, Buffalo Creek, and North Indian Creek.[28] This area contained the one government-ordered road that crossed the Appalachian Mountains to Burke County, North Carolina. Although the court assigned several overseers to the Burke County road, little action was taken on other transmontane routes to the North Carolina piedmont.[29] In short, residents like David Deaderick used roads that connected to neighboring counties and to about four hundred square miles within Washington County. However, settlement was unevenly distributed within this area. With the population concentrated along the principal waterways and at the county seat of Jonesborough, the roads serviced those regions to the exclusion of others.

During the rest of the 1780s, however, the transportation and communication network grew in both scope and density.[30] Deaderick could travel farther east into the most mountainous portions of the county as well as take new branches off the earlier roads and reach nearby locations more easily. In some cases, the court ordered new overseers for existing roads, and at other times it ordered roads to be surveyed because earlier requests never had been carried out or because an increase in traffic required the roads to be expanded. By the late 1780s, the southern part of the county, watered by the Nolichucky River and its principal tributaries, received new roads to new locations and began to develop an interconnecting set of roads similar to the area around the Watauga and Holston rivers.[31] The spiderweb of roads also began to develop around Sycamore Shoals, as residents could travel on new routes which pushed up the Doe River as well as westward to Gap Creek. By the end of the decade, new routes had expanded into the eastern, more mountainous regions of Washington County. The work proceeded slowly, however; the court had to request work on the first part of one road, extending about ten miles east of Sycamore Shoals, on three separate occasions.[32] Perhaps the difficulty in completing the road can be attributed to the difficult terrain (one traveler referred to Roan Creek as "the dismal place")[33] or to an insufficient number of workers. At any rate, this expanding network of roads, which included new routes extending both north (to the Holston River in Sullivan County) and southeast (through the mountains, following the Nolichucky to its headwaters), reached into new territory during the late 1780s.[34]

Such expansion did not occur in the 1790s. Although surveyors marked out two new roads near the most northeastern point in the state, no other roads extended the territorial boundaries of the transportation network during the decade. New roads cut across Washington County in different directions, especially south of Jonesborough, but these simply provided new ways to reach familiar destinations. In the vast majority of cases, the court either assigned new overseers to old roads or ordered new roads to be surveyed along previously requested routes. More than ever before, the court sought to build and maintain roads radiating from Jonesborough and connecting the settled portions of Washington County.[35] The road network had reached a plateau in its development. The court evidently had deemed the geographical scope sufficiently extensive, so its mission shifted to facilitating movement within the county by maintaining the existing set of roads and gradually supplementing them with interconnecting routes.

Distinct patterns emerge from mapping the development of this network over two decades. Clearly, most of the traffic ran along the valleys in the more open areas of Washington County. Many more roads linked the county to Sullivan in the north and Greene to the west than to the North Carolina piedmont. When the locations of all roads are considered, one can see a road network consisting of far more external connections which led to the north and west than ones that ran to the east, and internal connections which linked the population centers to settlements scattered about on the county's rivers and streams. By the turn of the nineteenth century, therefore, these Appalachian residents were "connected" with others in significant ways. The quality of these connections, however, must be analyzed before the road network can help us understand the community of Washington County.

On the Road in Washington County

A simple mapping of these early roads misrepresents how Washington County residents could or could not move about their region and hence distorts our view of the region's connectedness. The court records describe the road network only imperfectly. On the one hand, the minute books may underestimate the links connecting residents. Many roads are described as running between the farms or mills of two individuals; when these locations cannot be mapped, neither can the road. One suspects that a road has been created, but exactly where is not known. In addition, the county court recognized only public roads; residents certainly used a private, informal network of trails and paths. Therefore, areas of upper East Tennessee that seem to lie outside the transportation system actually may have been tied in.

On the other hand, one can easily overestimate the connections implied by the roads. The mere existence of such roads does not mean easy travel. The county court occasionally had difficulty getting a road established; the court, for example, had to call the same jury repeatedly to survey the same stretch of road.[36] Once surveyed and marked, the roads often were maintained poorly. "We the grand jurymen," Frank Allison reported in 1798, "present the road from Hock Beckens to John Brown's out of repair and Abednego Hail is the overseer." At times, "a tree top and some other impediments" were found blocking roads and as a result the grand juries typically reported that "the citizens passing and travelling ... with their horses, carts, carriages, and waggons could not ... go, return, pass, ride, and labour without great damage."[37] If they were fortunate, after fines were levied, the good citizens would have the road fixed shortly afterward.

Even when roads were not out of repair, travelers had difficulty moving on them. Francis Asbury, the Methodist bishop who roamed throughout the United States for over forty years, passed through upper East Tennessee several times. By the time he reached the Holston River on September 26, 1801, he had "ridden about one hundred miles in the last four days; the roads equal to any in the United States for badness." These words came from a man who had traveled the length of the United States from Massachusetts to Georgia many times. On another trip to the Sycamore Shoals area in 1806, he endured "rough roads, and a wild country, rocks, ruts, and sidelong difficult ways, sometimes much obscured; it was thus I lost my way, and traveled twenty miles farther than I needed."[38]

Perhaps the most telling incidents are those in which Asbury had to pass through forests and over mountains in order to go between upper East Tennessee and North Carolina. On one trip in the early spring of 1797, the rain had swollen a branch of the Toe River so that it was "rocky, rolling, and roaring like the sea." After crossing it several times, Asbury and his companions climbed to the summit of Yellow Mountain. "We found it so rich and miry that it was with great difficulty we could ride along." It was then "pitch, slide, and drive to the bottom." When crossing the Great Toe, his horse "locked one of his feet in a root" but managed to free himself. The next day, they began "to scale the rocks, hills, and mountains, worming through pathless woods. . . . I had to step from rock to rock, hands and feet busy; but my breath was soon gone, and I gave up the cause, and took my horse again." At last they made it to the Doe River and followed it to Sycamore Shoals. "I was much spent with the labours of this day," he concluded.[39]

François André Michaux also left a detailed account of his journey across these mountains. The Frenchman left Jonesborough on September 21, 1802, and arrived in Limestone Cove "benumbed with cold by the thick fog that reigns almost habitually in the vallies of these enormous mountains." Even this route, established early in the county's history, had its problems. "The road, or rather the path, begins to be so little cut that one can scarce discern the track for plants of all kinds that cover the superficies of it." Michaux had to use an axe to chop through the "twisting and interwoven" branches of rhododendron shrubs which towered as high as twenty feet over the path. "The torrents that we had continually to cross added to the difficulty and danger of the journey," Michaux added, for their horses risked slipping on the "loose round flints concealed by the ebullition of the waters with which the bottom of these torrents are filled."[40]

Michaux left Limestone Cove the following morning, "after having made the most minute inquiry with regard to the path I had to take." Given the steep grade of the path, "it is with great difficulty a person can sit upon his horse, and . . . half the time he is obliged to go on foot." By noon he reached the summit of the mountain, which he "recognized by several trees with '*the road*' marked on each." After descending the other side, "I had again, as the evening before, to cross through forests of *rhododendrum*, and a large torrent called Rocky Creek, the winding course of which cut the path in twelve or fifteen directions." Each crossing was a trial, as was finding the path on the other bank. "The entrance was frequently concealed by tufts of grass or branches of trees, which have time to grow and extend their foliage, since whole months elapse without its being passed by travellers." Once Michaux emerged from this most mountainous section of the crossing, he could reflect upon his experiences:

> I then perceived the imprudence I had committed in having exposed myself without a guide in a road so little frequented, and where a person every moment runs the risk of losing himself on account of the sub-divisions of the road, that ultimately disappear, and which it would be impossible to find again, unless by being perfectly acquainted with the localities and disposition of the county, where obstacle upon obstacle oppose the journey of the traveller, and whose situation would in a short time become very critical from the want of provisions.[41]

Such difficulties in moving through this region must have been experienced, too, by the local residents.

Mountain residents familiar with the "disposition of the county," however, would not have suffered such confusion over which path to take. This "local knowledge" distinguishes the travel experiences of county residents (who have left no surviving accounts) from those of visitors such as Asbury and Michaux. One also must consider the visitor's purpose in traveling. Individuals like Asbury, who traveled merely to reach the next destination, well may have been annoyed by the delays caused by the environment. Such frustration may have spilled out in the subsequent diary entry and thus would have colored the historian's view of the experience. These idiosyncrasies within published accounts force one to look carefully through the "lens" of history. Those who moved at a more leisurely pace perhaps did not see the road in the same way. Although certainly interested in reaching their destination, such travelers also may have been intrigued by what they found along the way. From this perspective, travel may have seemed less taxing.

The Road Network and Early Appalachian Communities

How, then, does this examination of roads speak to the question of isolation and integration in upper East Tennessee during the last decades of the eighteenth century?

Clearly, the region was not sealed off from the surrounding counties and states. The external links created by the mere existence of public roads establishes a degree of connectedness that refutes popular assumptions of extreme isolation. Yet the difficulties encountered while creating, using, and maintaining this limited set of roads argues for a powerful sense of remoteness. Furthermore, because the physical setting of ridges and valleys directed roads along northeast-southwest lines, travel in other directions was impeded. Crossing the mountains posed such a formidable task that relatively few individuals, using even fewer roads, attempted travel between this part of Tennessee and northwestern North Carolina. Internal road connections radiated from Jonesborough like spokes around a wheel's hub, but steep mountains and narrow valleys discouraged road surveyors from penetrating certain parts of the county. Thus, while the extent and quality of the roads made it possible to enter and move about much of upper East Tennessee, the convoluted land on which the roads were built helps explain why movement was so difficult. Measuring this geographical dimension leads one to place upper East Tennessee somewhere in the middle on the scale of connectedness, perhaps weighted slightly toward the "integration" pole.

The patterns of the roads also reveal something of the human weave of Washington County communities. Fifteen persons were listed at least three times as starting or ending points for roads from 1778 to 1800. One might expect these men to be prominent landowners and among the region's earliest settlers; as such, they could persuade the court to build roads to their property. Indeed, several of these fifteen men fell into this category. James Stuart, county surveyor and justice of the peace, owned seven tracts of land covering 7,400 acres and property worth a total of about £16,000 in 1779. Robert Young owned three 640-acre tracts, one slave, twenty horses, and thirty-one cattle, all worth £5,642 in 1779. John Tipton, militia colonel and clerk of the court, lived nearby on 2,000 acres of land. Abednego Inman, another early settler, owned 450 acres of land on Big Limestone Creek, two slaves, seven horses, and eight cattle, valued at £2,418 in 1781. Charles Robertson, a justice of the peace who hosted the Washington County court's first session in his home, owned £2,382 worth of property in 1778.[42] In forty-four cases, the court assigned either surveyors or overseers to roads which had one of these five men as a terminus.

Yet not all of the fifteen men who appeared frequently in the road requests owned thousands of acres and dozens of head of livestock. In 1790, Hugh Campbell had one hundred acres, and Ninian Hoskins owned no land at all.[43] In all likelihood, roads ran to these and other people less for their political influence than for their geographical location. Many of the roads which ended at an individual's residence also were located on waterways: William Dovere lived on Buffalo Creek, John Parkson on the Doe River, and Peter French on Cherokee Creek, to name just a few.[44] The termini of other roads were identified as a river, creek, ford, or mill, so it seems likely that the majority of the roads in Washington County went where they did because they connected with waterways as essential sources of power and sustenance. Given the physical characteristics of

Washington County and the needs of its residents, a smaller number of roads to these locations would have been surprising.

The road network shaped the communities of Washington County in other important ways. One can deduce a sense of Gemeinschaft from the network of roads set out around the county seat of Jonesborough. With ready access to one another, people made face-to-face contacts at the courthouse, the general stores, and the taverns. The roads helped to develop common interests and, as noted earlier in Thomas Bender's definition, "a network of social relations marked by mutuality and emotional bonds." Furthermore, the difficulty of traveling on the roads, especially when crossing the mountains to North Carolina, fostered a sense of Gemeinschaft in upper East Tennessee more generally. The physical barrier of the mountains could turn the residents' economic interests, for example, to the north and west (toward the more open and rolling valleys of Sullivan and Greene counties) and away from the North Carolina counties to the south and east.

At the same time, however, one can also see Gesellschaft relationships at work. Area residents might use the roads for commercial reasons and have no intention of enriching their local network of social relations. The roads allowed Washington County residents to pursue interests that connected them not with neighbors, but with distant places. For example, David Deaderick advertised in Knoxville (about one hundred miles away) that he had received "a very handsome and general assortment of goods" from Philadelphia and Baltimore for his store in Jonesborough. He also shipped local produce out of the region, sending hemp to Richmond, Virginia, on occasion. In 1801, Deaderick paid John Gifford for "hawling 3007 lbs. from Philadelphia to Jonesborough" and John Masengale for "holing 1294 lbs. from Richmond to Jonesborough."[45] In this case, Deaderick made local connections in order to serve distant ones.

Clearly, both Gemeinschaft and Gesellschaft relationships existed for each individual living in upper East Tennessee at this time. The same person whose economic interests pointed him toward the livestock markets in Charleston, South Carolina, also saw himself as a county taxpayer, as a member of the local militia, and as a neighbor. Each of these dimensions—the economic, political, social, and geographical—contributes to the mixture of Gemeinschaft and Gesellschaft that connects the inhabitants of the region. A community, after all, need not be grounded in a territory of only one size. The Washington County resident lived concurrently in communities the size of his valley, his civil district, his county, and his interstate markets. John Fox, Jr., and other writers describe the residents' world as sharply circumscribed, but the early road network prevents this characterization from being applied accurately to upper East Tennessee.

By looking at Appalachian communities through interdisciplinary lenses, we no longer need to accept blindly the long-standing explanations that shape modern stereotypes. Disciplines such as geography and sociology help historians look beyond concepts like "remote isolation" and "closed community" and help them "see" more clearly how perceptions of a region may develop. The framework for connectedness and a balanced theory of community provide one promising approach, but other issues still need to be addressed. What happens when one looks through the lenses at a different place, somewhere even more mountainous or a region with no court-ordered roads? Consider, too, what happens when the historian looks through the lenses and sees an inhabitant like David Greer, the "hermit of Big Bald." How do theories of community incorporate one who was "thought to be somewhat deranged (according to one diarist), separates himself from the rest of the population in 1802, clears nine acres of land, and lives for 20 or 30 years past near the top of the Bald Mountain . . . entirely alone?"[46] While Jonesborough is connected in many ways, Greer is much less so. Could residents such as he, living in the most rugged portions of the mountains, serve as the basis for subsequent images of the entire Appalachian region? The interdisciplinary lenses of geography, sociology, and history, focused on questions such as these, will help us understand not just rural settings like early Appalachia but also the rich diversity that comprises the southern colonial backcountry.

Notes

I would like to thank the University Press of Kentucky for permission to reprint material that first appeared in a different form in my book, *Two Worlds in the Tennessee Mountains: Exploring the Origins of Appalachian Stereotypes* (1997). I also thank David Barnes of Deasy GeoGraphics Laboratory, Pennsylvania State Univ., for producing the maps.

1. John Fox, Jr., "The Southern Mountaineer," *Scribner's Magazine* 29 (Apr. 1901): 390, 392.
2. Will Wallace Harney, "A Strange Land and Peculiar People," *Lippincott's Magazine* 12 (1873): 429–38. For a thorough treatment of local color writers and the time period, see Henry D. Shapiro, *Appalachia on Our Mind: The Southern Mountains and Mountaineers in the American Consciousness, 1870–1920* (Chapel Hill: Univ. of North Carolina Press, 1978). Americans have a long history of perceiving Southern Appalachia and its residents as being different; examples from primary sources dating back to the colonial period are contained in Robert J. Higgs and Ambrose N. Manning, eds., *Voices from the Hills: Selected Readings of Southern Appalachia* (New York: Ungar, 1975). Cratis D. Williams provides the first modern treatment of the subject in "The Southern Mountaineer in Fact and Fiction" (Ph.D. diss., New York Univ., 1961). For the persistence of such images, see John Solomon Otto, "'Hillbilly Culture': The Appalachian Mountain Folk in History and Popular Culture," *Southern Quarterly* 24 (1986): 25–34.
3. Fox, "Southern Mountaineer," 392.
4. George A. Hillery, Jr., "Definitions of Community: Areas of Agreement," *Rural Sociology* 20 (1955): 117. For a recent overview of historians' work on community, see Dwight W. Hoover, "Community Studies," in *Encyclopedia of American Social History*, ed. Mary K. Cayton, Elliot Gorn, and Peter Williams (New York: Scribner's, 1993): 297–305. Provocative studies of community theory in colonial America include Darrett B. Rutman and Anita H. Rutman, *A Place in Time: Middlesex County, Virginia*,

1650–1750 (New York: Norton, 1984); Lois Green Carr, Russell R. Menard, and Lorena S. Walsh, *Robert Cole's World: Agriculture and Society in Early Maryland* (Chapel Hill: Univ. of North Carolina Press, 1991).

5. Colin Bell and Howard Newby, *Community Studies: An Introduction to the Sociology of the Local Community* (New York: Praeger, 1971): 31.
6. Thomas Bender, *Community and Social Change in America* (Baltimore, Md.: Johns Hopkins Univ. Press, 1978): 6–7.
7. Gunnar Almgren, "Community," in *The Encyclopedia of Sociology*, ed. Edgar F. Borgatta and Marie L. Borgatta (New York: Macmillan, 1992), 244.
8. For a brief overview, see Almgren, "Community." For different examples of this approach, see Colin Bell and Howard Newby, eds., *The Sociology of Community: A Selection of Readings* (London: Frank Cass, 1974). For a recent contribution to this topic, see Michael M. Bell, "The Fruit of Difference: The Rural-Urban Continuum as a System of Identity," *Rural Sociology* 57 (1992): 65–82.
9. Ferdinand Tonnies, *Community and Society (Gemeinschaft und Gesellschaft)*, trans. and ed. Charles P. Loomis (New York: Harper and Row, 1957), 33–34. These two forms of social organization can be confused, because the Gesellschaft "superficially resembles the Gemeinschaft in so far as the individuals live and dwell together peacefully. However, in the Gemeinschaft they remain essentially united in spite of all separating factors, whereas in the Gesellschaft they are essentially separated in spite of all uniting factors" (64–65). Further confusion can arise in this essay because I use the term "community" in a much broader sense than does Tonnies. In an attempt at clarity, when referring to Tonnies's ideas I use his German terms (*Gemeinschaft* and *Gesellschaft*) rather than the English translations.
10. Almgren, "Community," 244.
11. Overviews of this topic include Jess Gilbert, "Rural Theory: The Grounding of Rural Sociology," *Rural Sociology* 47 (1982): 609–33; and Gene F. Summers, "Rural Sociology," in Edgar F. Borgatta and Marie L. Borgatta, *Encyclopedia of Sociology*, 1685–94.
12. Bender, *Community and Social Change in America*, 45–51.
13. Robert Gross, *The Minutemen and Their World* (New York: Hill and Wang, 1976); Christine Leigh Heyrman, *Commerce and Culture: The Maritime Communities of Colonial Massachusetts, 1690–1750* (New York: Norton, 1984); Carr, Menard, and Walsh, *Robert Cole's World*.
14. Christopher Lasch, *The True and Only Heaven: Progress and Its Critics* (New York: Norton, 1991), 142.
15. Bender, *Community and Social Change in America*, 33.
16. Tonnies, *Community and Society*, 232.
17. For a fuller treatment of this road network, see David C. Hsiung, *Two Worlds in the Tennessee Mountains* (Lexington: Univ. Press of Kentucky, 1997), ch. 2.
18. Paul M. Fink, "Jacob Brown of Nolichucky," *Tennessee Historical Quarterly* 21 (1962): 237–43.
19. Cora Bales Sevier and Nancy S. Madden, *Sevier Family History, with the Collected Letters of Gen. John Sevier . . .* (Washington, D.C.: Kaufmann Printing, 1961): 26–34.

20. Samuel Cole Williams, ed., "Journal of Events (1825–1873) of David Anderson Deaderick," East Tennessee Historical Society's *Publications*, no. 8 (1936): 122n1. For the Shenandoah Valley and the Great Wagon Road, see Robert D. Mitchell, *Commercialism and Frontier: Perspectives on the Early Shenandoah Valley* (Charlottesville: Univ. Press of Virginia, 1977).
21. This road appears on Marshall Wilson, "Map of Early Settlements of East Tennessee, previously a part of North Carolina and of the Territory of the U.S. South of the River Ohio, Series 1–To End of Year 1776," n.d., in McClung Collection, Lawson-McGhee Library, Knoxville, Tenn.
22. William Edward Myer, "Indian Trails of the Southeast," map in *42nd Annual Report*, Bureau of American Ethnology, Smithsonian Institution (Washington, D.C.: U.S. Government Printing Office, 1928) 801–2; and Wilson, "Map of Early Settlements."
23. *Goodspeed's History of Tennessee* (Chicago: Goodspeed Publishing Co., 1887); Mrs. Charles Fairfax Henley, "Maj. Charles Robertson, and Some of His Descendants," *American Historical Magazine* 3 (1898): 22–23.
24. The 1778 population estimate appears in *Goodspeed's History of Tennessee*, 891. The 1791 figure comes from Mary H. McCown et al., comps., *Washington County, Tennessee, Records*, vol. 1: "Washington County List of Taxables, 1778–1801" (Johnson City, Tenn.: Privately printed, 1964), vi–vii. The 1800 figure can be found in U.S. Bureau of the Census, *Census of the United States*, 1800. For land area, see *Rand McNally Commercial Atlas and Marketing Guide* (Chicago: Rand McNally, 1987): 522.

    The North Carolina General Assembly created Washington County first in 1777; it sliced off Sullivan and Greene counties in 1779 and 1783, respectively. The Tennessee Legislature, after statehood in 1796, created Carter County out of eastern Washington County that same year, running a boundary line generally south and west from Sycamore Shoals. See John Trotwood Moore and Austin P. Foster, *Tennessee: The Volunteer State, 1796–1923* (Chicago: S. J. Clarke, 1923), vol. 1, ch. 23. The following analysis of the road network to 1800 includes the territory of what becomes Carter County after 1796.
25. Feb. 23, 1779, Washington County, Court of Pleas and Quarter Sessions, Minute Book, 1778–1785, prepared and typed by the Tennessee Historical Records Survey, Works Projects Administration, and microfilmed by the Tennessee State Library and Archives, Nashville, roll 85. References to local "hands" responsible for the roads near their homes are scattered throughout the court's minute book.
26. The secondary sources used to locate the roads include: *Goodspeed's History of Tennessee*; Mildred Kozsuch, ed., *Historical Reminiscences of Carter County, Tennessee* (Johnson City, Tenn.: Overmountain Press, 1985); Samuel Cole Williams, *History of Johnson City and Its Environs* (Johnson City, Tenn.: Watauga Press, 1940); *History of Washington County, Tennessee, 1988*, comp. Watauga Association of Genealogists—Upper East Tennessee (Johnson City, Tenn.: N.p., 1988); and Sevier and Madden, *Sevier Family History*.
27. Various maps were used: A reproduction of an 1828 map of Washington County; P. T. Samuel, "Washington County, Tennessee, Post Offices, 1796–1900"; and Nat E. Hyder, Mildred Kozsuch, and Alan Park, "Early Carter County, Tennessee," all

in the Archives of Appalachia, Sherrod Library, East Tennessee State Univ., Johnson City, Tenn. A hand-drawn map in the Samuel Cole Williams Collection, Box 4, acc. no. 85–13, Tennessee State Library and Archives, Nashville. Topographical maps produced by the U.S. Geological Survey. Wilson, "Map of Early Settlements of East Tennessee." Myer, map of "Indian Trails of the Southeast."

28. For the road to Sullivan County, see Washington County, Court of Pleas and Quarter Sessions, Minute Book, 1778–1785, Aug. 24, 1780; for Greasy Cove, see Nov. 26, 1778; for Big Limestone Creek and Greene County, see May 30, 1781, and Nov. 1, 1784. For links to the Great War Path, see May 26, 1778; Feb. 27, 1781; Feb. 3, 1783; and Aug. 24, 1780. For connections to Sycamore Shoals and other destinations, see Nov. 25, 1779; Feb. 4, 1783; Nov. 4, 1782; Aug. 4, 1783; and Feb. 5, 1784.

29. *State Records of North Carolina*, ed. Walter Clark (Goldsboro, N.C.: Nash Brothers, 1905), 24:135; Nov. 25, 1779, Washington County, Court of Pleas and Quarter Sessions, Minute Book, 1778–1785. Samuel Cole Williams, ed., "Executive Journal of Governor John Sevier," East Tennessee Historical Society's *Publications*, no. 1 (1929): 109; Elmer T. Clark et al., eds., *The Journal and Letters of Francis Asbury* (Nashville, Tenn.: Abingdon Press, 1958) 2:261, n. 116.

30. A map of these new roads must be particularly sketchy because of the chaos engendered by the State of Franklin movement in upper East Tennessee, which destroyed the 1785 and 1786 Washington County court records. Two sets of records were kept during 1787 and early 1788, one by those maintaining allegiance to North Carolina and another by those seeking independence. Since only the former set of minute books survives, the description of the road network likely reflects a minimum of what local government accomplished. By the end of 1788, however, Washington County once again was united under the North Carolina government and keeping one set of records. See Samuel Cole Williams, *History of the Lost State of Franklin*, rev. ed. (New York: Press of the Pioneers, 1933).

31. See esp. the sessions for Feb., May, and Aug. 1788 and Feb. 1789, Washington County, Court of Pleas and Quarter Sessions, Minute Book, 1787–1798.

32. Feb. 5, 1787; Aug. 6, 1787; May 1788 sessions, Washington County, Court of Pleas and Quarter Sessions, Minute Book, 1787–1798.

33. Elmer T. Clark et al., *Journal and Letters of Francis Asbury*, 1:631.

34. See May 7, 1787, and Feb. and May 1789 sessions for roads from Sycamore Shoals north to Indian Creek; Nov. 11, 1789, for Jonesborough towards Ross's iron works on the north fork of the Holston; May 15, 1788, for the southeastern route from Greasy Cove to Cane Creek; all in Washington County, Court of Pleas and Quarter Sessions, Minute Book, 1787–1798.

35. These roads appear in nearly every session; see Washington County, Court of Pleas and Quarter Sessions, Minute Book, 1787–1798 and 1798–1799.

36. Road from James Stuart's plantation to the head of Indian Creek, June 4, 1783; Nov. 4, 1783; and Feb. 5, 1784, Washington County, Court of Pleas and Quarter Sessions, Minute Book, 1778–1785.

37. Frank Allison was foreman in "Presentment of Grand Jury," Nov. 1798, Washington

County Court Records, Archives of Appalachia, box 247, folder 10. For the tree top, see Nov. 14, 1804, Carter County, Court of Pleas and Quarter Sessions, Minute Book, 1804–1805. For reports by grand juries, see Washington County Court Records, Archives of Appalachia, box 230, folder 1.
38. Elmer T. Clark et al., *Journal and Letters of Francis Asbury*, 2:308, 2:517.
39. Ibid., 2:124–25. This trip probably followed a path and not a public road. In this portion of the county, as shown above, the court endorsed few roads.
40. François André Michaux, *Travels to the West of the Allegheny Mountains* . . . (London, 1802); reprinted in Reuben Gold Thwaites, ed., *Early Western Travels, 1748–1846* (New York: AMS Press, 1966), 3:283 (page references are to reprint edition).
41. Ibid., 3:284–85.
42. McCown, "Washington County List of Taxables" 10–45, 73. For offices held, see pp. 248–49 and *Goodspeed's History of Tennessee*, 891, 894–895.
43. McCown et al., "Washington County List of Taxables," 60, 72.
44. Aug. 6, 1787; Aug. 8, 1787; and May 14, 1788, Washington County, Court of Pleas and Quarter Sessions, Minute Book, 1787–1798.
45. *Knoxville Gazette*, July 14, 1792; Paul M. Fink, *Jonesborough: The First Century of Tennessee's First Town* (Johnson City, Tenn.: Overmountain Press, 1989), 75, cites this information from Deaderick's 1801 daybook.
46. The diarist, David Anderson Deaderick, is the son of the Jonesborough merchant mentioned earlier. For the quotation, see Samuel Cole Williams, "Journal of Events (1825–1873) of David Anderson Deaderick," 127. Note 10 in this edited version of the Deaderick diary and Pat Alderman, "Hermit of Big Bald," in his *Greasy Cove in Unicoi County: Authentic Folklore* (Johnson City, Tenn.: Overmountain Press, 1975), n.p., contain the background information on Greer.

Between Two Cultures: Judge John Martin and the Struggle for Cherokee Sovereignty

Elizabeth Arnett Fields

In the opening years of the nineteenth century, the vast lands of the Cherokee, which at one time had ranged from Virginia through Kentucky, Tennessee, and the Carolinas south to Georgia, had been reduced to a fraction of their original size. Throughout the eighteenth century, the Cherokee population had shifted first west and then south, as the Cherokee sought abundant game and stayed ahead of white settlement.[1] By 1785, when the first treaty between the Cherokee and the United States was enacted, Cherokee territory had been reduced by more than two-thirds. Subsequent treaties further reduced the Cherokee Nation's resources. After the Treaty of 1819, Cherokee land consisted of approximately twelve thousand square miles, centered on the Cherokee town of New Echota in northeastern Georgia. Throughout this time, the U.S. pursued a policy of "pacification" and "civilization" in dealing with the Five Civilized Tribes of the eastern United States (Cherokees, Chickasaws, Choctaws, Creeks, and Seminoles). Of these five tribes, the Cherokees most enthusiastically embraced the U.S. policy, taking advantage of the farm implements and training supplied by the U.S. to create an agriculture-based economy similar to that of the southern U.S. The tribe's emerging upper class, composed largely of men of mixed white and Cherokee ancestry, took great pride in the advancement of the Cherokees. Elias Boudinot, editor of the *Cherokee Phoenix* newspaper, boasted in his *An Address to the Whites* (1826) of the progress made by the Cherokees. His address contained an accounting of the material wealth accumulated by the Cherokees, including numbers of livestock, plows, sawmills, grist mills, looms, schools, and other signs of civilization.[2]

It is not surprising that, as U.S. policy shifted toward removal in the years between 1817 and 1830, Cherokee leaders felt confident of their ability to convince the U.S. to allow them to stay on their current lands, since the Cherokees had "progressed" so far. John Ross, the principal chief of the Cherokee Nation from 1828 to 1866, at one time even believed that statehood within the U.S. was a viable option for the Cherokee Nation. The struggle for Cherokee autonomy and the fight against removal lasted until the Trail of Tears in 1838.

The years leading up to the Trail of Tears were turbulent ones for the Cherokee Nation, as the Cherokees became caught between two cultures—their traditional ways of life and those of white society. Contributing to the turmoil was the fact that many of the Cherokee leaders themselves were products of both cultures. Most of these men chose to honor their Cherokee heritage, no doubt because Cherokee society is matrilineal and their Cherokee ancestry came from their mothers. However, it was largely their white ancestry which made possible their material wealth and their educational backgrounds. This article examines the years from the Treaty of 1819 to the Trail of Tears, using one of the pivotal figures in the struggle for Cherokee sovereignty, Judge John Martin, to illustrate how their cultural conflicts shaped the motivations of the Cherokee leaders.

Usually identified merely as the first chief justice of the Cherokee Supreme Court, Judge John Martin has remained a minor figure in Cherokee history. Although an influential member of the Cherokee Nation—he was a circuit judge, served on the first Supreme Court of the Cherokee Nation, was elected treasurer of the Nation, represented the Nation on several delegations to Washington, and helped to form the republican government of the Nation, both in the East and in the West—the details of his life largely have remained unexplored by historians. He died relatively young, only a few years after his emigration from Georgia to present-day Oklahoma in 1837. His early death may well account for his relative obscurity in the annals of Cherokee history.

Judge John Martin is mentioned in nearly all works on the history of the eastern Cherokee Nation prior to 1839. Most of these references are brief notes, recounting simply that Martin was elected to various positions within the Cherokee Nation or that he represented the Nation on a number of delegations to Washington, with little substantial information about Martin himself. Piecing together a reliable account of Judge John Martin's life proves problematical. The basic outlines are easily drawn, especially his involvement in the politics of the Cherokee Nation. However, in-depth information is somewhat elusive.

Judge John Martin was a product of two conflicting worlds. Only one-eighth Cherokee, well-educated, blonde, and blue-eyed, John Martin easily could have passed for white. He was wealthy by any standards of the day, being a slave owner whose plantations produced nearly seven thousand bushels of corn and wheat in 1834. At one time, apparently he made the decision to leave his Cherokee heritage behind, even taking an oath to support the U.S. Constitution. However, within a few years he changed his mind and abandoned his home to move within the boundaries of the Cherokee Nation. Subsequently he relinquished three other homes, as the Cherokees were forced off their land by the white settlers of Georgia. For years, as a leader of the Cherokee Nation, he fought for U.S. recognition of Cherokee sovereignty, but finally he gave up and emigrated west of the Mississippi two years before the Trail of Tears. How did John Martin come to these decisions? The answers may never be known fully, but the facts of his life provide some clues.

According to the inscription on his tombstone, Judge John Martin was born on October 20, 1784. His father was a white trader from Virginia named John "Jack" Martin. Jack was the brother of Gen. Joseph Martin, the first agent to the Cherokees after the American Revolution. Until recently, most scholars believed that Judge Martin's father was in fact Joseph Martin, not his brother Jack.[3] The preeminent Cherokee genealogist, Emmet Starr, listed Joseph as Judge Martin's father in his *History of the Cherokee Indians* (1921). Starr's sources were sketchy at best; the chaos of the Trail of Tears and the post-removal fighting among factions of the Cherokee Nation served further to confuse genealogical records. Starr's main source appears to have been an obituary for one of Judge Martin's sons, which was published in the *Cherokee Advocate* on November 18, 1891. This obituary incorrectly identified Gen. Joseph Martin as Judge John Martin's father.[4] However, documents in the Georgia State Archives clearly indicate that Judge John Martin's father was Joseph's brother, not Joseph himself. In 1831, when Georgia's Gov. George Gilmer was seeking a peaceful solution to the removal crisis, he sought information about Cherokee leaders who, if in favor of removal, might be influential in convincing other Cherokees to emigrate voluntarily. Judge John Martin was one of the Cherokees whom Gilmer investigated. Several letters in the Georgia State Archives, written to Gilmer in 1831, discuss Martin and his family. One letter does not name Judge Martin's father but states that he was "the brother of Joseph Martin the first Agent of the Cherokee Nation after the Revolution." Another letter describes Judge John Martin's father as "a white man, of the same name with the son."[5]

Gen. Joseph Martin, Judge Martin's uncle, began his work among the Cherokee during the American Revolution, in about 1775. General Martin had the unique distinction of holding commissions as a brigadier general in the militias of both North Carolina and Virginia. Following the Revolution, he served as an agent to the Cherokee from these states. Because he ran a "constant risk of assassination" (mostly from British agents) in his work, Joseph Martin gained the protection of the Cherokee by marrying into one of the Nation's most powerful clans. In December 1780, the Ghigau, the "Beloved Woman" of the Cherokee, and her family were taken prisoner. They were placed under the protection of Joseph Martin at his home on Long Island on the Holston River (present-day Kingsport, Tennessee). Joseph Martin subsequently married the Ghigau's daughter, Elizabeth Ward. Exactly when Joseph's brother, Jack, first arrived in the Cherokee Nation is unknown; but, by 1780 at the latest, Jack was living in the Cherokee Overhill Towns along the Hiwassee, Little Tennessee, and Tellico rivers in what is now southeastern Tennessee, "primarily occupied as a trader." Jack Martin also married into the Cherokee Nation.[6]

Judge John Martin's mother, Susannah Emory, was one-quarter Cherokee. Her maternal grandfather was a Scotsman named Ludovic Grant, who arrived in South

Carolina in 1716 as a prisoner of war of the British. After serving his indenture, Grant became a trader among the Cherokee, married a Cherokee woman, and lived in the Cherokee Nation for the rest of his life. His daughter married a white man named William Emory. Their daughter, Susannah, was married three times: first to Capt. John Stuart, then to Richard Fields, and finally to Jack Martin, all white men. Children from all three marriages proved to be leaders among the Cherokee.[7]

The birthplace of Judge John Martin is undetermined. It is known that Judge Martin grew up in the Tugaloo River region, along the present-day Georgia–South Carolina border, and that he eventually established a plantation in the nearby Nacoochee Valley. Patricia Lockwood, a descendant of Judge Martin who has done extensive research on his life, believes that Judge Martin was born in the Overhill Towns and moved south to the Tugaloo region in 1789, when he was five years old. Gen. Joseph Martin had interests in the Tugaloo region; and, at the end of his agency in 1789, he turned most of his efforts to those interests. Lockwood surmises that, due to the close relationship between the brothers, Jack moved to the Tugaloo area at about the same time as Joseph, bringing his Cherokee family with him.[8]

However, Lockwood's explanation does not accord with traditional Cherokee family dynamics. Judge John Martin's mother had been married twice before her marriage to Jack Martin. It would have been unlikely that she would move, with her children from her two previous marriages, to a new area in order to follow her husband. Such a move would have cut her off from the traditional support she would have received from her brothers and maternal uncles. A more logical explanation is that, well before 1789, Jack Martin moved to the Tugaloo region, where Susannah Emory was living when they married, and that their son, the future Judge John Martin, was born there in 1784. This explanation is further supported by a letter to Governor Gilmer, in which Samuel Wales asserts that Judge John Martin was born in "Habersham County." At the time Wales wrote the letter, Habersham County encompassed both present-day Habersham and White counties, which include the Tugaloo River region.[9]

There is evidence that Gen. Joseph Martin paid considerable attention to the education of his Cherokee children, even taking one son back to Virginia with him. Although Jack Martin apparently never returned to Virginia, he was a man of some wealth and would have provided for the education of his children. It is most likely that Judge John Martin received his early education at home from a white tutor, a practice common among Cherokees of wealth. He probably attended a school outside the Cherokee Nation for his later education. Gen. Benjamin Cleveland related to Governor Gilmer in 1831 that he [Cleveland] had gone to school with Martin. The location of this school is undetermined. John Ross, a close friend of Martin's, attended the missionary-run academy at South West Point, Tennessee (now Kingston). Perhaps they were schoolmates for a time.[10]

Martin probably was raised mostly by his mother and her brothers, along with his two sisters and his mother's children from her two previous marriages (two half-sisters and six half-brothers), according to Cherokee custom. Both his parents died when he was relatively young. His mother died when he was an adolescent, and after her death he was raised by his brother-in-law, a white man named Jeter Lynch, the husband of his older sister Nancy. Judge Martin's father died when he was "almost grown," probably in 1801 or 1802.[11]

Little else is known about Judge John Martin's life until he emerged as an influential member of the Cherokee Nation in 1818. Martin's name is conspicuous only by its absence in the military service records of the War of 1812. During the Creek War of 1813–14, approximately five hundred Cherokees fought in the service of the U.S. under Andrew Jackson's command. Two of Martin's half-brothers were volunteers in the Cherokee Regiment. His cousin, James Martin, served as quartermaster for Col. Gideon Morgan during the brief war. John Martin, however, apparently did not volunteer for military service. Starr and others list Martin as a signer of the Treaty of July 8, 1817. However, a copy of the treaty reveals that it was signed by his cousin James, not by John. Martin's name does not appear in the records of the Cherokee Indian Agency in Tennessee, an agency of the War Department established in 1801, until he was named as a member of the Cherokee delegation to Washington in December 1818.[12]

By December 1818, when he was appointed to the Cherokee delegation to Washington, Martin had become one of the ruling elite of the Cherokee Nation. He had established a plantation in the Nacoochee Valley on Sautee Creek, in what is now White County, Georgia. As a member of the Cherokee delegation to Washington, Martin was one of the signers of the Treaty of February 27, 1819. The land on which his Sautee Creek plantation stood was ceded to the U.S. in this treaty. As allowed by the treaty, Martin chose to remain in his home even though it was no longer within the Cherokee Nation boundaries. On March 6, 1819, while still in Washington, Martin informed Col. Return J. Meigs, the U.S. agent to the Cherokee, that he intended to reside there permanently and so accepted a reservation of 640 acres. In accepting the reservation, Martin became a citizen of the U.S., albeit as a free person of color.[13]

Both the Treaty of 1817 and the Treaty of 1819 were attempts by the federal government to "denationalize" the Cherokees. By granting reservations of land to the Cherokees who wished to remain on their land, the U.S. hoped to assimilate the Cherokees into the general population.[14] The effort failed for a number of reasons. The Cherokees, although now citizens of the U.S., were considered under U.S. law to be free persons of color. Living among whites, the Cherokees found themselves unwanted and often unfairly treated. In his autobiography, Georgia's Gov. George Gilmer offered an illuminating glimpse of how white Georgians regarded the Cherokees: "The question was tauntingly put to Georgians, Why not let the Cherokees remain among you?—Why not foster and improve them, and let them add to your numbers and wealth? Our villifiers seemed, in their clamor against us, to have forgotten that there was no interchange of the productions of labor between the Indians and others; that they were without wealth, and were incapable of acquiring any; and that they had remained ignorant savages, notwithstanding the constant efforts to change them into better beings."[15] For a man of

John Martin's stature, better educated and wealthier than most whites, this attitude would have been especially hard to accept. As early as May 1819, Martin complained to Colonel Meigs that white Georgians were forcing Cherokees out of their homes. Evidently, such incidents continued to occur; within a few years, most Cherokees, John Martin among them, abandoned their reservations and moved west to within the reduced boundaries of the Cherokee Nation.[16]

Another factor in the failure of the federal government's policy of "denationalization" was that Georgians took considerable exception to the federal government's grants of land within the state of Georgia to the Cherokees. Georgians felt that the federal government had no right to give their land away, especially to Indians. Whether intentionally or not, much of the land reserved for the Cherokees in the two treaties actually was sold or granted by Georgia to its white citizens. The federal government was slow to survey the land involved, and any unsurveyed land was considered fair game by Georgia officials.[17]

Definitely by the spring of 1822 and possibly as early as 1820, John Martin had given up his reservation and moved his family sixty miles west to the Coosawattee River area in present-day Murray County, Georgia, within the reduced boundaries of the Cherokee Nation.[18] Lockwood believes that Martin's decision to move was based upon his personal experience and first-hand observation of the treatment that Cherokees received from their white neighbors. She surmises that Martin's experiences during this time led to his conscious decision to become an active political leader in the Cherokee Nation. This explanation does in some way account for his lack of political involvement prior to 1819.[19]

After moving to the Coosawattee River area, Martin firmly established himself as a leader of the Cherokee Nation. During the time from the Treaty of 1819 to the removal of the Cherokees from east of the Mississippi in 1838, the Cherokee Nation formed a republican government, patterned after that of the U.S. Judge Martin was an active participant in this new government. In 1820, the National Council of the Cherokee Nation divided the Nation into eight districts and created positions for eight district and four circuit judges to preside over the legal matters of the Nation. John Martin was the circuit judge for the Coosawattee and Amohee districts in 1822. In November 1822, the council created a superior court, composed of the four circuit judges. When the first session of the Cherokee Supreme Court was held in Newtown (New Echota) in October 1823, John Martin was one of the three Supreme Court judges present. In 1825, Martin was appointed a member of the committee which laid out the lots in the Nation's new capitol, New Echota. In February 1827, following the death of Principal Chief Charles Hicks, John Martin was appointed treasurer pro tem of the Nation (Starr asserts that Martin had held the position of treasurer earlier, too, and had been elected to that position in 1817). In May 1827, Martin was elected a delegate from the Coosawattee District to the Cherokee Constitutional Convention later that year.[20]

At the time of his appointment as treasurer in February 1827, Martin then held four official positions in the Nation's government, three too many, in the opinion of some Cherokees. In a letter to the editor of the *Cherokee Phoenix*, entitled "Money and Principles," an incensed member of the Nation, who signed his letter "A Cherokee," complained, "The signers of the Constitution . . . were so careful to distribute offices so that one man should not hold more than one constitutional appointment . . . in what way then can [Martin's] acceptance of the treasury be safely accounted for, if it be not that friends exalt high: and that emolument of office has induced an abandonment of principles."[21] In addition to the treasurer's position, Martin was a presiding circuit judge, a judge of the Supreme Court, and a public turnpike keeper on the Federal Road. The position of treasurer had an annual salary of $350. Whether the judicial positions were paid as well is unknown; presumably Martin was entitled to keep a portion of the proceeds of the turnpike revenue. During the next meeting of the General Council, in October 1828, Martin was elected treasurer and replaced as circuit and supreme court judge. He continued to maintain the turnpike.[22]

As the national treasurer, Martin was responsible for such actions as leasing turnpikes on the federal roads that ran through the Cherokee Nation, leasing ferries, collecting the federal annuity paid to the tribe by the U.S., and collecting debts owed to the Nation by various individuals. While John Martin was the national treasurer, the Cherokee Nation went heavily into debt. In 1830, following the passage of the Indian Removal Bill, the U.S. Treasury stopped paying the federal annuity to the Nation. President Andrew Jackson directed Secretary of War John Eaton to take this action to prevent the Cherokee leaders from effectively governing their nation. Jackson hoped to force the Cherokees to accept the U.S. removal policy. Claiming that the Eastern Cherokee Nation no longer existed and therefore neither did its treasury, the U.S. offered to divide the annuity among all members of the Nation and pay each his or her individual share. This per capita amount came to approximately 45 cents for each Cherokee. The Cherokee leaders refused to accept this per capita payment; and John Ross, the principal chief, repeatedly sued for payment of the entire annuity, $6,666, to Treasurer John Martin. The money remained unpaid and untouched in a Nashville bank for five years. John Martin remained the Nation's treasurer until his emigration westward in the spring of 1837.[23]

Until at least 1832, the Cherokee leaders were united in their stand against removal. Under the Treaty of 1817, the U.S. granted land in Arkansas to individual Cherokees who wished to emigrate. Approximately three thousand Cherokees took advantage of the U.S. offer between 1817 and 1828. However, in 1819, the Cherokee Nation passed a law denying Cherokee citizenship to anyone who enrolled for emigration or accepted a reservation within ceded lands under the Treaties of 1817 and 1819. This law was aimed specifically at stopping the voluntary emigration of Cherokees to west of the Mississippi. In 1828, the Cherokee National Council went even further, extending the death penalty to any Cherokee who negotiated to sell land within the Nation.[24]

In May 1830, the U.S. Congress passed the Indian Removal Bill, which called for the removal of the Five Civilized Tribes from east of the Mississippi. Three days after this bill was passed, Georgia asserted its authority over the 4,600,000 acres of Cherokee land in northwestern Georgia. Surveyors were dispatched to divide the land into 160-acre lots, to be given away to Georgia citizens by lottery. These actions, coupled with the discovery of gold in 1829, led to a veritable flood of whites into the Cherokee Nation. For whatever reason, the task of keeping white intruders out of the Cherokee Nation fell to the State of Georgia. The state militia, known as the Georgia Guard, arrived in the Cherokee Nation in early 1831. Of course, given the state's actions to remove the Cherokees, the Georgia Guard, as an agency of the state government, did more to harass the Cherokees than to expel intruders. For example, in February 1831, after lodging members of the guard at his plantation on the Coosawattee, John Martin was arrested on "merely suspicion" and held overnight. Other prominent Cherokees, including Martin's son-in-law, John Adair Bell, similarly were harassed by the Georgia Guard.[25]

To address the actions taken by the State of Georgia against the Cherokee Nation, John Ross sent a delegation to Washington in December 1831. This delegation—all hand-picked by Ross as men he could trust—consisted of Judge John Martin, John Ridge, and Ross's nephew, William Shorey Coodey. Although the delegation did not return to the Cherokee Nation until June 1832, it accomplished little. Following the U.S. success in removing the Creeks from east of the Mississippi, the Cherokees lost much of their support in Washington.[26]

John Ross, the principal chief, did not give up the fight against removal, however. Using the federal government's own legal tactics, Ross hoped to prove that the Cherokee Nation was capable of self-government and, under U.S. law, had the right to be autonomous. Two U.S. Supreme Court decisions, *Cherokee Nation v. Georgia* in 1831 and *Worcester v. Georgia* in 1832, upheld the sovereignty of the Cherokee Nation. Following these decisions, Ross believed that the U.S. would protect the Cherokee from actions by the states of Georgia, Tennessee, and North Carolina and by the Territory of Alabama to take over Cherokee land.[27] President Andrew Jackson, of course, had no intention of doing anything of the sort. In fact, Jackson was rumored to have remarked, upon being told of the *Worcester v. Georgia* ruling, "[Supreme Court Justice] John Marshall has made his decision; let him enforce it if he can."[28] Even after Jackson's inaction became evident, Ross continued to believe that the struggle for Cherokee sovereignty could succeed. His apparent strategy was to outlast Jackson's presidency.[29]

Other Cherokee leaders, however, became convinced of the futility of Ross's course of action, and so the Cherokee Nation divided into two factions. Ross and his followers continued to fight against removal. The other faction, led by John Ridge and his father, realized that the U.S. was not going to take any action to protect the Cherokees from the flood of whites coming into Cherokee land. Removal, therefore, was inevitable. The main concern of the Ridge, or Treaty, Party, was to negotiate terms for removal that were as favorable as possible to the Cherokee Nation. It was probably during the winter of 1831–32, which John Ridge spent in Washington as a member of the Cherokee delegation, that he became convinced that removal was the Cherokee's only option, even though he and his father did not formally break with John Ross until November 1834.[30]

Historians have long struggled to characterize the two political factions of the Cherokee Nation, Ridge's Treaty Party and Ross's National Party. Both factions were led by men who were the wealthiest and most acculturated among the Cherokee Nation, slave owners with large plantations. These men were mostly of mixed white and Cherokee heritage and had been educated at schools outside the Cherokee Nation. Some historians have charged that the leaders of one faction or the other had lost touch with (or had never known) traditional Cherokee ways of life, that they felt no connection to the Cherokees' "ancestral lands," and that their political actions were motivated largely by concern for their own material wealth.[31]

In fact, evidence suggests that the leaders of both factions did have the best interests of the Cherokee people as a whole at heart. John Ross perhaps was somewhat naïve and idealistic in his dealings with the U.S., but he had the support of a majority of Cherokees, both those of mixed heritage and full-bloods. On the other hand, John Ridge had been an ardent supporter of the fight for Cherokee sovereignty; but, once convinced that it was useless, he was an equally passionate advocate for a favorable removal treaty, despite the reality that he was espousing what essentially amounted to treason. It must have been a difficult, even heart-wrenching, decision for John Ridge and the other members of the Treaty Party to come to the conclusion that they would have to give up their land in the East. More than two years elapsed from the time John Ridge first began to consider the fight against removal hopeless to the time when he finally moved against John Ross by forming the Treaty Party.[32]

In the spring of 1835, the two rival factions both sent delegations to Washington. On March 14, 1835, the Treaty Party members signed a treaty which ceded all Cherokee lands east of the Mississippi in exchange for lands in the West and five million dollars, subject to ratification by the Cherokee Nation at the National Council meeting in October 1835. This treaty, like two earlier treaties with similar terms, was rejected by the Nation.

In December 1835, John Ross himself led a delegation to Washington once again to seek support for the cause of Cherokee sovereignty. Judge John Martin also served on this ill-fated delegation. While the delegation was in Washington, leaders of the Treaty Party took advantage of the principal chief's absence and signed the treaty which had been rejected by the National Council the previous October. This treaty, signed on December 28, 1835, at New Echota, with less than five hundred Cherokees (out of a population of over seventeen thousand) in attendance, became known among members of the National Party as the "Christmas Trick." John Ross and the other members of the National Party spent the next three years striving to prove the Treaty of New Echota invalid and to renegotiate with the U.S.[33]

Evidence suggests that, despite his presence in Washington as a member of the National Party delegation and his participation in a protest against the Treaty of

New Echota, Martin, as early as February 1835 and perhaps even earlier, had begun to realize the inevitability of removal. Martin apparently tried for a time to steer a neutral course, but eventually he threw his lot with the Treaty Party and decided to emigrate westward. Two of Martin's sons-in-law, John Adair Bell and George Washington Adair, were signers of the Treaty of New Echota. Their influence must have played a part in Martin's change of heart. Martin's family was extremely important to him; in fact, his private life suggests much about his political motivations.[34]

Judge John Martin had two wives, sisters named Lucy and Nellie McDaniel, and eight children by each wife. One descendant dates his two marriages as having taken place in 1807 and 1810, respectively. However, it is far more likely that Martin married both of his wives at the same time. The traditional marriage customs of the Cherokee involved a succession of monogamous relationships (serial monogamy), as practiced by Martin's mother. However, polygamy often was practiced by "Cherokee men of standing and importance ... Polygamous wives were commonly sisters who had been taken in marriage on the same occasion." By John Martin's generation, the influence of missionaries and other whites in the area had made monogamy the more widespread practice. The fact that Martin had two wives must have played a large part in his decisions to remain within the Cherokee Nation.[35]

After the move to the Coosawattee River area, between 1819 and early 1822, Martin's two families lived on farms approximately fifteen miles apart. His wife Nellie and her children lived at a plantation on the Coosawattee River, where the Federal Road crossed the river. It was at this plantation that Martin kept a gate on the turnpike. Lucy and her children lived fifteen miles south on Salequoyah (Salacoa) Creek, where the Sally Hughes (Tennessee) Road crossed the creek. Both these homes were far grander than the homes owned by average Cherokees. Of course, Judge John Martin was not a typical Cherokee; he was a wealthy and well-educated planter. During the years that he lived at Coosawattee, he and his families built both plantations into prosperous farms.[36]

The 1835 Census Roll of Cherokees East of the Mississippi and the Cherokee Property Valuations completed in 1837 provide evidence of Martin's prosperity. The Coosawattee plantation had twenty-eight buildings (house, kitchen, smoke house, slave cabins, stables, barns, and chicken coops) and 300 acres in cultivation, plus peach and apple orchards. The main dwelling was a two-story frame house, valued at four thousand dollars. Six thousand bushels of corn and thirty-five bushels of wheat were harvested from the Coosawattee plantation in 1834. The Salequoyah plantation was somewhat smaller, with only eleven buildings and 110 acres in cultivation. Between these two plantations, Martin and his wives owned eighty-nine slaves.[37]

By 1835, when the census was taken, five of Martin's daughters were married and living in homes of their own. All the daughters settled near their parents—two in Salequoyah, one in Coosawattee, and two in other nearby communities. Martin's daughters apparently married well, although none of their husbands was quite as wealthy as their father. Four of the five were slave owners. Three of Martin's son-in-laws were leaders among the Cherokee: Joseph M. Lynch, who served as the national marshal, and George Washington Adair and John Adair Bell, both of whom signed the Treaty of New Echota in 1835. Bell became a leader of the Cherokee Nation in the West following removal.[38]

One source of evidence especially revealing about Judge John Martin's personal motivations is his dealings with Christian missionaries. No evidence exists to suggest that Martin was baptized into the Christian faith. In fact, it is quite clear that he never renounced his polygamous marriages. He had an on-again, off-again relationship with the Christian missionaries in the Cherokee Nation, suggesting that he was more interested in how he and his families could benefit from their association with the missionaries than in spiritual salvation. At times, his attitude towards the missionaries was nothing short of antagonistic. At other times, he encouraged their work in the Cherokee Nation, even offering financial support. Martin's support of the missionaries most likely stemmed from an interest in seeing his children well educated. The 1835 census illustrates how important education was to Martin; in that year, all but three of his children were literate (and presumably the non-readers were the youngest children, not yet old enough to read).[39]

As early as February 1822, a Presbyterian missionary considered opening a school near Martin's home in Coosawattee. Although Martin expressed his personal interest in the school and even offered to pay the teacher's salary, the school never opened. A little over a year later, in April 1823, Baptist missionaries did establish a school in Coosawattee. Schoolmaster Thomas Dawson counted at least one of Martin's children among his students. However, Dawson soon was recalled by the Baptists to Valley Town, and the Coosawattee school was forced to close in September that same year. Following the closure of the Baptist school, Martin expressed his willingness to support an American Board (Congregationalist) teacher at Coosawattee, offering one hundred dollars a year plus board. The American Board, however, did not take him up on his offer. In 1826, one of Martin's daughters attended the American Board mission school at Carmel; but, sometime later that year, Martin became "opposed to missions" (or at least to the minister at Carmel) and withdrew his daughter from the school. He then hired a tutor for his children, and later Methodist Episcopal missionaries established a school at his home. This school did not last much longer than either of the two previous ones. In 1828, two of his daughters attended a Baptist school at Valley Town, presumably boarding at the school. Sometime later, his daughters Nancy and Rachel attended Miss Sophia Sawyer's school in New Echota, run by the American Board.[40]

Martin's involvement with the missionaries in the Cherokee Nation was not limited to the pursuit of educational instruction for his children. Around April 1823, Coosawattee became a major stop on the Baptist preaching circuit. Ministers Evan Jones and Jesse Bushyhead visited Coosawattee twice on each complete circuit. John Martin's Salequoyah plantation also was a station on that preaching circuit. In addition, at least two of Martin's daughters were married by missionaries. Rev. Dickson C. McLeod, a Methodist Episcopal minister, married George Washington Adair and Martha Martin in 1829. In 1831, Charlotte Martin's marriage to Joseph M. Lynch was solemnized by Rev. Evan Jones. Judge Martin even served as vice-president of the Cherokee Sunday School of Mount Wesley, a Methodist Episcopal organization overseen by Reverend McLeod. The fact that the missionaries apparently ignored Martin's polygamy is not surprising, especially if he had married both wives at the same time. When first seeking guidance from their home churches, missionaries were advised that polygamous Cherokees who wished to become Christians must set aside all wives except the one first married. If the wives were married at the same time, this solution was impossible. Therefore, as a practical solution, missionaries often overlooked or turned a blind eye to the practice of polygamy among the Cherokee. In addition, as familiar as Judge Martin was with white society, he would have realized that "setting aside" one wife would have made her children illegitimate in the eyes of white society.[41]

As a result of the 1832 Cherokee Land Lottery conducted by the State of Georgia, John Martin's families were forced out of their Georgia plantations. The first drawings in the Cherokee Land Lottery were held on October 22, 1832. By law, those drawing the Cherokee land lots could not take possession of their new property until it was abandoned by the Cherokees. However, even before the lottery drawings were completed in May 1833, whites flooded into the Cherokee Nation. Many Cherokees found themselves thrown out of their own homes, while the Georgia Guard, ostensibly charged with upholding the law, looked the other way. John Martin, John Ross, and other wealthy Cherokees tried to help Cherokees who were evicted by paying for litigation to stay the evictions. The legal expenses were supposed to be paid by "public moneys," but the Cherokee treasury was empty, so Martin and the others paid for it out of their own pockets. Their efforts were unsuccessful.[42]

John Martin lost the house on Salequoyah Creek sometime in 1833 or early 1834. According to local tradition, the James M. Erwin family moved to "a fine plantation in the fertile bottom lands of Salacoa Valley" in 1838. The Erwin family owned this land well into the twentieth century, and its location does correspond to contemporary accounts of Martin's Salequoyah home. However, exactly who forced Martin and his family out of their home some four or five years earlier is unknown. The circumstances surrounding Martin's eviction from the Coosawattee house, however, are well documented. The Coosawattee house became part of one of the largest antebellum plantations in Georgia. Farish Carter had traveled through the region before the land lottery, and after the lottery he purchased a total of fifteen thousand acres from lottery winners. All of John Martin's land, as well as that of several other Cherokees, was included in Carter's new land holdings.

In January 1835, Farish Carter requested, through the commander of the Georgia Guard, that the Martin family vacate its home. Martin appealed to Georgia's Gov. Wilson Lumpkin, who interceded on his behalf. Since Governor Lumpkin had given some degree of protection from white intruders to members of the

Treaty Party, the fact that Lumpkin did intercede on Martin's behalf would suggest that Martin had, at that time, already switched his allegiance to the Treaty Party (or at least that Lumpkin believed he had). In a letter to the Georgia Guard's Commander William Bishop, Lumpkin advised Bishop that Carter had agreed to allow Martin and his family to remain in the Coosawattee plantation through the end of 1835, "provided he used his influence to bring our Indian affairs to a final issue." Other evidence, however, indicates that the Martins in fact were dispossessed of their home in February 1835.[43]

The Martin family reestablished itself briefly in Tennessee's Red Hill Valley in 1836. Later known as the Byrd Hambright place, Martin's Tennessee home was located on the Hiwassee River in present-day Bradley County. The 1837 Cherokee Property Valuations offer a brief description of this farm, evidently much smaller than either of the Georgia plantations. The main dwelling was a "hewed log house" valued at five hundred dollars, compared to the two-story frame house in Coosawattee, which had been valued at four thousand dollars.[44]

As previously noted, Martin gave signs of his sympathy for the Treaty Party as early as February 1835, even though another two years would pass before he emigrated westward. His responsibilities to the Cherokee Nation as national treasurer and his responsibilities to his family most likely were the reasons for that delay (most members of the Treaty Party emigrated in early 1836). Martin's concern for the well-being of his family, and for his children's futures, no doubt was at the heart of his decision to leave the eastern Cherokee Nation. After watching Cherokee neighbors and relatives lose their homes to white Georgians in the Nacoochee Valley in the early 1820s and then seeing the same thing happen again in the 1830s, Martin must have realized that the National Party was fighting a losing battle. Being evicted from his own home only would have convinced him further that emigrating was the right course of action. In addition, as already mentioned, two of Martin's sons-in-law had signed the Treaty of New Echota, which meant that those two daughters and their families would be moving to the West. Many factors went into Martin's decision to abandon the fight for Cherokee sovereignty, but his family's welfare was probably the most important.

By late 1836, Judge John Martin had begun to prepare to move his family to the West. Throughout 1836, Cherokees had been subjected to increased harassment from U.S. soldiers under the command of Gen. John Wool, stationed in the Cherokee Nation to assist in the removal. Martin was no exception. Late one night in December, members of the Cherokee General Council met with Martin at his home in Red Hill to settle his accounts as national treasurer before his emigration. U.S. soldiers surrounded the house, arrested Martin and the other members of the General Council, and confiscated the account books and other official papers. General Wool released the men but kept the papers for some time, threatening the Cherokee with further arrests if they did not cooperate. In March 1837, accompanied by at least one son-in-law (George W. Adair), John Martin led a group of three hundred Cherokee families overland to the western Cherokee Nation.[45]

Because the Cherokee Nation as a whole owned the land in the East, individuals were not compensated for the loss of their land. However, the U.S. did pay individual Cherokees for the improvements they had made to the land, including houses and other buildings, cleared land, orchards, and fences. Martin received compensation for all three plantations, as well as rent on his property, amounting to a total of $22,400. He took his slaves with him to the western Cherokee Nation.[46]

In the western Cherokee Nation, the Martins settled in Grand Saline, near present-day Locust Grove, Oklahoma, on the Saline River. Martin was as active in the establishment of the new government in the West as he had been in the East. In 1839, Martin was elected the first chief justice of the Cherokee Supreme Court, a position he held until his death in 1840 (the position of chief justice had not existed before, although the Supreme Court had been created in 1822). Judge John Martin died of "brain fever" three days before his fifty-sixth birthday, on October 17, 1840, and was buried at Fort Gibson.[47]

Judge John Martin's lifetime was a turbulent period for the Cherokee, especially the years from the Treaty of 1819 until the forced removal of the Cherokee from their eastern lands in 1838. In many ways, Judge John Martin epitomizes the struggle that the Cherokee leaders faced during that time. In addition to the division between the Cherokee leaders, there was a deeper, more fundamental division within the Cherokee Nation. Following the deaths of Cherokee chiefs Pathkiller and Charles Hicks in 1827, full-blood Cherokees began to voice opposition to the changes that the Cherokee Nation was making in order to win autonomy from the U.S. They felt that these changes, such as establishing a republican form of government and writing laws, meant losing their identity as Cherokees. The full-blood Cherokees, who were a majority of the Nation's population, also opposed removal.[48] As previously mentioned, most of the Cherokee leaders were of mixed white and Cherokee heritage, and were the wealthiest and most acculturated men in the Nation. How could any of these men, whether fighting against removal or supporting a removal treaty, claim to represent the interests of the average Cherokee?

Judge John Martin could have chosen any of a number of different courses of action other than becoming politically involved in the Cherokee Nation. He could have emigrated to Arkansas under either the Treaty of 1817 or the Treaty of 1819. He could have remained on his Sautee Creek reservation. He could have "set aside" one of his wives in order to pass for white. Yet Martin did none of these things. Instead, he deliberately chose to become a leader of his mother's people. His choice must have taken a toll on every member of his family. Everything that is known about Martin's life, public and private, suggests that he was a pragmatic man. Undoubtedly, Martin believed that he could use his white heritage, his wealth, and his education to the advantage of the Cherokee people and that the Nation would benefit from his leadership. Martin fought long and hard against removal, at great personal cost, evidently even after he was convinced that the struggle for Cherokee sovereignty was a lost cause. In the end, however, Martin could not deny the inevitability that the U.S. would succeed in removing the Cherokees from their eastern lands, and so he elected to emigrate to the West of his own accord.

Notes

1. Richard Pillsbury, "The Europeanization of the Cherokee Settlement Landscape Prior to Removal: A Georgia Case Study," *Geoscience and Man* 23 (1983): 60.
2. Douglas C. Wilms, "Cherokee Land Use in Georgia Before Removal," in *Cherokee Removal: Before and After*, ed. William L. Anderson, 3–9 (Athens: Univ. of Georgia Press, 1991); Theda Perdue, *Slavery and the Evolution of Cherokee Society, 1540–1866* (Knoxville: Univ. of Tennessee Press, 1979), 54–55.
3. Patricia Lockwood, "Judge John Martin: First Chief Justice of the Cherokees," *Chronicles of Oklahoma* 64 (1986): 61.
4. Emmet Starr, *History of the Cherokee Indians* (Oklahoma City: Warden Co., 1921; reprinted Millwood, N.Y.: Kraus Reprint Co., 1977), 305; *Cherokee Advocate* (Tahlequah, Cherokee Nation), Nov. 18, 1891.
5. George R. Gilmer, *Sketches of Some of the First Settlers of Upper Georgia, of the Cherokees, and the Author* (Baltimore, Md.: Genealogical Publishing Co., 1965), 311–13; J. E. Hays, *Cherokee Indian Letters, Talks and Treaties, 1786–1838* (Atlanta: Georgia Department of Archives and History, 1939), 289–90.
6. Stephen B. Weeks, "General Joseph Martin and the War of the Revolution in the West," in *Annual Report of the American Historical Association for the Year 1893*, 410–20; Vicki Rozema, *Footsteps of the Cherokee* (Winston-Salem, N.C.: John F. Blair, 1995), 126–28; Letter from Patricia Lockwood to Elizabeth Arnett Fields, Aug. 8, 1993.
7. Lockwood to Fields, Aug. 8, 1993; John Bartlett Meserve, "Chief Dennis Wolf Bushyhead," *Chronicles of Oklahoma* 14 (Sept. 1936): 349–50.
8. Lockwood to Fields, Aug. 8, 1993; Hays, *Cherokee Indian Letters*, 289–90.
9. Hays, *Cherokee Indian Letters*, 289–90.
10. Ibid., 289; Gary E. Moulton, *John Ross, Cherokee Chief* (Athens: Univ. of Georgia Press, 1978), 6–7
11. Hays, *Cherokee Indian Letters*, 289; Lockwood to Fields, Aug. 8, 1993.
12. Index to Compiled Service Records of Volunteers in the War of 1812, RG 94, National Archives; Henry Thompson Malone, *Cherokees of the Old South: A People in Transition* (Athens: Univ. of Georgia Press, 1956), 71; Charles J. Kappler, comp. and ed., *Indian Treaties, 1778–1883* (New York: Interland Publishing, 1972), 140–44; Return J. Meigs to John C. Calhoun, Dec. 19, 1818, in Records of the Cherokee Indian Agency in Tennessee, 1801–1835, Records of the Bureau of Indian Affairs, RG 75, National Archives.
13. Lockwood, "Judge John Martin," 63–64; Hays, *Cherokee Indian Letters*, 172, 289; Mary B. Warren and Eve B. Weeks, *Whites Among the Cherokee* (Danielsville, Ga.: Heritage Papers, 1987), 98.
14. William G. McLoughlin, "Experiment in Cherokee Citizenship, 1789–1839," *American Quarterly* 33 (1981): 3–5.
15. Gilmer, *Sketches of Some of the First Settlers*, 246–47.
16. Lockwood to Fields, Aug. 8, 1993; John Martin to Return J. Meigs, May 17, 1819, in Records of the Cherokee Indian Agency in Tennessee, 1801–1835, Records of the

Bureau of Indian Affairs, RG 75, National Archives; McLoughlin, "Experiment in Cherokee Citizenship," 24.
17. Gilmer, *Sketches of Some of the First Settlers*, 255–56; McLoughlin, "Experiment in Cherokee Citizenship," 6–12. The vast majority of reservations granted were "life reservations." In other words, upon the death of the reservee, ownership of the land reverted to the State of Georgia. Martin's reservation, however, was a fee-simple reservation (he could have sold the land if he had chosen to).
18. Paul Kutsche, *A Guide to Cherokee Documents in the Northeastern United States* (Metuchen, N.J.: Scarecrow Press, 1986), 181. In Oct. 1823, Martin received $2,000 compensation from the U.S. government for the Sautee Creek land; see "Purchase of Reservations of Indian Lands in Georgia," Letters Received by the Office of Indian Affairs, 1824–1881, Records of the Bureau of Indian Affairs, RG 75, National Archives.
19. Lockwood to Fields, Aug. 8, 1993.
20. Malone, *Cherokees of the Old South*, 80–84; Cherokee Advocate Office, *Laws of the Cherokee Nation: Adopted by the Council at Various Periods* (Tahlequah, Cherokee Nation: Cherokee Advocate Office, 1852), 28; William G. McLoughlin, *Cherokee Renascence in the New Republic* (Princeton, N.J.: Princeton Univ. Press, 1986), 392; John Ross, *The Papers of Chief John Ross*, ed. Gary E. Moulton (Norman: Univ. of Oklahoma, 1985), 1:128, 1:758; Starr, *History of the Cherokee Indians*, 50–53.
21. *Cherokee Phoenix* (New Echota, Cherokee Nation), Feb. 28, 1828.
22. *Cherokee Phoenix*, Oct. 22, 1828; Ross, *Papers*, 1:147.
23. *Cherokee Phoenix*, Nov. 19, 1830; William G. McLoughlin, *Cherokees and Missionaries, 1789–1839* (New Haven, Conn.: Yale Univ. Press, 1984), 253; Ross, *Papers*, 1:220–23, 1:489.
24. Kappler, *Indian Treaties*, 140–44; McLoughlin, "Experiment in Cherokee Citizenship," 5; Kenneth Penn Davis, "Chaos in the Indian Country: The Cherokee Nation, 1828–35," in *The Cherokee Indian Nation: A Troubled History*, ed. Duane King (Knoxville: Univ. of Tennessee Press, 1979), 130.
25. Douglas C. Wilms, "Georgia's Land Lottery of 1832," *Chronicles of Oklahoma* 52 (1972): 52–55; *Cherokee Phoenix*, Feb. 12, Feb. 19, and Apr. 16, 1831.
26. Samuel Carter, III, *Cherokee Sunset: A Nation Betrayed* (Garden City, N.Y.: Doubleday, 1976), 127–28; Thurman Wilkins, *Cherokee Tragedy: The Ridge Family and the Decimation of a People* (Norman: Univ. of Oklahoma Press, 1986), 230–38; Lockwood, "Judge John Martin," 67.
27. McLoughlin, *Cherokee Renascence*, 390–91, 438–47; Wilkins, *Cherokee Tragedy*, 235–36.
28. Wilkins, *Cherokee Tragedy*, 236.
29. Moulton, *John Ross*, 55–59.
30. Carter, *Cherokee Sunset*, 127–28; Moulton, *John Ross*, 50–51; Wilkins, *Cherokee Tragedy*, 233–41.
31. Perdue, *Slavery and Evolution of Cherokee Society*, 68–69; Morris L. Wardell, *A Political History of the Cherokee Nation, 1838–1907* (Norman: Univ. of Oklahoma Press, 1938), 8–10.
32. Moulton, *John Ross*, 50–58; Wilkins, *Cherokee Tragedy*, 233–41.
33. Grant Foreman, *Indian Removal: The Emigration of the Five Civilized Tribes of Indians*

(Norman: Univ. of Oklahoma Press, 1953), 264–69; Moulton, *John Ross*, 72–73; Wilkins, *Cherokee Tragedy*, 287–89.

34. Wilson Lumpkin, *The Removal of the Cherokee Indians from Georgia* (New York: Dodd, Mead & Co., 1907), 311; Wilkins, *Cherokee Tragedy*, 237–38, 299, 334; Warren and Weeks, *Whites Among the Cherokees*, 182–83.

35. George Morrison Bell, Sr., *Genealogy of "Old and New Cherokee Indian Families"* (Bartlesville, Okla.: Privately published, 1972), 290; McLoughlin, *Cherokees and Missionaries*, 204–5; William Jasper Cotter, *My Autobiography* (Nashville, Tenn.: Publishing House Methodist Episcopal Church South, 1917), 74–75.

36. Census Roll of the Cherokee Indians East of the Mississippi (Henderson Roll), 1835, 55–57, Records of the Bureau of Indian Affairs, RG 75, National Archives; Cherokee Property Valuations, 1837, Murray County, Georgia, #57, and Cass County, Georgia, #27, Records of the Bureau of Indian Affairs, RG 75, National Archives; Charles O. Walker, *Cherokee Footprints: The Principal People, "Ani-Yunwiya"* (Jasper, Ga.: Privately published, 1988), 99.

37. Census Roll of the Cherokee Indians East of the Mississippi (Henderson Roll), 1835, 55–57; and Cherokee Property Valuations, 1837, Murray County, Georgia, #57 and Cass County, Georgia, #27. It is tempting to assign ownership of both the plantations and the slaves to Martin; however, it is far more likely that Martin himself saw the land and the slaves as the property of his wives (see Perdue, *Slavery and the Evolution of Cherokee Society*, 51).

38. Census Roll of the Cherokee Indians East of the Mississippi (Henderson Roll), 1835, 54–57; Ross, *Papers*, 2:726.

39. Census Roll of the Cherokee Indians East of the Mississippi (Henderson Roll), 1835, 55–57.

40. Robert G. Gardner, *Cherokees and Baptists in Georgia* (Atlanta: Georgia Baptist Historical Society, 1989), 101–38; McLoughlin, *Cherokees and Missionaries*, 228; Kutsche, *Guide to Cherokee Documents*, 205; Althea Bass, *Cherokee Messenger* (Norman: Univ. of Oklahoma Press, 1936), 120.

41. Gardner, *Cherokees and Baptists*, 106, 186–90; Walker, *Cherokee Footprints*, 1:99; *Cherokee Phoenix*, July 1, 1829; Oct. 8, 1830; Dec. 31, 1831; McLoughlin, *Cherokees and Missionaries*, 204–5.

42. H. David Williams, "Gambling Away the Inheritance: The Cherokee Nation and Georgia's Gold and Land Lotteries of 1832–1833," *Georgia Historical Quarterly* 73 (Fall 1989): 520–36; Carter, *Cherokee Sunset*, 146; McLoughlin, *Cherokee Renascence*, 437; Elias Boudinot, *Cherokee Editor: The Writings of Elias Boudinot*, ed. Theda Perdue (Knoxville: Univ. of Tennessee Press, 1983), 229.

43. Burton J. Bell, *1976 Bicentennial History of Gordon County, Georgia* (Calhoun, Ga.: Gordon County Historical Society, 1976), 322; Ross, *Papers*, 1:432; Lumpkin, *Removal of the Cherokee Indians*, 312–14; Perdue, *Slavery and the Evolution of Cherokee Society*, 66–67; Cherokee Property Valuations, 1837, Murray County, Georgia, #57.

44. Ross, *Papers*, 1:552; Don L. Shadburn, *Cherokee Planters in Georgia, 1832–1838* (Roswell, Ga.: W. H. Wolfe Associates, 1990), 243; James F. Corn, *Red Clay and Rattlesnake*

Springs (Cleveland, Tenn.: Walworth, 1959), 48; Cherokee Property Valuations, 1837, Bradley County, Tennessee, #157; and Murray County, Georgia, #57.
45. Ross, *Papers*, 1:489; Moulton, *John Ross, Cherokee Chief*, 81; Kutsche, *Guide to Cherokee Documents*, 252; R. Halliburton, Jr., *Red Over Black: Black Slavery Among the Cherokee Indians* (Westport, Conn.: Greenwood Press, 1977), 59.
46. Lockwood, "Judge John Martin," 69; Belle K. Abbott, "Cherokee Indians in Georgia," *Atlanta Constitution*, Oct. 27–Dec. 1, 1889.
47. Wardell, *A Political History of the Cherokee Nation*, 50; McLoughlin, *Cherokee Renascence*, 407; Starr, *History of the Cherokee Indians*, 292; Foreman, *Indian Removal*, 238.
48. McLoughlin, *Cherokee Renascence*, 390–96.

Folk Art, Architecture, and Artifact: Toward a Material Understanding of the German Culture in the Upper Valley of Virginia

Donald W. Linebaugh

Thomas Jefferson argued in 1817 that "foreigners" should distribute themselves sparsely among the natives of the United States: "It's better to discourage the settlement of foreigners in large masses, wherein, as in our German settlements, they preserve for a long time their own languages, habits, and principles of government."[1] This statement suggests that German settlers in Virginia did not readily embrace the dominant English culture. However, until the 1960s, histories of settlement in the Valley of Virginia postulated that Germans relatively quickly were absorbed into the Anglo-American mainstream. More recently, the pendulum seems to have swung back toward Jefferson's view, with historian Klaus Wust arguing that "the process of integration was neither as inevitable nor as automatic as the theories of Americanization have assumed in the past."[2]

Current material culture scholarship has sustained Wust's position, suggesting that acculturation of German immigrants was a gradual process and not a sudden dissolution of traditional ethnic values within the American melting pot.[3] However, questions regarding the direction, speed, and degree of cultural mixing remain largely unasked and unanswered. By suggesting that acculturation was a positive and necessary change, earlier studies have denied the possibility of a heterocultural existence for these groups.[4] Even the term *acculturation* can be problematical, in that it implies a view of cultural mixing based on cultural biases and attitudes that promote the inevitable absorption of a minority culture by the dominant culture.

How, then, to study the intermixture of German and English culture in the upper Valley of Virginia? One possible starting point is the work of Pennsylvania German folk artist Lewis Miller. A frequent traveler to the Valley of Virginia during the nineteenth century, Miller, in a number of sketches and illustrations, recorded his views and experiences as a member of the German American community. By means of an interdisciplinary approach that combines Miller's sketches with historical and archaeological data, it may be possible to begin constructing a chronology of cultural changes and exchanges in this multidimensional community. Investigation should focus on contextualizing the community to view how internal and external symbols of the cultures compare and contrast over time. In this regard, archaeological studies of the farmsteads sketched by Miller could add an important temporal, geographical, and economic dimension to the equation. Archaeology also can help concentrate the investigation on the full range of individuals within the community and on individual responses to ethnic identity.[5] Albert Tillson, Jr., has noted obvious source problems in studying the ethnic dimension of the region's "humbler inhabitants." He explains that the: "poverty of lower-class settlers may have limited their preservation of cultural traditions. On the other hand, as elite groups became more fully Anglicized, common folk may have resented and resisted this assimilation as a violation of their ethnic identity."[6] The interdisciplinary study of the farmsteads that make up the ethnically and economically diverse communities found in the Valley of Virginia offers real potential for exploring cultural changes in these communities; we can enhance our understanding of them, that is, by capitalizing on the evidence contained in such sources as the Miller drawings, historical documents, and archaeological sites.

Lewis Miller was born in 1796 in York, Pennsylvania, the tenth and youngest child of German immigrant parents. His father, the master at the German Lutheran Parochial School, saw that Lewis received a literary and classical education and then apprenticed him to his elder brother to learn the "art and mystery of house-carpentering."[7] The dialect poet Henry L. Fisher, the artist's friend, has suggested that Miller fruitfully practiced his carpentry trade and was "employed at most, if not all, of the principal public buildings and many of the private homes erected in York during that period."[8]

Beginning in the early part of the century, and especially on visits to nearby towns in south central Pennsylvania, Miller began recording the events, people, and places that formed his daily experience. In 1840, Miller departed York for the grand tour of Europe. During this one-year journey, which included his ancestral city of Strassburg, Germany, Miller visited the principal countries, sketching the "picturesque European landscapes and recording their historical associations."[9] Following his overseas visit, Miller continued to travel, visiting New York in 1842 and New Jersey in 1847.

From at least the early 1830s until 1880, the bachelor Miller documented trips to visit his three brothers who had settled near Christiansburg in the Valley of Virginia. The products of these expeditions are two manuscripts, *The Sketchbook of Landscapes in the State of Virginia* (1853) and the *Virginia Sketchbook* (1856–57).[10] Historians Harry L. Rinker and Richard M. Kain have noted that Miller's Virginia sketches depict "people of Pennsylvania-German descent, whose stern values the artist shared. His sketches are chiefly of rural towns and individual farms on which are a residence, a large barn, outbuildings, occasionally a mill, and a well-kept garden. Neatness, order, and prosperity predominate. The artist, a devout Lutheran, found in the Virginia landscape the orderliness in both nature and society that was stressed in Lutheran theology."[11] Manuscript historian Daniel Porter adds, however, that "practical jokes, hangings, floods, table manners, craftsmen at work, people at worship—all were within the province of the pen and brush of Lewis Miller."[12]

Sadly, few attempts have been made to use Miller's work in approaching problems central to understanding the German culture in nineteenth-century America.[13] From a cultural history perspective, Miller's drawings allow us to glimpse brief moments across the landscapes of Pennsylvania and Virginia. These drawings, which contain highly accurate, detailed depictions of people and places throughout the Valley of Virginia, provide an unusual source of evidence to test assumptions about the problematical cultural integration of Germans in Virginia. By correlating Miller's sketches with extant structures and period documentation, for example, scholars can identify changes in the cultural landscape, notably in farmstead building traditions and spatial organization. The farmsteads that he sketched in Montgomery County, Virginia, can be verified on period maps and plotted on modern United States Geological Survey quadrangles. The Widow Murray house, for example, described by Miller as facing the turnpike road, four miles from Christiansburg, is shown at that location on an 1864 map of the county by Confederate cartographer J. F. Gilmer.[14]

Miller's texts also reflect changes in language use among his subjects, as speech shifted from High German to English. A native-born American who spoke and wrote in English and German,[15] Miller was raised in a bilingual and bicultural atmosphere. Fisher, the dialect poet, recounted that "as a rustic poet and writer of popular German songs, Louie Miller had few superiors."[16] His songs and poems span a wide range of styles and types, including both secular and sacred.[17] Miller's captions and narratives display a wide linguistic range—from formal and dialectal German to Latin and English. The Pennsylvania German dialect appears to have continued in use in the homes of valley residents into the twentieth century, while High German persisted in churches until at least the 1850s and 1860s. Language traditionally has been an important yardstick by which to measure the blending of cultures. Scholars have used language, such as the persistence of High German in churches or the degradation of German in older residents (speaking a "poor sort" of German), to support their theories concerning a loss of German culture and integration into the dominant English culture. Miller's narratives and sketches chronicle many disputes about language use. In "The Synod, A Senate of the German Reformed Church, ca. 1828," for example, he records that "[Rev.] Vonderschold is on the floor saying this is A German Synod and he hopes that the business will be done in the German language. Mr. Schmaltz saying he not understand what is going on." Here Miller switches to German, writing, "Rev.

Vonderschold. Warum geht er nicht in die deutsche Schule und lernt (Why doesn't he attend the German school and learn [the language])."[18] Miller ends by stating that the theological seminary moved to York in 1828 and has a library of four thousand volumes, "chiefly in the German language."[19]

The fine detail of Miller's work provides a unique opportunity to analyze the process of change at the individual and household level. Anthropologist Fredrik Barth, who points out that it is "not societies and cultures that change initially, but individuals and households experimenting with changes,"[20] has argued for a process-oriented approach to change that focuses on individuals and networks as the units of study, rather than on cultures and societies. Processes of change at the individual and household level will, he suggests, help scholars perceive continuities between emerging institutional forms and those that preceded them.[21]

A potential problem with this type of approach to acculturative change involves selection: which actors and events are important to study? In the case of the Miller data for the upper Valley of Virginia, the actors and events are linked to the experiences of a relatively well-traveled bachelor. Miller's circle of acquaintances in Montgomery County represents a specific network of individuals in the community, including Germans, Scots-Irish, and English, but this group may not be representative of the community at large. While questions of representativeness remain unanswered, the series of human and institutional linkages provided by Miller's drawings and texts promises to offer connections to the folk culture of the community not found in other sources. The Miller drawings also provide a visual framework for multiple aspects of the acculturative process, including language, religion, and other material signs and symbols of German ethnic identity.

Like language, religion was an important cultural tradition that bound the German settlers. Historian Timothy L. Smith has commented that ethnic allegiance was "determined largely by the immigrants' identification with a particular religious tradition. The appeal of common language, national feeling, and belief in a common descent was sufficient in only a few minor cases to outweigh the attraction of religious affiliation as an organizing impulse."[22] Similarly, historian Klaus Wust reports that "in every settlement the German church was the spiritual, educational, and social center, and very few people remained outside its influence."[23] Religion appears to be an important internal cultural feature that continued to provide a framework for German group identity throughout the nineteenth century. Archaeologist Gary G. Robinson has noted that both religion and language were central to the maintenance of the ethnic boundaries of the mid-nineteenth-century German Lutheran community of Frankenmuth, Michigan.[24] Examination of the church records extant for Montgomery County Lutheran and German Reformed congregations will assist in further linking the individuals in Miller's work to each other, to specific religious organizations, and to extended family kinship networks.

In addition to highlighting language use and religious practice, previous investigations have acknowledged the central importance of farms and farming to the acculturation of the Virginia Germans. The farm was a primary unit of spatial or-

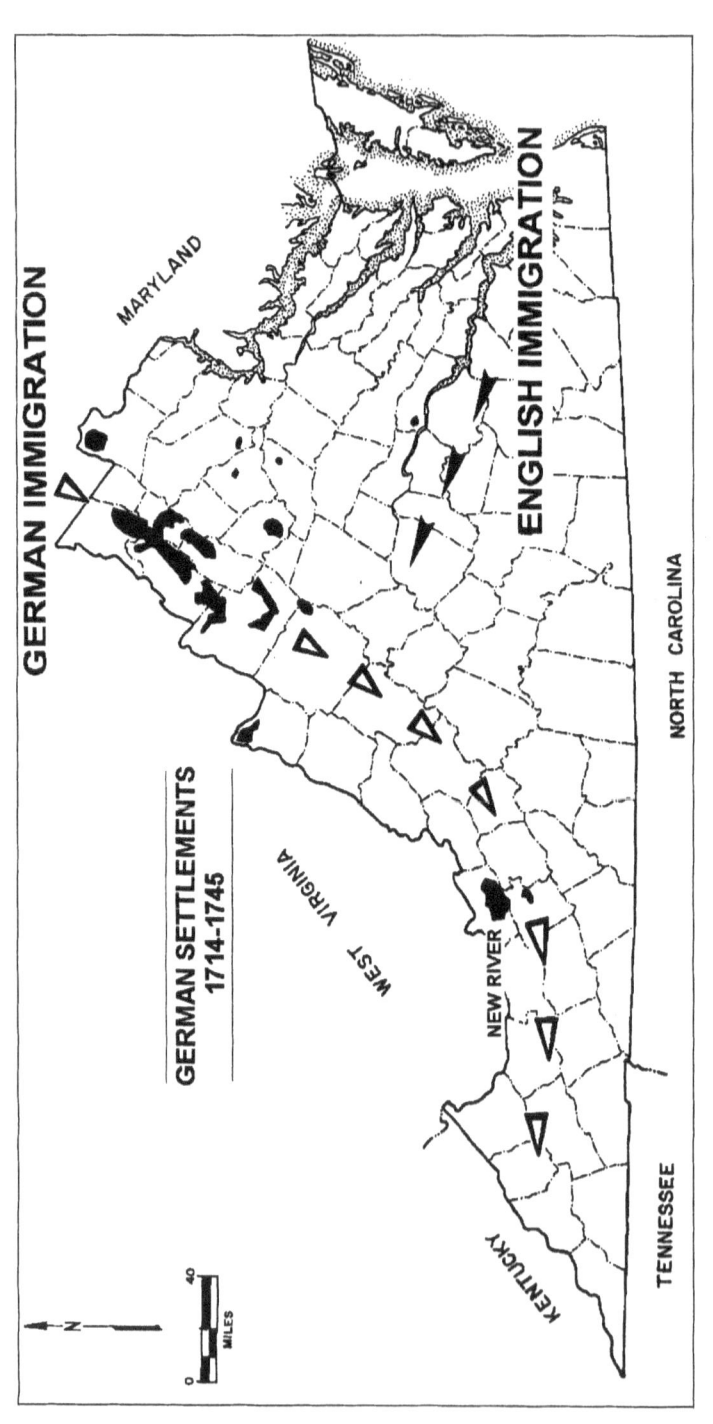

Map 11.1. Map of German and English immigration into the Valley of Virginia, with German settlements, ca. 1714–45. Drawn by John D. Roberts, adapted from Klaus Wust, *The Virginia Germans* (Charlottesville: University Press of Virginia, 1969), 23.

ganization for individuals in these German groups, ordering daily life and reflecting values and beliefs associated with work, animals, and land. German farmsteads in the valley were exceptional for their small size and high levels of production.[25] This pattern of small, highly productive farms began during the eighteenth century, when German immigrants followed the limestone soils of southern Pennsylvania into the Shenandoah Valley and quickly set to farming the land. The settlement pattern of small individual farms scattered in rural community enclaves continued south and west through the valley, with a major settlement at New River in Montgomery County (map 11.1).

Wust and others suggest that this pattern of separated individual farmsteads was a New World manifestation that differed from traditional German settlements formed around nucleated groupings of residential structures and communal land holdings. A study of German settlement patterns by Robert Dickinson, however, suggests that the relatively solitary farmstead, or *Einzelhof*, encountered in the Valley of Virginia was a historic rural settlement type in Germany. The Einzelhof pattern emerged during the Middle Ages through the process of forest clearance and subsequent movement of people from parent villages onto the cleared land.[26] Far from fostering close communal ties among the Germans in Virginia, the dispersed farmsteads kept their inhabitants relatively isolated from the encroaching English world.

Architectural historian Edward Chappell has argued in his essay, *Acculturation in the Shenandoah Valley: Rhenish Houses of the Massanutten Settlement*, that Germans experienced increased acculturative pressure from the dominant culture in the late eighteenth century. He notes that the result of this pressure was not the total abandonment of the German culture, but a masking of public expressions such as language and architecture. The house, a very public and visible symbol, he argues, was at first modified to conform to Anglo-American aesthetics. Eventually the German style was abandoned altogether. Chappell identifies the *Flürkuckenhaus* as the primary model for German and Swiss houses in America throughout most of the eighteenth century. The Flürkuckenhaus's primary characteristics are an unbalanced plan, asymmetrical fenestration, off-center internal chimney, first-floor kitchen, and stone or log construction with limestone foundations (fig. 11.1). Lewis Miller illustrated several of these structures in Pennsylvania during the early nineteenth century (fig. 11.2)—a time when, according to Chappell, the Flürkuckenhaus in its pure form was beginning to disappear or to incorporate Anglo-American forms and characteristics. Chappell asserts that an Anglo-derived I-house plan was embraced by making alterations to the Flürkuckenhaus, and that this later completely replaced the earlier traditional form. The I-house consists of symmetrical elevations, balanced plan, central entrance passage, gable chimneys, and a kitchen ell or detached kitchen (fig. 11.3). Though Chappell has argued that "the tenacious adherence to the I-house form in the Valley represents a conscious replacement of the symbols of the old ethnic cultures,"[27] it is as yet unclear whether it represents a specific step toward an Anglo-American ideal.

The I-house and the Flürkuckenhaus in both their pure and hybrid forms, along with the dispersed farmstead arrangement discussed by Dickinson, figure in the cultural landscape of Germans in south central Pennsylvania. In fact, William Weaver has argued that the three- to four-room Pennsylvania German House plan, Chappell's Flürkuckenhaus, was largely a product of the immigrant culture in central Pennsylvania.[28] The most common room arrangement in central and southern Germany, Weaver asserts, was the two-room plan: "a room called the Stube (store room) and one called the Küche (hearth room)."[29] This arrangement, he argues, was expanded to the three- or four-room plan in Pennsylvania. Settlers coming to the Valley of Virginia from southern Pennsylvania, then, already may have begun to modify their European cultural traditions to fit the New World experience, due to both cultural and environmental differences.

According to Chappell, the southern and western portions of the Valley of Virginia appear to have made the transition in outward symbols in the early nineteenth century, while the northern portions nearer to southern Pennsylvania were slower to change. The increasing presence of Anglo Virginians in the southern valley probably had some effect on the German community, particularly in terms of emphasizing cultural differences such as housing and farming behavior. Vir-

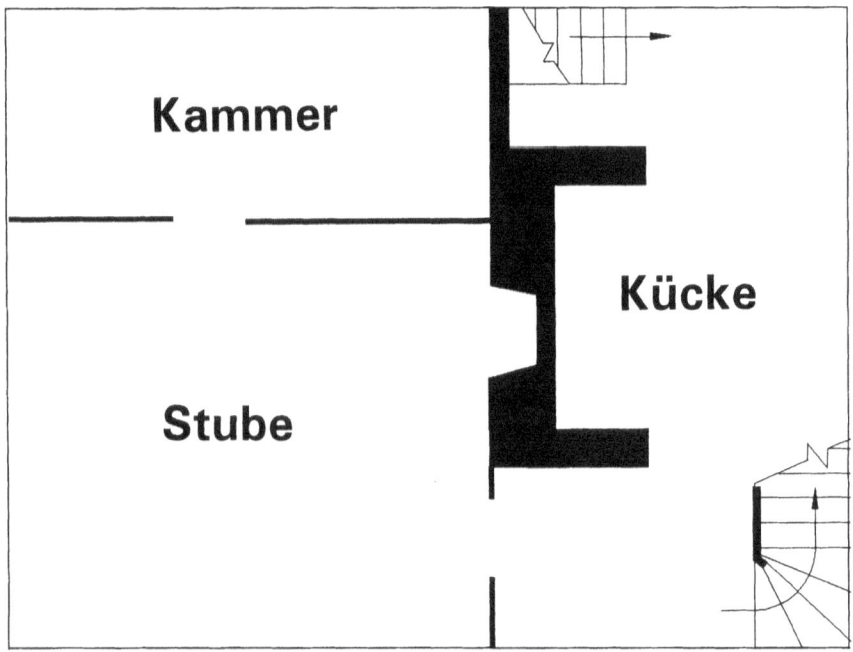

Fig. 11.1. First-floor plan, Andrew Keyser House, Virginia, ca. 1765. Drawing by John D. Roberts, adapted from Edward A. Chappell, "Acculturation in the Shenandoah Valley: Rhenish Houses of the Massanutten Settlement," *Proceedings of the American Philosophical Society* 124 (1980): 74.

ginia Germans may have become more aware of cultural differences as the two groups began to settle in closer proximity and live together as a community.

Lewis Miller's drawings of farmsteads in the upper valley in the 1830s to 1870s suggest that the German house was changing during this period to reflect (at least externally) the I-house plan. These drawings, which show houses and farmsteads retaining numerous German traits, also suggest that the overall transformation to

Fig. 11.2. Home of the Geiger family, York County, Pennsylvania, ca. 1810. Detail of drawing by Lewis Miller (1796–1882). Used by permission of the Historical Society of York County, Pennsylvania.

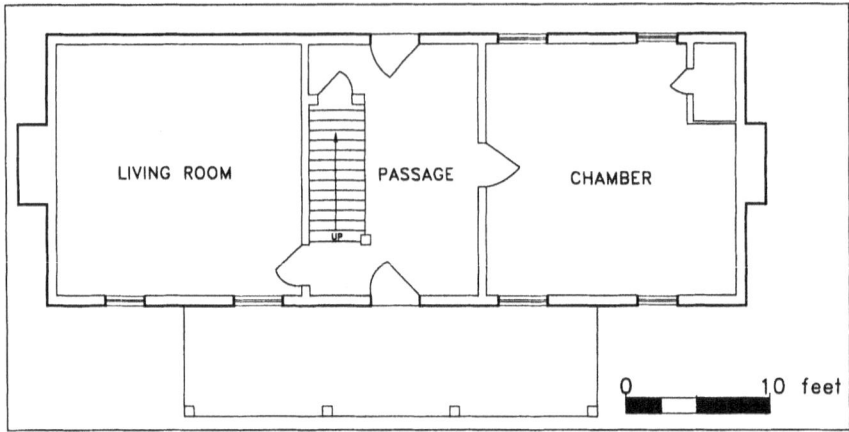

Fig. 11.3. First-floor plan, Lanier House, Dinwiddie County, Virginia, Period I, ca. 1850. Drawing by John D. Roberts.

Fig. 11.4. Mrs. Widow Wade House and Mill, Montgomery County, Virginia, ca. 1850. Drawing by Lewis Miller (1796–1882). Used by permission of the Abby Aldrich Folk Art Center, Williamsburg, Virginia.

a specifically Anglo configuration was not complete, even by the late nineteenth century. Specifically, the drawings illustrate the survival of features such as central chimneys, German roofing systems and log construction techniques, the three-room Flürkuckenhaus plan, large animal barns and sheds, and a clustered farm-building layout combining work and domestic spaces. In fact, the drawings hint that the Germans of the valley and their neighbors may have been living a more multicultural and international existence than previously has been thought. Klaus Wust has asserted this type of multicultural experience in Wythe County, stating that "they were able to create their own German environment without ... remaining outside the community at large."[30]

Miller's sketch of the Widow Wade House, located one mile north of Christiansburg, was drawn around 1850. It shows a fenced yard surrounding a house with interior end chimneys, asymmetrical three-bay elevation, and off-center entrance (fig. 11.4). The elevation of this house, as well as its door placement, suggests a possible interior Flürkuckenhaus plan. The addition of a rear ell may indicate that the cooking function had been moved from its traditional location.

Fig. 11.5. The residence of John Craig, Hamten Meadow, Montgomery County, Virginia. Drawing by Lewis Miller (1796–1882). Used by permission of the Abby Aldrich Folk Art Center, Williamsburg, Virginia.

A large pole barn with vertical siding sits in the foreground, while the three-story Wade's Mill is found slightly to the right of center.

The John Craig farmstead, "Hamten Meadow," also located near Christiansburg, often served as Miller's valley residence. Miller's niece Emmeline, daughter of Dr. Joseph Miller, was married to John Craig. The drawing from around 1860 suggests the presence of several dwelling houses on the property, a relatively common occurrence on these German farmsteads as families expanded (fig. 11.5).[31] A two-story brick I-house dominates the foreground scene, with two one-and-a-half-story dwellings in fenced yards to the rear. Also dotting the landscape are numerous log outbuildings, including a barn, as well as more fence lines. Lewis Miller wrote of the farm in 1851, "I am often in a dream in John Craig's meadow gathering flowers."[32] In another Miller sketch dated 1865, we see on the Craig farm a mill used for grinding sugar cane (fig. 11.6), as well as male and female figures in German-style hats and clothing.

The Zoll farmhouse, located west of Christiansburg along the New River, is a two-story log structure with a covered porch and one-story rear ell (fig. 11.7). The building has a three-bay symmetrical façade and exterior end chimney. Two log

Fig. 11.6. "On the Farm of Missters [sic], Emmeline Craig," ca. 1865. Drawing by Lewis Miller (1796–1882). Used by permission of the Virginia Historical Society, Richmond.

Fig. 11.7. The residence of Mr. Zoll at New River, Montgomery County, Virginia, n.d. Drawing by Lewis Miller (1796–1882). Used by permission of the Virginia Historical Society, Richmond.

outbuildings complete the complex, both with extended kicked eaves suggestive of German roof framing.[33] The building to the right of the grouping is likely a barn, while the intermediate structure with chimney is possibly a summer kitchen.

The Ingles property, farmed by Mr. Jones, is also sited on the bank of the New River. This large farm is dominated by a two-story hipped roof house with two-story rear ell (fig. 11.8), a symmetrical three-bay front façade, and interior end chimneys. The farm complex consists of nine buildings, including a two-story asymmetrical log structure that may be an earlier dwelling. The small building to the right of the dwelling house is probably an animal shed; a large log barn is located on the far left.

The residence of the "late Mr. Haymacker" was drawn by Miller in August 1856. The farm was located about three miles north of Christiansburg along the road to the Yellow Sulphur Springs resort. The two-story farmhouse has an asymmetrical front façade, exterior end chimneys, and a kicked roof at the eaves (fig. 11.9). Outbuildings include a log house, possibly the original dwelling, and a small log shed with vertical siding.

A sketch titled "The Residence of Mr. Lenard," drawn around 1870, depicts a farmstead located six miles outside of Christiansburg. This farmhouse, built using log construction, has an asymmetrical front elevation (fig. 11.10) and a roof with a possible kick at the eave.[34] While no chimneys are visible on the main house, the rear ell, or attached single-story addition, appears to have a large chimney for cooking purposes. Three other outbuildings complete the complex.

The "Residence of Mr. Etzler," drawn about 1870, was located five miles from Christiansburg. It apparently is a central-passage plan dwelling with a single exterior gable-end chimney and a rear ell (fig. 11.11). The foundation of the house and ell is limestone, as is the ell chimney. The ell and the outbuildings appear to have been built using traditional log construction techniques. The exterior gable-end chimney probably is constructed of brick and therefore may be a later addition. The log outbuilding to the left of the main house ell is possibly a summer kitchen with a stone chimney. A fenced garden or small field appears in front of the house.

The selected Miller drawings and preliminary historical and architectural research for this study suggest that architecture and farmstead layouts in the southwestern portion of the Valley of Virginia reflect less than a total merger of the German and English cultures as late as the final quarter of the nineteenth century. The

Fig. 11.8. Ingles farm on the bank of New River, Montgomery County, Virginia, n.d. Drawing by Lewis Miller (1796–1882). Used by permission of the Virginia Historical Society, Richmond.

Fig. 11.9. The residence of Mr. Haymacker, Montgomery County, Virginia, ca. 1856. Drawing by Lewis Miller (1796–1882). Used by permission of the Virginia Historical Society, Richmond.

drawings also raise many questions concerning the actual processes of cultural mixing. While an outward sign such as architecture may signal an inward accommodation with the dominant Anglo culture, in the valley Germans the extent of assimilation remains unclear. Rather than a specific Anglo-American aesthetic[35] emphasizing symmetry, balance and order, and refinement, the architectural changes embraced by these Germans in fact may signal the impact of a more international architectural style and culture. The architectural features represented in the valley I-house, after all, had a large worldwide distribution by the early nineteenth century. Inasmuch as changes already were under way in Europe when many German immigrants made the crossing to America, it should not surprise us to see them integrated into building traditions from Pennsylvania to the Midwest.[36]

The addition of a rear or side ell to a house with German characteristics is an interesting change in this regard. Why did the Virginia Germans almost universally reconfigure the internal spatial layout of their homes through the adoption of the rear-ell kitchen addition? The hot and humid Virginia environment may have played a part in moving the kitchen away from the main body of the dwelling, but this change occurs in Pennsylvania, too.[37] Architectural historian Mark R. Wenger has suggested that this reorientation may be related to the worldwide trend toward banishment of work

Fig. 11.10. The residence of Mr. Lenard, near Christiansburg, Montgomery County, Virginia, ca. 1870. Drawing by Lewis Miller (1796–1882). Used by permission of the Abby Aldrich Folk Art Center, Williamsburg, Virginia.

Fig. 11.11 The residence of Mr. Etzler, near Christiansburg, Montgomery County, Virginia, ca. 1870. Drawing by Lewis Miller (1796–1882). Used by permission of the Abby Aldrich Folk Art Center, Williamsburg, Virginia.

from polite spaces, discussed by Richard Bushman in *The Refinement of America*.[38] Likewise, the Germans may have used this reconfigured space to embrace the centrality of entertaining in Anglo Virginian culture.

The acculturation of Germans in the Valley of Virginia may have been tentative, and it need not be taken as evidence of a desire for assimilation or a bid for membership in the dominant Anglo culture. Recent studies of ethnic groups have shown that acculturation can occur without a change in values and need not lead to assimilation on the part of the group or the individual.[39] As mentioned above, the rear-ell kitchen is accepted in German housing in Pennsylvania even within Amish and Mennonite communities that are non-assimilative of Anglo cultural traditions in general. Lewis Miller's drawings and Chappell's architectural data both suggest a reorganization of food preparation activities within the dwelling, as central fireplaces were relocated to the gable ends and kitchens were moved to rear ells. This change is also seen in the German farmhouse of southern Pennsylvania, with the movement of the *Vorhof* or *Vorplatz*, the kitchen yard, to a position adjacent to the rear ell. Therefore, it is important to sort out the types of changes acceptable to the Germans in the valley, why they were acceptable, and the speed of their implementation.

Additional interdisciplinary research utilizing the Lewis Miller drawings and other German material culture is needed to answer questions about culture change in the Valley of Virginia. A constructive line of inquiry would be to trace—both historically through documents and physically through archaeology—the farms and families mentioned in the sketchbooks. Such research might enable us to gauge the extent of the social and cultural experimentation of individuals who inhabited these farms. To understand the processes of valley cultural mixing in more detail, it will be necessary to focus on demographic particulars and on the geographical mobility of individuals. How, in other words, does one's age affect speed of acculturation and retention of previous traditions?

Archaeological work on the German farmsteads in Virginia and even in Pennsylvania is very limited. In the upper Valley of Virginia, however, the visual framework and community network provided by Miller's sketches offers archaeologists a range of temporally and culturally associated farmstead sites. Archaeologist John S. Wilson recently examined the research potential (based on factors such as the existence and extent of county records, length of the occupation, type of occupation, and type of superstructure demolition) of the thousands of late-eighteenth- and nineteenth-century farmstead sites across the country.[40] The ideal site, Wilson notes, would possess excellent documentary records and would have been destroyed by a catastrophic event such as a fire after a relatively short overall occupation (twenty years or less) by a single family.[41] While these ideal sites are relatively rare, the Montgomery County farmsteads illustrated by Miller may rank as better than most. Unlike many farmstead sites in Virginia, these have the potential for excellent documentation—including court records, church records, and diaries, not to mention Miller's art—of the owners' and tenants' lives. While many of the Miller farms will be multifamily sites, the families often will prove to have lived in separate dwellings and outbuildings in different areas of the farmyard (see figs. 11.7 and 11.8). The length of occupation and type of destruction of the property will vary and should be a consideration in selecting specific sites for excavation. Finally, a "good" site may allow for more specific control in artifact recovery, to aid in addressing elusive issues of material culture and ethnicity through both intersite and intrasite comparison. The recovery of environmental artifacts, or *ecofacts*, for example, can document the occupants' foodways.

Additional historical documents research can be combined with the Miller drawings to establish the social context of each site and to lay out, as completely as possible, community institutions and kinship networks. The extensive decorative arts of the Germans present a wide range of markers linked to participation in German cultural traditions, while the presence of American and English material culture may document the degree of participation in the larger economy of Anglo Virginia. Archaeologists James Gibbs and Tara Pettit, working at the Reiff site in western Maryland, have found that, while over 50 percent of the ceramics in the assemblage are redwares of local manufacture, the site's occupants also regularly purchased and utilized English ceramics in quantity.[42] Of specific interest here may be English ceramics with patterns—"Gaudy Dutch," for example—imitative of a German aesthetic. Artifact assemblages also can establish building function and activity areas related to farming and domestic employment. The material and historical analysis of German farmsteads should provide an index to the movement of Pennsylvania German–produced goods from markets in southern Pennsylvania, Maryland, and North Carolina to communities in the valley. This analysis would chronicle, too, the establishment of similar craft traditions, such as the potteries of the Bell family.[43] Artifacts of particular interest might include redware and stoneware ceramics from the potteries of southern Pennsylvania and the Moravian communities of North Carolina; ironware, particularly stove plates and parts; ceramic stove tiles; tinware; gun parts; decorated gravestones; and glassware. This type of assemblage can be combined with documented museum collections of German crafts containing furniture, Fraktur, and textile arts. Such close temporal, geographic, and cultural control, achieved through artifact dating and documents such as the Miller drawings, should yield comparative assemblages that can be applied directly to addressing questions of cultural interaction and integration.

Archaeological data may provide an opportunity to juxtapose differences in things found in the house or "private sphere of life" with more public artifacts such as buildings and landscapes. Disjunction between these records may be significant for addressing issues of belief and value retention in immigrant German communities, in terms of individual and household experimentation and community continuity. How much control did German individuals or the community at large have in the acceptance or rejection of Anglo Virginian cultural traits? Studies of German Hutterite communities have verified the practice of controlled acculturation, in which the group accepts a cultural behavior or convention from another group, but integrates that convention into its existing value system.[44] This allows the group to maintain an autonomous social system yet incorporate cultural traits and behavior patterns of the surrounding culture.

It appears from initial study of Miller's drawings that the intermixing of German and English cultural communities in the Valley of Virginia is a much more complex and variable process than previously understood. The blending of German cultural traditions and newer international architectural styles as late as the end of the nineteenth century suggests that German cultural identity continued to exist and evolve, even at this relatively late date. As increasing study occurs relating to questions concerning resistance to, or acceptance of, Anglo-American cultural traits in the German community, Miller's drawings offer new opportunities to comprehend multiculturation in the Valley of Virginia.

Notes

1. Thomas Jefferson, 1817, quoted in Klaus Wust, *The Virginia Germans* (Charlottesville: Univ. Press of Virginia, 1969), 107.
2. Wust, *Virginia Germans*, 186.
3. Edward A. Chappell, "Acculturation in the Shenandoah Valley: Rhenish Houses of the Massanutten Settlement," *Proceedings of the American Philosophical Society* 124, no. 1 (1980): 55–89.
4. Philip Gleason, "American Identity and Americanization," in *Harvard Encyclopedia of American Ethnic Groups*, ed. Stephan Thernstrom (Cambridge, Mass.: Harvard Univ. Press, 1980), 32–58.
5. Dell Upton, "Ethnicity, Authenticity, and Invented Traditions," *Historical Archaeology* 30, no. 2 (1996): 5.
6. Albert H. Tillson, Jr., "The Southern Backcountry: A Survey of Current Research," *Virginia Magazine of History and Biography* 98, no. 3 (1990): 396.
7. Robert P. Turner, ed., *Lewis Miller: Sketches and Chronicles* (York, Pa.: Historical Society of York County, 1966), xvi.
8. Preston Barba and Eleanor Barba, "Lewis Miller, Pennsylvania German Folk Artist," *Pennsylvania German Folklore Society, Publications* 4 (1939): 11.
9. Donald A. Shelley, "Lewis Miller: An Introduction," in Robert P. Turner, *Lewis Miller: Sketches and Chronicles*, xvii.
10. Lewis Miller, *Sketchbook of Landscapes in the State of Virginia*, 1853, in collection of Abby Aldrich Rockefeller Folk Art Center, Williamsburg, Va.; Lewis Miller, *Virginia Sketchbook*, 1856–57, in collection of Virginia Historical Society, Richmond.
11. Harry L. Rinker and Richard M. Kain, "Lewis Miller's Virginia Sketchbook: A Record of Rural Life," *Antiques* 119, no. 2 (1981): 396–401.
12. Daniel Porter, "Folk Art as Manuscripts: The Works of Lewis Miller," *Manuscripts* 13 (1961): 13.
13. Elizabeth Dabney Coleman, "Southwest Virginia's Railroad," *Virginia Cavalcade* 2, no. 4 (1953): 20–28; Richard M. Kain, "Stalking Nineteenth-Century Virginia with Sketchbook and Pen," *Colonial Williamsburg Today* 1, no. 4 (1979): 6–8; Porter, "Folk

Art as Manuscripts," 13–19; William M. E. Rachal, "A Trip to the Salt Pond: The Rewards of a Vacation Ride from Christiansburg to Mountain Lake in 1853, Portrayed in Sketches by Lewis Miller," *Virginia Cavalcade* 2, no. 2 (1952): 22–27; Lyle Royster, Jr., and Pamela Hemenway Simpson, *The Architecture of Historic Lexington* (Charlottesville: Univ. Press of Virginia, 1977); Bob Thompson, ed., "York, Pennsylvania: Lewis Miller Remembers," *Washington Post Magazine*, Mar. 8, 1992, pp. 21, 38.

14. Jeremy F. Gilmer, *Map of Montgomery County* (Richmond, Va.: Confederate Engineer Bureau, Richmond, 1864). On file, Virginia Historical Society, Richmond.
15. Preston Barba and Eleanor Barba, "Lewis Miller," 10–11.
16. Henry L. Fisher, quoted in Shelley, "Lewis Miller: An Introduction," xiv.
17. Shelley, "Lewis Miller: An Introduction," xiv.
18. Robert P. Turner, *Lewis Miller: Sketches and Chronicles*, 109.
19. Ibid.
20. Alexander M. Ervin, "A Review of the Acculturation Approach in Anthropology with Special Reference to Recent Change in Native Alaska," *Journal of Anthropological Research* 36, no. 1 (1980): 49–70.
21. Fredrik Barth, "On the Study of Social Change," *American Anthropologist* 69, no. 6 (1967): 661–69.
22. Timothy L. Smith, "Religion and Ethnicity in America," *American Historical Review* 83 (1978): 1169.
23. Wust, *Virginia Germans*, 129.
24. Gary G. Robinson, "Material Culture and Settlement Pattern Among the Germans in the New World: The View from Frankenmuth, Michigan," in *Spatial Patterning in Historical Archaeology: Selected Studies of Settlement*, ed. Donald W. Linebaugh and Gary G. Robinson (Williamsburg, Va.: King and Queen Press, 1994), 97.
25. Herrmann Schuricht, *History of the German Element in Virginia* (Baltimore, Md.: Theo. Kroh and Sons, 1898), 1:96–97.
26. Robert E. Dickinson, "Rural Settlement in the German Lands," *Annals of American Geographers* 39, no. 4 (1949): 262.
27. Chappell, "Acculturation in the Shenandoah Valley," 56.
28. William Woys Weaver, "The Pennsylvania German House: European Antecedents and New World Forms," *Winterthur Portfolio* 21, no. 4 (1986): 243–64.
29. Ibid., 253.
30. Wust, *Virginia Germans*, 101.
31. Scott M. Hudlow and Charles M. Downing, "A Phase II Architectural Evaluation of the Potential Crockett/Reed Creek Rural Historic District Associated with the Proposed Ground Wave Emergency Network Tower, Wythe County, Virginia," report on file, William and Mary Center for Archaeological Research, Williamsburg, Va., 1992, p. 9.
32. Rinker and Kain, "Lewis Miller's Virginia Sketchbook," 397.
33. Chappell, "Acculturation in the Shenandoah Valley," 59.
34. Ibid.
35. Carl Lounsbury and Mark R. Wenger, personal communication, 1993.

36. Ibid.
37. Chappell, "Acculturation in the Shenandoah Valley," 61; Donald W. Linebaugh, "'All the Annoyances and Inconveniences of the Country . . . Thunder, Heat, and Troublesom Vermin': Environmental Factors in the Development of Outbuildings in the Seventeenth- and Eighteenth-Century Chesapeake," *Winterthur Portfolio* 29, no. 1 (Spring 1994): 1–18.
38. Mark R. Wenger, personal communication to Linebaugh, 1993.
39. Raymond H. C. Teske, Jr., and Bardin H. Nelson, "Acculturation and Assimilation: A Clarification," *American Ethnologist* 1 (1974): 365.
40. John S. Wilson, "We've Got Thousands of These! What Makes a Historic Farmstead Significant?" *Historical Archaeology* 24, no. 2 (1990): 23–33.
41. John S. Wilson, "We've Got a Thousand of These," 30.
42. James G. Gibb and Tara D. Pettit, "Consumer Choice and Locally-Made Coarse Earthenwares in Western Maryland, 1800–1850" (Paper presented at the annual meeting of the Middle Atlantic Archaeological Conference, Ocean City, Md., Apr. 8, 1995).
43. A. H. Rice and John Baer Stoudt, *The Shenandoah Pottery* (Strasburg, Va.: Shenandoah Publishing House, 1929).
44. Teske and Nelson, "Acculturation and Assimilation," 357.

Epilogue: Interdisciplinary Dialogues on the Southern Colonial Backcountry, 1893–1998

Warren R. Hofstra

The year 1993 marked the centennial of Frederick Jackson Turner's famous address, "The Significance of the Frontier in American History."[1] The Chicago World's Columbian Exposition provided the venue for Turner's presentation. This quadricentennial commemoration of European contact with the New World embodied Turner's theme of the triumph of civilization over savagery in the progressive settlement of the North American continent. Visitors to the exposition moved initially through a series of ethnographic displays about the world's peoples. Only after they "progressed" through several degrees of savagery did they finally ascend to the White City, where the marvels of modern science and technology could, presumably, be fully appreciated.

The Columbian quincentenary of the 1990s has lacked any similar tangible expression of modern ideology, but the debates surrounding this anniversary nonetheless have served to intensify recent interest in the backcountry frontier. The mood, however, has been far less sanguine. Columbus's late-twentieth-century detractors quite rightly have pointed out that the Columbian invasion of European cultures, peoples, and diseases was a death march—not a triumphal procession—for North America's native inhabitants. A postmodern reading of Turner's thesis thus produces very different conclusions about the consequences of the frontier for American life.

Despite his critics, Turner was no exposition shill mindlessly heralding the blessings of progress. Behind his assertions about the significance of the frontier lay a sophisticated argument about how the frontier ought to be studied, one that holds important implications for today's scholarship. More than a decade of earlier work had led Turner to the conclusion that the study of the frontier not only ought to be interdisciplinary but inherently was interdisciplinary. The study of the past could not be left to historians alone. Environmentally unique frontiers and sectional cultures left in the wake of their passing were cumulatively responsible, Turner held, for a distinctive American civilization whose regions required collaborative study among historians, social scientists, and natural scientists.[2] Thus, if the essays in this volume do indeed initiate an interdisciplinary dialogue on the southern colonial backcountry, they are at least one hundred years in fulfilling Turner's promise.

As a student in Herbert Baxter Adams's seminar at Johns Hopkins University, Turner had imbibed the heady principle that "history is past politics and politics present history." During his first years at the University of Wisconsin, however, his horizons stretched beyond political history. In a short essay published in the *Wisconsin Journal of Education* in 1891, he argued that young historians were about "to rewrite history from the economic point of view." Because this perspective directed attention to labor and production, "the focal point of modern interest is the fourth estate, the great mass of the people," he went on to say. Turner then reversed Adams's formula and asserted that "far oftener than has yet been shown have these underlying economic facts affecting the bread-winners of the nation, been the secret of the nation's rise or fall." In this nexus of economic and political history lay the imperative for interdisciplinary collaboration:

> First we recognize why all the spheres of man's activity must be considered. Not only is this the only way in which we can get a complete view of the society, but no one department of social life can be understood in isolation from the others. The economic life and the political life touch, modify and condition one another. Even the religious life needs to be studied in conjunction with the political and economic life, and vice versa. Therefore all kinds of history are essential—history as politics, history as art, history as economics, history as religion—all are truly parts of society's endeavor to understand itself by understanding its past.

To achieve this wider conception of history, Turner understood very well that all sources—artifactual and documentary, material and mental—were essential: "To the historian the materials for his work are found in all that remains from the ages gone by—in papers, roads, mounds, customs, languages; in monuments, coins, medals, names, titles, inscriptions, charters; in contemporary annals and chronicles, and finally in the secondary sources or histories in the common acceptance of the term. Wherever there remains a chipped flint, a spear-head, a piece of pottery, a pyramid, a picture, a poem, a coloseum [sic], or a coin, there is history."[3]

At the heart of Turner's appeal for applying a wide variety of academic disciplines to the study of the American people—not just political leaders—was yet another seminal idea that connected human history with the natural environment. The year following "The Significance of History" and still a year before "The Significance of the Frontier," Turner published in *The Aegis*, a University of Wisconsin undergraduate newspaper, an essay entitled "Problems in American History."

Here he pointed out that American history is "at bottom the study of European germs developing in an American environment." Equating germs with the seeds of civilization, this study arguably was a "new" history. "Little has yet been done," he continued, "toward investigating the part played by the environment in determining the lines of our development." Realizing the part, however, required collaboration across academic and scientific disciplines: "When the geologists, the meteorologist, the biologist, and the historian shall go hand in hand in this study, they will see how largely American history has been determined by natural conditions." Discerning that different environments could produce different regional cultures, Turner went on to make the link between interdisciplinary work, sectionalism, and American historical development. "The evolution of sections in our history," he proclaimed, "is a far deeper fact than the development of state particularism, for whatever force the latter had came in a large degree from its association with sectionalism."[4]

Although it contradicted his own thinking, the essay in *The Aegis* impressed Adams greatly and led directly to Turner's invitation to develop his ideas further before the American Historical Association meeting the next year in Chicago at the Columbian Exposition. In the well-known story, Turner took that opportunity to argue the frontier thesis that the encounter between European peoples and American environments produced democratic institutions and a unique national character. America therefore was very different from Europe. The fate of this idea of American exceptionalism worked out during an ensuing century of scholarship has produced yet another argument for the necessary collaboration of many disciplines in the study of the southern colonial backcountry.

Although some scholars have deplored the alleged failure of the new social history and modern community studies to yield any original generalizations for early American history, the past thirty years of scholarship in these fields has produced the overwhelming conclusion that the communities of Puritan New England and the plantation South were characterized more by continuity with origins in England than by discontinuity.[5] America simply was far less exceptional than previously believed or than Turner argued. If diffusion, more than insularity, has characterized American development, then colonial communities must be studied as complex aggregations of cultural traits diverse and distant in origin. Although unique as cultural fusions, these communities were nonetheless derivative.

Insofar as the town in New England and the county in the South have served as the units of investigation, community studies have been the special preserve of historians, because, quite conveniently, town and county also have been the political entities generating and preserving the documentary records upon which historians rely. This was not so for the eighteenth-century interior. As Michael J. Puglisi points out in chapter 2 of this volume, there are "inherent difficulties in attempting to impose the town-study model on the backcountry." Pioneer settlers occupied landscapes in which the fluid geography of ethnicity, kinship, congregation, and economic reciprocity defined the contours of new communities.[6] In early Tennessee, for instance, David C. Hsiung finds that each resident "lived concurrently in communities the size of his valley, his civil district, his county, and his interstate markets" (ch. 9). The initial focus of social relations and economic interdependence remained within what some geographers have termed "open-country neighborhoods," despite the efforts of colonial authorities to overlay the traditional political units of town, county, and parish on the backcountry.[7] Amid the "documentary riches" these polities generated, "there is no simple way to isolate information concerning a single frontier settlement," according to Turk McCleskey (ch. 3). The autonomy and spatial distinctiveness of these neighborhoods, as fusionist societies poorly articulated in the early county systems of government and record keeping, thus force historians into collaborations with ethnohistorians, geographers, anthropologists, and archaeologists more accustomed to evaluating cultures and communities within self-determined boundaries and more adept at plotting cultural diffusion across large areas.

As historical interest swept in a broad arc from New England to the Chesapeake and finally reached the backcountry in the late 1980s, scholars of the frontier have come full circle. They have arrived at the position Frederick Jackson Turner identified a century ago, finding his arguments for interdisciplinary work largely intact and unexplored. Now his exhortation is seconded by modern scholarship. New work recognizes that an interdisciplinary approach can give a fuller picture of the backcountry—one attuned more to the autonomous cultures of its varied peoples than to the inevitable domination of a single civilization.[8]

What, then, is the picture the essays in this volume have presented of the backcountry? Where, in other words, have they led recent scholarship?

All of the essays in this book presuppose the regional integrity of the eighteenth-century southern backcountry. They demonstrate that it was a place as well as a process. It can be studied all in a piece. This idea is by no means new. For Turner, the Old West could be "appreciated only by obliterating the state boundaries which conceal its unity."[9] Backcountry society, in other words, was shaped more by common characteristics than by political divisions. A half-century later, Carl Bridenbaugh, in *Myths and Realities: Societies of the Colonial South*, defined the backcountry as a unified region of diverse peoples distinct from the Chesapeake and Carolina lowcountries.[10] What is new are the subsequent contributions from social scientists leading toward more precise regional definitions and more sophisticated understandings of interrelated economic and social functions within regions. Geographers—from Fred Kniffen and Henry Glassie beginning in the 1960s, to Wilbur Zelinsky in the 1970s, and Terry G. Jordan and Matti Kaups more recently—have plotted cultural traits (such as settlement patterns, economic activities, building traditions, kinship systems, ethnic customs, political procedures, and religious practices) to map out an Upland South regionally distinct in the cultural geography of early America.[11] Explaining aggregations of traits in terms of migration patterns or diffusion from cultural hearths, these social scientists have delineated more precisely the eastern boundaries of the backcountry, described a fluid or permeable northern perimeter, and postulated a western frontier defined more by zones of cultural and environmental encounters than by fixed boundaries.

Working within the culture-area concept and gathering information on social and economic developments, ethnicity, and material culture, historical geographer Robert D. Mitchell suggests that diffusionist approaches reveal unity only as a self-fulfilling prophecy. It is no surprise that, in focusing on and plotting the diffusion of specific traits, social scientists find a connection between pattern and space. More detailed examinations of specific places within the backcountry, Mitchell argues, betray greater regional diversity in the combinations and recombinations of varied peoples and lifeways.

The backcountry west of Augusta, Georgia, as Edward J. Cashin describes it, certainly was a region of cultural fusion. The town had been established in the 1730s "for the better regulation of the Indian trade" (ch. 4) and helped to maintain Indian independence within its hinterland lying between the Savannah and Ogeechee rivers. Newcomers, mainly from Virginia, migrating south after the Proclamation of 1763 and the Creek land cessions of that year, brought new influences into the region—namely, the Virginia plantation, evangelical religion, and an intolerance of Indians. The result was what Cashin calls a "social revolution," as white settlers, very different from the older residents of Augusta and in conflict with the Indians, asserted their control over the territory, ultimately allying with radical Whigs in the lowcountry during the American Revolution. In this way the region west of Augusta demonstrated a cultural uniqueness at the same time that its history was shaped by migration and the diffusion of cultural traits. Therefore Mitchell can accept the geographer's concepts of cultural core and trait diffusion from core to peripheral areas, while also calling for a greater attention to place. The notion that regions are bounded by the extent to which cultural traits diffuse, then, is accepted widely throughout the social sciences.

Collectively, these geographers and historians have affirmed that the backcountry was regionally distinct and that it cannot be viewed simply as a western extension of British colonial America.[12] At the same time, however, the West became an integral part of the United States during the early national era. Elizabeth Arnett Fields, for instance, describes the Cherokee struggle for sovereignty that collapsed in the 1830s before the onslaught of land-hungry Georgia settlers and a federal government bent on Indian removal. The failure of the Cherokees can be seen, too, as the assertion of a national dominion and as a form of sectional unification at the expense of cultural diversity and the autonomy of native peoples.

Likewise, separatist movements, although entertained from time to time west of the thirteen original states, never gained any widespread currency. Sectional politics also were muted, as agricultural economies based on grains and livestock spread across the Midwest and as the cotton plantation expanded throughout the Lower South, the interior upcountry, and the Old Southwest. Monica L. Beck makes this point in her account of the reordering of the settler landscape of upcountry South Carolina following the arrival of cotton culture and plantation slavery. Planters asserted control over land and society in part by constructing carefully organized complexes of domestic and agrarian structures based on Georgian principles of social hierarchy. Thus, from the geographer's perspective, the United States became more a confederation of regions than a union of states, and the colonial southern backcountry played a key role in defining the emerging regional patterns. A backcountry created, on the one hand, by the spread and aggregation of cultural traits and, on the other, by the integration of political sections is a region whose study naturally would bring together the interests of geographers and historians.

The essays in this volume have led contemporary backcountry scholarship to a region that not only could be defined spatially but also was developing in time throughout the eighteenth and early nineteenth centuries. The frontier, then, represented a process happening in place. "By the time of the American Revolution, much of the South Carolina interior had been occupied by immigrants of European origin, and the region was well on its way toward becoming an integral part of the expanding European world economy," writes Kenneth E. Lewis. "Such a process occurs among complex societies as they attempt to recreate themselves in the face of the attenuated conditions encountered at the periphery of settlement" (ch. 6). Key concepts here are *integration* and *recreation*—that is, regional consolidation progresses as societies attempt to recreate themselves.

Taken together, the historical and archaeological perspectives presented by Elizabeth Fields and Monica Beck, for instance, provide powerful testimony for a process of social recreation that extends far beyond any frontier stage of development. That process reorders the backcountry through the imposition of both national authority and a landscape expressing the hierarchical domination of a planter class. Thus the frontier is not simply a growing place, but it is one undergoing an ordering process that results in both replication and reformulation in the colonizing society.

In this study of change and development, historians, geographers, archaeologists, ethnohistorians, and others have an excellent opportunity for collaboration. But the record of collaboration in the past, as some scholars remind us, has not been good. "History is a difficult pursuit," Henry Glassie points out. "For that reason the vanguard of social science has been in full retreat from history for most of our century. Left in the path of that movement is a critique of history.... The first charge is that of unexplained process. It is intellectually unsound to develop a narrative of change through time without first accounting for the system that is undergoing and enabling change.... How can you study change before you know what is changing?" But by the time Glassie issued this charge in his *Folk Housing in Middle Virginia* (1975), historians, according to David Hackett Fischer, already were deeply committed to studying change:

Then, in the decade of the 1960s, something new began to happen. Young scholars in Europe and America were inspired by the French school of the *Annales* to invent a new kind of history which differed from the old paradigm.... This new history was not really about the past at all, but about change—with past and present in a mutual perspective. It was not a story-telling but a problem-solving discipline. Its *problematiques* were about change and continuity in the acts and thoughts of ordinary people—people in the midst of others; people in society. The goal of this new social history was nothing less than an *histoire totale* of the human experience. To that end, the new historians drew upon many types of evidence: documents, statistics, physical artifacts, iconographic materials and much more.

What for Henry Glassie was a system of cultural traits became a total history in Fischer's thinking, but the message was clear: historians were beginning to take into account the analyses of social scientists, and both groups shared an interest in explaining change.[13]

David Hsiung has provided a good example of where disciplinary integration, in the study of change, can lead. In his examination of northeastern Tennessee, he describes how the elaboration of a road system forms part of a developmental process in which a transportation infrastructure emerges to carry goods and ideas within communities and between regions. Borrowing sociological concepts, he directs his developmental narrative toward an analysis of cultural isolation in Appalachia. His conclusion is that the elaboration of both internal and external communications networks diminished the remoteness of the frontier by encouraging face-to-face interactions within communities and by facilitating selective market contacts with more distant entrepôts. Similarly, Charles H. Faulkner points out that, within a few years of the founding of Knoxville, Tennessee, merchants had overcome regional "transportation barriers" and were importing a large variety of manufactured goods into the emerging town from distant Atlantic markets (ch. 8).

An expanding road system represents only one aspect of the ordering process in the backcountry. The notion, pertinent to both analytic and narrative studies, that change leads toward greater social stability and community cohesion opens many new avenues for cooperation among historians and social scientists. Essays in this volume suggest that this collaboration can be especially fruitful in three areas of frontier development: the establishment of power relationships along lines of gender, class, and race; the adjustment of ethnic identity within a pluralistic society; and the establishment of towns.

Taverns, like roads, in the thinking of Daniel B. Thorp, helped order the backcountry around "places in which people most often gathered and ... neighborhoods developed" (ch. 5). But Thorp views class and gender divisions evident in tavern life as potentially destabilizing. Taverns certainly created cultural arenas where social roles could be played out as dramatically and symbolically as in the more frequently studied courthouses and churches of the colonial South. Tavern life, in fact, may have been especially revealing of widespread patterns of authority, because power relationships were more apparent in the daily jostlings of ordinary people than in the dictates of officials. Tavern keepers, unlike justices or clergymen, did not possess the authority to suppress dissension and discontent, which then could flow freely in their establishments. Growing class distinctions in tavern life and restrictions on the use of taverns by women, however, failed to threaten what Thorp calls the "basic stability of backcountry society" (ch. 5). Thus privilege and exclusion were indicative of the progressive articulation, not the disarticulation, of social and political order.

Turk McCleskey illuminates another aspect of the power of social class: the influence that land surveyors and speculators wielded over the distribution of property. This elite sought to replicate the deferential, hierarchical order of Chesapeake society on Virginia's frontier in Augusta County by managing access to ungranted lands. The authority of these officials was less than absolute, however, because families, in order to settle together, could and did exercise the option of paying higher prices for isolated land far from centers of power. Settlers were motivated more by the nonmarket impetus of acquiring sufficient property to secure collective economic competence and family cohesion than by conformity to deferential social relations. In linking kin networks to settlement patterns, they imprinted their own order on the land; but at the same time, they produced the ordered society that powerful men desired.

Archaeologist Charles Faulkner concurs with McCleskey on the social construction of land distribution, observing that the "idealized view of the frontier is of egalitarian pioneers carving out their niches in the wilderness, but in reality their destiny was often controlled by an oligarchic ruling class of white males in the nascent towns" (ch. 8). In Knoxville, this class was composed of Anglo-American businessmen, professionals, and landowners who dominated local affairs with little apparent dissent. Archaeological investigations reveal that, while these elite men and women often lived in crude log and frame houses, their "wealth and social status seems to have been more easily expressed by the luxury goods present in significant quantities on domestic sites." Thus the development of merchant commerce, facilitated by road improvements, helped to order the backcountry through social stratification and conspicuous consumption. Monica Beck makes a similar point when she observes that the "clustering of numerous brick outbuildings around the Brattons' Georgian-style home was impressive, and implied the presence of a successful and powerful family in control of their landscape" (ch. 7).

In ordering the frontier, ethnicity cannot be considered separately from class and gender. The essays in this volume indicate that, despite the disproportionate share of power exercised on the frontier by officials with English backgrounds over settlers from the north of Ireland or the German Palatinate, these non-English peoples represented a subversive force. As Edward Cashin demonstrates, settlers in the Georgia backcountry rejected the authority of the colonial governor when he acted in the interest of Indian tribes and Indian traders. Backcountry peoples, in effect, created their own order by siding with the rebels during the American Revolution.

At other times, the official culture of Anglo America, although outwardly adopted by Scotch-Irish and Germanic peoples, was undermined by their private application of traditional norms. In his study of the Lewis Miller drawings, Donald W. Linebaugh, for instance, applies the sociological distinction between assimilation and acculturation to demonstrate that, for Virginia Germans, acculturation proceeded separately from assimilation. They adopted outward signs of economic success, such as the rationally ordered I-house, while maintaining distinctly Germanic patterns of life within the house. An interdisciplinary approach that correlates Miller's sketches with historical research, archaeological data, and extant structures leads Linebaugh to envision "constructing a chronology of cultural changes and exchanges" in the "cultural landscape, notably in farmstead building traditions and spatial organization" (ch. 11). Other authors in this volume also document outward conformity but inner autonomy among German peoples. According to Daniel Thorp, North Carolina Germans avoided taverns except in Moravian communities, where church-run establishments sold more beer than did any other Rowan County enterprise.

For a developing frontier, the study of town founding and growth requires the collaboration of many disciplines. On the one hand, this process composes a narrative of concentrating population, trade, and wealth; on the other, it reflects deep systemic changes in social structure and an evolving market economy. Laying out towns in the backcountry often followed rural settlement by several decades and marked the achievement of a threshold population in the countryside.[14] The lag behind rural settlement and the emergence of a functional hierarchy of urban places also reflected incremental increases in surplus agricultural production, as Kenneth Lewis argues in his case study of Camden. Lewis contends that urban development followed the transition to capitalism in the countryside. Thus, marketplaces in towns appeared only after commercial markets penetrated rural economies, where household production and local exchange based on use value traditionally prevailed. Whereas Charles Faulkner argues that urbanization in the backcountry proceeded hand in hand with an emerging import trade in elite goods for the upper classes, Lewis suggests that the growth of the export trade facilitated town founding and growth.

Towns had other functions that interdisciplinary approaches can flesh out. Chief among these was the replication of civic culture. Augusta, for instance,"gradually assumed the requisites of a proper British town," according to Edward Cashin (ch. 4). Kenneth Lewis points out that the features of a proper town, such as churches, schools, courthouses, jails, shops, and stores, in addition to a market and fairground, made Camden "the initial center of urban activities in the South Carolina backcountry" (ch. 6). Likewise, Charles Faulkner demonstrates that the fledgling town of Knoxville was promoted by its merchants as a "'civilized' place like the secure towns they had left behind east of the mountains" (ch. 8).

Perhaps most symbolic of the progressive order that towns brought to the frontier were their grid street plans. From an anthropological perspective, Lewis argues (ch. 6) that the grid "controlled expansion" and created a compact settlement permitting social and economic development. According to Faulkner, "the street grid and establishment of courthouses and other public buildings symbolized order and security, as well as the town's central position in the frontier economy" (ch. 8).

One lesson to be derived from the fascination with founding towns in the wilderness, so evident in many of the papers in this collection, is that a town must be studied not in isolation but as an integral part of a rural landscape, in which production and consumption made town life possible. Settlement pattern, landscape, and material culture long have been the special domains of geography, archaeology, and anthropology. But these terms are neither obscure nor alien to historians, and during the past twenty years historians have made perhaps the greatest strides in gaining a working knowledge of material culture studies, partly because they have had the farthest to travel. Whereas the social sciences are more inclined to view landscape as the consequence of economic function, historians can contribute a developmental perspective in which landscape evolution is preconditioned by political or social change. As Michael Puglisi has reminded us, cultural assumptions and economic expectations "can be just as influential as material conditions" (ch. 2).

Here, too, roads provide a case in point. Road networks certainly do develop as communications systems linking economic nodes in space. But these networks also emerge with the settlement of an area, as regulated by the county courts and those who have influence in the courts. In the eighteenth century, the laying out of roads was a political process proceeding from a road petition, to the court appointment of a road overseer to "view, mark, and lay off" a route, and finally to the empowerment of that overseer to order out the labor of nearby taxpayers to construct and maintain the road. Routes were determined not only by terminus points and the constraints of intervening terrain, but also by the influence of those living near the road and their interest in acquiring or denying public access to private resources. Road networks therefore encode a community consensus finely attuned to cultural assumptions and economic expectations, as well as material conditions. Roads might appear as only a minor element in the much larger landscape panorama of the southern colonial backcountry, but they provide an excellent beginning point for interdisciplinary dialogue.

What, then, is the answer to the question: Where have the articles in this volume led recent scholarship? What, in other words, have interdisciplinary perspectives contributed to the study of frontier communities? None of the articles in this volume, it should be pointed out, has been researched and written by an interdisciplinary team of scholars. Thus, what is interdisciplinary in them lies partly in their juxtaposition in the table of contents, and partly in all that can be drawn from each one, which, when recombined with selections from other articles, represents new perspectives. The result is more of a challenge than a conclusion.

The work of geographers and archaeologists challenges historians to think more carefully about precisely what is changing when they describe change. Historians, say social scientists, ought to ask how communities are structured and how the elements of structure contribute to community function. Historians might inquire how communities are organized in space and what space, or distance, might mean to pioneer peoples. Answers to these questions would give historians of frontier communities a stronger sense of place and a better understanding of how one place varies from another. Historians also might learn how places are woven together in regions and how people define a regional identity. Describing national identity comes more easily for historians—in Turner's facile handling, it readily was seen as a product of the frontier process. But Turner and historians ever since have struggled in identifying the traits that make up regions. Finally, taking Turner up on his own advice about interdisciplinary work might help historians write regional histories of, for instance, the southern backcountry or even of the nation as a composite of regions.

Working with historians might encourage social scientists to seek continuity, not only in space but in time. Geographers and archaeologists might learn to craft narratives that describe the establishment of frontier communities as an ordering process. Fulfilling an obligation to interpret the patterns their research reveals, social scientists thus might look to the past for contingencies in time that explain contiguities in space.

Combining the perspectives of place and process, inherent in the grouping of these essays, indeed can produce some new views. New perspectives could link the establishment of towns such as Augusta, Georgia, to a process of ordering Anglo-American relations with Indians. That process broke down under the force of settlement expansion and cultural intolerance, culminating over the course of a century in the removal of Native Americans from the entire Southeast. Likewise, distant places such as Camden and Knoxville can be seen as connected in a process of frontier expansion, initiated in the quest for export commodities and reaching farther and farther into the American interior as settlement communities created their own demand for import commodities. In a similar manner, settlement expansion can be seen as a blending of settler desires to establish kinship communities, replicate familiar landscapes, or take advantage, in myriad ways, of economic opportunities unleashed as new places emerged around accustomed institutions ranging from taverns to towns. Historians, ethnohistorians, geographers, anthropologists, and archaeologists have much to learn from one another.

For Frederick Jackson Turner, studying the frontier through an interdisciplinary dialogue was no idle or academic exercise. "Each age writes the history of the past anew with reference to the conditions uppermost in its own time," he wrote early in his career. "The aim of history, then, is to know the elements of the present by understanding what came into the present from the past."[15]

Turner began his most famous essay with a reference to the recent statement by the superintendent of the U.S. Census that, based on the 1890 statistics, "there can hardly be said to be a frontier line."[16] If, as Turner stated, the democratic institutions and national character of America had developed out of the frontier experience, what would be their fate in the urban, industrial nation America was fast becoming in the 1890s—the nation enshrined at the World's Columbian Exposition? As the primary concern of the progressive movement, this question brought Turner's view of history into the center of the most perplexing issues and the most significant debates of his own day. What remains to ask of the essays in this volume, then, is where they lead modern scholars in the future study of the frontier.

For Turner and his contemporaries, settling the frontier meant the triumph of civilization—one civilization, Western civilization. Defeated in the conquest of the American interior were its "savage" peoples. Most men and women in Turner's society would have thought this victory inevitable, due to the unquestioned superiority of civilization over savagery. Such logic certainly seemed to justify Indian removal in the 1830s and reservation policies underwritten by wars of extermination later in the nineteenth century. Although they admitted that civilization had evolved out of savagery, Turner's contemporaries nonetheless held the essentialist view that human differences could be ascribed to the varying positions of dissimilar peoples on the evolutionary ladder. Differences in position they equated with differences in race. Even so, evolution was progress. The long transition from savagery to civilization was marked continually by the replacement of what were regarded as inferior economic, social, political, and religious institutions by superior ones. From this point of view, the demise, if not the intentional destruction, of American Indian lifeways was considered a benefit to native and Anglo-American peoples alike. Thus the Dawes Severalty Act of 1887 sought to dismantle tribal culture in favor of the nuclear family and to replace hunting and gathering lifeways with small-farm agriculture and private property, in patterns consistent with contemporary American norms.

The century since Turner's work on the significance of the frontier has witnessed a paradigm shift in the way human differences are explained. This shift is as profound as any intellectual revolution in human history, including the rise of rationalism in the eighteenth century and Darwinian science in the nineteenth. That the world's peoples think and act differently is seen today as a product of culture. Culture is a set of learned behaviors, conditioned by nature and environment, which, when meshed together in a functional system, equip a people collectively to sustain life and elaborate upon living through art, politics, religion, and the means to achieve security, if not comfort. Cultural relativism requires that differing lifeways be regarded as equally viable vehicles for achieving these objectives. Equal viability, however, does not necessarily presuppose moral neutrality, and one of today's central controversies involves decisions on when to let other people alone and when to intervene in the name of values such as freedom, justice, and equality, or rights to life, liberty, and the pursuit of happiness.

Another of today's controversies concerns the multicultural construction of American identity. If different cultures possess equal rights to exist, then the nation cannot claim one cultural identity to the exclusion of others. But this argument flies in the face of a long tradition of Anglo-American domination. Not surprisingly, multiculturalism has become a flash point in the culture wars of the late twentieth century. Diversity raises the question of how far the nation can go in acknowledging the mutual integrity of all peoples contained within it. Is America strictly an English-speaking nation, or should Spanish be taught as a second language in public schools? Is black English, or Ebonics, a separate language? Do we recognize Native American or African origins of modern lifeways, or was American society born solely on Plymouth Rock or Jamestown Island? These are only some of the questions that divide Americans today along the fault lines of multiculturalism, but the point is that America's identity at the end of the American century is up for grabs.

The authors of essays in this volume, as well as other scholars, are concerned—like Turner and his contemporaries—for the prospects of American institutions and national identity in a future that looks quite different from the past. A quick review of the previous century reveals an important lesson: not only has the concept of culture replaced the evolutionary paradigm of savagery versus civilization, but also diverse American cultures have persisted, despite the overwhelming force leveled against them in the name of this paradigm. The Dawes Act, for instance, proved a failure; and, since New Deal legislation such as the Indian Reorganization Act of 1934, the federal government progressively has recognized the legality and viability of tribal culture. Similarly, African American culture heroically has survived racism in the twentieth century and overcome virulent attempts to exclude blacks from every source of influence or advantage in American economic, social, and political life. In Canada, Quebec separatists have demonstrated vividly the power of cultural persistence and have threatened to redefine Canadian nationality by establishing an independent government. Separatists among American Indians and black nationalists have made similar attempts in the United States. These efforts raise troubling questions about national identity in the future. Will cross-cultural ties among groups dispersed across the earth's surface during the diaspora of post-Columbian imperialism prove stronger than political boundaries? Will nations such as the United States follow Yugoslavia and the Union of Soviet Socialist Republics in fragmenting into enclaves of competing ethnic groups given to hostility and warfare? Or should conformity to an Anglo-American heritage be enforced by law and by the return to a triumphal narrative of national history?

It is precisely the diversity of the American past and its constituents that engages historians and social scientists today and demands explanations for ethnic and cultural pluralism. And it is toward a fuller account of American multiculturalism that the essays in this volume point modern scholarship. Multicultural study is inherently interdisciplinary. If scholars heed Turner's hundred-year-old call to begin an interdisciplinary dialogue and, like him, aspire to understand the present by knowing the past, then new work in the humanities and social sciences must accept that the eighteenth-century backcountry is "back" from only one point of view. Our perspective on a moving, developing region of cultural encounter must acknowledge the integrity of all peoples, encompass the exchange of cultural information among these peoples, and comprehend the creation of diverse sectional identities within a polyglot nation.

These efforts should produce some tangible results in the future. New work presented in this volume has important implications for the discussion of cultural boundaries by restoring narrative continuity and human agency to the process of regional definition and evolution. Donald Linebaugh's research, for instance, points toward a "process-oriented approach to change that focuses on individuals and networks as the units of study, rather than cultures and societies" (ch. 11). Regions need not be defined solely through the abstract process of trait diffusion. In the final analysis, traits do not diffuse, people move. What, then, causes people to move? In the backcountry, as elsewhere in early America, people for the most part moved to better their circumstances. Narrative approaches can add to discussions of regionality a causal mechanism for why—as opposed to how—the southern backcountry developed as a discrete and diverse region: why distinctive landscapes appeared, and why culturally adaptive traits could—as opposed to did—diffuse across the landscape.

Population movements, of course, can be explained on scales larger than personal ambition. A backcountry that was settled for political purposes and for imperial objectives related to escalating conflicts among European powers and Native Americans is a backcountry whose regional distinctiveness has its origins in forces beyond the collective motives of migrant peoples or the spatially restricted distributions of cultural traits. As a result of present efforts, future scholarship no doubt will move beyond the backcountry to conceive of a North American interior, seen from the multiple perspectives of English, French, Spanish, and Native American interests, as both contested spaces and zones of encounter.

Earlier generations of imperial historians were fascinated by the clash of empires in America, but a new imperial history of the frontier could trace the origin of American encounters, exchanges, and contests to the centers of power in Native American and European societies. Current scholarship can inform future work with the lesson that the outcome of the clash was not foreordained and had much to do with the cultures of diverse peoples and their power to persist. In this way we can come to understand better the ancient origins of modern multiculturalism and, like Turner, address the anxieties of the future through an appraisal of the past.

Notes

1. Frederick Jackson Turner, "The Significance of the Frontier in American History," in Frederick Jackson Turner, *The Frontier in American History* (New York: Holt, Rinehart and Winston, 1920), 1–38. The essay was originally published in the *Annual Report of the American Historical Association for the Year 1893* (Washington, D.C., 1894), 197–227.

2. Ray Allen Billington, *Frederick Jackson Turner: Historian, Scholar, Teacher* (New York: Oxford Univ. Press, 1973), 82–107.
3. Frederick Jackson Turner, "The Significance of History," *Wisconsin Journal of Education* 21 (Oct.–Nov. 1891): 230–34, 253–56. Quotations appear on pp. 230–34.
4. Frederick Jackson Turner, "Problems in American History," *The Aegis*, Nov. 4, 1892; reprinted in Frederick Jackson Turner, *The Early Writings of Frederick Jackson Turner*, comp. Everett E. Edwards (Madison: Univ. of Wisconsin Press, 1938), 71–83. Quotations appear on pp. 74–75, 78 in the reprint edition.
5. Critiques of the new social history appear in Richard R. Beeman, "The New Social History and the Search for 'Community' in Colonial America," *American Quarterly* 24 (fall 1977): 422–43; Darrett Rutman, "Assessing the Little Communities of Early America," *William and Mary Quarterly* 3d ser. 43 (Apr. 1986): 163–78; Michael Zuckerman, "The Fabrication of Identity in Early America," *William and Mary Quarterly* 3d ser. 34 (Apr. 1977): 183–214. Other authors have stressed the contributions of social history research in linking American societies to English sources. See David Grayson Allen, *In English Ways: The Movement of Societies and the Transferral of English Local Law and Custom to Massachusetts Bay in the Seventeenth Century* (Chapel Hill: Univ. of North Carolina Press, 1981; New York: Norton, 1982); James Horn, *Adapting to a New World: English Society in the Seventeenth-Century Chesapeake* (Chapel Hill: Univ. of North Carolina Press, for the Institute of Early American History and Culture, 1994); Kenneth A. Lockridge, *A New England Town: The First Hundred Years* (New York: Norton, 1970); Sumner Chilton Powell, *Puritan Village: The Formation of a New England Town* (Middletown, Conn.: Wesleyan Univ. Press, 1963).
6. Richard R. Beeman, *The Evolution of the Southern Backcountry: A Case Study of Lunenburg County, Virginia, 1746–1832* (Philadelphia: Univ. of Pennsylvania Press, 1984), 29; Warren R. Hofstra, "Land, Ethnicity, and Community at the Opequon Settlement, Virginia, 1730–1800," *Virginia Magazine of History and Biography* 98 (July 1990): 423–48; James T. Lemon, *"The Best Poor Man's Country": A Geographical Study of Early Southeastern Pennsylvania* (Baltimore, Md.: Johns Hopkins Univ. Press, 1972; New York: Norton, 1976), 1–117.
7. Conrad Arensberg, "American Communities," *American Anthropologist* 57 (Dec. 1955): 1143–62.
8. Gregory H. Nobles's 1989 review of recent literature on the eighteenth-century backcountry can be used as a starting point for modern frontier studies. See Nobles, "Breaking into the Backcountry: New Approaches to the Early American Frontier," *William and Mary Quarterly* 3d ser. 46 (Oct. 1989): 641–70.
9. Frederick Jackson Turner, "The Old West," in *The Frontier in American History*, Turner, 67–125. Quotation appears on pp. 68–69.
10. Carl Bridenbaugh, *Myths and Realities: Societies of the Colonial South* (Baton Rouge: Louisiana State Univ. Press, 1952).
11. Henry Glassie, *Pattern in the Material Folk Culture of the Eastern United States* (Philadelphia: Univ. of Pennsylvania Press, 1969); Terry G. Jordan and Matti Kaups, *The American Backwoods Frontier: An Ethnic and Ecological Interpretation* (Baltimore, Md.: Johns

Hopkins Univ. Press, 1989); Fred Kniffen, "Folk Housing: Key to Diffusion," *Annals of the Association of American Geographers* 55 (Dec. 1965): 549–77; Wilbur Zelinsky, *The Cultural Geography of the United States* (Englewood Cliffs, N.J.: Prentice-Hall, 1973).

12. The alternative view that society and economy in the southern backcountry became increasingly similar to patterns of Chesapeake life during the course of the eighteenth century has been argued effectively by historian Jack P. Greene. See Greene, "Independence, Improvement, and Authority: Toward a Framework for Understanding the Histories of the Southern Backcountry during the Era of the American Revolution," in *An Uncivil War: The Southern Backcountry during the American Revolution*, ed. Ronald Hoffman, Thad W. Tate, and Peter J. Albert, 3–36 (Charlottesville: Univ. Press of Virginia, for the U.S. Capitol Historical Society, 1985); Jack P. Greene, *Pursuits of Happiness: The Social Development of Early Modern British Colonies and the Formation of American Culture* (Chapel Hill: Univ. of North Carolina Press, 1988).

13. Henry Glassie, *Folk Housing in Middle Virginia: A Structural Analysis of Historic Artifacts* (Knoxville: Univ. of Tennessee Press, 1975), 8; David Hackett Fischer, *Albion's Seed: Four British Folkways in America* (New York: Oxford Univ. Press, 1989), viii–ix.

14. Delayed town founding was evident in the early Shenandoah Valley. See Warren R. Hofstra and Robert D. Mitchell, "Town and Country in Backcountry Virginia: Winchester and the Shenandoah Valley, 1730–1800," *Journal of Southern History* 59 (Nov. 1993): 619–46.

15. Frederick Jackson Turner, "Significance of History," 233.

16. Frederick Jackson Turner, "Significance of the Frontier," 1.

Selected Bibliography

ARTICLES

Arensberg, Conrad. "American Communities." *American Anthropologist* 57 (December 1955): 1143–62.

Barth, Fredrik. "On the Study of Social Change." *American Anthropologist* 69, no. 6 (1967): 661–69.

Bassin, Mark. "Turner, Solov'ev, and the 'Frontier Hypothesis': The Nationalist Significance of Open Spaces." *Journal of Modern History* 65 (1993): 473–511.

Beeman, Richard R. "The New Social History and the Search for 'Community' in Colonial America." *American Quarterly* 24 (Fall 1977): 422–43.

Bell, Michael M. "The Fruit of Difference: The Rural-Urban Continuum as a System of Identity." *Rural Sociology* 57 (1992): 65–82.

Brown, Ralph Hall. "Materials Bearing upon the Geography of the Atlantic Seaboard, 1790 to 1810." *Annals of the Association of American Geographers* 28 (1938): 201–31.

Calmes, Alan. "The British Revolutionary War Fortifications at Camden, South Carolina." *Conference of Historic Site Archaeology, Papers* 2 (1968): 51–55.

Carr, Lois Green, and Lorena S. Walsh. "The Planter's Wife: The Experience of White Women in Seventeenth-Century Maryland." *William and Mary Quarterly* 3d ser. 34 (1977): 542–71.

Chappell, Edward A. "Acculturation in the Shenandoah Valley: Rhenish Houses of the Massanutten Settlement." *Proceedings of the American Philosophical Society* 124 (1980): 55–89.

Clark, Andrew H. "Geographical Change—A Theme for Economic History." *Journal of Economic History* 20 (1960): 607–16.

———. "Suggestions for the Geographical Study of Agricultural Change in the United States, 1790–1840." *Agricultural History* 46 (1972): 165.

Conzen, Michael P. "The Historical Impulse in Geographical Writing about the United States,

1850–1990." In *A Scholar's Guide to Geographical Writing on the American and Canadian Past*, Research Paper No. 235, edited by Michael P. Conzen, Thomas A. Rumney, and Graeme Wynn, 3–90. Chicago: Dept. of Geography, Univ. of Chicago, 1993.

Crass, David Colin; Bruce Penner; Tammy Forehand; Lois Potter; and Larry Potter. "A Man of Great Liberality: Recent Research at George Galphin's Silver Bluff." *South Carolina Antiquities* 27, nos. 1–2 (1995): 26–41.

Deetz, James. "American Historical Archaeology: Methods and Results." *Science* 239 (1988): 362–67.

De Vorsey, Louis, Jr. "Indian Boundaries in Colonial Georgia." *Georgia Historical Quarterly* 54 (1970): 63–78.

Earle, Carville, and Ronald Hoffman. "Staple Crops and Urban Development in the Eighteenth Century South." *Perspectives in American History* 10 (1976): 7–78.

Ernst, Joseph A., and Harry Roy Merrens. "'Camden's Turrets Pierce the Skies!': The Urban Process in the Southern Colonies during the Eighteenth Century." *William and Mary Quarterly* 3d ser. 30 (1973): 549–74.

Faulkner, Charles H. "The Urban Farmstead in Knoxville, Tennessee: Pattern and Process in a Mid-South City." *Ohio Valley Historical Archaeology* 7-8 (1993): 17–23.

Forbes, Jack D. "Frontiers in American History and the Role of the Frontier Historian." *Ethnohistory* 15 (1968): 203–35.

Friis, Herman R. "A Series of Population Maps of the Colonies and the United States, 1625–1790." *Geographical Review* 30 (1940): 463–70.

Harris, R. C. "The Simplification of Europe Overseas." *Annals of the Association of American Geographers* 67 (1977): 469–83.

Harris, R. C., and L. Guelke. "Land and Society in Early Canada and South Africa." *Journal of Historical Geography* 3 (1977): 135–53.

Hart, John Fraser. "The Spread of the Frontier and the Growth of Population." *Geoscience and Man* 5 (1974): 73.

Henretta, James A. "Families and Farms: *Mentalité* in Pre-Industrial America." *William and Mary Quarterly* 3d ser. 35 (1978): 3–32.

Hillery, George A., Jr. "Definitions of Community: Areas of Agreement." *Rural Sociology* 20 (1955): 111–23.

Hofstra, Warren R. "Adaptation or Survival?: Folk Housing at Opequon Settlement." *Ulster Folklife* 37 (1991): 36–61.

———. "Land, Ethnicity, and Community at the Opequon Settlement, Virginia, 1730–1800." *Virginia Magazine of History and Biography* 98 (1990): 423–48.

Hofstra, Warren R., and Robert D. Mitchell. "Town and Country in Backcountry Virginia: Winchester and the Shenandoah Valley, 1730–1800." *Journal of Southern History* 59 (1993): 619–46.

Hudson, John C. "Migration to an American Frontier." *Annals of the Association of American Geographers* 66 (1976): 242–65.

Jordan, Terry G. "Preadaptation and European Colonization in Rural North America." *Annals of the Association of American Geographers* 79 (1989): 489–500.

Kniffen, Fred. "Folk Housing: Key to Diffusion." *Annals of the Association of American Geographers* 55 (1965): 549–75.

Kniffen, Fred, and Henry Glassie. "Building in Wood in the Eastern United States: A Time-Place Perspective." *Geographical Review* 56 (1966): 40–66.

Landsman, Ned C. "*Albion's Seed: Four British Folkways in America*—A Symposium." *William and Mary Quarterly* 3d ser. 48, no. 2 (1991): 253–60.

Lemon, James T. "Early Americans and Their Social Environment." *Journal of Historical Geography* 6 (1980): 115–31.

———. "Household Consumption in Eighteenth-Century America and Its Relationship to Production and Trade: The Situation among Farmers in Southeastern Pennsylvania." *Agricultural History* 41 (1967): 59–70.

Lockwood, Patricia. "Judge John Martin: First Chief Justice of the Cherokees." *Chronicles of Oklahoma* 64 (Summer 1986): 60–73.

McCleskey, Turk. "Rich Land, Poor Prospects: Real Estate and the Formation of a Social Elite in Augusta County, Virginia, 1738–1770." *Virginia Magazine of History and Biography* 98 (1990): 449–96.

McDonald, Forrest, and Ellen Shapiro McDonald. "Ethnic Origins of the American People, 1790." *William and Mary Quarterly* 3d ser. 37 (1980): 179–99.

McLoughlin, William G. "Experiment in Cherokee Citizenship, 1789–1839." *American Quarterly* 33 (1981): 3–25.

Meinig, Donald W. "The American Colonial Era: A Geographical Commentary." *Proceedings of the Royal Geographical Society of Australasia, South Australian Branch* 59 (1957–58): 1–22.

———. "The Continuous Shaping of America: A Prospectus for Geographers and Historians." *American Historical Review* 83 (1978): 1186–1217.

Merrens, Harry Roy. "Historical Geography and Early American History." *William and Mary Quarterly* 3d ser. 22 (1965): 529–48.

———. "Source Materials for the Geography of Colonial America." *Professional Geographer* 15 (1963): 8–11.

Mikesell, Marvin W. "Comparative Studies in Frontier History." *Annals of the Association of American Geographers* 50 (1960): 62–74.

Mitchell, Robert D. "American Origins and Regional Institutions: The Seventeenth-Century Chesapeake." *Annals of the Association of American Geographers* 73 (1983): 404–20.

———. "The Commercial Nature of Frontier Settlement in the Shenandoah Valley of Virginia." *Proceedings of the Association of American Geographers* 1 (1969): 109–13.

———. "From the Ground Up: Place, and Diversity in Frontier Studies." In *Diversity and Accommodation: Essays on the Cultural Composition of the Virginia Frontier*, ed. Michael J. Puglisi, 23–52. Knoxville: Univ. of Tennessee Press, 1997.

———. "The Shenandoah Valley Frontier." *Annals of the Association of American Geographers* 62 (1972): 475–76.

Mitchell, Robert D., and Warren R. Hofstra. "How Do Settlement Systems Evolve? The

Virginia Backcountry during the Eighteenth Century." *Journal of Historical Geography* 21 (1995): 123–47.

Mitchell, Robert D., and Milton B. Newton. *The Appalachian Frontier: Views from the East and the Southwest.* Historical Geography Research Series, no. 21 (London: Institute of British Geographers, 1988), 1–64.

Newton, Milton B. "Cultural Preadaptation and the Upland South." *Geoscience and Man* 5 (1974): 143–54.

Nobles, Gregory H. "Breaking into the Backcountry: New Approaches to the Early American Frontier, 1750–1800." *William and Mary Quarterly* 3d ser. 46 (1989): 641–70.

Perkins, Elizabeth A. "The Consumer Frontier: Household Consumption in Early Kentucky." *Journal of American History* 78 (1991): 509–10.

Pillsbury, Richard. "The Europeanization of the Cherokee Settlement Landscape Prior to Removal: A Georgia Case Study." *Geoscience and Man* 23 (1980): 59–69.

Porter, Daniel. "Folk Art as Manuscripts: The Works of Lewis Miller." *Manuscripts* 13 (1961): 13–19.

Pudup, Mary Beth. "The Boundaries of Social Class in Preindustrial Appalachia." *Journal of Historical Geography* 15 (1989): 139–62.

Purvis, Thomas L. "The European Ancestry of the United States Population, 1790." *William and Mary Quarterly* 3d ser. 41 (1984): 85–101.

Rinker, Harry L., and Richard M. Kain. "Lewis Miller's *Virginia Sketchbook*: A Record of Rural Life." *Antiques* 119, no. 2 (1981): 396–401.

Rutman, Darrett. "Assessing the Little Communities of Early America." *William and Mary Quarterly* 3d ser. 43 (April 1986): 163–78.

Schulz, Judith J. "The Hinterland of Revolutionary Camden, South Carolina." *Southeastern Geographer* 16 (1976): 91–97.

Shammas, Carole. "How Self-Sufficient Was Early America?" *Journal of Interdisciplinary History* 13 (1982): 252–53.

South, Stanley. "The Ceramic Forms of the Potter Gottfried Aust at Bethabara, North Carolina, 1755–1771." *Conference on Historic Site Archaeology, Papers* 1 (1967): 33–52.

Steiner, Michael C. "The Significance of Turner's Sectional Thesis." *Western Historical Quarterly* 10 (1979): 437–66.

Thorp, Daniel B. "Doing Business in the Backcountry: Retail Trade in Colonial Rowan County." *William and Mary Quarterly* 3d ser. 48 (1991): 387–408.

Tillson, Albert H. "The Southern Backcountry: A Survey of Current Research." *Virginia Magazine of History and Biography* 38 (1990): 387–422.

Turner, Frederick Jackson. "Geographical Interpretations of American History." *Journal of Geography* 4 (1905): 34–37.

———. "Problems in American History." *The Aegis*, November 4, 1892. Reprinted in Frederick Jackson Turner, *The Early Writings of Frederick Jackson Turner*, compiled by Everett E. Edwards, 71–83. Madison: University of Wisconsin Press, 1938.

———. "Report on the Conference on the Relation of Geography and History." *American*

Historical Association Annual Report 1 (1907; Washington, D.C.: American Historical Association, 1908): 45–48.
———. "The Significance of History." *Wisconsin Journal of Education* 21 (October–November 1891): 230–34, 253–56.
Ulrich, Laurel Thatcher. "Of Pens and Needles: Sources in Early American Women's History." *Journal of American History* 77 (1990): 200–207.
Weaver, William Woys. "The Pennsylvania German House: European Antecedents and New World Forms." *Winterthur Portfolio* 21, no. 4 (1986): 243–64.
Whittenburg, James P. "Planters, Merchants, and Lawyers: Social Change and the Origins of the North Carolina Regulation." *William and Mary Quarterly* 3d ser. 24 (1977): 215–38.
Williams, H. David. "Gambling Away the Inheritance: The Cherokee Nation and Georgia's Gold and Land Lotteries of 1832–1833." *Georgia Historical Quarterly* 73 (Fall 1989): 519–39.
———. "Georgia's Land Lottery of 1832." *Chronicles of Oklahoma* 52 (1972): 52–60.
Wilson, John S. "We've Got Thousands of These! What Makes a Historic Farmstead Significant?" *Historical Archaeology* 24, no. 2 (1990): 23–33.
Zierden, Martha, and Linda F. Stine. "Historical Landscapes through the Prism of Archaeology." In *Carolina's Historical Landscapes*, edited by Linda F. Stine, Martha Zierden, Lesley Drucker, and Chris Judge, xi–xvi. Knoxville: University of Tennessee Press, 1997.
Zuckerman, Michael. "The Fabrication of Identity in Early America." *William and Mary Quarterly* 3d ser. 34 (April 1977): 183–214.

Books, Dissertations, and Theses

Anderson, William L., ed. *Cherokee Removal: Before and After*. Athens: University of Georgia Press, 1991.
Allen, David Grayson. *In English Ways: The Movement of Societies and the Transferral of English Local Law and Custom to Massachusetts Bay in the Seventeenth Century*. Chapel Hill: University of North Carolina Press, 1981; New York: Norton, 1982.
Bailyn, Bernard. *The Peopling of British North America: An Introduction*. New York: Alfred A. Knopf, 1986.
Bailyn, Bernard, and Philip D. Morgan, eds. *Strangers Within the Realm: Cultural Margins of the First British Empire*. Chapel Hill: University of North Carolina Press, 1991.
Bass, Althea. *Cherokee Messenger*. Norman: University of Oklahoma Press, 1936.
Beeman, Richard R. *The Evolution of the Southern Backcountry: A Case Study of Lunenburg County, Virginia, 1746–1832*. Philadelphia: University of Pennsylvania Press, 1984.
Bell, Colin, and Howard Newby. *Community Studies: An Introduction to the Sociology of the Local Community*. New York: Praeger, 1971.
———, eds. *The Sociology of Community: A Selection of Readings*. London: Frank Cass and Co., 1974.

Bender, Thomas. *Community and Social Change in America*. Baltimore, Md.: Johns Hopkins University Press, 1978.
Berry, Brian J. L. *Geography of Market Centers and Retail Distribution*. Englewood Cliffs, New Jersey: Prentice-Hall, 1967.
Billington, Ray Allen. *Frederick Jackson Turner: Historian, Scholar, Teacher*. New York: Oxford University Press, 1973.
Binford, L. R. *For Theory Building in Archaeology*. New York: Academic Press, 1977.
Bivens, John F., Jr. *The Moravian Potters of North Carolina*. Chapel Hill: University of North Carolina Press, 1972.
Boudinot, Elias. *Cherokee Editor: The Writings of Elias Boudinot*. Edited by Theda Perdue. Knoxville: University of Tennessee Press, 1983.
Boyd, William K., ed. *Some Eighteenth-Century Tracts Concerning North Carolina*. Raleigh: North Carolina Historical Commission, 1927.
Brennan, Thomas. *Public Drinking and Popular Culture in Eighteenth-Century Paris*. Princeton, New Jersey: Princeton University Press, 1988.
Bridenbaugh, Carl. *Myths and Realities: Societies of the Colonial South*. Baton Rouge: Louisiana State University Press, 1952; New York: Athenaeum, 1963.
Brown, Richard Maxwell. *The South Carolina Regulators*. Cambridge, Massachusetts: Belknap Press of Harvard University Press, 1963.
Bushman, Richard. *Refinement in America: Persons, Houses, Cities*. New York: Alfred A Knopf, 1992.
Butzer, Karl. *Archaeology and Human Ecology: Method and Theory for a Contextual Approach*. Cambridge, England: Cambridge University Press, 1982.
———. *Environment and Archaeology: An Introduction to Pleistocene Geography*. London: Methuen, 1965.
Carr, Lois Green; Russell R. Menard; and Lorena S. Walsh. *Robert Cole's World: Agriculture and Society in Early Maryland*. Chapel Hill: University of North Carolina Press, 1991.
Cappon, Lester J., ed. *Atlas of Early American History: The Revolutionary Era, 1760–1790*. Princeton, New Jersey: Princeton University Press, 1976.
Carter, Samuel, III. *Cherokee Sunset: A Nation Betrayed*. Garden City, New York: Doubleday, 1976.
Cashin, Edward J., ed. *Colonial Augusta: "Key to the Indian Country."* Macon, Georgia: Mercer University Press, 1986.
Chalkley, Lyman. *Chronicles of the Scotch-Irish Settlement in Virginia*. Baltimore, Maryland: 1912. Reprint, Genealogical Publishing Company, 1980.
Cherokee Advocate Office. *Laws of the Cherokee Nation: Adopted by the Council at Various Periods*. Tahlequah, Cherokee Nation: Cherokee Advocate Office, 1852.
Clark, Peter. *The English Alehouse: A Social History, 1200–1830*. London: Longman, 1983.
Clarke, D. L., ed. *Models in Archaeology*. London: Methuen, 1972.
———. *Spatial Archaeology*. London: Academic Press, 1977.
Corn, James F. *Red Clay and Rattlesnake Springs*. Cleveland, Tennessee: Walworth, 1959.
Crass, David Colin; Bruce R. Penner; Tammy R. Forehand; John Huffman; Lois J. Pot-

ter; and Larry Potter. *Excavations at New Windsor Township, South Carolina.* Savannah River Archaeological Research Heritage Series 3. Columbia: South Carolina Institute of Archaeology and Anthropology, University of South Carolina, 1997.

Deaderick, Lucille, ed. *Heart of the Valley: A History of Knoxville, Tennessee.* Knoxville: East Tennessee Historical Society, 1976.

Deetz, James. *In Small Things Forgotten: The Archaeology of Early American Life.* New York: Anchor Press/Doubleday, 1977.

De Vorsey, Louis, Jr. *The Indian Boundary in the Southern Colonies, 1763–1775.* Chapel Hill: University of North Carolina Press, 1966.

Doerflinger, Thomas M. *A Vigorous Spirit of Enterprise: Merchants and Economic Development in Revolutionary Philadelphia.* Chapel Hill: University of North Carolina Press, 1986.

Eiseley, Loren. *The Night Country.* New York: Charles Scribner's Sons, 1971.

Ekirch, A. Roger. *"Poor Carolina": Politics and Society in Colonial North Carolina.* Chapel Hill: University of North Carolina Press, 1981.

Farmer, Charles J. *In the Absence of Towns: Settlement and Country Trade in Southside Virginia, 1730–1800.* Lanham, Maryland: Rowman and Littlefield, 1993.

Ferguson, Leland. *Uncommon Ground: Archaeology and Early African America, 1650–1800.* Washington, D.C.: Smithsonian Institution Press, 1992.

Fischer, David Hackett. *Albion's Seed: Four British Folkways in America.* New York: Oxford University Press, 1989.

Foreman, Grant. *Indian Removal: The Emigration of the Five Civilized Tribes of Indians.* Norman: University of Oklahoma Press, 1953.

Gibson, James R., ed. *European Settlement and Development in North America: Essays on Geographical Change in Honour and Memory of Andrew Hill Clark.* Toronto, Canada: University of Toronto Press, 1978.

Glaab, Charles N., and A. Theodore Brown. *A History of Urban America.* New York: Macmillan, 1967.

Glassie, Henry. *Folk Housing in Middle Virginia: A Structural Analysis of Historic Artifacts.* Knoxville: University of Tennessee Press, 1975.

———. *Pattern in the Material Folk Culture of the Eastern United States.* Philadelphia: University of Pennsylvania Press, 1968.

Gray, Lewis Cecil. *The History of Agriculture in the Southern United States to 1860.* 2 volumes. Washington, D.C.: Carnegie Institute, 1933; reprinted, Gloucester, Massachusetts: Peter Smith, 1958.

Green, Stanton W., and Stephen M. Perlman, eds. *The Archaeology of Frontiers and Boundaries.* Orlando, Florida: Academic Press, 1985.

Greene, Jack P. *Imperatives, Behaviors, and Identities; Essays in Early American Cultural History.* Charlottesville: University Press of Virginia, 1992.

———. *Pursuits of Happiness: The Social Development of Early Modern British Colonies and the Formation of American Culture.* Chapel Hill: University of North Carolina Press, 1988.

Greene, Jack P., and J. R. Pole, eds. *Colonial British America: Essays in the New History of the Early Modern Era.* Baltimore, Maryland: Johns Hopkins University Press, 1984.

Gross, Robert. *The Minutemen and Their World.* New York: Hill and Wang, 1976.

Halliburton, R., Jr. *Red Over Black: Black Slavery among the Cherokee Indians.* Westport, Connecticut: Greenwood Press, 1977.

Hatley, Tom. *The Dividing Paths: Cherokees and South Carolinians through the Era of Revolution.* New York: Oxford University Press, 1993.

Hays, J. E. *Cherokee Indian Letters, Talks and Treaties, 1786–1838.* Atlanta: Georgia Department of Archives and History, 1939.

Higgs, Robert J., and Ambrose N. Manning, eds. *Voices from the Hills: Selected Readings on Southern Appalachia.* New York: Ungar, 1975.

Hoffman, Ronald; Thad W. Tate; and Peter J. Albert, eds. *An Uncivil War: The Southern Backcountry during the American Revolution.* Charlottesville: University Press of Virginia, 1985.

Hooker, Richard J., ed. *The Carolina Backcountry on the Eve of the Revolution: The Journal and Other Writings of Charles Woodmason, Anglican Itinerant.* With an introduction by Richard J. Hooker. Chapel Hill: University of North Carolina Press, 1953.

Horn, James. *Adapting to a New World: English Society in the Seventeenth-Century Chesapeake.* Chapel Hill: University of North Carolina Press, for the Institute of Early American History and Culture, 1994.

Hsiung, David C. *Two Worlds in the Tennessee Mountains: Exploring the Origins of Appalachian Stereotypes.* Lexington: University Press of Kentucky, 1997.

Hume, Ivor Noël. *A Guide to Artifacts of Colonial America.* New York: Alfred A. Knopf, 1969.

Jordan, Terry G., and Matti Kaups. *The American Backwoods Frontier: An Ethnic and Ecological Interpretation.* Baltimore, Maryland: Johns Hopkins Univ. Press, 1989.

Jackson, James Brinckerhoff, *Discovering the Vernacular Landscape.* New Haven, Connecticut: Yale University Press, 1984.

Kappler, Charles J., comp. and ed. *Indian Treaties, 1778–1883.* New York: Interland Publishing, 1972.

Kessel, Elizabeth A. "Germans on the Maryland Frontier: A Social History of Frederick County, Maryland, 1730–1800." Ph.D. diss., Rice University, 1981.

King Duane, ed. *The Cherokee Indian Nation: A Troubled History.* Knoxville: University of Tennessee Press, 1979.

Klein, Rachel N. *Unification of a Slave State: The Rise of the Planter Class in the South Carolina Backcountry, 1760–1808.* Chapel Hill: University of North Carolina Press, 1990.

Kutsche, Paul. *A Guide to Cherokee Documents in the Northeastern United States.* Metuchen, New Jersey: Scarecrow Press, 1986.

Ledgerwood, Mikle David. "Ethnic Groups on the Frontier in Rowan County, North Carolina, 1750–1778." Master's thesis, Vanderbilt University, 1977.

Lemon, James T. *The Best Poor Man's Country: A Geographical Study of Early Southeastern Pennsylvania.* Baltimore, Maryland: Johns Hopkins University Press, 1972.

Lewis, Kenneth E. *The American Frontier: An Archaeological Study of Settlement Pattern and Process.* Orlando, Florida: Academic Press, 1984.

———. *Camden: A Frontier Town in Eighteenth-Century South Carolina*. Anthropological Studies No. 2. Columbia: South Carolina Institute of Archaeology and Anthropology, University of South Carolina, 1976.
Linebaugh, Donald W., and Gary G. Robinson, eds. *Spatial Patterning in Historical Archaeology: Selected Studies of Settlement*. Williamsburg, Virginia: King and Queen Press, 1994.
Lumpkin, Wilson. *The Removal of the Cherokee Indians from Georgia*. New York: Dodd, Mead and Company, 1907.
Malone, Henry Thompson. *Cherokees of the Old South: A People in Transition*. Athens: University of Georgia Press, 1956.
Manners, Robert A., ed. *Process and Pattern in Culture: Essays in Honor of Julian H. Steward*. Chicago: Aldine, 1964.
McDonald, Michael J., and William B. Wheeler. *Knoxville, Tennessee: Continuity and Change in an Appalachian City*. Knoxville: University of Tennessee Press, 1983.
McLoughlin, William G. *Cherokee Renascence in the New Republic*. Princeton, New Jersey: Princeton University Press, 1986.
———. *Cherokees and Missionaries, 1789–1839*. New Haven, Connecticut: Yale University Press, 1984.
Meinig, D. W. *The Shaping of America: A Geographical Perspective on Five Hundred Years of History*. Volume 1: *Atlantic America, 1492–1800*. New Haven, Connecticut: Yale University Press, 1986.
———. *The Shaping of America: A Geographical Perspective on Five Hundred Years of History*. Volume 2: *Continental America, 1800–1867*. New Haven, Connecticut: Yale University Press, 1993.
Meriwether, Robert L. *The Expansion of South Carolina, 1729–1765*. Kingsport, Tennessee: Southern Publishers, 1940.
Merrell, James. *The Indians' New World: Catawbas and Their Neighbors, from European Contact through the Era of Removal*. Chapel Hill: University of North Carolina Press, 1989.
Merrens, Harry Roy. *Colonial North Carolina in the Eighteen Century: A Study in Historical Geography*. Chapel Hill: University of North Carolina Press, 1964.
———. *The Colonial South Carolina Scene: Contemporary Views, 1697–1774*. Columbia: University of South Carolina Press, 1977.
Miller, David Harry, and Jerome O. Steffen, eds. *The Frontier: Comparative Studies*. Norman: University of Oklahoma Press, 1977.
Miller, Lewis. *Sketchbook of Landscapes in the State of Virginia*. 1853. In collection of Abby Aldrich Rockefeller Folk Art Center, Williamsburg, Va.
———. *Virginia Sketchbook*. 1856–57. In collection of Virginia Historical Society, Richmond.
Mitchell, Robert D. *Commercialism and Frontier: Perspectives on the Early Shenandoah*. Charlottesville: University Press of Virginia, 1977.
———, ed. *Appalachian Frontiers: Settlement, Society and Development in the Preindustrial Era*. Lexington: University Press of Kentucky, 1991.

Mitchell, Robert D., and Paul A. Groves, eds. *North America: The Historical Geography of a Changing Continent.* Lanham, Maryland: Rowman and Littlefield, 1987.
Morgan, John. *The Log House in East Tennessee.* Knoxville: University of Tennessee Press, 1990.
Moulton, Gary E. *John Ross, Cherokee Chief.* Athens: University of Georgia Press, 1978.
North, Douglass C. *The Economic Growth of the United States, 1790–1860.* New York: Norton, 1966.
Perdue, Theda. *Slavery and the Evolution of Cherokee Society, 1540–1866.* Knoxville: University of Tennessee Press, 1979.
Powell, Sumner Chilton. *Puritan Village: The Formation of a New England Town.* Middletown, Connecticut: Wesleyan University Press, 1963.
Puglisi, Michael J., ed. *Diversity and Accommodation: Essays on the Cultural Composition of the Virginia Frontier.* Knoxville: University of Tennessee Press, 1997.
Quimby, Ian M. G., ed. *Ceramics in America.* Report of Winterthur Conference, 1972. Charlottesville: University Press of Virginia, 1973.
Ramsey, J. G. M. *The Annals of Tennessee.* Knoxville: East Tennessee Historical Society, 1967.
Ramsey, Robert W. *Carolina Cradle: Settlement of the Northwest Carolina Frontier, 1747–1762.* Chapel Hill: University of North Carolina Press, 1964.
Rice, A. H., and John Baer Stoudt. *The Shenandoah Pottery.* Strasburg, Virginia: Shenandoah Publishing House, 1929.
Rorabaugh, W. J. *The Alcoholic Republic: An American Tradition.* Oxford, England: Oxford University Press, 1979.
Ross, John. *The Papers of Chief John Ross.* Volume 1. Edited by Gary E. Moulton. Norman: University of Oklahoma, 1985.
Rountree, Helen C., ed. *Powhatan Foreign Relations.* Charlottesville: University Press of Virginia, 1993.
Rozema, Vicki. *Footsteps of the Cherokee.* Winston-Salem, North Carolina: John F. Blair, 1995.
Rutman, Darrett B., and Anita H. Rutman. *A Place in Time: Middlesex County, Virginia, 1650–1750.* New York: Norton, 1984.
Savage, William W., Jr., and Stephen I. Thompson, eds. *The Frontier: Comparative Studies.* Volume 2. Norman: University of Oklahoma Press, 1979.
Sauer, Carl O. *Land and Life: A Selection from the Writings of Carl Ortwin Sauer.* Edited by John Leighly. Berkeley: University of California Press, 1963.
Schulz, Judith J. "The Rise and Decline of Camden as South Carolina's Major Trading Center, 1751–1829: A Historical Geographic Study." Master's thesis, University of South Carolina, 1972.
Schuricht, Herrmann. *History of the German Element in Virginia.* Volume 1. Baltimore, Maryland: Theo. Kroh and Sons, 1898.
Schuyler, Robert L., ed. *Historical Archaeology: A Guide to Substantive and Theoretical Contributions.* Farmingdale, New York: Baywood Publishing Company, 1978.
Sellers, Leila. *Charleston Business on the Eve of the American Revolution.* Chapel Hill: University of North Carolina Press, 1934.
Shadburn, Don L. *Cherokee Planters in Georgia, 1832–1838.* Roswell, Georgia: W. H. Wolfe Associates, 1990.

Shapiro, Henry D. *Appalachia on Our Mind: The Southern Mountains and Mountaineers in the American Consciousness, 1870–1920*. Chapel Hill: University of North Carolina Press, 1978.
Silver, Timothy H. *A New Face on the Countryside: Indians, Colonists and Slaves in the South Atlantic Forests, 1500–1800*. New York: Cambridge University Press, 1990.
Simmler, L., ed. *Lois Green Carr: The Chesapeake and Beyond—A Celebration*. Crownsville: Maryland Historical and Cultural Publications, 1992.
South, Stanley. *Method and Theory in Historical Archaeology*. New York: Academic Press, 1977.
———. *Spanish Artifacts from Santa Elena*. Anthropological Studies No. 7. Columbia: South Carolina Institute of Archaeology and Anthropology, University of South Carolina, 1988.
———, ed. *Pioneers in Historical Archaeology: Breaking New Ground*. New York: Plenum Press, 1994.
Starr, Emmet. *History of the Cherokee Indians*. Oklahoma City: Warden Company, 1921; reprinted Millwood, New York: Kraus Reprint Company, 1977.
Steffen, Jerome O. *Comparative Frontiers: A Proposal for Studying the American West*. Norman: University of Oklahoma Press, 1980.
Stilgoe, John R. *Common Landscape of America, 1580–1845*. New Haven, Connecticut: Yale University Press, 1982.
Teute, Frederika J. "Land, Liberty and Labor in the Post-Revolutionary Era: Kentucky as the Promised Land." Ph.D. diss., Johns Hopkins University, 1988.
Thompson, Peter J. "A Social History of Philadelphia's Taverns, 1683–1800." Ph.D. diss., University of Pennsylvania, 1989.
Thorp, Daniel B. *The Moravian Community in Colonial North Carolina: Pluralism on the Southern Frontier*. Knoxville: University of Tennessee Press, 1989.
Tillson, Albert H. *Gentry and Common Folk: Political Culture on a Virginia Frontier, 1740–1789*. Lexington: University Press of Kentucky, 1991.
Tonnies, Ferdinand. *Community and Society [Gemeinschaft und Gesellschaft]*. Translated and edited by Charles P. Loomis. New York: Harper and Row, 1957.
Turner, Frederick Jackson. *The Frontier in American History*. New York: Holt, Rinehart, and Winston, 1920.
———. *The Significance of Sections in American History*. New York: Henry Holt and Company, 1932.
Turner, Robert P., ed. *Lewis Miller: Sketches and Chronicles*. York, Pennsylvania: Historical Society of York County, 1966.
Upton, Dell, and John Vlach, eds. *Common Places: Readings in American Vernacular Architecture*. Athens: University of Georgia Press, 1986.
Wagstaff, J. M., ed. *Landscape and Culture: Geographical and Archaeological Perspectives*. Oxford, England: Basil Blackwell, 1987.
Wardell, Morris L. *A Political History of the Cherokee Nation, 1838–1907*. Norman: University of Oklahoma Press, 1938.
Wilkins, Thurman. *Cherokee Tragedy: The Ridge Family and the Decimation of a People*. Norman: University of Oklahoma Press, 1986.

Williams, Cratis D. "The Southern Mountaineer in Fact and Fiction." Ph.D. diss., New York University, 1961.

Williams, Michael A. *Homeplace: The Social Use and Meaning of the Folk Dwelling in Southwestern North Carolina.* Athens: University of Georgia Press, 1991.

Williams, Samuel Cole, ed. *Early Travels in the Tennessee Country, 1540–1800.* Johnson City, Tennessee: Watauga Press, 1928.

Wust, Klaus. *The Virginia Germans.* Charlottesville: University Press of Virginia, 1969.

Zelinsky, Wilbur. *The Cultural Geography of the United States.* Englewood Cliffs, New Jersey: Prentice-Hall, 1973; rev. ed., 1992.

 *Contributors*

MONICA L. BECK received her M.A. in anthropology from the University of South Carolina, where she later worked at the South Carolina Institute of Archaeology and Anthropology, University of South Carolina. She currently is historic site archaeologist for Old Dorchester State Park in Summerville, South Carolina. Her research interests continue to focus on multiethnic aspects of the colonial frontier.

RICHARD D. BROOKS received his B.A. degree in English from Kentucky Wesleyan College in 1972. He is administrative manager of the Savannah River Archaeological Research Program, South Carolina Institute of Archaeology and Anthropology, University of South Carolina, where he has worked as a historian since 1977. His current research is based on excavations of a Welshman's cattle ranch located in the Central Savannah River Valley and dating to around 1745–82.

EDWARD CASHIN has written extensively about the southern colonial frontier. He currently is director of the Center for the Study of Georgia History at Augusta State University.

DAVID COLIN CRASS holds an M.A. degree in anthropology, with a concentration in historical archaeology, from the College of William and Mary in Virginia. His Ph.D. in anthropology is from Southern Methodist University. He is the archaeological services unit manager, Historic Preservation Division, Georgia Department of Natural Resources. He has published in the fields of historical archaeology, social history, collections management, and material culture.

CHARLES H. FAULKNER is professor of anthropology at the University of Tennessee, Knoxville. He received the Ph.D. in anthropology from Indiana University, has been named a Chancellor's Research Scholar and a Phi Kappa Phi Faculty Lecturer, and has authored and edited 20 books and monographs and 78 articles on prehistoric and historical archaeology. His current research involves the historical archaeology of early Knoxville, early historic architecture of East Tennessee, cave archaeology, and prehistoric rock art.

ELIZABETH ARNETT FIELDS received her M.A. in applied history from the University of South Carolina. She currently is director of the Main Street Program in Lancaster, Texas.

WARREN R. HOFSTRA is professor of history at Shenandoah University in Winchester, Virginia. He holds an M.A. degree from Boston University and a Ph.D. from University of Virginia. In addition to teaching in the fields of American social and cultural history, he directs the Community History Project of Shenandoah University. His research and writing focus on regional studies, with an emphasis on the Shenandoah Valley. He has published in the fields of social and economic history, material culture, geography, and archaeology.

DAVID C. HSIUNG, the Newton and Hazel Long Associate Professor of History at Juniata College, earned his B.A. degree from Yale and his Ph.D. from the University of Michigan. His book, *Two Worlds in the Tennessee Mountains: Exploring the Origins of Appalachian Stereotypes* (1997), won the 1996 Appalachian Studies Award from the University Press of Kentucky and the Appalachian Studies Association. His current project explores historical methodology as revealed in studies of relations between Indians and colonists on the Pennsylvania frontier during the eighteenth century.

KENNETH E. LEWIS received an M.A. degree in anthropology from the University of Florida and holds a Ph.D. from the University of Oklahoma. He currently is associate professor of anthropology at Michigan State University. He has maintained a long-term geographical research interest in British colonization in the South Carolina backcountry. His current archaeological work at Camden is concerned with the role of frontier processes in the evolution of this central colonial settlement.

DONALD W. LINEBAUGH received his M.A. in anthropology and Ph.D. in American Studies from the College of William and Mary. He is currently director of the Program for Cultural Resource Assessment and assistant professor of anthropology at the University of Kentucky. He has written numerous journal articles and, with Gary Robinson, edited *Spatial Patterning in Historical Archaeology: Selected Studies of Settlement* (1994). His research interests include the history of historical archaeology, early settlement in the Chesapeake region, German settlement and material culture, environmental archaeology, and the archaeology of early industry.

TURK MCCLESKEY received a B.A. degree in history from the University of Texas at Austin in 1975 and a Ph.D. in history from the College of William and Mary in 1990. His research and writing focus on the eighteenth-century colonial American frontier. He is associate professor of history at Virginia Military Institute.

ROBERT D. MITCHELL, professor of geography at the University of Maryland, College Park, has a long-standing interest in the European colonization of the southern backcountry. A former trustee of the Museum of American Frontier Culture in Staunton, Virginia, he is author of *Commercialism and Frontier: Perspectives on the Early Shenandoah Valley* (1977) and, most recently, "From the Ground Up," in *Diversity and Accommodation: Essays on the Cultural Composition of the Virginia Frontier*, edited by Michael J. Puglisi (1997). Mitchell also edited *Appalachian Frontiers: Settlement, Society, and Development in the Preindustrial Era* (1991), and, with Paul A. Groves, *North America: The Historical Geography of a Changing Continent* (1987).

MICHAEL J. PUGLISI holds a B.A. degree in history from James Madison University and received his Ph.D. from the College of William and Mary in Virginia. He currently is vice-president for academic affairs and associate professor of history at Virginia Intermont College. He is author of *Puritans Besieged: The Legacies of King Philip's War in the Massachusetts Bay Colony* (1991) and editor of *Diversity and Accommodation: Essays on the Cultural Composition of the Virginia Frontier* (1997).

STEVEN D. SMITH currently is head of the Cultural Resource Consulting Division of the South Carolina Institute of Archaeology and Anthropology, University of South Carolina. He received his B.A. in history from Virginia Military Institute in 1973 and his M.A. in archaeology from the University of Kentucky in 1983. He has conducted archaeological research in Louisiana, Mississippi, Missouri, Kentucky, Indiana, South Carolina, North Carolina, and Georgia. He has published numerous reports and articles on Upland South farmsteads and American military sites.

DANIEL B. THORP is associate professor of history at Virginia Polytechnic Institute and State University at Blacksburg. He is author of *The Moravian Community in Colonial North Carolina: Pluralism on the Southern Frontier* (1989) and several articles about the colonial backcountry.

MARTHA A. ZIERDEN is curator of historical archaeology at the Charleston Museum, where she works in archaeological research, curation, and exhibition. Her research interests include landscape studies, refinement and material culture, urban life, and African American society. She has conducted numerous archaeological investigations of sites in Charleston and other urban centers.

Index

acculturation, xxiv
activity area, xxii
African-American, 45, 79, 110–36, 144–45
Alabama, 7
Alabama, Mobile, 73
alcohol, 76–86
alehouses, 76–86
Allegheny Mountains, 3
American Rectangular Land Survey System, 9
Ancrum, Lance, and Loocock (merchants), 94
Anglican, 98
Appalachian Mountains, 137, 161, 162–81
artifacts, archaeological, xiv–xvi, 87–108, 118–36, 146–61

bakery, 94, 99
Baptist, 18, 72
barley, 92
barns, 6–8, 46
Bartlam, John, 99
beer, 76–86
Beverley, William, 57, 63
Beverley Manor, 57, 59, 63–64
blacksmith, 99
Blount, William, xxii–xxiii, 137–61
Blue Ridge Mountains, 57, 137
Boas, Franz, xvi
Boone, Daniel, 168
Borden, Benjamin, Jr., 57
Borden's Land, 57, 59, 64
brandy, 76–86
Bratton, Col. William, 113–36

brewery, 94, 99
Brims ("Emperor" of Creek Indians), 69
British Coercive Acts, 73
buttons, brass, xx

cabinetware, 26
Calhoun, James E., 111
capitalism, 42, 87–107
Carolina, xvii, 24, 26
cattle, 5, 18, 24–25
ceramics, 99, 146–61, 217
cereals, 3
Cherokee Phoenix, 182
Cherokee War, 15, 70
china, 26; *see also* porcelain
Civil War, 112
claret, 81
Clark, Peter, 76
club, 81
coffee, 82
Colono Ware, 118–20
commodities, 88
corn, 5, 12, 15, 24, 81, 92
cotton, xvii, 73, 108–36, 225–26
Crackers, xix, 69–75
creolization, xxiv, 111
cultural ecology, xxi, 49

deerskin, 92, 142
dendrochronology, 46
distillery, 94, 99
domain, 11

dram-shots, 76–86
Dutch, 79

ecology, 22, 45
eggnog, 81
England, 78, 81–82
English, xvii, 3, 6, 18, 76–86, 144, 234
entrepôt, 88, 92, 94, 95, 101
ethnic, xvii, xviii, xx, xxiv, 6, 16, 18, 38, 41, 45, 47, 76–86, 109–36, 145, 225, 228
exchange value, 90–91
export, 87–107

Fairfax, Thomas, 6th Lord, 23; *see also* Northern Neck Proprietary
farm, xvii, xxii, xxiii, 5, 14, 24, 79, 90–136, 138, 200–20, 226
fauna, archaeological, 118–20, 153–55
Fauquier, Gov. Francis, 59
features, archaeological, 111, 118–20, 146–61, 216–17
flax, 92
Florida, 71; Kingsley Plantation, 110; Pensacola, 73; St. Augustine, 110
flour, 15, 24, 93, 143, 144
France, Paris, 76
French, 23, 72, 79, 112, 144, 234
frontier, xiii, xvi, xviii, xxi–xxii; comparative analysis of, 13–21; defined, 2, 38
furnishings, 80–81, 115–26

Galphin, George, xxi–xxii, 71
Gemeinschaft, xxii, 43, 162–81
gender, xx, 26, 82–83, 145, 151, 153, 156, 227
Geographic Information Systems, 23, 43
Georgia, 182–99, 225, 231; Altamaha River, 71; Augusta, xix, xx, 11, 69–75, 225; Cannon's Point Plantation, 119; Coweta Town, 70; New Echota, 182; New Savannah, 70; Ogeechee River, 71–72; Queensborough, 71; Saint Mary's River, 71; Savannah, xix, 73, 124, 143; Wrightsborough, 71, 73
German, xvii–xviii, xxiv, 3, 18, 23, 25, 46, 76–86, 138, 142, 200–20, 228–29
Gesellschaft, xxii, 43, 162–81
grains, 5, 15–16, 20, 92, 101
grasses, 5
Great Awakening, 72
Great Wagon Road, 77–79, 108, 168
groggeries, 76–86

Habersham, James, 69, 73
hemp, 24
Henry, Jim, 114
hogs, 5
housing, xxii, 6, 8, 26, 45–46, 71, 100, 109–36, 137–61, 200–20, 228–29
Huguenot, 112
hyperdiffusionists, xvi

imports, 87–107
indentured servants, 111
Indians, xvii, xix, xxiii, 22, 38–40, 44–45, 58, 63, 69–75, 168, 228, 231; Catawba, 39, 92–93, 118; Cherokee, xxiii, 16, 22, 69–75, 137, 151, 182–99, 225; Cherokee Judge John Martin, xxiii, 182–99; Chickasaw, 70, 182; Choctaw, 182–87; Creeks, xix, xxii, 69–75, 151, 182; Five Civilized Tribes, 182; Iroquois, 2; Monacan, 40; Seminole, 182; *see also* Native Americans
indigo, 18, 94
inns, 76–86, 92, 97, 99, 142
inventories, probate, xix, xx, 20, 26, 76, 83, 112, 123, 145
Irish Protestants, 71, 79

juleps, 81

Kentucky, 5–6, 10, 26, 65, 182
Kershaw, Joseph, xxi, 87–107
kiln, pottery, 102
Knox, Henry, 137
Knoxville Gazette, 138–39, 143–44, 151, 154

livestock, 5, 12, 20, 163, 175
Louisiana, New Orleans, 144
Lowrance, Alexander, 78–82
Lowrance, John, 78–82
lumber, 92
Lutheran, 203–20

Madeira, 81
magazine, 97
Marx, Karl, xxvi
Maryland, 6, 8, 12, 13, 16, 18, 20–22, 77, 217; Baltimore, 20, 24–25, 143; Frederick, 21; Hagerstown, 21; St. Mary's County, 165
Massachusetts, Boston, 124; Plymouth, 110, 173
McGillivray, Lachlan, 71
mead, 80–81
merchant, xix, xxi, 87–107

merchant-planter, xx
metropolitan fashion, 81–82
militia, xxiii, 27, 59, 73, 79
mill, 92
Miller, Lewis, xxiv, 200–20
mirror, xx
models, archaeological, xv
Moravians, 16, 25, 40–41, 76–86, 92, 139, 141–42, 229

National Historic Preservation Act, 110
Native Americans, xvii, xxiii, 111–12, 118, 127, 231, 234
North Carolina, 7–8, 14, 16, 18, 20–21, 27, 71, 118, 144, 175–76, 184, 189, 217, 229, 231; Bethabara, xx, 76–86, 92; Catawba River, 77; Fayetteville, 20; Irish Settlement, 79, 81; New Bern, 20; Rowan County, 16, 76–86; Salem, 77–78; Salisbury, 77–79, 81; Shallow Ford, 78; Wachovia, 40–41, 77; Winston-Salem, 76–86; Yadkin River, 77, 79
Northern Neck Proprietary, 23

Oglethorpe, James, 70
Ohio River, 137
Ohio Valley, 8, 12
Oklahoma, 183–99
open-country neighborhoods, 22, 25
orchards, 5
ordinaries, 76–86, 142
Ozarks, 7

patent, land, 58–60
Patton, James, 57, 59
pearlware, xx, 146–61
Pennsylvania, xvii, 3, 5–12, 14, 16, 18, 56, 62, 77; Philadelphia, 15, 24–25, 76, 78, 82, 94, 142, 143, 176, 201, 216
pewter, 26
plantation, xvii, xix, xxii–xxiii, 5, 12, 14, 16, 18, 20, 108–36, 182–99, 225–26
plats, xix, 58–68
population profiles, 25
porcelain, xx, 146–61; see also china
pottery factory, 99
Presbyterian, 18, 23, 141, 192
public houses, 76–86, 142
punch, 81

Quaker, xxi, 18, 23, 25, 71, 92, 97
quitrent, 58–59, 64

real estate, xviii, 26, 41–42, 56–68
Regulators, 27, 80, 112
Rhode Island, Providence, 124
rice, 12, 15, 18, 91, 112, 118
roads, 162–81, 227, 230
rum, 70, 76–86
rye, 81

sanger, 81
Savannah River, xx, 16, 18, 69–70, 72–73, 76
Scotch-Irish, xvii, 3, 11, 18, 23, 38, 46, 48, 76–86, 120, 138, 229
Scots, xvii, 80
Scots-Irish, iii, 108–36, 144, 203
Scottish, 18, 79–80, 121, 144; Highlanders, 18
section, 2, 3
settlement patterning, 88–107
Seven Years' War, 24, 58, 64
Sevier, John, 139, 168
shoemaker, 99
slavery, xxi, xxii, 12, 20, 24, 108–36; see also slaves
slaves, xxii, 5, 20, 92, 108–36, 144, 146, 148–49, 156; see also slavery
sling, 76–86
Smoky Mountains, 137
South Carolina, xviii, 7, 8, 10, 12, 15–16, 18, 21, 39, 69, 71, 108–36, 144–45, 182, 226; Allen Plantation, 110; Blackstock, 114–15; Brattonsville, xxii, 108–36; Broad River, 101; Camden, xxi, 14, 15, 25, 87–107, 110, 229, 231; Catawba Path, 92, 94, 97–98; Charles Town, 112; Charles Towne, 110; Charleston, xx, xxiii, 15, 18, 20, 24, 92, 94, 101, 124, 143, 176; Charlestown, 69–70, 81; Cheraw, 94; Chester County, 126, 128; Clinkscales Farm, 110; Congaree River, 94; Craven County, 112; Finch Farm, 110; Fort Moore, 70; Fredericksburg Township, 92, 101; Georgetown, 94; Granby, 94; Herndon Plantation, 115; Houser House, 110; Long Canes, 70; Millwood Plantation, 110; New Windsor, xx, xxvi, 110–11; Pee Dee River, 92, 94, 101; Pine Tree Creek, 92; Pine Tree Hill, xxi, 92–107; Redcliffe Plantation, 110; Rosemont Plantation, 110; Saluda River, 101; Santa Elena, 110; Santee River, 112; Saxe Gotha, 110–11; Spiers Landing, 119; Stewart Plantation, 116; townships, xviii, 92; Union, 115–16; Wateree River, 92, 94, 101; Waxhaws, 94; Winnsboro, 114, 116; Woodward, 115
Spanish, 71, 234

speculators, land, 56–60, 62, 64, 137–61, 228
spirits, 76–86
status, xix, xxii
Steele, Elizabeth, 77
Steele, William, 77, 79–82
stemware, xx
stoneware, salt-glazed, xx
store, 87–107

tailor, 99
tanning, 92, 143
taverns, xx, 76–86, 99, 139, 141–42, 227–28
tea, xix, 72, 151–54
teacups, xx
Tennessee, xvii, xxii, xxiii, 5–6, 10, 26, 42–43, 46, 58, 65, 182, 189, 224, 227; Hermitage, 110; Knoxville, xxii, 137–61, 228, 231; Nashville, 143–44; Tennessee River, 137–38; Washington County, 162–81
tippling house, 139, 141
tobacco, 5, 12, 15, 18, 20, 24, 73, 94
toddy, 76–86
towns, xxi, 14–16, 20, 23–25, 41, 76–86, 87–107
trade, xix, xxi, xxii, 40, 69–75, 89–107, 225
traders, xix
transportation, 42–43, 87–107, 162–81, 227, 230
Turner, Frederick Jackson, xvi, xviii, xxiv, 1–4, 8, 10, 13, 26, 36–38, 40–41, 49, 138, 221–36

Ulster, 46
Upland South, 7–8, 11, 12, 38, 156, 224

urbanization, xxi, xxvi, 13–15, 20, 24, 76–86, 87–107, 137–61, 229–30

vegetables, 92
vegetation cover, 22, 44
Virginia, xvii, xviii, xxii, 5–10, 13–14, 16, 18, 20, 23, 40, 46, 56, 62, 64, 72, 77, 112, 146, 171, 184, 225, 228, 229; Alexandria, 20, 24–25; Fredericksburg, 24; Holston River, 58; James River, 57, 59–60, 62, 64; Kingsmill, 110; Lexington, 21, Maury, River, 57; Monticello, 110; New River, 57–58, 62; Norfolk, 20; Petersburg, 20; Richmond, 143; Roanoke River, 16, 18, 56, 58–60, 62, 64; Roanoke, Valley, 39; Shenandoah Valley, xvii, xviii, xx, xxiii, xxiv, 3, 6, 9, 12, 15–16, 18, 20–22, 24–27, 41–42, 44, 56, 62, 76, 168; Valley of, 8, 200–20; Williamsburg, 110; Winchester, xviii, 23–25

Washington, D.C., xxiii
Welsh, 79
West Indies, 93
Western Great Road, 77–78
wheat, xxi, 14–15, 18, 20, 24, 92–94, 101
whiskey, 72, 76–86
White, James, 137–61
wine, 81
worldview, Georgian, 109–36
Wright, Gov. James, 69, 72–73

Yamasee War, 69–70

The Southern Colonial Backcountry was designed and typeset on a Macintosh computer system using PageMaker software. The text is set in Jenson, and the ornaments are set in Arabesque Ornaments and Caslon Ornaments. This book was designed by Todd Duren, composed by Kimberly Scarbrough, and manufactured by Thomson-Shore, Inc. The recycled paper used in this book is designed for an effective life of at least three hundred years.

www.ingramcontent.com/pod-product-compliance
Lightning Source LLC
Chambersburg PA
CBHW030309080526
44584CB00012B/496